Perils of Perestroika

Viewpoints from the Soviet Press, 1989-1991

Edited by
Isaac J. Tarasulo

A Scholarly Resources Inc. Imprint
Wilmington, Delaware

The paper used in this publication meets the minimum requirements of the American National Standard for permanence of paper for printed library materials, Z39.48, 1984.

First published 1992
Printed and bound in the United States of America

Scholarly Resources Inc.
104 Greenhill Avenue
Wilmington, DE 19805-1897

Library of Congress Cataloging-in-Publication Data

Perils of Perestroika : viewpoints of the Soviet press, 1989–1991
edited by Isaac J. Tarasulo.
p. cm.
Translated from the Russian.
Includes bibliographical references and index.
ISBN 0-8420-2380-1 (cloth). — ISBN 0-8420-2398-4 (pbk.)
1. Soviet Union—Politics and government—1985. 2. Perestroika—Soviet Union. 3. Glasnost. I. Tarasulo, Isaac J., 1939–
DK286.5.P49 1992
947.085'4—dc20 91-20267
CIP

The following articles were reproduced with the permission of the original publishers or authors, and the underlying material is subject to Soviet copyright:

Alexander Shchelkin, "The Dynamics of Freedom," *Sovetskaya Kultura*, March 31, 1990.
A. Kuznetsov, "Not All Theaters Are Erotic," *Komsomolskaya Pravda*, July 28, 1990.
Yevgeny Yevtushenko, "A Nation Begins with Its Women," *The Literary Gazette International*, no. 2, March 1990.
Ivan Dzyuba, "A Commonwealth of Cultures," *The Literary Gazette International*, no. 2, August 1990.
Oleg Moroz, "Vilnius: A Night in Spring," *The Literary Gazette International*, no. 1, May 1990.
Piatras Keidoshus and Vitautas Petkiavicius, "Confessions of a 'Renegade,' " *Literaturnaya Gazeta*, no. 1, January 1991.
Patriarch Alexei II, "Faith without Action Is Dead," *Izvestiya*, June 16, 1990.
"A Letter from Russia's Writers," *Moskva*, no. 5, 1990.
R. Safarov, "Looking Around at the Pass," *Pravda*, July 28, 1990.
Alexei Kiva, "Will the Party Catch Up with *Perestroika*?" *Izvestiya*, July 19, 1990.
Alexander Tsipko, "Do We Need Yet Another Experiment? Ideological Paradoxes of Reform," *Rodina*, no. 1, January 1990.
Oleg Kalugin, "The KGB Has Not Changed Its Principles . . . Yet," *Komsomolskaya Pravda*, June 20, 1990.
Nina Andreyeva, "The Striving for Truth Has Not Yet Been Suppressed," *Molodaya Gvardiya*, no. 2, February 1990.
Ilya Zaslavsky, "Enough Talk! Let's Get to Work!" *Demokraticheskaya Rossiya*, no. 4, October 1990.
Nina Maksimova, "The Strike: Sketches for a Portrait of a Phenomenon," *Eko*, no. 11, November 1989.
Boris Pinsker and Larisa Piyasheva, "Property and Freedom," *Novy Mir*, no. 11, November 1989.
Yuri Orlik, "To Heaven on Ration Cards," *Izvestiya*, March 30, 1990.
M. Lapitsky, "Why They Work Better Than We Do," *SSHA*, no. 2, February 1990.
Georgy Podlesskikh, "Finding a Steward for the Land," *Moskva*, no. 10, October 1989.
Sergei Novikov, "Help! The Dollars Are Coming!" *The Literary Gazette International*, no. 1, August 1990.
Stanislav Shatalin, "The Risk of Going Over to a Market Economy Is Less Than the Cost of Marking Time," *Izvestiya*, April 22, 1990.
Alexei Arbatov, "How Much Defense Is Sufficient?" *International Affairs*, April 1989.

Yuri Lyubimov, "Enough Defense, Not Enough Competence," *Kommunist Vooruzhennykh Sil*, no. 16, August 1989.

Stanislav Kondrashov, "From the Shadows of the Unknown: Flashes of Openness in the Realm of Military Secrets," *Novy Mir*, no. 8, August 1989.

Igor Malashenko, "Russia: The Earth's Heartland," *International Affairs*, no. 7, July 1990.

Anatoly Butenko, "A Time to Learn What the Events in Eastern Europe Are Telling Us," *Nedelya*, no. 11, 1990.

Irina Lagutina, "Nation on the Eve of War: Subjective Notes on the Margins of Letters from Strangers," *New Times*, no. 3, January 1991.

Mikhail Gorbachev, "Gorbachev Talks to Workers at the Izhora Plant," *Sovetskaya Rossiya*, August 20, 1989.

Boris Yeltsin, "There Won't Be a Civil War," *Ogonyok*, no. 12, March 16–23, 1991.

Alexander Yakovlev, "On the Threshold of Momentous Changes," *Izvestiya*, May 31, 1990.

Yegor Ligachev, " 'I Believe in the People's Soul and Reason,' " *Pravda*, June 18, 1990.

Yegor Ligachev, "Ligachev Addresses the Constituent Congress of Russian Communists," *Moscow TV Service*, June 20, 1990.

Andrei Sakharov, "Dimensions of Freedom," *Ogonyok*, no. 31, 1989.

About the Editor

A native of the Soviet Union, Isaac J. Tarasulo was educated at the University of Leningrad and at Yale University, from which he received a Ph.D. in Russian history. He also has been a research fellow at the Kennan Institute for Advanced Russian Studies. Since 1986, Dr. Tarasulo has been director of the Bethesda Institute for Soviet Studies, a nonpartisan research organization. He is also editor of *Gorbachev and Glasnost: Viewpoints from the Soviet Press* (Wilmington, DE: Scholarly Resources, 1989).

Contents

Editorial Note

I have selected these thirty-three articles published in Soviet mainstream newspapers and magazines in 1989, 1990, and 1991 to reflect best the most important developments taking place in the Soviet Union today. These articles express various points of view, from moderate and reformist to conservative. With *glasnost* resulting in an escalating number of new publications, it is difficult to include all interpretations of current events.

Ten of the articles were translated by me; Thomas M. Starker of Little Rock, Arkansas, translated eleven documents; and eight were taken from Soviet publications that are printed in English as well as in Russian. Translation of the remaining four articles was done by FBIS (Foreign Broadcasting Information Service), a U.S. government agency.

Most of the articles have been carefully abridged to fit space requirements. All editorial interpolations within the documents are confined to footnotes or brackets. Footnotes are mostly the editor's addition; the occasional footnote found in an original document is always identified as such. Boldface is occasionally used to indicate emphasis that was in the original document; footnotes clarify when this occurs. Transliteration was based on the Library of Congress system, with a few modifications to conform to generally accepted usage.

Acknowledgments

I would like to express my gratitude to Thomas M. Starker for his swift and flawless translation of eleven articles for this volume. Stuart Anderson provided editorial assistance in preparing the introductory essays. And, as always, Tricia Andryszewski worked very hard to prepare this book.

I also would like to note the efforts of Carolyn J. Travers, managing editor at Scholarly Resources, as well as Ann M. Aydelotte and Sharon L. Beck, whose assistance at every editorial stage was invaluable.

Introduction

Mikhail Gorbachev came to power in March 1985 but did not initiate fundamental reforms until nearly five years later. Crucial reforms in the direction of a parliamentary democracy and a market economy finally began in 1989 and 1990. Early 1991 brought some steps backward in the reform process, but by the summer positive signs toward reforms could again be seen. Revolutionary changes have been accompanied by the rapid destruction of the old regime and the unraveling of the Russian-Soviet empire. It is as if Russia were spiraling backward toward its pre-1917 pattern of development.

Reading the Soviet newspapers and magazines these days, we can learn significant facts to which official Soviet historians intentionally have not drawn our attention. It is surprising that so much space in the media is still taken up with debates over distant historical events. These endless discussions between conservatives and liberals concerning the revision and interpretation of history continue because crucial decisions regarding the future have yet to be made.

Six critical years of change and turmoil have produced a distinctly new situation in the Soviet Union that no one could have predicted. Surprises have followed one another in dizzying succession. Dramatic events have led to the mass migration and uprooting of hundreds of thousands of people. National conflicts have created at least six hundred thousand refugees, the Chernobyl disaster has forced the relocation of entire communities, and many of the Soviet soldiers and officers returning home with their families after fifty years of a de facto occupation of Eastern Europe have become essentially homeless. Miners striking for political and economic change in the hot summer of 1989 marked the disappearance of a sacrosanct prohibition.[1] Demands for independence are loud and clear: The union republics are attempting secession, and even the autonomous republics are now proclaiming themselves to be union republics.[2]

This period of political reforms and elections has been accompanied by a rebirth of spiritual life and religion. Ominously, the political struggle among nascent political parties has been characterized by a great deal of intolerance. New social mores and attempts to introduce a rule of law have been subjects of turbulent debate. The dismal failure of Soviet domestic policy contrasts markedly with widely perceived Soviet achievements in foreign policy. This incongruity was underlined when Gorbachev was awarded the Nobel Peace Prize at the same time that he was asking for economic assistance from abroad. A growing pessimism is sweeping the USSR; the road to democracy is long and tortuous, and the country is drinking its cup of bitterness and sorrow to the dregs.

This book, a sequel to *Gorbachev and Glasnost: Viewpoints from the Soviet Press* (Scholarly Resources, 1989), includes thirty-three articles published in the Soviet press between 1989 and 1991. The articles are grouped into five chapters by topic. The major Soviet publications with the largest numbers of subscribers are represented; there also exists a burgeoning number of independent publications, too numerous for all of them to be included here. Because the Soviet press has greater freedom than ever before, it is difficult to include all materials deserving attention. Bibliographies at the end of each chapter suggest additional reading.

In Chapter 1 the issues of building a civil society based on the rule of law, changing attitudes toward women, and new attitudes toward religion are addressed. In addition, three articles are devoted to various points of view on the divisive

---

[1] In March 1991 the miners of Siberia again proclaimed a political strike, this time demanding that Gorbachev resign.

[2] Union republics represent the major nationalities that make up the Soviet Union. Autonomous republics, each of which is attached to a union republic, represent smaller nationalities.

relationships between the various nationalities and the Russians.

Chapter 2 deals with the process by which the Communist party is rapidly losing its grip on power. The continuing revision of Soviet history has even led to attacks on Lenin, the founder of the Soviet state; thousands of his statues have been removed from city and village squares, especially in the republics outside of Russia proper. Politically, the Communist party is split between moderates and conservatives. R. Safarov's letter (Doc. 9) and Alexei Kiva's article (Doc. 10) express the hope of the moderates that Gorbachev's leadership will continue and that the party will finally adjust to the new realities. The party apparatus is identified with the bankrupt command-administrative system, and the notion of pluralism increasingly gains currency in the country. Abolition of Article 6 of the Soviet constitution (which mandated the "leading role" of the Communist party) has led to quick endorsement by reformers for a multiparty system, as well as to growing demands for depolitization of the army, navy, Ministry of Internal Affairs, and KGB. Alexander Tsipko's article (Doc. 11) even advances the argument that Marxism itself, the last sacred cow, can make no relevant contribution in resolving current Soviet problems.

The selections in Chapter 3 hotly debate such issues as the transition to a regulated market economy, privatization of the economy, giving land to peasants, and leasing enterprises to their employees. One of the Soviet Union's foremost economists, Stanislav Shatalin, speaks about the introduction of a market system in the USSR (see Doc. 21). Boris Pinsker and Larisa Piyasheva's article (Doc. 16) deals with the fundamental question of the significance of various forms of property. Also discussed in this chapter are strikes, the rationing system, and the benefits of attracting foreign capital.

Foreign policy and military issues are dealt with in Chapter 4. The question of Soviet-American military parity remains a controversial issue debated both here and elsewhere by the military and by foreign policy experts. Innovative explanations of the importance of *glasnost* in foreign policy are presented by Stanislav Kondrashov in Document 24. Finally, the lessons of the loss of Eastern Europe are analyzed by Igor Malashenko and Anatoly Butenko in Documents 25 and 26.

Chapter 5 deals with the appearance of such political personalities as Boris Yeltsin, Yegor Ligachev, Alexander Yakovlev, and Andrei Sakharov and their roles in the rebirth of competitive politics in the USSR. This concluding chapter also evaluates the personal evolution and internal contradictions of Mikhail Gorbachev, a reformer and an *apparatchik* in one person.

RUSSIA IS NOW AT A CROSSROADS: One way leads to reform, and another returns to the totalitarian system. A pendulum swinging from left to right, from liberal hopes to conservative angst, has become the metaphor of the Soviet political system. This system was challenged in three extraordinary days—August 19–21, 1991—when Soviet tanks rolled into Moscow in an attempt by the conservative forces to stop the disintegration of the USSR and the further weakening both of the Communist party's role in the society and of the cause of socialism. Unlike the 1964 coup d'état against Nikita Khrushchev, this one was not directed against Mikhail Gorbachev personally. On the contrary, the plotters pressed Gorbachev to join them. It seems that they were puzzled by his refusal. Thus, the true role of the Soviet president in these events is, at least, dubious. Any Western politician in his place would have resigned immediately.

Three institutions—the KGB, the army, and the party—appeared badly compromised by the coup. Gorbachev had been warned countless times that no meaningful progress would be possible without dismantling the KGB. As for the army, Gorbachev himself contributed heavily to its politicization by calling up regular army units and troops of the Ministry of Internal Affairs to quell ethnic disorders. His political blunder of bringing fifty thousand troops to Moscow on March 28, 1991, to prevent a demonstration by Boris Yeltsin's supporters was one step toward a civil war.

The biggest loser appeared to be the Communist party, with unprecedented assaults on its property and power. Even Gorbachev suggested that the party was involved in the coup, and he solemnly resigned as its general secretary and dissolved the Central Committee. Nevertheless, it is too early to predict its dissolution. Millions of people still believe in its ideology and benefit from its power.

The coup came as a surprise to most observers, including the experts on the Soviet Union. Warnings were discounted by the Western media as not being factual, even when they came from Eduard Shevardnadze and Alexander Yakovlev. With the end of Gorbymania, the Western press found its new hero in the president of Russia, Boris Yeltsin. Several days after August 21 showed that he was in charge, with a shaken Gorbachev having mostly symbolic power. Indeed, the quick dissolution of the party and its *apparat* showed at the same time that anyone in power would not care much about constitutional arrangements. The funeral procession of the three young martyrs with their coffins covered in red fabric recalled the imagery of the October Revolution.

Why did this August coup fail so quickly and decisively? Was it because of democracy, television, and Yeltsin? Rather, other reasons are more crucial. First, there is a deep aversion among the Russian people toward unleashing civil war and bloodshed among themselves; and second, Gorbachev's refusal to lead the coup deprived it of legitimacy and increased dissension among its leaders and the military. Moreover, Yeltsin, at the center of resistance to the coup, incessantly called for the restoration of Gorbachev to power. Whatever the victory of democracy in the Soviet empire, in this period of instability we may be separated from the emergence of a truly civilized democratic society by several decades and generations of strife and civil war. At this point in time it is difficult to assess the true significance of the events of these three days in August that changed the Soviet Union.

Our seventy-year-old social experiment has turned out to be an extension of the worst features of the Russian autocracy and the Russian bureaucratic machine. Communism on our Russian soil has brought human life to the point of complete folly. The reality is absurd, and the people in it are absurd.

Anatoly Sobchak,
mayor of Leningrad
and People's Deputy

Chapter One

The Emergence of a Civil Society

Crushed Hopes

Russia is in the midst of a new Time of Troubles.[1] For the second time in this century it has lost its sense of national purpose. Ideological and national conflicts have become intertwined, and as a result liberals, conservatives, and various ethnic groups are holding each other responsible for the country's present quandary. While free political and philosophical discussions were practically forbidden for many years, insular nationalist tendencies of all kinds developed among various nationalities and groups.

Over the past few years conservatives have been alarmed by and have mobilized against two key developments: 1) the identification of socialism with both the crimes committed under Joseph Stalin and the rampant corruption and inefficiency of Leonid Brezhnev's regime; and 2) the hopes Soviet citizens have pinned on a market economy rescuing the country's future. The desire to preserve the Russian empire intact is a common denominator for the "monarchists," those who desire a return to a strong, autocratic Russian state, such as Alexander Nevzorov, a popular television reporter from Leningrad, as well as for the Communists, including the leaders of the Soviet military. The conservatives ground many of their arguments in alleged

---

[1]In late sixteenth- and early seventeenth-century Russia, popular uprisings and foreign invasions followed one another. This period of turmoil is called the Time of Troubles.

Russophobia, the belief that the Russian Republic is in such a miserable economic condition because Russians are hated and exploited by other ethnic groups. Conservatives are well represented among the KGB, the police, Afghan war veterans, and trade union officials. They see Russophobia everywhere, and they accuse their enemies—"left radicals," Jews, and the Baltic peoples—of trying to sell Russia's natural resources to cooperatives and to the West.[2] The greatest irony of all is that the conservatives endeavor to speak in the name of workers against a new bourgeoisie. Conservative press organs include, among others, all of the military press, especially *Krasnaya Zvesda* and *Kommunist Vooruzhennykh Sil.*

The most vicious ideological struggle is taking place among Russian writers: between the proreform writers' societies, such as April and Memorial, and the rabidly conservative official board of the writers of the Russian Republic. These deep divisions could be labeled a literary "civil war." The conservative writers (see Doc. 8), in the guise of patriotism, are allowed to criticize the new Soviet system. They extol such "traditional" values as the Russian soul, the rural village, the workers, and the army, while they condemn "seducers of souls," lovers of rock music and the West, Jews, members of the interregional group in the parliament, and reserve particular contempt for market economists like Leonid Abalkin, Abel Aganbegyan, Nikolai Shmelyov, and Tatyana Zaslavskaya.

The conservatives seem to have no ideology or arguments with which to respond to the new ideas and revelations about the past, so they are forced to resort to old strategies. Although they attack the reforms, they rarely mention Gorbachev by name. Like the czarist secret police at the beginning of this century, the conservatives have started a debate about anti-Semitism and Russophobia in order to discredit the reformers and thus derail reforms. The conservatives have chosen Jews as their particular target. Soviet Jews are the only ethnic group whose problems are not discussed in the Soviet press; it is presumed that nothing is wrong with their status, despite their wholesale flight from the country. Pamyat, which openly conducts anti-Semitic campaigns, operates freely, and the sentencing of Russian nationalist Konstantin Smirnov-Ostashvili on October 12, 1990, to two years in prison (for anti-Semitic activities and for stirring up nationalist discord) amounted to nothing more than a slap on the wrist.

Mikhail Gorbachev's position on the "Jewish question" is similar to his stance on the economy. He is trying to be neutral. He has ignored all appeals by reformers to speak out against the conservatives, Pamyat, and anti-Semitism. In a not-very-subtle signal to Russian nationalists, late in the 1980s he awarded Hero of Socialist Labor

---

[2]See Vladimir Lichutin's "Happiness Cannot Be Found Outside," *Sovetskaya Rossiya*, October 15, 1989, which argues that Russia should not try to follow or catch up with the West and that reformers are chameleons who do not cherish traditions.

medals to the Russian conservative writers Valentin Rasputin, Vasily Belov, Yuri Bondarev, and Victor Astafiev. Even though Valentin Rasputin has openly expressed sympathy for Pamyat and has signed the nationalist "Letter from Russia's Writers" (Doc. 8), Gorbachev appointed him, in March 1990, a member of the Presidential Council. At the same time Gorbachev did not appoint any reformers, despite their considerable electoral successes and the corresponding electoral defeats of the conservatives.

Attempted reforms have resulted in the weakening of central imperial authority. Nationalist riots in Alma-Ata, Kazakhstan, in December 1986 were an early sign of impending trouble on a large scale, a signal mostly missed by the Soviet leadership. The central authorities have showed an unusual helplessness in their attempts to resolve disturbances in Nagorno-Karabakh, which began in February 1988 and which continue still. When Soviet troops used nerve gas and shovels in Tbilisi in April 1989, killing twenty demonstrators, the survival of the empire was jeopardized. Since then, national relations have gone rapidly downhill. Riots against Armenians in Baku, Azerbaijan, on January 13, 1990, led to Soviet troops storming Baku, which only aggravated the situation.

Each interethnic conflict has its roots in an accumulation of long-standing problems. The authorities were aware of these problems but did nothing to prevent an explosion. One of the bloodiest clashes took place in June and July of 1990 in the cities of Osh and Uzgen, in Kirghizia, between ethnic Uzbeks and the Kirghiz. Hundreds of people were killed or mutilated, and thousands of families became refugees.

Unfortunately, it can be argued that many of the republics reaching for independence have displayed almost as much intolerance as have their Soviet rulers. In such places as the Baltic republics, Moldavia, and Georgia, local leaders are pushing out Russians and other minority nationalities and are denying nonnatives equal rights. This enables the Soviet central government to assume the role of defender of the minorities, and to play on the conflicts among large and small nationalities. The most effective weapon of local governments has been the laws on state language. It works the same way in Canada or Czechoslovakia as it does in Lithuania or Kirghizia: Changes in the official status of language exacerbate tensions and polarize the population. The hasty promotion of local languages over Russian helped the conservatives, the supporters of the centralized system, to organize their actions. Russians are fleeing from Central Asia and the Caucasus, but they are likely to fight resolutely in the Baltics.[3]

The leaders of the nationalist movements have failed to recognize that the only way to true independence and freedom for their regions is

---

[3]The reasons for this include the sizable ethnic Russian population of the Baltic states, their strategic importance, and their long history of domination by Russia. Also, Russians perceive the Balts as more civilized and less intimidating than the Islamic peoples of the USSR.

the victory of democratic forces in the Soviet Union as a whole (see Doc. 4). Lithuania (see Docs. 5, 6) is a case in point. Lithuania was independent for only twenty years during the last three centuries, so there is not much experience in nation building there. The inflexible policies of the Lithuanian leaders may unfortunately only delay true independence for the Lithuanian people. In case of armed Soviet intervention, no other country is likely to come to Lithuania's aid. The attempts to gain independence made by the president of the Supreme Soviet of Lithuania, Vitautas Landsbergis, and his associates may well bring them inadvertently together with Gorbachev in the final defeat of all efforts for democratic reform.

Since 1988, 950 people have been killed, more than 9,000 have been wounded, and more than 600,000 have become refugees as a result of ethnic conflicts.[4] The Soviet leadership enjoys far better relations with the heads of foreign countries, including Germany, than it does with the leaders of many Soviet republics.

The ethnic conflicts are partially caused by the lack of democratic political culture and by economic difficulties. In a country just starting on the road to democracy, it is easier to communicate with and to mobilize people on ethnic grounds than on the basis of ideological, political, or philosophical ideas. There is no question that economic difficulties and national tensions are connected. The ethnic problems are clearly exacerbating the economic crisis, but to what extent the reverse is true remains to be proven. In the eyes of many nationalities, the USSR looks like a loser economically, and this provides little incentive to stay in the federation. According to *Pravda*, there are 6,000,000 jobless in Central Asia and Kazakhstan. In Uzbekistan, in the city of Fergana alone, there were approximately 170,000 jobless before ethnic unrest was ignited by a dispute at a fruit market, allegedly over a dish of strawberries.

The Baltic republics are a special case, since their annexation by the Soviet Union in 1940 was never formally recognized by the United States. In August 1989 the Central Committee issued a statement on the situation in the Baltics, warning that a cession can only be accomplished by mutually agreed-upon procedures. Then, in September 1989, the long-awaited party *plenum* adopted the Central Committee's platform "National Policy of the Party in Contemporary Times" and created a special department on national relations within the Central Committee. In order to placate the Baltic nationalists, an attempt was made on November 27 to give the Baltic republics something definite in the form of a Supreme Soviet law entitled "On the Economic Independence of Lithuania, Latvia, and Estonia." On January 11, 1990, Mikhail Gorbachev visited Lithuania, the most militant of the Baltic republics. Although no one could accuse Gorbachev and the Kremlin of passivity on the Lithuanian question, all

---

[4] *Argumenty i Fakty*, no. 41, 1990.

of their feverish efforts did not prevent Lithuania's proclamation of independence on March 11, 1990.

Two weeks later, a virtual state of war erupted between the Gorbachev government and the Lithuanian Republic, attracting the attention of the entire world. First, Soviet tanks passed near the parliament building in Vilnius in the middle of the night (see Doc. 5). Then came a month-long fuel blockade. In response to these actions, President Vitautas Landsbergis sought world attention and international diplomatic recognition for his country, and he encouraged its youth to avoid the Soviet army's draft. Western leaders proved to be unwilling to take Lithuania's side at the risk of losing Gorbachev's support for their actions in the Persian Gulf crisis, and toward the end of 1990 Gorbachev sent more troops to the Baltics. The Lithuanian independence movement began to splinter (see Doc. 6). On January 13, 1991, the Soviet militia attacked a television station in Vilnius, killing fourteen and wounding hundreds. Only one week later, on January 20, Soviet troops attacked the Ministry of Internal Affairs in Riga, Latvia (the Soviet military had been refused supplies in Latvia since November 1990). These two "Bloody Sundays"—recalling the first, on January 22, 1905, when czarist troops fired on peaceful demonstrators—were roundly condemned by the public in the Soviet Union as well as elsewhere in the world. Gorbachev quickly retreated, claiming to have had no advance knowledge of the attacks.

In contrast to the situation in the Baltics, the question of Russia's independence from the USSR could be viewed as a theater of the absurd. Given the centralized nature of political power in the Soviet Union, the notion of Boris Yeltsin's Russia and the Kremlin's USSR operating as two parallel centers of power is totally unworkable. In his meeting with Britain's foreign secretary, Douglas Hurd, on September 13, 1990, Yeltsin stated that Russia would agree to let the Kremlin manage defense, the KGB, Aeroflot, communications, transportation, energy, and foreign affairs. The rest would be the domain of the Russian Republic. This is a new and unprecedented definition of sovereignty; no one knows how such a separation of powers could ever be achieved, even if the Kremlin were not to have objections. Although this arrangement would still give the Kremlin leader more power than the U.S. president has over each of the fifty states, the Soviet Union's historical, political, and social traditions make this a totally different case.

Complaints of oppression are the driving force behind the demands for independence by all the republics. The same complaints are heard from the Russian Republic, although the country as a whole is more often called Russia than it is called the USSR. Is it a Soviet or a Russian empire? Have the Russians suffered because of their imperial ambitions or because maybe they have been oppressed by the Uzbeks or the Lithuanians? Is it necessary to have separate Russian and Soviet Communist parties, parliaments, or academies of science? Probably not, since 96 percent of all members of the existing Academy of Science work and live in the Russian Republic. Nonetheless, on December 9, 1989, the Central Committee *plenum* decided to create a Russian bureau of the CPSU as a concession to Russian nationalism.

In June 1990 the first session of the Russian Supreme Soviet elected Boris Yeltsin as its chairman, in spite of the conservative resistance. Enjoying democracy, the deputies of the Russian parliament formed thirty-two separate groups according to their different political views, with "Democratic Russia" and "Democratic Platform in the CPSU" representing the liberals, and "Marxist Platform in the CPSU" and "Communists of Russia" run by conservatives.

More recently, a union treaty, designed by Gorbachev to resolve national disagreements by distributing responsibilities between the Kremlin and the union republics, was considered by the Supreme Soviet on November 30, 1990, and by the 4th Congress of People's Deputies of the USSR, convened on December 17, 1990. It was too little, too late. After significant concessions by Gorbachev on the issue of sovereignty, it seems that nine republics are ready to sign a new union treaty, probably by midsummer of 1991. The agreement, known as "9 + 1," was reached at the Moscow suburb of Novo-Ogarevo on April 23, 1991.

Ultimately, the national movements have proven to be counterproductive to the cause of reform. The original aim of the various people's front movements was to help *perestroika*. Instead they turned into national parties, which slowed reforms, created social tensions, economic problems, and forced migrations, which may finally contribute to their own defeat. By concentrating prematurely on only their own needs, the national movements may have fatally weakened the democratic liberal forces in the Soviet Union. It was perhaps unrealistic to expect that out of the ruins of such an imperial monster would easily be born democratic and free states.

The Emergence of a Civil Society

We are witnessing the birth of a civil society in the Soviet Union. New notions of *glasnost* and democratization are contributing to a different approach to religious, political, and social issues, although Soviet leaders are extremely cautious concerning the social experimentation needed to bring about a civil society (see Doc. 1). Fundamental legal issues such as property, land, the federal structure, and social mores have come under intensified scrutiny. There are, of course, specific features of the Soviet Union (such as *propiska*, the permission to live in a particular town and apartment) which are not compatible with the principles of a civil society. The restrictions on where one can live inside the country are augmented by restrictions on emigration. After two years of discussion, the legislature finally passed the new law on emigration on May 20, 1991. However, it will take effect only on January 1, 1993.

Respect for law and for due process has always been marginal, both in Russia and in the Soviet Union at large. It will be especially difficult to build a society obedient to laws in the face of the recent dramatic increase in crime. The rise of organized crime is especially worrisome. Former Prime Minister Nikolai Ryzhkov was forced to admit: "We are losing the war against crime."[5]

The status of women is changing, and shifts in public attitudes toward sex and morality are apparent (see Docs. 2, 3). For the first time, it has become possible to discuss openly women's drinking and drug problems, prostitution, and abortion. The first Moscow beauty pageant, held in June 1988, was a vivid indication that Western culture has arrived in Russia. In the spheres of politics and economics, the equality of women remains a chimera. For example, while they constitute 30 percent of all party members, women hold only 6 percent of the positions of responsibility.[6]

Religion

Since Gorbachev's historic meeting with Russia's Patriarch Pimen and several members of the Holy Synod on April 27, 1988, relations between the Russian Orthodox church and the world's most militant atheist state have improved considerably (see Doc. 7). The church's prestige further increased with the numerous celebrations marking the millennium of Orthodoxy, most notably with the ceremony at the Bolshoi Theater on June 10, 1988, in which Raisa Gorbachev participated. Since then, Bibles have been printed, imported into the country, and even given out on the streets. The number of baptisms has nearly doubled, from 682,427 in 1986 to 1,142,693 in 1988, largely because of the celebration of the millennium and also because it is no longer required to register baptisms with the local authorities. The USSR's first Sunday school was opened in Moscow in the fall of 1989 by the Church of Glory to the Resurrection of Our Lord.[7] Religious weddings are on the rise as well.[8]

With the increased freedom of action, however, new problems have arisen. The Orthodox church has had to deal with separatist tendencies in the Ukrainian dioceses as well as with attempts by the Russian Church Abroad to gain a foothold in the Soviet Union. A nationalist wing in the Russian Orthodox church, led by Father Hermogen, lends strong support to right-wing Russian nationalists. It will take time for the church to cleanse itself of KGB appointees, who virtually ruled the church until recently. The Russian people will not

---

[5] Ibid., no. 29, 1990.

[6] *Soviet Life*, June 1990.

[7] Ibid., August 1990.

[8] *Argumenty i Fakty*, no. 41, 1990.

fully trust the spiritual leadership of the Orthodox church until it becomes more independent of political authorities. The murder of the priest Alexander Men on September 9, 1990, is still under investigation. Because of his democratic views (still rare among the clergy) Father Men—a Jew by birth—was threatened by Russian nationalists and was hated by the conservative clergy. Nonetheless, so far the Russian Orthodox church has been more supportive of Gorbachev than of his opponents, although the church's political acceptability is so new that the struggle is just beginning. On Easter Sunday 1991, for the first time in seventy-three years, at least two high-ranking officials—Boris Yeltsin and Prime Minister Valentin Pavlov—attended Easter church services.

Glasnost

Nikita Khrushchev's "thaw," considered by some to be a forerunner of *glasnost*, pales in comparison to the veritable information explosion now taking place in the Soviet Union. *Glasnost* truly flourished in 1989 and 1990. All of Alexander Solzhenitsyn's works were published in full—a true test of *glasnost*. And the changes occurring in the Soviet press are breathtaking. A wide diversity of views is now expressed in "alternative" newspapers, magazines affiliated with new political parties and social movements, and in a variety of journals copublished with Western publishers. Recently created news agencies such as Interfax and Postfactum quickly gained wide recognition. Although the new publications have very limited resources and circulation, their emergence is clearly a step in the right direction. The biggest *glasnost* revelations thus far have been admissions of the 1940 massacre of Polish officers in Katyn Forest and of the Soviet collaboration with Nazi Germany in secret clauses of the 1939 Nazi-Soviet nonaggression pact.

Beginning steps have been taken toward institutionalizing freedom of the press and toward freeing the press from the daily control of the Communist party. Gorbachev's decree of July 14, 1990, eliminating party control over television and radio in the USSR, and the Law of the Press and Other Means of Mass Information promulgated on August 1, 1990, were significant, although neither has been fully implemented.

As a result of *glasnost*, Kremlinology is rapidly dying of natural causes. Kremlinology, an ambivalent science, flourished because of the scarcity of information about the internal affairs of the Soviet Union. *Glasnost* has created a glut of valuable data about both the past and the present, rendering the speculations of Kremlinologists unnecessary. Furthermore, the mechanisms of power under Gorbachev operate in a completely different fashion than was the case in the past, making previous knowledge virtually irrelevant. Analysts of the Soviet Union have to change their methods to operate in the new environment.

Parliamentary System

The transition from a single-party state to a multiparty state under the rule of law is a protracted and complex process. It began in the spring of 1989 with elections for the first Soviet parliament, the Congress of People's Deputies. Then, there was a sudden leap from a scarcity to an overabundance of political activity. In just one year, two Supreme Soviet sessions and two Congress of People's Deputies sessions took place, and numerous elections were held. Deputies who simultaneously hold other positions were overwhelmed. There were constant complaints that procedural arguments were taking too much time. Televised in full, the debates at the first session of the Congress of People's Deputies shook the world. After several sessions, the country discovered new talents—leading speakers such as Deputy Prime Minister Leonid Abalkin and Anatoly Sobchak, a lawyer who has since become Leningrad's mayor. Numerous laws prepared by government bureaucrats and often not yet finished were quickly approved. The rudimentary parliamentary system revived the forgotten notion of opposition, which came to be represented by an interregional group of deputies. The real strength of this nascent opposition has been its ability to bring people to the streets, as it did for demonstrations on February 4, May 1, and July 5, 1990. That the demonstrations were allowed to proceed is itself a break with the recent past. Conservative forces, remembering the past (when all votes in the Supreme Soviet were unanimous), complained at the 2d Congress of People's Deputies about the decreased representation of the workers in the highest elected bodies.

Perceptions about the Soviet Union have shifted, both inside the country and abroad. The dissolution of external and internal empires, the new sense of moderation in foreign affairs, the arms control agreements, the reunification of Germany, the weakening of the authority of the Communist party, the new social and ethical values—all have fallen on the shoulders of the Soviet people in quick succession.

The collapse of authority is an indisputable fact. Although nobody at present doubts Gorbachev's authority, he nevertheless does not exercise his powers and endlessly postpones making important and inevitable choices. Thus, the new institutions of government, from the untried institution of the presidency to the Congress of People's Deputies, have not yet gained significant popular acceptance. For most of the Soviet people, a substandard system that functions is better than chaos. At issue is not so much the competence of the leaders as uncertainty about the outcome of evolutionary processes that may take a very long time. Fear of violence is widespread, and the concern about the possibility of civil war seems more and more realistic. A revolution is taking place, but one without leadership, without a revolutionary party, and without a clue as to where it will end. The past six years have changed the Soviet Union more than did the previous several decades.

1

The Dynamics of Freedom

Alexander Shchelkin

Sovetskaya Kultura
March 31, 1990

The most significant task facing the Soviet Union today is the establishment of a civil society based on compromise and tolerance. This has never before existed in Russia. The first step in this direction is the adoption of extensive legislation to introduce the rule of law—a process that is taking place at an extremely slow and cautious pace. For the past thousand years of Russian history, the ruler's wishes have taken precedence over the laws of the land.

A civil society is needed to restrict the power of the state vis-à-vis the individual. In this article, Alexander Shchelkin argues that the Soviet people paid an enormous price to build socialism and that the results were negative. Shchelkin unfavorably contrasts the passive attitude of the Soviet leadership with the active stance of President Franklin D. Roosevelt during the Great Depression. He shares the pessimism of Stanislav Shatalin (see Doc. 21) as to whether a civil society can be created within the USSR's existing sociopolitical system.

"Tomorrow There Will Be a Big Fight"

A historical necessity is stepping on our heels. We have begun quite actively to disassemble the old economic system and part of the political system. Clearly, however, we have procrastinated in devising the legal foundation of the new kind of society that we have finally dared to call "democratic socialism." The call to accelerate *perestroika* has therefore sounded just in time. Sluggishness in approving fundamental laws threatens to create so many social "long-term construction projects," requiring continuous repairs, that we run the risk of spending all of our energy and reserves of initial optimism.[1]

The magnitude of our doubts and our propensity for cautiousness deserve to be cited in the *Guinness Book of*

[1]Large construction projects in the USSR often are stretched out for decades and are synonymous with inefficiency, procrastination, and waste.

World Records. However, the time has come when he who does not take risks runs even greater risks. We cannot afford, at this time, to label our indecisiveness circumspection or even foresight.

Yes, today we are in crisis. This happens periodically with any nation, but not every nation suffers from atrophy of political will and an inclination to overcautiousness. When the Great Depression of 1929 to 1932 caused the American economy to decline by almost one third, Franklin Roosevelt spent no time searching for a panacea. He simply experimented. His motto was, "The most important thing is to do at least something!" But we have hypnotized ourselves with excessive concern about unforeseen consequences, forgetting that the right to make mistakes is a sacred prerogative of the initiators of *perestroika*, provided of course that we react to mistakes with *glasnost*, tolerance, impartial analysis, and action, and do not fall prey to panic and hysterics.

To feel the pulse of history is the obligation, rather than the privilege, of the major players in this drama. You cannot admire a nation in which the leaders' instinct for self-preservation is elevated to the status of the highest political wisdom and an uncompromising willingness to take risks proportional to the historical challenge is perceived as irresponsibility and a maximalist approach. According to the law promulgated by the renowned Solon, each inhabitant of Athens during civil disorders was obliged to state which of the opposing sides he supported. We would be naive if we considered this law to be only a pro forma gesture. Today, in the epoch of *perestroika*, political success depends on making correct political choices rather than on swinging from one extreme to another. It also depends on the correct choice of laws, which will bring us to a new civil condition and a new state of public order, protected and supported by compromise and tolerance. However, the road to such a state of affairs will surely be fraught with struggle.

"Tomorrow there will be a big fight." With these words, the academician Andrei Sakharov passed into immortality.[2] For this courageous and wise man, the struggle was not an end in itself, but rather the means of achieving a civilized and lawful order. Sakharov's political vision of humane conditions

---

[2]These were reported as the last words Sakharov spoke before he died.

for mankind is embodied in his draft of a new Soviet constitution.

What Comes after the "Civil Twilight"?

Today we often speak of the epochal character of the current moment, and I ask myself what about it is epochal? Not our discovery of the ancient truth that society should be governed by principles and laws, not by people. That truth was enunciated long ago by Aristotle. But with what difficulty do we arrive at this discovery? The root of our difficulties lies deep in ourselves—and not in the native conservatives[3] engaging in political activism at all levels. Bulat Okudzhava sings in one of his songs: "Why do you place your palm guiltily over your heart? Brother, you cannot recover what you did not lose."[4] In struggling to win civil and legal dignity, we will encounter this problem—gaining what we never lost.

In the history of our fatherland we have had few experiences with the concept of a civil society: the liberal reforms of the 1860s; Stolypin's innovative changes at the beginning of this century; experiments with the functions of the Duma after the revolution of 1905; the Constituent Assembly of 1917, which was freely elected but never allowed to function.[5] Prerevolutionary Russia earned the right to a bitter joke: "There are four systems of law and order. In Britain, everything is allowed, except what is forbidden. In Germany, everything is forbidden, except what is allowed. In France, everything is allowed, including even what is forbidden. In Russia, everything is forbidden, even that which is allowed." Alas, in postrevolutionary times nothing happened to change this bitter joke. Under the Russian Empire, hundreds of people were deprived of their civil rights

---

[3]"Native conservatives" refers to those who oppose any changes toward democracy in the Western sense of the word. They are opposed by Soviet "democrats."

[4]From the song "The Faraway Road."

[5]Petr Stolypin, Russian prime minister (1906-1911), tried to save Russia from its impending revolution by repression and halfhearted reforms. The Duma was the first Russian parliament. Between 1906 and 1917, four Dumas were elected in Russia, but the czar could not get used to sharing power and dissolved each of them. The Constituent Assembly was freely elected at the end of 1917. The Bolsheviks did not possess a majority in it, so they simply disbanded it by military force.

under the law despite the objections of a democratic Russian intelligentsia. Under Stalin, the entire country underwent "civil execution" without benefit of trial or investigation.

We surrendered our power and freedom with our own hands, without foreign intervention. We surrendered ourselves first to the harsh principles of class intolerance and later to an "administrative serfdom" tailored to the needs of the party, state, economic, and military *nomenklatura*.

In view of all of this, should anyone be surprised that we are entering into our new legal future with virtually no foundation of philosophical perceptions about the basics of civil life? Open the five-volume *Philosophical Encyclopedia*, published in our country from 1960 to 1970. In all editions, there is an entry on "civil war," but one can find no entry on "civil society." The same is true of the information jungle of the *Great Soviet Encyclopedia*, but one can encounter there something painfully familiar: "civil twilight." This is, in fact, an astronomical phenomenon, but in a symbolically fortuitous way, it sounds almost like the "twilight of civil society."

Any idea that is relentlessly imposed on society in spite of resistance and rejection ends up being a caricature of itself. Such is the fate of many of our ideological innovations. But some ideas are not subject to this verdict of history. Such is the idea of a civil society.

"Let the Game Be Honest!"

So what do we have here? Is it sufficient to say that the essence of a civil society is a free man?

No matter what the existentialists wrote about the burden of freedom, anyone who has lived in a stifling atmosphere of fear and public hypocrisy would hardly be inclined to make such a careless philosophical interpretation of this highest value of existence.

An innate Jesuit trickery of the native weltanschauung is that it sets too many traps for human freedom;[6] indeed, we easily sell it in exchange for a cozy comfort, full security, the benefits of state sinecures, etc. Our senses are so lulled by the mythology of social insurance that we respond meekly to the stridently sweet melody of freedom. Much has been said in

---

[6]Jesuit trickery, in Russian parlance, signifies a combination of foul play and perfidy.

the history of human culture about freedom as a necessary condition for human existence. But no condition is a guarantee. A free person poses a dilemma that agonized thinkers of the past. Remember [Fyodor] Dostoyevsky and his Grand Inquisitor's thoughts about how much freedom demands. First of all, man has to be protected from himself and from other free men. The bearded anarchists have numerous reasons for their dissatisfaction with the state, but until now the state has been the only bulwark against the self-destruction of society in a war of all against all. Nonetheless, no matter how order is established it immediately becomes a new threat to the freedom of man; this time the threat emanates from the state. All arguments asserting the impossibility of obtaining individual freedom in society come from the devil. Too often this sophism served as a convenient argument for politicians in support of a mechanistic structure of social existence that treats individuals as cogs in a state machine. A civil society, on the other hand, vigilantly guards the independence of the individual from encroachment by the Leviathan of state power.

All of the architects of a civil society—[Thomas] Hobbes, [John] Locke, [Charles] Montesquieu, and others—were motivated by a passionate desire to establish a human order based on freedom and the unfettered activity of citizens. The state was to act as a guardian of justice, to prevent the clash of private and corporate interests from erupting in civil war. The English poet William Blake expressed this philosophical postulate in a shining metaphor: "When the wide world became crowded for men, time came to proclaim: Let the game be honest!"

Our consciousness is not yet able to comprehend all the subtleties of the operations of a civil society concerning the state, as practiced by the civilized world. The essential strategy is to use the state only as much as is required to prevent freedom from slipping into anarchy, while at the same time keeping the state within its legitimate limits to ensure that it will not be transformed from a servant into an arbitrary master. A civil society knows only one way to win in this game with the state, and that is to create a rule of law.

A rule of law does not impose any objectives on its citizens, nor does it require them to make sacrifices in the name of a bright future; it simply gives them rights. Each person chooses and formulates his own objectives. A state without laws attempts to force politicized goals on its people and torments them by constantly changing the goals.

On the Other Side of Common Sense

When the academician Stanislav Shatalin asks, "Is it possible in principle to take our country out of crisis within the framework of the existing sociopolitical system?" he is, in effect, posing the question of how long we will postpone our entry into a civil society. Our lack of attention to the idea of a civil society is not acceptable. The price will be excessive in economic, political, moral, and psychological terms. It is high time for all native conservatives who have made a cult of their doctrinaire beliefs to understand that there is only one dignified and serious way to oppose a civil society, and that is to accept it as a historical inevitability.

The civilized world did not destroy a civil society. The sacrifice of economic and political freedom is too high a price to pay for the problematic "bright future," for the potential of state socialism. It is clear that to link the solution of fundamental human problems with the total destruction or dissolution of property is functionally equivalent to the notion that the best cure for dandruff is the guillotine. Life has shown us that there are less drastic ways.

A civil society cannot be "nationalized" in the same way as plants, railroads, or the mail service. The solution lies not in elevating the state to a position of absolute power but in helping the state to carry out its genuine function—democracy. With the help of democracy, the state can mobilize all the available energy of civil society and direct it in a civilized channel, creating as necessary remedial institutions and a system of checks and balances.

It is now clear that the dismantling of numerous economic and political institutions of a civil society that occurred in Russia seventy years ago was not critical for the creation of healthy conditions. In the beginning a modest measure was instituted—workers' control over private enterprise. Before it was over, we had a total nationalization of the means of production, even at the village level, where the peasants were simply cheated. The final result is well known: A monopoly in all spheres of life ended in the stagnation of the whole of society. Let us consider another example. Lenin suggested that the principles of ideology be applied only to the party's literature. His successors outdid him; they leveled all lay literature with the party yardstick. Another fact: We started with the slogan about the dictatorship of the proletariat and ended with the dictatorship of the secret police, with law and rights relegated to the "department of unnecessary things."[7]

Is there any need to continue this sorrowful list of victories on the other side of common sense? Must we continue to prolong the "civil twilight"? It would be much more reasonable to create a legislative foundation of economic and political freedom, so that a civil society could come into existence. Certainly, it is unquestionably true that freedom by decree will not become an integral part of society if society is not yet mature enough for it. However, it is also unquestionably true that the struggle for freedom is in itself a maturational process, an acquisition that no one will give up.

---

[7]A reference to Yuri Dombrovsky's masterful novel *The Department of Unnecessary Things* (Moscow, 1989), which describes Stalin's system as rule by an Antichrist, in which laws are included among unnecessary things.

2

Not All Theaters Are Erotic

A. Kuznetsov

Komsomolskaya Pravda
July 28, 1990

Although the country was going through a severe crisis, President Gorbachev took the time in December 1990 to read before the Supreme Soviet letters complaining about pornography. On December 5 he issued a decree outlining a program to combat pornography and establishing a Public Morals Protection Committee under the auspices of the Ministry of Culture. Two prominent members of the former Presidential Council, Yevgeny Primakov and Valentin Rasputin, were put in charge.

The shift from a hypocritically puritan socialist society to democracy is naturally accompanied by a more open interest in sex. Video clubs showing mainstream Western movies are becoming the most important entertainment for males in the Soviet Union. Severe economic problems and the lure of hard currency have resulted in an increase in prostitution. Soviet children learn a lot about Lenin, but nobody ever tells them about sex! Nor do adults have an opportunity to discuss their intimate problems with trained physicians. According to the older Communists and conservatives, it is *glasnost* that created this turmoil.

Dear Editor!

I read in your newspaper Mr. V. Shtyryakhov's letter, "Eroticism Is a Weapon, Too," and, word of honor, I shed a tear. I congratulate you wholeheartedly! I have been subscribing to *Komsomolka*[1] for more than twenty years, but a more hypocritical article I have not read, not even during the stagnation period!

It seems that, instead of nuclear weapons, now there is an erotic weapon. All must stand as one on the front line of struggle! Destroy the weapon and multiply chastely, like flowers and leaves! Remove eroticism from the big screen, from the newspaper pages, from the theaters, from the beaches, and from spouses' beds! And only then will we eradicate sexual crimes!

---

[1]A diminutive form of the newspaper's name, *Komsomolskaya Pravda*.

Our ancestors, as well as the Americans' ancestors, paid for freedom with their lives. And we, in exchange for our new-found freedom, are inundated by the naked thighs of Moscow beauties, leading all of society to dwell on but one thought: Whom should we rape today? Isn't it too primitive? Isn't it too pitiful a price for freedom?

The image of part or all of a woman's naked body is not eroticism! The description of the sexual act in literature is not eroticism, but rather naturalism. Eroticism is a depiction and a glorification of sensual love; it is not bestiality! I will swear that in the Soviet Union not one erotic movie or play has been produced, nor has one truly erotic book been published!

I can assure you, Mr. Shtyryakhov, that nobody forces sexual permissiveness into the public consciousness. To do so would be possible only through cruel repression and animal fear, which is never 100 percent effective in any case; society is never a unified conglomerate but consists instead of individuals. The more a person is cultured and educated, the more difficult such mind control is to achieve! Take our society in the 1930s: With education averaging four to seven years and with no culture, there was fertile ground for the forcible manipulation of thought. It happened! It also happened that sixty million people disappeared! And a lot of our citizens believed sincerely that their parents, children, relatives, and friends were indeed German and Japanese spies, Trotskyites, terrorists, or simply enemies of the people.[2]

And, in another example, how many times were we told in the mass media, literature, movies, and television that dear Leonid Ilyich [Brezhnev] was a smart, handsome, and courageous champion (of what?), a true Leninist (and who are the rest?), and a loyal proponent (of what?)? At the same time, society was laughing at him openly and telling anecdotes (at his expense). Why? Society had become more cultured and educated. And there was no fear anymore, only disdain.

I do not think that, at present, our society can still be afraid of anything! The genie has been let out of the bottle, and to put it back again would be very difficult! It might be also dangerous! And, Mr. Shtyryakhov, do not presume to speak for all of society, because we have plenty of cowards

---

[2]"Enemies of the people" was a vague accusation in Stalin's time to justify the repression of millions.

and scoundrels, traitors and conformists, rapists and murderers. Speak only for yourself.

I, for example, will never assault a woman after watching erotic videotapes or looking at nudes on a calendar. It is not eroticism that provokes sexual crimes, but our low culture, savagery and dullness, permissiveness, absence of authoritative powers, uncertainty about the future, and the deep moral and ethical crisis in our country! As a result we have a rapid rise in serious crimes!

Religion will not help us here, because it is not a panacea for all problems. Simply put, the church is now as much in fashion as are acid-washed jeans in the Riga market in Moscow. Before, we criticized the church and praised the bureaucrats, now it's vice versa.

I'd like to quote one sentence from your letter: "I suspect you are right that the term 'full freedom of creativity,' which has been talked about so much recently, should not signify a full freedom of artists to do anything they want."

The artist can only be called an artist when he has full freedom in his work. Otherwise he becomes a craftsman or, what is even more terrible, a flattering servant. Talent does not owe anything to anyone. It cannot be nurtured; one either has it or not. This is a notion that stands above classes, systems, and politics!

In dark, cruel medieval Spain *Don Quixote* suddenly appeared—a humanistic, light, and kind novel. And in the nice, staid tulip country of Flanders appeared the no-less-famous novel, *The Legend of Ulenspiegel*, all stained with blood, smelling of burned human flesh, pain, and suffering!

If these novels had been written by "assignment," the result would have been the opposite. These novels would not have become jewels of world literature.

Should we see everywhere and in everything the intrigues of the command administrative system? According to you, a naked back on the screen amounts to a conspiracy. A beauty pageant is a malicious plot. An erotic calendar in the metro is simply a terrible scheme. If there is a plot, where are the enemies—enemies of society, enemies of the people? Maybe everything is much simpler. Perhaps what we observe today is the expression of the "forbidden fruit syndrome." All of it will pass; we'll become more cultured, free, quiet, and we won't snivel because of every miniskirt, be enraged because of eroticism, write ludicrous mad letters to newspapers, and confuse low-quality cooperative goods with the arts.

But when will this happen? Until we live in such a dark and boring reality, Mr. Shtyryakhov, we should allow our youth to enjoy themselves by truly looking at beautiful men, women, and life. You remember Dostoyevsky's words: "Beauty will save the world!" It is truly so! When one sees a beautiful woman, one immediately forgets about increasing her role in society and about a positive outcome for the Food Program. And, in a further advantage, one's stomach suffers less from hunger, and one stops running to the stores. Instead, one lovingly feels the awakening of his primal animal instincts!

So let's be gentlemen. Don't deprive a Soviet woman of her only joy (she is already left without sausage). Let her, one who shares our misfortunes, have plenty of at least these things! And we men will go on somehow.

The roots of amorality in our country lie not in eroticism and pornography but in an agonized economy and an absence of ideals. We can do anything. We can forbid eroticism, put underwear and a Russian blouse on the statue of David and an old-fashioned swimsuit on Aphrodite. We can dress Danae in a deep-sea diving suit, close all cinemas and TV stations, and I assure you there will be no drop in sexual crimes.

A crisis of ideas brings about a crisis of authority, which in turn results in a moral and ethical crisis in society. We are all guilty in this! Some are guilty because they rule, and others because they allowed the first ones to rule!

Enough of screams, and appeals, and false threats ascribed to a nonexistent weapon. It is high time to learn to think and build, but not to restructure.

With erotic regards,

A. Kuznetsov, director
Palace of Culture, Moscow province

3

A Nation Begins with Its Women

Yevgeny Yevtushenko

The Literary Gazette International
no. 2, March 1990

The image of the Soviet woman as overworked, overweight, tired, and unable to take proper care of herself is widely known. More and more, the miserable situation of women in the Soviet Union has become a subject of public discussion. March is the month in which men pay lip service to women, buy them perfumes and flowers, so that they can exploit them mercilessly throughout the rest of the year. Poet Yevtushenko, once a favorite of Soviet youth and of the Slavic studies departments of American universities, is no stranger to controversy. Although he had promised himself never again to become embroiled in public issues, he could not help but speak up once more, for women. They have borne the burden of Soviet history through repressions, collectivization, and industrialization. Even wider job opportunity has turned out to be a punishment, since a great number of women work in undesirable occupations that in most of the civilized countries employ only men, while access is still denied to many professions. The appalling shortages of consumer goods are a greater burden for women, who still do most of the housework. Women are not very active in political life, and the Soviet Union is clearly behind the Western nations in the number of prominent positions held by women.

How long can we continue fobbing off the fair sex with cakes on birthdays and flowers on the Eighth of March?[1] It is high time we revised our attitude toward our womenfolk.

After my last two articles, "Servile Patience" and "Unmannerliness of Upbringing," I rashly declared that I had had it, I was through with journalism and was going to commit myself wholly to poetry. But it turned out to be easier said than done. For a long time I've been haunted by a line from a half-forgotten poem of mine: "A nation begins with its women." This article was not planned for any particular occasion: Instead of March, the traditional month for public

[1]The Eighth of March is celebrated in the Soviet Union as International Women's Day, an official holiday.

praise of women, it was born late in April, amid the smell of the sticky new leaves and the first violets pushing their way through last year's grass.

The very first picture you have of your nation and indeed of humanity is your mother's blurred face bending over you in your crib. You have been pushed out of her womb into the world, and your first cry of distress means: "I want to go back inside!" Mother is our first native country. How naturally the two notions go together in the word "motherland." And the famous wartime poster "Your Motherland Is Calling" had an emotional impact as well as a political one, for it touched some of the deepest chords of the human heart. A nation truly begins with its women.

One of my earliest memories goes back to 1937, when I was four. Both of my grandfathers had been arrested, and I remember Mother and me standing in an endless line in a street with the poetic name of Sailor's Serenity. In her hand she held a food parcel she hoped to be allowed to pass on to her father. As far as the eye could see in the blue-grey mist of the half-drizzle, half-snow, there were only women, women, women, and all with parcels. Not a single man. The men were afraid. Only women had the courage to inquire and to beg for their parcels to be accepted. All of them—mothers, wives, fiancées, daughters—they all became mothers of their arrested men.

The Bolshevik Revolution proclaimed that women were to be emancipated. But it did not mean, when Soviet peasants had their internal passports taken away and were thus chained to their collective farms, that peasant women could keep their passports. With all due respect for the talent of our sculptor Vera Mukhina, whenever I see her gigantic and dynamic bronze duo *Worker and Kolkhoz Woman* I am invariably depressed by the thought that this monumental beauty did not possess even an identification card. Women on the farm were enslaved by a new landowner, the state; women at factories were enslaved by the new industrialist, the state. The law of the land proclaimed, "Those who don't work, don't eat," and in effect insisted that every woman must go out to work. But isn't motherhood itself a full-time job? The housewife, the mother of a family has all but disappeared, and the few remaining specimens feel totally out of place, like class misfits. Even poets, instead of worshiping femininity, the fragile, vulnerable, tender, and passionate woman, glorified her physical strength, her political awareness, her industrial achievements, and her heroism in overcoming adversity.

Far from being placed on a pedestal, women were effectively demoted to the mere equal of men.

Characteristically, in Soviet high society the "privileged" position of the women was in effect a special brand of serfdom. The popular singer V. Davydova-Mchedlidze, a favored acquaintance of Stalin, recalls that her chauffeur asked her to intercede with the premier on behalf of his father, who had been convicted in the drive to wipe out independent farmers as a class. She broached the subject with Stalin, and she never saw the chauffeur again. Stalin was in the habit of humiliating his party associates. With sadistic refinement, he accused Foreign Minister [Viacheslav] Molotov's and Chairman [Mikhail] Kalinin's wives of being foreign spies, jailed one, and exiled the other. He even arrested, just in case, the wife of his totally devoted secretary, [Alexander] Poskrebyshev.

The official ban on abortions that we had for so many years (lifted in the mid-1950s) was not only an outrage to a woman's dignity. It also spelled almost certain death for countless women who were forced to apply to dubious midwives and assorted charlatans. On coeducational schools, or rather the lack of them: Several generations of boys and girls were brought up in an abnormally segregated system (coeducation was instituted in the mid-1950s), thereby aggravating the alienation between men and women.

True attempts were made to liberate women from heavy physical labor, for example in mines. The famous wagon women of the miners' folk songs became a thing of the past. The men who took their place had no intention of working for the same low wages, and eventually they got their raise.

Inevitably the question comes up: Why is it that for so many years women have been paid less for exactly the same work? Even now, women's salaries and wages average only 60 percent of men's. Is it because men's work is harder? Or is it because highly paid positions are mostly occupied by men? I think the main reason is male chauvinism.

My first election platform, printed in *Ogonyok* magazine, contained a promise to get a ban on the use of women for heavy physical labor. The letters that I got in response stunned me with their tragic futility: Women wrote that only such jobs could earn them a decent living, and a ban would be disastrous.

Yet a typical Soviet woman holds down three jobs at once: the one for which she gets money; then the job of standing in endless lines and dragging home shopping bags of food; and finally care of the children, the home, and particularly the kitchen.

A few years ago on a visit to East Berlin, I dropped in at a small shop not far from my hotel. Not that I was planning to buy anything; I was simply driven by our purely Soviet habit of staring at foreign goodies. It wasn't any special outlet, nor was it a hard-currency store for foreigners. And yet it boasted some two dozen varieties of sausage. Suddenly I heard a dull thud behind me. There on the floor was a girl in her early twenties. From her standard hairdo, the pattern of her silk dress, her dull beige-colored sandals, and many other less obvious details I recognized a compatriot. Up until then I had read in nineteenth-century novels about girls passing out from an overwhelming emotion, but this was my first encounter with a swoon. As the girl came to, her lips feebly whispered: "Why? Why?" When she had sufficiently recovered, I took her to a nearby café. I was intrigued: What had happened, what was behind the enigmatic "Why?" The girl told me that she was from a collective farm in the Altai region of Siberia, where she operated a tractor and a harvester combine. She was earning enough, she said, and for her "achievements in socialist labor" she had been "rewarded" with the trip to East Germany. But when she saw the shops bursting with sausages, cheeses, and other things she had never even heard of, and all to be bought without any lines, it was too much for her. "I can't understand it," she said. "It's we who won the war and they who lost it! Not that I begrudge them their high living standard but why must our life be so hard? Why?" With a sigh I thought, thank goodness she hadn't gone to West Berlin, where one fancy-foods store has no fewer than five hundred varieties of sausage!

But why is our life so hard? What did we do to deserve such a life?

In the weekly *Ogonyok* Academician Stanislav Shatalin cites an appalling figure: The unsatisfied consumer demand of the Soviet people now exceeds seventy billion rubles.

Nobody is saying, of course, that men don't suffer from the continuous shortages. But women obviously bear the brunt. It is they, after all, who are constantly seeking and finding ways out of the situation. Foreigners are surprised at how smart a lot of Soviet women look these days. If they only knew what a struggle it is, how much ingenuity stands behind every detail of a Soviet woman's costume. Foreigners admire the hospitality and culinary talents of our women; they have no idea to what lengths they must go to find all those little tidbits (which, incidentally, would grace a royal banquet). A Russian woman shops for the home, for the children, for her husband, and only then for herself. Try getting a kilo of frankfurters, half a dozen boxes of detergent, a pack of disposable diapers, some razor blades, and a pair of nice-looking shoes that don't cost the earth—all in one round of shopping! For the back-breaking job of supply sergeant alone, every Soviet woman ought to be getting a full pension in addition to her pay. Why can't the bringing up of a child at least to the age of one be equated with a paying job in the state sector?

While disastrously trailing behind the other industrialized countries economically, we lead the world in divorce rate. And yet why? A major factor is the explosive charge of mutual irritation yielded up from the thousand little cares of everyday life in crowded living conditions—a sure killer of romance. When each family member has his or her own separate room to sulk in during a set-to, there is more opportunity for mutual resentment to be dissipated. But what if there is only the one room—with one's aging parents or in-laws sharing the space besides? In a recent poll many Soviet women cited constant friction with in-laws as a main cause of divorce.

Women in the United States, by contrast, almost never mention this as a divorce factor. How come? Simply because most American newlyweds immediately hive off, and relationships with in-laws remain quite amicable, whereas so many young couples here have to live with their parents and in-laws for years, if not decades.

Our women get so exhausted from housework, shopping, and crowded conditions (also tension because of in-laws, relatives, and callous husbands, to say nothing of stress at their regular jobs) that they often prematurely lose their femininity. Chasing around to find a good face cream to preserve a youthful complexion, they age even faster. Giving women the right to buy a bottle of French perfume in exchange for a specified amount of waste paper and scrap iron! Is that the best the Soviet state can do to show its respect (much vaunted, by the way) for women? Even Kafka and Orwell in their most hideous nightmares could not imagine such a thing.[2]

I'm afraid that, with all due respect, just a few women members of the Congress of People's Deputies and other female public figures cannot champion all the causes of Soviet women. We need an association: Women for Women's Rights. We need women in all echelons of power. And just because Mrs. Nasriddinova, the high-ranking official in Uzbekistan, was once convicted for corruption and embezzlement, what have all the other women got to do with it? We haven't got a single woman minister in central government, not a single woman editor in chief of a national paper. What we need, of course, are not merely women's representatives who would meekly rubber-stamp government decisions. Unfortunately, some yes-women of this sort were handpicked to take part in the 19th Party Conference because they wouldn't pronounce a single word in defense of women's rights. Even what the women delegates talked about in the lobby often boiled down to complaints that there was no privileged shop made available for them as was the usual practice at party congresses. Don't get me wrong, I don't mean to ridicule those milkmaids, crane operators, cotton pickers, and others who were delegated to the conference from places where the shops simply never have babies' rompers, children's soap, or ladies' boots of any decent quality. But why then delegate working women who obviously had only a vague idea of the unprecedented political struggle going on in the Kremlin for their own future and for the future of their children?

We had the same situation at the [first session of the] Congress of People's Deputies: Many of the women delegates were, no doubt, excellent milkmaids and textile workers, but I'm not at all sure how many of them were aware of their history-making legislative mission. On the other hand, many able women candidates for the congress—candidates with a message—were blocked by the conservative district electoral commissions. I was impressed, for example, by the environmental and moral programs proposed by Mrs. Maria Cherkassova of Moscow's Liublino constituency and by Mrs. Ussova in Mytishchi. Fortunately, the local bureaucrats were unable to thwart Mrs. Alla Yaroshinskaya of the Ukraine's

---

[2]Kafka and Orwell both wrote fictional accounts of societies in which individual autonomy was restricted unbearably.

Zhitomir province, fondly called "our Alla" by her constituents.

Still, I don't lose hope that our women deputies will rally together and pick those who are best suited to represent their interests. Women from a factory or a farm might suddenly become leaders of the women's cause, but for heaven's sake let's cast off the blinders of reverse class prejudice which have done our society so much harm. More often than not, women from the professional classes and the intelligentsia can defend the interests of milkmaids, crane operators, and cotton pickers much better than they themselves can.

And it's time we men came down a peg or two, it's time we stopped being such condescending male chauvinists when discussing the role of women in society. How long can we continue fobbing off the fair sex with cakes on birthdays and flowers on the Eighth of March?

It's high time we revised our attitude toward our womenfolk. After all, a nation begins with its women. But a nation that doesn't respect its women can hardly hope to be respected by others.

4

A Commonwealth of Cultures

Ivan Dzyuba

The Literary Gazette International
no. 2, August 1990

This article, a measured response to the Russian nationalists and their arguments, was written by a former dissident who for years was persecuted by the authorities and who is now a prominent opposition leader.[1] It is directed against Russian nationalism's pretense of a "special historical mission." Dzyuba compares the Russian nationalists with the notorious Black Hundreds who tried to salvage the Russian Empire. He points out that the smaller nations of the Soviet Union have not benefited at all from their natural resources, unlike such Third World nations as the Arab countries of the Middle East.

Dzyuba believes that it is pointless and immoral to argue over which people suffered most from the October Revolution and from Stalinism. He also points out that it would be inappropriate to contrast the disintegration of the Soviet empire with the integration processes under way in Western Europe. In his view, Russian patriots have themselves caused "Russophobia" by spreading greatly exaggerated claims (see, for example, Doc. 8) that Russia has selflessly helped everyone.

There has been a recent trend to reconsider the Soviet Union's future in the light of national revivals going on in the republics. Even people who not long ago were uncomfortable with the word "national" (let alone in conjunction with "revival") are now speaking along these lines. But what are the realities of these revivals? If national revival means a popular effort to achieve real political, economic, and cultural sovereignty, we are (bearing in mind the Ukraine) still far from this goal.[2]

---

[1]Ivan Dzyuba's *Internationalism or Russification*, written in 1965 and translated and published in London in 1968, argues that Stalin had distorted Lenin's principles concerning nationalities. For this and for other activities he was persecuted by the Soviet authorities and briefly imprisoned in 1973.

[2]Although Ukrainian nationalism was and is very strong, it is more difficult to separate this republic from the USSR than the others because its economic, social, and cultural ties with Russia are diverse and strong, and because Russification was more successful there than it was in the Baltic republics and the Caucasus.

Some of the preconditions necessary for revival exist already. They are becoming more firm before our eyes. Most significantly, national self-awareness and civic activism are growing in the context of anxiety over the status of the individual republics and the entire union's future.

Our hopes for a national revival are directly connected with the fate of *perestroika*. Its collapse would mean the collapse of our hopes and the loss of what little we have. National revival can be brought about with years of constructive effort and purposeful work. There is no place for mass hysteria or passions. These things are not only fruitless but also often dangerous. This is especially true of state-making in the present situation of exacerbated interethnic relations. These nationalist emotions are destructive when someone tries to harness them to fulfill some "historic mission."

It seems that history's lessons have never registered in our minds. We remember the Black Hundreds from our classrooms, and we condescendingly think that it was just a band of social outcasts. Not a bit of it! It was a powerful social movement, a quite popular, ultranationalist movement with a sophisticated, broad ideological foundation. The Black Hundreds were guided by masters of social and national demagogy. Their task was to save the czarist empire from the threatening revolution. They were to direct the people's protest and anger away from the regime and against such "agitators" as the revolutionary intelligentsia, "Jew-Freemasons," and "foreigners oppressing the Russian people." Aren't we today witnessing the birth of a new variant of this movement? In any case, the movement's main ideas have currency again.

But is it only in this corner that trouble lurks? Have the attempts of one people to bring unfounded and unverified charges against another people helped to create mutual understanding?

It seems to me that here we approach the main source of stereotypes, falsifications, and myths in overly nationalistic self-awareness. We need to think about the situation. Every republic and every autonomous region has enough resources and every people has enough productivity and intelligence not only to escape poverty but also to flourish in the modern world. If the United Arab Emirates achieved their level of wealth due to only one resource—oil—then why hasn't black gold made Azerbaijan, Bashkiria, Poltava province, and other places wealthy? Why has "white gold"—cotton—brought nothing but suffering to the peoples of Central Asia? And what does the "hard currency workshop" of the Soviet Union—Yakutsk—have for all her diamonds, furs, and gold? These kinds of questions can be raised about any republic or any people. Where does all the incalculable natural bounty and incredible human effort go? It is consumed by the incredibly wasteful command system of bureaucracy!

It is completely immoral to make an issue over which people suffered most from the monstrous social experiments engineered by Stalin. But an issue is made! As if one could calculate human grief. Can we gauge the Ukraine's misfortunes (three famines, including the manmade one of 1932–33; the destruction of the intelligentsia; fascist occupation; and the present-day ecological damage, including Chernobyl) against the misfortunes of the Russian people or the woes of Byelorussia or the Crimean Tatars? No. It is better to look for small joys to share than to count our sorrows.

I find the statements of Russian patriots concerning "Russophobia" peculiar. I have the impression that some people very much want Russophobia to spread and are ready to do anything to stimulate it. Let's think soberly: What good can come of the wildly exaggerated thesis that Russia has always helped and saved everyone, and now, when she has given away all she had, she gets ingratitude in return and is left alone to wrestle with her fate?

In the first place, Russia has in no way been left alone with all her problems. Aren't other republics, particularly the Ukraine, assisting in her revival? I won't even mention Russia's use of Tyumen and Northern and Far Eastern oil resources. Second, we do not need an emotional reaction to the real instances of Russophobia. What is needed is a deep sociological, historical, and psychological analysis of the origins of such anti-Russian feeling. Furthermore, I feel that much of the blame for strained interethnic relations falls on those Russians living in the other republics. Due to arrogance or lack of culture they do not respect or take an interest in the life, language, and culture of the local population. Third, much is made over the assistance given to less developed regions after the revolution. Yes, Russia helped, as did the Ukraine and other "strong" republics. What is so odd about this? After all, little Sweden gives aid to African peoples where there is no historical bond, and this aid has no strings attached.

Unfortunately, patriotism for parts of the intelligentsia has reached the point where offense is taken at the mention of completely genuine historical facts. For instance, they find it hard to swallow that Russian great-power chauvinism and Russian nationalism ever existed. It has always been assumed that only other peoples were nationalistic. People do not think about the fact that the Russian Empire was a prison for many peoples. To deny this, to try to soften the harsh realities of czarism, is to insult the memory of thousands and millions of the best sons of Russia's peoples (including the Russians themselves). These persons dedicated their lives to the freedom of their own peoples and the creation of a future—alas, still not realized—brotherhood of nations.

We cannot move toward a new union on this kind of ideological and psychological foundation. Interethnic conflicts, especially the criminal and bloody ones, cast a disturbing light on the general nationalities problem. They create an atmosphere of ill will. They put people who are speaking out for their native language and culture in the Ukraine, Moldavia, and other republics in an extremely difficult position. Certain parts of society come to think that such people are themselves guilty of creating difficulties and hostility. Thus new myths are formed.

Another negative factor in the nationalities issue is the irresponsible action of certain elements in the republics themselves. In particular, adventuristic and provocative slogans have been giving national movements a militaristic or malicious character.

Still another factor that complicates interethnic relations is national demoralization. This phenomenon of self-denial even reaches the level of "self-devouring" (especially in the Ukraine). For a long time our society fought nationalism. Under the cover of this struggle, national self-awareness was eradicated. Today we must constantly remember the catastrophic perversions of the clampdown on nationalism. Even the word "nationalism" has become empty and stereotyped. This is very dangerous. We must give the word an objective, clearly defined content. Furthermore, actions taken against nationalism must be more sophisticated and tactful. They should not confuse right and wrong.

The main source of interethnic complications, however, is the set of unsolved political, socioeconomic, and ecological problems facing the Soviet Union. The concealment of facts and the falsification concerning the economy, particularly concerning the financial relations between the center and the republics, create tension. Ideological complications arise out of this economic situation. This, in turn, exacerbates interethnic relations.

Opponents of nationalities' individual development often refer to West European unification. But those who want to defuse national self-awareness seem to forget that the union of Western Europe is based on the political and cultural independence of its various peoples. Although they have a unified health care system, for instance, West European peoples do not in any way have the same health standards. Moreover, these countries jealously preserve their own sovereignty. They are not willing to recognize any hegemony in Europe, be it political, cultural, or linguistic. So there is no reason to place our hopes on a natural course of events, to wait while political and economic emancipation leads to linguistic and cultural independence. We have to work from both ends.

This does not mean that culture and language are secondary in a nation's emancipation. Indeed, culture sparks this process and is its crown of success. Statehood is not the final guarantee of a people's way of life; it is only a precondition. Only a complete, globally significant culture guarantees a people's way of life. Culture is the fundamental expression of a people's creativity and the chief goal of historical development. It is also the best means by which we can be understood by other nations. In this way, perhaps we could really help them.

5

Vilnius: A Night in Spring

Oleg Moroz

The Literary Gazette International
no. 1, May 1990

A column of eighty to one hundred Soviet tanks rolled past the Lithuanian parliament barely two weeks after Lithuania proclaimed its independence on March 11, 1990. This article and interview accurately present a picture of sacrificial determination coupled with absolute helplessness. The independence of Lithuania was hanging in the balance. President Vitautas Landsbergis, a former professor of musicology, expressed surprise that it was necessary to send so many tanks, when thirty soldiers armed with submachine guns would have been sufficient to arrest everyone.

The events described in this document were only a warning of bloodier days to come. On January 13, 1991, Soviet troops killed thirteen Lithuanians who had captured and were attempting to control a local television station in Vilnius. One week later, five people were killed during an assault by Soviet militia on the Ministry of Internal Affairs in Riga, Latvia.

The interview was scheduled for Friday, March 23, at 10 P.M. This is not an unusual hour for Professor Vitautas Landsbergis, president of the Lithuanian Supreme Soviet, since lately he's been working around the clock. My colleague Pyatras Keidoshius and I stationed ourselves at his door, but we were not too optimistic about seeing him soon, as the session of the Soviet was still under way. Then we learned that he unexpectedly had to appear live on Canadian television at 10 P.M. He excused himself and left the session, explaining to us on the way out, "Today I'll have to work on and on. So please wait, we'll talk later."

His reception room is staffed with two secretaries. One, the more imposing Regina, is the Supreme Soviet president's secretary proper. The other one, Yadwiga, is—as I gathered—Landsbergis's assistant for Sajudis (Lithuanian Movement for *Perestroika*). She was hired only recently, and her duties could be described as consultative and advisory.

People kept entering his study, without previous announcement or even a knock at the door (which, by the way, wouldn't be audible from his desk: The study is enormous). The visitors were of two kinds: bearded men in elegant suits—some were deputies, or leaders of Sajudis, or both; and young men with a student-like appearance, dressed in athletic suits, or jeans—Sajudis activists and, some, functionaries of the Supreme Soviet *apparat*.

At about half past one the reception room became more animated, with more people in it than usual. The general conversation carried overtones of anxiety. The people spoke Lithuanian, but from snatches of English and Russian I deduced that something was up on the Kaunas-Vilnius highway.

After a while, Yadwiga approached me and said, "I am sorry we've made you wait so long, but the president will not be able to see you. Tanks are approaching Vilnius from Kaunas."

"Tanks?!" My drowsiness completely vanished.

"Yes, many of them. People have been calling in. Someone counted more than eighty."

"Not again!" I was terrified. "You shouldn't have done it," I said involuntarily.

"Done what?" said Yadwiga without understanding.

"What was done on the eleventh of March. Weren't you already moving toward what you wanted? Economic and political independence? Why did you precipitate events?"

"But someone had to begin. How much longer could we endure?"

Yadwiga was weeping. One of the boys began to draw the blinds. Blackout. Just in case.

I wandered off into the building. The news had spread quickly. Groups of journalists and functionaries of the Soviet stood everywhere, discussing the situation. There were no signs of panic, just weary waiting and curiosity about the debacle.

A small car flashed out of the dark and sped across the square, right up to the entrance. Without pausing to kill the engine, a youth sprang out, darted past the stupefied guards, and ran up the stairs—five at a leap—to the second floor. There, in imitation of ancient Greek runners with tidings, he threw himself down, exhausted, before Landsbergis's door. Regaining wind, he sat cross-legged on the floor, slapped it with both hands, and pronounced one word: "Tanks!" He was certain that his was the first warning we'd heard.

At five minutes past 2 A.M., Landsbergis came out of his study.

"Is the situation becoming more complicated?" I asked him.

"Yes," he answered reluctantly. "You see, we'd be wasting time if we proceeded with the interview now. Who'll publish all this if I'm arrested? Who needs an interview with a detainee?"

"Did you try to contact Gorbachev?"

"No," he said uncertainly, shrugging his shoulders.

At 2:30 A.M., Landsbergis addressed the Supreme Soviet. He told the deputies that a column of tanks was approaching the city. Its purpose was unknown; they had received no information whatsoever. He had repeatedly asked the military to keep him informed of the force's every move within the republic, but despite all assurances that such information would be provided, this had not been done.

The Supreme Soviet voted that, if through certain coercive measures its rights to function and to voice freely the will of the people should be infringed upon, it vest the Washington representative of the independent Lithuanian Republic, Mr. Stasis Losoraitis, with emergency powers in representing the restored Lithuanian Republic.

Evidently remembering my question, Landsbergis asked the deputies if they thought he should call Gorbachev. The entire audience responded as one: "It's of no use."

The telephones continued. The tanks were drawing nearer. Thirty miles . . . twenty . . . ten. . . .

Five minutes later Prime Minister Kazimiera Prunskiene passed by the journalists and, knowing her sacred duty to keep the press informed, told us that in five minutes we'd know whether the tanks would skirt the city on their way to one of the garrisons, or would enter it. There were many, many tanks—eighty to a hundred.

Mechanically, I made sure my press card was in my pocket. A ridiculous gesture. As if I didn't know how it would be: Tanks and combat groups pull up. Boys in mottled uniforms infiltrate every crevice of the building, spreading out over all staircases. Then you get it in the teeth, a gun butt in your back and a boot somewhat lower. Only after that does the who-is-who procedure begin.

At about twenty minutes to 4 A.M. I went outside. In the air hung the continuous hum of motors. They were about to appear. The head tank whirled on its tracks and came straight at me. Its flaring headlights were blinking; I dodged away. My imagination had got the better of me; it was only a cab. I went back. Meanwhile the hum never abated, but it also did not rise.

Ten minutes later I went outside again. The noise was considerably lower. Some people were running toward me. I caught a boy by the sleeve.

"What's up? Where are they?"

"Off to the garrison, north of the city," he panted, waving in that direction.

"Thank God! We're safe!"

I saw Prunskiene on the second floor and, relieved, asked in jest, "Danger over?"

"It's over, but there's nothing to be happy about," she answered seriously.

4:30 A.M. Landsbergis appeared and gave Regina a handwritten sheet to type: The answer to Gorbachev about registering volunteers who, should it prove necessary, could take part in maintaining public peace and order.[1]

Here I saw my chance and immediately approached him. "I think my time has finally come?"

He nodded readily. "I've just cabled Gorbachev: We have no military forces. The tanks approaching the capital of the Lithuanian Republic have no business here. Why so many? Thirty men with automatic machine guns could easily seize everything and take everyone here captive. We don't intend to put up resistance."

We sat down at his desk. The table lamp revealed his pale grey face, puffy from lack of sleep. On their tiny personal computers, foreign correspondents were hastily pecking away, trying to make it before the "tanks—reached—the parliament line."

Interview with the President of the Supreme Soviet of Lithuania, Vitautas Landsbergis

Moroz: Mr. President! I respect the right of all those in Lithuania—and in other republics of the USSR—who seek to live better than they do at present and to determine their own fate. The question here is: How should this be achieved? By the line of action the Lithuanian leadership has already

---

[1]Gorbachev had demanded that Landsbergis stop recruiting volunteers for the Lithuanian militia. Landsbergis replied with a conciliatory offer to negotiate, but he maintained that Lithuania had the right to recruit volunteers to man its borders and customs stations.

taken? I have my doubts. Don't you? Do you consider your steps the only ones that could have been taken?

President: To my mind we have not made mistakes. The issue of separation is one of paramount importance. The time has come to abandon the rebellious and revolutionary traditions of the past and to deal with the situation in terms of law and reason. I see separation as based on the free expression of the absolute majority's will, with the procedure of the separation and the expression of will thoroughly reasoned by the legislature.

Moroz: Why did you prefer unilateral action to a calm bilateral consideration of the issue?

President: Because the law on leaving the Soviet Union does not concern us. We are not members of the Soviet Union. We did not enter it, but were invaded and annexed. We don't want to be involved in an ambiguous situation. Moreover, its stipulations are such that no one would ever be able to leave.

Moroz: Please elaborate.

President: For example, the mandatory joint agreement with all the other republics concerning the right to freedom.

Moroz: But the law has not been passed yet; it is only a draft. You could participate in the discussion, present your demands, and possibly come to some sort of an understanding.

President: We saw this understanding, when other laws were being discussed. Besides, in seeking some minor concessions we might give the impression that we recognize as valid the jurisdiction of the USSR.

Moroz: But such recognition has repeatedly been confirmed; the Lithuanian Supreme Soviet again and again has voted for union-wide decisions.

President: True, but you know the value of such voting. It's worth nothing.

Moroz: You do realize that you are putting Gorbachev in a difficult position?

President: No. It was Comrade Stalin who did that. He put the country in a very nasty situation. We want to help this country divorce and free itself from its criminal heritage. Then we are reproached. Why should we want to help the country become more civilized?

Moroz: When I say you are putting Gorbachev in a difficult position, this is what I mean: As I see it, if the president of the USSR agrees to Lithuania's version of separation, it means that he must also agree to have the state fall apart, because Estonia, Latvia, Georgia, etc. will immediately follow in Lithuania's tracks. Of course, it can be construed that eventually, and in accordance with resolved legal procedure, certain republics will separate, remaining within either the federation or a confederation, if they don't leave completely. But this process must not have the potential to completely dismantle the country. I don't think any leader would agree to this. That's why he is acting so resolutely and firmly.

President: If you think the republics will begin to depart one by one—that's your business. I personally do not know how things will develop. And why is Gorbachev's position difficult? Was the British government in a difficult position when its colonies had to be freed? Was France in a difficult position when Indochina, and especially Algeria, had to be freed? Of course, for General [Charles] de Gaulle it was a serious problem, but he coped. Why shouldn't Mikhail Gorbachev try to deal with it in the same spirit? Perhaps he's simply unable. If so, that's too bad.

Moroz: How would you deal with it in his place?

President: Well, I'd at least make an effort.

Moroz: As a politician, don't you have the feeling that you will fail at this endeavor which you've undertaken?

President: I don't see how whether I fail or not is crucial. Do you think the Decembrists failed?[2]

Moroz: In a sense, yes.

President: Does that mean they shouldn't have done what they did?

Moroz: How far ahead had you thought this through before resolving on the step taken on March 11th? Did you expect the measures that followed?

President: Not specifically. But, by and large, we had foreseen that there would be counteraction. Some measures—economic difficulties, instigation of national hatred—were used as threats before, too. So, to a certain extent, we had prepared ourselves for this.

Moroz: How far are you ready to go in challenging the center?

President: We have no such notion as "center."

Moroz: What about Moscow?

---

[2]This refers to a failed coup attempted in December 1825 by Russian officers who supported democratic reforms against Czar Nicholas I.

President: Moscow for us is the capital of a big neighbor with whom we'd like to maintain the friendship and harmony of good neighbors, but not as subordinates, not as a landlord's farmhands.

Moroz: At what point would you be ready to abandon your separation plans and go into reverse gear?

President: I cannot conceive of such a situation.

Moroz: Tanks just went past this building. A lot of tanks.

President: Well, what of it? What can they do? This is absurd. They can raze us, crush us, but that doesn't solve the problem.

Moroz: Are you able to foresee developments? What will happen to Lithuania in half a year? In a year?

President: I think we'll be negotiating with the Soviet Union. Some of the relevant issues will have been solved. Or perhaps all. This will depend on developments within the Soviet Union and, of course, in the world.

I think the world will soon see that we are not undermining Gorbachev but helping him. We have constantly been helping the Soviet Union to wake up. Generally speaking, Gorbachev has so far been conducting it all wisely. At present they are attempting to put him in an ambiguous position, specifically as regards Lithuania. Mikhail Gorbachev deserves great respect. He has often impressed us as a person superior to his handicapping political entourage.

6

Confessions of a "Renegade"

Piatras Keidoshus and
Vitautas Petkiavicius

Literaturnaya Gazeta
no. 1, January 1991

This interview with one of the founders of the informal movement Sajudis, Vitautas Petkiavicius, reveals the serious political disagreements among the Lithuanian people regarding the policies and methods of their president, Vitautas Landsbergis. It was inevitable that Sajudis, a widely based movement for independence, would one day split into an array of political parties. It should also not be a surprise that the national states that are trying to assert themselves are utilizing the same coercive tactics as Russia had done before, as they are saddled with the same deficient political culture and intolerance. This slows down and may even reverse the process of achieving genuine independence and democracy in the Baltic republics.

Keidoshus: In an interview with the *Litaratura ir Mianas* weekly you said: "Sajudis has told us all a big lie. It had declared in its program that it wouldn't try to seize power, but now it has done just that." And then you go on to say: "Never before has Lithuania been ravaged—either materially or morally—so much as today." How did it happen that you and your colleagues' brainchild, on which the whole of Lithuania is pinning so much hope, has turned into a "deceiver and robber"?

Petkiavicius: True, I'm one of the founders of Sajudis, but neither our program nor our actions had even a hint that we would some day fight Stalinism with Stalin's methods. I firmly believe that violence inevitably turns any goal into a lie. Sajudis was born as the Lithuanian people's bid for freedom. We had no intention of glorifying anyone, nor did we wish to humiliate anyone, for we knew that Lithuania needed all her children equally—the righteous and the erring. We had a burning desire to give everyone a chance to help revive Lithuanian society, regardless of their ethnic background, political or religious beliefs, or social status. However, leadership in Sajudis was gradually taken over by a bunch of demagogues who didn't care about the movement's original essence, its program and aspirations. They simply said: "The political situation has changed and now we are going to dictate our will." The new leaders pushed aside the scholars and writers who had founded Sajudis. They used its more obedient members to establish an elite ruling party, which they called Independence. It's the same old joke: A revolution is prepared by intellectuals, carried out by fanatics, while its results are used by con men. Probably this should have been expected, because we've lived for too long with a triple straitjacket: party commitment, coercion, and fear. We were deceived by our own political ignorance, and those who told the biggest lies and promised more than the others got to the top, while those who warned that the road to independence is long and hard were pushed aside and trampled underfoot.

Landsbergis hasn't been in power for even six months, but collections of his speeches are already coming out in mass editions, like Lenin's, Stalin's, and Brezhnev's used to be. His followers use hunger strikes to unseat the government he doesn't like. Writers who dared to criticize him are disgraced and blacklisted. Sinister pickets are staged outside the windows of those who had the courage to protest. The republic's radio and television networks taken over by Landsbergis pour dirt over dissenters, branding them "enemies of the people."

What democracy, what law-abiding state can you talk about when the amended penal code of October 4 specifies imprisonment, expropriation, and execution for dissent? Truly, history is repeating itself.

How come the majority in Lithuania puts up with this situation? Because our ambitions prevent us from admitting our mistakes. It's clear as daylight that, as a result, the old dictatorship has been replaced by a new one, which has already played economic and political havoc.

Alexander Solzhenitsyn warned in his most recent article that politics is not the most important thing in life, it's not something that can give happiness to the people at large. The more society is engulfed by political struggle, the less there's room for spirituality, culture, and intellectualism. This inevitably results in mass apathy and consequently stagnation.

A nation's spiritual resurgence is impossible to expect in the midst of mass rallies and demonstrations. It will take time before people can decide for themselves who is who. But we will experience such a resurgence, of that I am sure, especially if we don't sit by and twiddle our thumbs. We need to patiently explain to people the state of affairs as we see it.

Keidoshus: What, then, has happened to the Lithuanian intelligentsia, or rather a section of it? In the stormy months of 1988 before the first session of the new parliament, the intellectuals would applaud every move made by Sajudis, and rise to the defense of their heroes and brothers-in-arms if they were attacked from any quarter. Now that power has been won and independence declared (March 11), there suddenly appears this appeal signed by intellectuals whose authority is well-nigh indisputable. Most of them were in at the birth of the movement, and some of them did not even conceal their anti-Communist sentiments. The appeal contains words like these: "Regrettably, not all of us favor democracy, legality, truth, and mutual respect. Some are obviously making a bid for personal glory." And that's when the campaign against those who signed the appeal began, didn't it? Incidentally, some of the critics were intellectuals, too, yesterday's teammates, you might say. What is this, growing pains? Or a natural process of polarization? Or a general sobering up?

Petkiavicius: Frankly, most of my colleagues are either disappointed or intimidated by what's been going on here. The image of Lithuania, carefully nurtured by the politicians, as a lovely, quiet, peaceful, but long-suffering nation is, with the rise of critical sentiment, turning into that of a blind, unheeding mob with a singular lack of memory. Then there's the well-rehearsed technique of intimidation, the revanchist tendencies, the anti-Communist hysteria. Put all that together and you get the situation that faces intellectuals today.

Most of them are Communist party members, though I must say they did not join to further their careers, but out of a deep desire to help the country in whatever way they could. Doing nothing in those conditions would, in their opinion, have been a greater sin. They worked hard to awaken national awareness, and to help Lithuanians preserve their cultural heritage. For this they were criticized, even hounded, and this went on for many years. Only the love of their countrymen and their gratitude gave them the strength to go on, deepening their conviction that Stalinism couldn't last forever, that justice would triumph. When Sajudis was born and their program was published, these people so devoted to their ideal were the heroes of the day. Today, for expressing a single truthful thought, they are publicly rapped on the knuckles.

This is the reason, I think, why this group of people, founders of Sajudis and deputies, attempted to appeal to the people of Lithuania: Come to your senses, they said, democracy is in peril. Elect a new constitutional parliament, and have a thought for the future of Lithuania, not just in words but in actions as well. And these patriots were ridiculed and trampled underfoot, a smear campaign launched against them, their many years of devoted work called "kowtowing to the occupants."

I'm an old bird myself, so I'm not afraid of these little Fascists. That's why I can openly declare today that our ideal of independence cannot be harmed by anyone except ourselves, if we go on with this infighting and humiliation of nonindigenous people.

Another thing: As a rule, talent, kindness, individuality are things that develop when you can be by yourself if you want to. In any situation, talent must be allowed to be itself. Evil, on the other hand, and mediocrity and power are generally well organized. Add to that the terrible envy that consumes the nonentity, and the desire to be prominent, rich, and powerful, and you can explain the appearance of all those people and understand their hankering after power.

Keidoshus: In the talk you mentioned, you refer to the state of mind of a certain section of the Lithuanian public, declaring: "Today, though we fear these words, we have been caught up in mass hysteria, the herd instinct has taken over and politics has become a religion."

Petkiavicius: I am completing a book on the origins of Sajudis and its untimely demise. I have carefully studied the biographies of Stalin, Hitler, Mussolini, as well as the political trials that led to their rise. And I am tempted to remind my readers of what Hitler wrote: "The masses are capable of taking in very little," he wrote. "Their ability to understand is extremely limited, while their forgetfulness is colossal." The moral? "Only he who repeats ordinary things thousand of times over will be remembered. If one is to tell a lie at all, it might as well be a big lie. This is more likely to be believed than a piddling one." And further: "In case of failure, it is necessary to find an enemy immediately. If there is none, then one must be invented."

This, too, must sound familiar.

In our country, the real *perestroika* is so late in coming not just because Stalinists and those who did so well under Brezhnev are constantly obstructing progress. The trouble is that, together with all those who are honestly trying to push through the reforms, there exists an assortment of chameleons who want to be seen as leaders of the process, though they are the ones who in the past always stifled any new ideas.

It is a bitter thing to have to admit, but in Lithuania such people are having a field day. Their incompetence has already cost our economy billions of rubles. Yet we are still under the influence of mass rally euphoria, expecting all differences to fall away of themselves as soon as we become independent. Many people are still obsessed by the idea that if state institutions are replaced or somehow improved, that will automatically change everything!

Some Lithuanians think they want an improved version of the prewar Smetona regime,[1] others still hope to patch up communism. Russia is once again banking on a good general secretary or a czar. Nothing will come of it, either in Lithuania or in Russia, because history has yet to see an idea once discarded by a nation return there to be used again. Such ideas always leave the arena for good and all. What is needed is new ideas, for the moral and cultural resurgence of a people is never linked with mass movements or mass politicization. The last word, the decisive say for the future of our society lies not in good or bad organization, not in military discipline or unbridled anarchy. It lies in the inner potential of each of the individuals that make it up. That's why to the question "Can the leadership we now have take our republic to independence?" I answer in the words of the old quip: "Yes, but I'm sorry for the Lithuanians."

Keidoshus: We are considering our old literary values, such as socialist realism, with articles beginning to appear like the one in *Literaturnaya Gazeta* called "A Lament for Soviet Literature," by Victor Yerofeyev, in which he rejects all the literary methods previously favored.

Petkiavicius: You say we are rethinking our values? As I see it, values have very little to do with it. Talent confronted by organized mediocrity—that's an old, old story. Didn't the

---

[1]Antanas Smetona was a ruler of Lithuania for most of the period between World War I and World War II.

critics of the time write that Anton Chekhov would end his days in the gutter together with his writings? And they were wrong, weren't they? Did Lord Byron ever dream that he would be called the father of romanticism? He just lived according to the laws of his talent. What would you call Giovanni Boccaccio's *Decameron*—naturalism, realism, or some other "ism"? When the critics predict eternal glory for the works of their friends and other writers who think the same way as they do, I know that they will, with the same carefree hand, sign the death warrant of works by dissidents and whichever of their brethren may have a new literary approach. Socialist realism is nothing but a term, and a synthetic one at that. If you can write, then you will do so whether you have a label pinned on you or not.

So they can go ahead and hold a funeral mass for Soviet literature if they want, so long as they don't put a gag on those who don't agree with them, or try to bury the living. When a critic is unable to understand or analyze what the writer is saying, he has only one way of expressing his displeasure, and that is by making pseudoscientific forecasts—this author's books will live forever, that one's will be forgotten by tomorrow. There's nothing more behind all the mumbo jumbo.

Russian literature, and to some extent literary criticism, has always suffered from messianism. But that, I suppose, is the business of the Russians. We Lithuanians seem to be beset by delusions of grandeur, or the "European syndrome." Instead of the "historical basis" we are all so tired of, our critics now all tend to view a writer's work through the prism of nationalist revival. But what, after all, is nationalism? It has become fashionable to see it as an antidote to great-power chauvinism, but that is only the political aspect. What about the spiritual side? I see it as patriotism taken to the point of folly, which has nothing in common with either nobility of motive or high moral values. If national pride is ruled by wisdom, culture, and morality, it will never turn into nationalism. If it becomes a cult, it leads to strife, wars, and the killing of other people. This sickness now affects the entire Soviet Union, including Russia, because chauvinism is exactly the same as nationalism.

Many today adopt the trappings of nationalism to make their policies more attractive, turning our sacred patriotic feelings into a propaganda gimmick. Into the fray go the ready-made phrases our glib politicians need to arouse the public, but nobody looks ahead to the consequences.

Keidoshus: Could you tell us about your personal experience? What you have learned from the events of the recent past?

Petkiavicius: Now, when I seem at last to have reached the age of maturity, I understand that, whatever happens, you must remain true to yourself. It's a hard thing to do, but not impossible. It is even harder to expose your own ego to the public gaze. But perhaps hardest of all is to appear as the prophet of gloom among your own people, to sit down and quietly write "No" when everybody is screaming "Yes!" All the more so since the mob soon tires of anybody who seems too reasonable and sober-minded, preferring somebody more like themselves. This type of mutual attraction as a rule leads to anarchy, which is soon followed by dictatorship.

Keidoshus: They say you have left politics and public life and retired to your farm (the envious even speak of an "estate"), and that you now devote yourself to gardening and carpentry, that you keep bees and go berry picking and mushroom hunting.

Petkiavicius: Living on my "estate," I don't hide from people. The silence of the forest simply helps me to concentrate. And physical work keeps me sane. In our time, nobody can remain completely calm, a writer no more than anyone else. If, as in 1917, 1933, and 1940, people are again seized by the passion to destroy and annihilate, while politics becomes a religion, we would do well to remember the blessed words: "Forgive them, O Lord, for they know not what they do."

Think about them now—later might be too late.

7

Faith without Action Is Dead

Patriarch Alexei II

Izvestiya
June 16, 1990

This was the first interview of a newly elected patriarch of the Russian Orthodox church by a major newspaper in many decades. In these times of strong nationalism, it is remarkable that this head of the church was born into a family of Russified Germans. He quite honestly describes his difficult years of accommodation to the Soviet authorities. The patriarch expresses the hope that the church will play a more important role in the spiritual life of the country from now on. He acknowledges that only the first steps have been taken on this road. This interview was conducted on the Moscow-Leningrad night train by the correspondents G. Alimov and G. Charodeyev. In the morning, the patriarch was greeted by the new mayor of Leningrad, Anatoly Sobchak. The railroad station was decorated with flowers. The Russian Orthodox church has been readmitted into political life.

Izvestiya: Your Holiness, every believer approaches God by his own path. How did you come to worship Him?

Alexei: I became a servant of the church when I was six years old. At that time, a desire for pastoral service arose in me. The church in which I was baptized was located in Tallinn. My parents were profound believers.

My route to lifelong spirituality was defined by two pilgrimages to the Valaam Monastery on Ladoga Lake in 1938 and one year later, when I went there again with my parents. I was then nine years old, and I still remember very well that the beauty of the monastery left me with an unforgettable impression. The upper church had just been renovated, and it shone with red and gold. We left the monastery with sadness in 1939, and I felt that we would not return for a long time. So it was; the war began.

Izvestiya: You are coming to a city that has been very important in your life. Shortly, you will conduct your last religious services here.

Alexei: It was extremely difficult for me to leave Leningrad. The city on the Neva has played a very important role in my life. In 1946, I tried to enter the Leningrad Orthodox Seminary, but they did not accept me because I was not yet eighteen years old. However, the next year I was accepted by taking an exam for two years, advanced placement. I finished at the seminary in 1949, and a year later I was ordained into the priesthood. After many years of pastoral service in Estonia and administrative service in Moscow, I again returned to Leningrad in 1986. I cannot say that these four years have been easy. The church was still ignored by the authorities. Immediately upon my arrival, I decided to visit the city's mayor. I was told that this had never happened before and would never happen. A year later, I succeeded in meeting with the city officials. The mayor at the time asked me in surprise, "Is this your first time at City Hall?"

"Yes," I said, "they didn't allow me in."

He answered, "Hereafter the doors will always be open for you, day or night."

Indeed, these meetings started to occur regularly. Nonetheless, it was necessary to fight for our rights. The opinion persisted, for example, that there were already enough churches in the city. Only with great difficulty were we permitted to open the Cathedral of the Archangel Michael. The opposition came forth with many arguments; they insisted that we open an exhibition of children's paintings or a museum in the church. And, most significantly, they asserted that it was out of the question for a functioning church to be located on the Prospect of Young Leninists. I replied, "Then why is it that the Leningrad Cathedral can be located on the Square of Communards?"

Izvestiya: Why hasn't the church participated in charitable activities for so many years?

Alexei: For people of the church, it is always difficult to answer this question. It seemed that we excused ourselves from providing help to the sick, the old, the poor, prisoners, orphans, invalids, and to all suffering people in general. In the New Testament it is said, "Faith without action is dead." But our hands and feet were tied by the decree of 1929 on religious associations; this law directly prohibited the church from engaging in charitable activity and participating in the upbringing of children. The Soviet government took over all these functions. Now, in the period of *glasnost*, it has become clear that millions of destitute and sick people are in need of concrete assistance. Unfortunately, in the intervening years, people lost the habit of doing practical good. Therefore I see a great educational task for the Russian Orthodox church. We should not be ashamed of elevated sentiments; people must be educated to do good and to create it.

The church should now return to its traditional spheres of activity. From time immemorial the church has sponsored old-age homes, trade schools, temperance societies, and orphanages where children deprived of parental care could receive a worthy upbringing. All this must be restored. But today we begin with nothing, and we are only just taking the first few steps.

Izvestiya: Does the new legislation on freedom of conscience and religious organizations specifically take into account the interests of the Russian Orthodox church?

Alexei: We hope that the churches will finally be granted greater scope for social activity and for nurturing various age groups. We have some opinions regarding the new legislation, and we have expressed them on more than one occasion in public. The law that passed the first reading was not completely satisfying to us. If that version were to be accepted, it would be a step backward.

Izvestiya: Your Holiness, you met at the Kremlin with the president of the USSR. What questions did you put before him?

Alexei: Life itself presents many questions. For example, I expressed my anxiety concerning the situation in several provinces of the western Ukraine, specifically the problem with the Uniates. The establishment of parishes of the Russian Church Abroad inside the Soviet Union also worries us.[1] This is an obvious example of the split within the church. At a time when the processes of integration are occurring all over the world, we are experiencing disintegration in our society and in our church. We told the president about this.

Izvestiya: How do you see the role of the government in smoothing over these contradictions?

Alexei: I want to emphasize that we did not ask for help from the head of state. We only familiarized him with our position on all these questions.

Izvestiya: Which position do you personally, as patriarch, support concerning the settlement of the conflict between the Uniates and the Orthodox church?

---

[1]Uniates, also known as Catholics of the Eastern Rite, are former Russian Orthodox in the western Ukraine who submit to the authority of the Roman Catholic pope. The Russian Church Abroad is the Russian Orthodox church established in the United States and Canada.

Alexei: Only by peaceful dialogue and the renewal of the activities of the Quadrilateral Commission on the Uniate question (with the participation of representatives of the Vatican) will we be able to remove the tension that arose lately in the western Ukraine. These days I receive numerous telegrams about violent seizures of Orthodox churches by the Uniates. In such cases, political emotions and nationalism play an undesirable role, causing the deterioration of interfaith relations. If there is a further confrontation, it may lead to very sad consequences. We don't need a religious clash in the Soviet Union now.

Izvestiya: Are you prepared to meet with the Roman pope in order to discuss the mounting problems?

Alexei: We have urgently informed John Paul II about the results of the All-Lands Church Council in Moscow.[2] On the 25th of June, he will meet in Rome with the Uniate bishops. It is necessary for him to hear the unambiguous position of the Russian Orthodox church on this question. We, in our turn, were informed officially that the pope has approved the work of the Quadrilateral Commission, which was created expressly for the purpose of settling differences between the Orthodox and the Catholics of the Eastern Rite. We hope that he will encourage the Uniates to work with the commission and that all problems can be resolved by peace talks with the Russian Orthodox church. In my opinion, we should base our decision on the following criterion: If the majority of the parishioners are Eastern-Rite Catholics, then the churches should belong to them; in other cases, they should belong to the Orthodox. It is intolerable that in Lvov the Uniates took over all the churches and did not leave even one in which the Orthodox could worship. Since February, our priests in the western Ukraine have performed services in many places under the open skies. This is a violation of human rights, of religious principles, and of ethical norms.

Izvestiya: In the same message of the All-Lands Church Council we read, "Until recently, the activities of the parish were limited because, in many churches, important posts were occupied by nonmembers and sometimes by nonbelievers who had selfish goals." How would you comment on this?

---

[2]This refers to the council of all Russian Orthodox bishops, from all of the Slavic republics of the USSR.

Alexei: The All-Lands Church Council of 1945 approved a regulation on the management of the Russian Orthodox church, in which fathers superior of the churches were designated chairmen of the parish councils. In 1961 the authorities suddenly remembered that the Law on Religious Associations of 1929 had not been repealed. At that time, the priests were deprived of voting rights, and they lost the right to be members of the parish council or to be in the church Twenty.[3] All financial matters were placed in the hands of the lay people. Nevertheless, in some of the dioceses, the process proceeded normally and elections were held. Unfortunately, in several provinces, municipal authorities appointed chairmen of parish councils from among people alien to the church. They were pawns in the hands of the church commissioners appointed by the Soviets. The priests protested but were helpless. Just imagine, they were signing work contracts—an inherent violation of our canonical laws. The priest is hired to conduct a divine service! Inconceivable!

Izvestiya: And what is your point of view on internal church problems?

Alexei: There was a time when we were sharply criticized by the Russian Church Abroad and by the Western world in general. We were accused of betraying church interests. As a bishop's conscience demands, I must say that even in the most difficult times, we were trying to use to the maximum those opportunities that we had. But never were we traitors to the church! We understood that our church must find its place in Soviet society. Sometimes we were looked upon as second-class citizens. Nevertheless, we did not abandon our motherland, and not one clergyman became a traitor. We were always patriots of our country and carried the cross that fell to us.

It is easy for the representatives of the Russian Church Abroad to criticize us. They live abroad in safety, having abandoned the motherland in difficult times, during the years of revolution and Stalinism. We had an opportunity to conduct the service of God, although confined within our church walls. We unfailingly preached the word of God, held services in honor of Him, and presided at baptisms, weddings, and funerals. During baptisms, problems arose when it was

---

[3]The Twenty is an extended council to manage the church-related affairs of the parish.

necessary for parents to be present and to signify their approval with their personal signatures. These facts were immediately reported to the municipalities by the same lay people who were alien to the church. Then, the churchmen were reproached by the people, who said, "We had a wedding at your church, and you betrayed us." That is how we were portrayed in the eyes of the believers.

Izvestiya: Dostoyevsky once said, "Beauty will save the world." How do you interpret this saying?

Alexei: One of the church teachers of the early period remarked that the human soul is Christian by its nature. And if man had only followed the Christian ideals, then his soul would have stayed pure and beautiful. Not in vain did the Reverend Serafim Starovsky say, "Gather unto yourself a peaceful spirit, and thousands around you will be saved."[4] The more we sow the seeds of kindness around us, the more kindness will we receive ourselves. Today, unfortunately, we must admit that love among people is drying up. To restore love among people, to restore tolerance toward one another—that is what is needed today. These are the eternal shining ideals of humanity.

---

[4]On January 11, 1991, the Museum of the History of Religion in Leningrad solemnly returned the relics of Starovsky to the Russian Orthodox Church.

8

A Letter from Russia's Writers

Moskva
no. 5, 1990

This letter, a true manifesto, is the most significant statement by the Russian conservative and nationalist forces since the notorious Nina Andreyeva letter (see Doc. 13 for more information) published in *Sovetskaya Rossiya* on March 13, 1988. This letter was first published in *Literaturnaya Rossiya* on March 2, 1990, signed by seventy-four people; by the end of March, more than three hundred had signed it. It was later reprinted by other conservative publications. The main targets of this statement are moderate and liberal publications, such as *Izvestiya, Ogonyok, Sovetskaya Kultura*, and *Moskovskie Novosti*, which are accused of being racist, of denigrating the Russian people, and of glorifying the Jews and Zionism with the aim of undermining Soviet military power on orders from the West. This is a reaction to the ongoing revision of Soviet history and to the growing nationalism of the non-Russian nations of the USSR. Although its authors try to dissociate themselves from Pamyat, this letter is evidence that their differences are minor.

In recent years, under the banners of "democratization" and establishment of a "legal state," and with the slogans of a struggle against "fascism and racism," our country has seen an unleashing of forces of social destabilization. The frontline of this ideological *perestroika* has been occupied by heirs to blatant racism. Their dens are the central periodicals with multimillion circulations, and television and radio channels broadcasting over the entire country.

We are witnessing a mass victimization unprecedented in all of human history, deception and persecution of representatives of a country's native population. They essentially have been declared outlaws from the point of view of that mythical "legal state" which seems to leave no room for the Russians or for any other indigenous peoples of Russia.

Tendentious and brimming with national intolerance, conceit, and hatred, the publications *Ogonyok, Sovetskaya Kultura, Komsomolskaya Pravda, Knizhnoe Obozrenie, Moskovskie Novosti,* and *Izvestiya* and such magazines as *Oktyabr, Yunost, Znamya*, and others compel a conclusion that the Russian people is the most unwanted stepchild of the current "revolutionary *perestroika*." Representatives of its three living generations, starting from the veterans of the Great Patriotic War, who saved the world from Hitlerism, people from different walks of life and professions—Russian people—daily and without any objective reasons are called by the media "fascists" and "racists" or, with a visceral contempt, "Sharikov's children," the descendants of dogs.[1] This immediately brings to mind the propaganda terminology that Hitler applied to Russians, the "inferior" Slavic race.

Systematic racist vilification is directed against Russia's entire historical past, pre- and postrevolutionary periods alike. "Millennium-old slave," "the mute retort of slavery," "the serf soul of Russia," "What can a millennium-old slave give to the world?" Unfortunately these slanderous clichés about Russia and the Russian people, which deny not only the fact but also the possibility itself of Russia's positive contribution to world history and culture, define the attitude of the central periodical press and television to the great heroic working people who once bore on their shoulders the awesome burden of creating a multinational state.

"The Russian character has historically degenerated; to resuscitate it means to condemn the country once again to backwardness that may become chronic." This is what we read printed in Russian on paper manufactured from Russian forests. The very existence of a "Russian character," a Russian ethnic type, is branded inadmissible by this monstrous logic! The Russian people is declared to be a superfluous and profoundly undesirable one. "This is a people with a distorted national self-consciousness," conclude Soviet political personalities and journalists. Yearning to dismember Russia, to abolish this geopolitical concept, they call it: "a country populated by ghosts," Russian culture: a "booty," the millennium-old Russian statehood: a "utopia." In the official media, the desire to take Russians outside the scope of *homo sapiens* has acquired the marks of a racism so clinical, so maniacal that it seems to have no analogues among all the ancient records of raving misanthropy of the past. "Yes, yes, all Russian people are schizophrenics. They are half sadists craving unlimited power, half masochists craving bruises and chains." This Russian stereotype is deliberately disseminated

---

[1]In Mikhail Bulgakov's short story "Dog's Heart," a dog named Sharik is transformed into a vulgar proletarian with the habits of a KGB man.

by Moscow "humanists" in the media of the union republics to mobilize all the peoples of the country, including other Slavs, against their fraternal Russian people. The Russophobia of the USSR mass media has caught up with and outstripped any foreign, overseas anti-Russian propaganda. The distinguishing feature of the local defilers and slanderers is their denial of the true nature of their activities, denial of the undeniable fact of Soviet Russophobia, a disclaiming of their crime against Russia and the Russian people. Discriminated against in his real civil rights, denigrated as a "slave," as an "unreality" or a "ghost," the Russian is at the same time persistently branded an "imperial chauvinist" who threatens other nations and peoples.

With this end in mind, the history of Russia is being falsely and leeringly rewritten, the sacred heroism of Russian patriotic feelings is being interpreted as "genetic" aggressiveness, self-reliant militarism. "And who on earth hasn't she gone to war with?!" laments, with regard to the "bully" Russia, Alexander Yakovlev, member of the Politburo of the CPSU Central Committee, in *Literaturnaya Gazeta* (April 14, 1990). "And all of that is retained by the memory. It forms the consciousness, stays in the genetic pool. It is a psychological burden of a heritage."

Is it to relieve us of the genetic, psychological "burden" of patriotic battlefield glory that the central media are denying Russia equally her victory over Napoleon and her victory over Hitlerite Germany? Countless, indeed, are the examples of the shameless lies by the mass media that try to shout down Nikolai Karamzin's *History of the Russian State*, Alexander Pushkin's "To the Slanderers of Russia," Leo Tolstoy's *War and Peace*, and the still-living memory of our contemporaries.

Although openly sympathizing with the nationalist movements and fronts (from the Baltic to Moldavia and Transcaucasia) that are infused with Russophobic sentiments, the mass media mostly hush up the tragedy of the Russian people, of its great sacrifice in the past and present, of the numerous pogroms against the Russian populations of the union republics. Against the background of these pogroms organized in various regions of the country, and in the face of the thousands of Russian refugees denied shelter in their own country, the mass media multiply their crude provocations aimed at fostering aversion to Russians, picturing them in zoological terms as, for example, in the February 2, 1990, program of the "Vzglyad" TV magazine devoted to a soirée given by *Nash Sovremennik* magazine.[2] The bogeyman of Pamyat is being blown out of all proportions and passed off as a mighty aggressive force, sort of like Hitler's Abwehr.[3] The truth of the matter is that there are a few clowns who by no means express the views of an entire people—that is true, even leaving aside the undeniable fact that their homemade placards captured by TV cameras are not a bit more nationalistic than the slogans of many of the "democratic" "popular" fronts of the union republics.

Another example of a large-scale provocation insulting to many peoples of Russia is the concerted effort by mass media to denounce the Sixth Plenum of the Board of the Writers' Union of the Russian Republic as an "anti-Semitic orgy." Almost 70 percent of the participants of the *plenum* were representatives of the Russian Republic's fraternal literatures.

Deeply provocative and groundless are the charges alleging that the Board of the Russian Writers' Union was involved in the obstruction of the meeting of the Moscow writers' organization "April" by persons who are not even members of the Russian Writers' Union.[4]

Deeply provocative as well as importunate is the desire of a number of media outlets to cast the Russian Writers' Union as masquerading big mouths from a glamour-hungry faction of Pamyat, with a few habitual demonstrators.

A note is in order here: Attempts to escalate any thought about a rebirth of Russia, about her political and economic equality, the uniqueness of her historical path, and the distinctiveness of her national culture to the shrill level of the "shocking" placards of the notorious (while in fact unknown and probably self-proclaimed) types from Pamyat undoubtedly serve to cover up the true racism and neofascism whose considerable forces are united in the USSR Union of Zionists with its paramilitary Betar troops.[5] The central media, while hysterically screaming about the threat to mankind, to all the peoples of the USSR, from the odious

---

[2]The head of Soviet television and radio, a Gorbachev appointee, took this program off the air at the end of 1990.

[3]Hitler's military intelligence organization.

[4]A group of Pamyat supporters burst into this meeting and disrupted it with physical violence and anti-Semitic statements.

[5]The Union of Zionists was created in 1989. Betar, a youth group created in Riga in the 1920s, advocated a more resolute policy to settle Palestine and organized defense of Jewish neighborhoods.

members of Pamyat, invariably gloss over or brazenly embellish the ideological core of Zionism. They conscientiously distract our citizens' minds from the fact that the Betar organization legalized in the USSR not only is responsible for the racist slogans about the Jews being "chosen people" but also was involved in such feats as massacres in the Palestinian refugee camps in Sabra and Shatillah as well as hundreds of other bloody crimes and terrorist acts that more than once made the world shudder.

Leaving in the shadow the true brownshirts[6] of today, who have unconstitutionally broken into the heart of Russia—Moscow—under their cover of the Jewish-Zionist Congress of December 18–21, 1989,[7] who have launched their practical activity and ultraracist propaganda all over our country, the "progressive" press, including party publications, sows the blasphemous notion of **"Russian Fascism,"**[8] "the nazism of Russia," "the neonazism of Russia"—a phenomenon we have never had.

Speaking at the February *plenum* of the Central Committee of the CPSU, Academician Stanislav Shatalin harangued about his academician's "shame" for the decision of "Great-Russian chauvinists to revive national socialism on our Russian soil, which would be equivalent to national chauvinism."[9]

It is significant that at the *plenum* no one objected to the "shameful" academician and his irresponsible, groundless accusations. A "revival of national socialism on our soil" implies that national socialism existed here in the past; it would seem that the academician has at the very least confused nations, countries, and soils: Russia with Hitler's Germany, aggressors with their victims. Such absentmindedness may be natural in a learned man with his head in the clouds, but is it becoming to a CPSU Central Committee *plenum*? One is left to wonder what the Communist Stanislav Shatalin knows about the "Great-Russian" plans to conquer the world and subjugate other nations, which would be the hallmarks of chauvinism. And to whom does the scientist refer when he talks about "Great-

---

[6]"Brownshirts" is a nickname for Hitler's storm troopers.

[7]This congress of all the Jewish organizations in the USSR took place in Moscow. The conservative press criticized the authorities for permitting it, the first such event in fifty years.

[8]Emphasis here, and in other boldface passages below, was in original.

[9]Reported in *Pravda*, February 8, 1990.

Russian chauvinists" and Nazis so predatory that they have him blushing with shame for Russia?

In the absence of facts regarding "Great-Russian fascism," the sociopolitical motives of such fiction reveal themselves in the press. The daily *Izvestiya* (February 19, 1990) is "thrown into despair" at the sight of a harbinger of "trouble!" in the guise of "the slogan on the square," "a placard raised by a hooligan(!)" demanding "Russian teachers—for Russian schools." *Izvestiya* strikes the alarm in its review of letters to the editor: Behold, "Russian fascism!"

This newspaper, the organ of the Soviets of People's Deputies of the USSR, categorically denies Russians precisely the same basic social rights it goes out of its way to hail in any African country. It hails the strengthening of similar rights (albeit in an overwrought manner) in the Baltic republics, Armenia, and Georgia. For example, *Izvestiya* has failed to spot "fascism" in the speech given by Shalva Amonashvili at the 1st Congress of People's Deputies in which he advocated the "development of a Georgian school" that would not only teach in Georgian but also steep the pupils in Georgian national ideals, love of Georgia, and national pride.

We are forced to conclude that **the phantom of "Russian fascism" today is conjured up to justify the ongoing, and apparently intended to last forever, comprehensive discrimination against Russia**.

How innocent was the infamous protest against the creation of a Russian Communist party and even a Russian Academy of Sciences voiced at the February *plenum* of the CPSU Central Committee by the same Academician Shatalin immediately following his aspersions about "Great-Russian national socialism" and "national chauvinism"? As if it is by fascism—and little else—that the history of Russian academe has been distinguished from the time of Mikhail Lomonosov![10]

The phantom of "Russian fascism" was invented for a variety of purposes, including foreign policy purposes. Its authors believe it can, through the mass media, decisively **divert the attention of the peoples of our country from any external threat to the security of the state**.

At the same time, the phantom of "Russian fascism" and the "antifascist" hysteria in the Soviet mass media instigated

[10]Lomonosov was a prominent Russian scientist of the eighteenth century.

around this phony cause has the goal of **preempting the possibility of any alliances between our country and other** (primarily European) **nations in the case of a common external threat.**

The fiction of "Russian fascism" is shoved down our throats in order **to justify the destruction of the Soviet army, to undermine the defensive might of our country.**

Currently being planted in mass consciousness, here and abroad, the lie about "Russian fascism" has been elaborated, in particular, **for the sake of negating the international consequences of the Second World War, the results of the victory of the Soviet Union and the European nations of the anti-Hitlerite alliance—of all the peoples who arose to defeat fascist Germany. The provocative lie about "Russian fascism" is being advanced as a, profoundly humiliating to Russia, "moral background" for the reunification of Germany, as an ideological means of transforming a victorious nation into a nation disgraced by shame.**

Furthermore, spreading the lies about "Russian fascism" serves to **"rethink," to abolish as an event and as a criminal act such real occurrences as treason and collaboration with foreign companies and governments so as to betray the state interests of our country.**

As for domestic political consequences, the unbridled fabrications about "Great-Russian national socialism" **have dealt a blow as thoroughly calculated as never before to the traditional historical friendship of peoples in the Soviet country—all the peoples "brought together by the Great Russia"—who may now be doomed to a fatally adventurous political destiny.**

A more universal and far more objective and plausible conclusion that equally concerns our swarthy and fair-skinned compatriots should be drawn: The widely financed and technically equipped ideological anti-Russian campaign started in the USSR mass media can logically have but one practical result—establishment in Russia, and in the entire country, of an uninhibited "Pretoria regime." It does not take much perception to notice that hailed, with consistency and ingenuity, in the moral and political **tribunal** as "nationalist" ("chauvinist" after their own manner, and "racist") are **all** peoples of our country, though many of them are being used in the global anti-Russian campaign. Set against one another, and invariably against the fraternal Russian people, they will inescapably find themselves just as disposable as the Russian nation in the hands of the transnational extremists, the political gangsters of the ultraleft, tyrannical stripe. They will find their historical land, natural riches, and cultural values used as commodities of international speculation, a source of profits for the "we-are-all-just-one-mankind" mobsters from the "national liberation" movement and the mythical "democracy."

Is it not peculiar that the fabrication of the myth of "Russian fascism" is taking place against the backdrop of a speedy rehabilitation and unreserved idealization of Zionist ideology?

Such antihistorical, deliberate idealization is an old and tried means of creating the notion of a "superior" nation—an "*uber*"-nation. Uncritical, sugar-sweet, essentially obsequious to Jewishness in its past and present, its local and foreign varieties, including imperialism and Zionism, this idealization is transformed by the mass media into a touchstone of personal, social, and even professional standing for Soviet people of non-Jewish descent.

However, merely stating the fact, formally identifying the Jewish ethnicity of a person or a group condemns a Russian (or a Ukrainian, Byelorussian, Chuvash, Azeri, or anyone else) to the badge of an "anti-Semite." Any such objective statement is regarded as an assault on "human rights," on a recently invented "ethnic privacy"; it is a "malicious" violation thereof, which is somehow equal to a violation of doctor-patient confidentiality and, apparently, of state secrets. For the "rights" of a superior race embrace concealing one's ethnic background and profiting from its privileged status, ethnic imposture, hiding behind the name of another, and nationalist arrogance. The bottom line is a guaranteed freedom from any historical responsibility, let alone national repentance of the type now being extorted from other peoples, first of all from Russians.

Under these circumstances, even many honest Soviet Jews are not protected from charges of "anti-Semitism" with all their dire consequences.

Under these circumstances, even sympathy with the Palestinian Arabs fighting for their legitimate rights becomes "sowing ethnic strife in the USSR."

Under these circumstances, we must note with concern, especially suspect of a lack of due servility and obedience are Russians, those "millennium-old slaves"! Historical facts notwithstanding, they are accused of "visceral," congenital anti-Semitism. Meanwhile, the Jewish Scientific Center of the Soviet Sociological Association of the USSR Academy of Sciences publishes in *Vestnik Evreiskoi Sovetskoi Kultury* [The Herald of Soviet Jewish Culture] (no. 4, 1990) "data" compiled by Academician Tatyana Zaslavskaya[11] showing that Russia excels in "manifestations of anti-Semitism" (unfortunately left unspecified) above and beyond other Soviet republics.

In the old **distorting** mirror of mass media, "anti-Semitism," "racist madness," "Russian fascism," and "the nazism of Russia" appear, at close inspection, to be anything that is not advantageous—no, not to Jews—to Zionists. And, since the latter are narrowly tuned to the interests of the state of Israel, to the rapacious interests of the black sheep of the Jews, since they only stand to lose from the absence of anti-Semitism in Russia (which puts a brake on the emigration to Israel and hinders the assignment of privileged political refugee status to Jewish emigres from the USSR), the absence of anti-Semitism or—much worse—the admission of its absence in Russia is perceived as "anti-Semitism." Such is the casuistry of dirty nationalistic politics! Thus falsified are the true interests of the majority of Soviet Jews, who do not want to spit on their Russian motherland or to support the aggressive designs of Israel. Thus deliberately narrowed and distorted is the concept of fascism, which is in fact an objective one, to the point where it is reduced to "manifestations of anti-Semitism" and nothing else. We are to believe that the real fascism, all too familiar from the time of Hitler and Mussolini, confined itself to the persecution of one ethnic group only, targeted Jews alone, with the conclusion that "there can be no" fascism or nazism of the Zionist variety. Meanwhile, it is the latter brand that is responsible for numerous pogroms, some of them against the Jews themselves, for "cutting off the dry branches" of their own people in Auschwitz, Dachau, Lvov, and Vilnius.[12]

---

[11]Tatyana Zaslavskaya, for at least the last ten years a tireless reformer, has long been a favorite target of conservatives.

[12]Auschwitz and Dachau were Nazi concentration camps in Poland and Germany; in Vilnius and Lvov, Jews were massacred with the assistance of

With friendly contacts between the Soviet Union and Israel expanding beyond the will of the Russian people, the free export of Zionism into our country has become a menacing reality; its danger to all the peoples of our country has taken center stage.

Particularly revealing in this respect is the ad nauseam discussion in our mass media of a "law on anti-Semitism" that would specifically, exclusively protect one ethnic group only. Bringing up this less-than-vital narrow issue of a selective ethnic privilege or a special right to state protection is in itself indicative of the essentially nationalistic bias of much of the media. This prejudicially legalistic and nationalistically selfish issue is raised against the backdrop of the countless human losses being suffered by various peoples of our country (although not by the Jews).

It should be added, with regard to the "law on anti-Semitism" (which is being extorted by the mass media, a group of the people's deputies of the USSR, and a number of "democratic" fronts and movements), that this artificial law with no basis in real life is particularly dangerous to the Russian population, who suffered the full force of such a policy in the 1920s and 1930s. We know that it is in fact a **law of Russian genocide.**

We demand to put an end to the anti-Russian and anti-Russia ideological campaign in the press, on radio, and on television. We demand an immediate and explicit ban on all public manifestations of Russophobia throughout the entire territory of Russia and the other Soviet socialist republics.

We demand a distribution equitable to Russia of the means of mass media publishing, which would correspond to the material and economic contribution of the Russian Republic to the national paper output and which would actually serve the interests of the Russian people and the other peoples of the Russian Federation commensurate with their respective numbers. We demand equality of the Russian Republic with other republics of the union in the volume of television and radio broadcasting.[13] In the Russian

---

Lithuanian and Ukrainian collaborators. Soviet critics of the Zionist movement accuse it of cooperating with the Nazi extermination of Jews.

[13]The Russian Federation, or Russian Republic, includes sixteen autonomous republics named for other nationalities.

Republic the powerful media enjoying a monopoly over the formation of public opinion and the ideological education of the population **must be turned to face fully the pains, concerns, hopes, and national ideals of the Russian people and of other peoples of our federation who have securely bound their destiny with that of the Russians.**

The current ratio—**a circulation of 1.5 million of patriotic Russian-language periodicals to 60 million of Russian-language periodicals that propagate Russophobia and represent an insult to Russian national dignity** (and that not taking into account a sea of unofficial newspapers and magazines)—**is tolerable no more, for it is destructive to Russia**!

We appeal to all Russians, workers, peasants, and national intelligentsia: Despite all the sorrows, persecution, and humiliation that the twentieth century has visited upon our people, **always remember the national dignity of the Great Russians bequeathed to us by our glorious forefathers, by a millennium of Russian history.**

Daily remember that we Russians are a highly talented, heroically courageous people with a powerful spirit who know the joy of meaningful creative work. "Russian character," Russian heart, utter Russian devotion to **the truth**, Russian sense of fairness, compassion, honesty, and finally Russian patriotism, ineradicable and selfless—all that can never be obliterated from the treasury of the human spirit.

Let us arise! Let us take into our own hands the destiny of our motherland—Russia!

Bibliography

Al'bats, Yevgeniya. "According to Gender." *Ogonyok*, no. 10, 1990.
Soviet women are victims of a double standard.

Biryukov, Fedor. "A People's Tragedy." *Moskva*, no. 12, 1989.
Describes "the genocide of the Cossacks of the Urals and Don River by Communist commissars, who were mostly Jewish and inspired by Trotsky."

Bokhanov, Alexander. "There Lived A Boy." *Nedelya*, no. 1, 1991.
A sentimental story about the family of the last czar, focusing on Prince Alexei, heir to the throne. The author condemns the killing of the czar's family as a portent of the wave of killings that followed and as an example of the presumably Marxist doctrine that the life of an individual is not important. An unusual article for a centrist journal.

Bushin, Vladimir. "When Doubt Is Appropriate." *Nash Sovremennik*, no. 4, 1989.
A vehement defense of Stalin against all his critics, past and present, but in particular against the playwright Mikhail Shatrov.

Galperin, I., and Golik, Yu. "The Law without Illusions." *Izvestiya*, March 28, 1990.
In the midst of a fever of lawmaking by various Soviet legislatures, the authors warn about the necessity to formulate laws precisely, and they point to the controversial law against speculation.

Kaipbergenov, Tulepbergen. "Don't Look for the Last Scapegoat." *Sovetskaya Kultura*, March 31, 1990.
The USSR's national conflicts are caused by social, political, and ideological crises; a corrupt mafia and the bureaucracy are the beneficiaries.

Kapelyushny, Leonid. "A Road to Independence: The Lithuanian Situation in the Mirror of International Law." *Izvestiya*, March 28, 1990.
An interview with a Soviet official who describes the niceties of international law regarding the secession of Lithuania.

Kasparov, Harry. "The Eyewitness Account." *Moskovskie Novosti*, January 28, 1990.
A vivid depiction of the passivity and indifference of the central authorities during the anti-Armenian pogroms in Baku.

Khlystalov, Eduard. "The Secret of the Hotel Angleter." *Moskva*, no. 7, 1989.
The author claims that Jews may have killed the famous Russian poet Sergey Yesenin, rather than his death being an apparent suicide.

Kunitsyn, Ivan. "Here, Grandma, Is the Yuriev Day." *Yunost*, no. 4, 1989.

A critique of the Soviet passport and *propiska* (residency permit) systems.

Kuplevakhsky, Valery. "The War Reckoning." *Znamya*, no. 9, 1989.

A sad account of the plight of the disabled, aged, and wounded World War II veterans in the Soviet Union. Many of them live in former monasteries without modern amenities and without proper medical attention. Along with the deficit of consumer goods there is a deficit of kindness, charity, and gratitude in the Soviet Union.

Migranian, Andranik. "A Long Road to the European Home." *Novy Mir*, no. 7, 1989.

Suggests that during the transition from totalitarianism to democracy it might be necessary to go through an authoritarian period to carry out economic reform. Discusses the roles of the party, Gorbachev, the soviets, and elections in the reform process.

Nazarov, German. "Further . . . Further . . . Further . . . to the Truth." *Moskva*, no. 12, 1989.

The article claims that Yakov Sverdlov and other revolutionaries of Jewish origin committed atrocities in the civil war of 1918–1920 that surpassed the crimes of the Nazis.

Prokhanov, Alexander. "Notes of a Conservative." *Nash Sovremennik*, no. 5, 1990.

A brief and eloquent conservative manifesto against the destruction of the military-ideological empire.

Radyshevsky, Dmitry. "Moscow Bears, or an American Dream à la Lyubertsy." *Moskovskie Novosti*, no. 29, July 22, 1990.

The story behind the first Soviet football teams.

Rudakov, Andrei. "Crime in Moscow: Inventions and Reality." *Nedelya*, no. 11, 1990.

Militia General Alexei Bugaev describes various aspects of crime in Moscow.

Shafarevich, Igor. "Russophobia." *Nash Sovremennik*, no. 6, 1989.

A mysterious small people, the Jews, threaten once more the existence of the big people, the Russians.

———. "Two Roads to the Same Precipice." *Novy Mir*, no. 7, 1989.

The author views the command-bureaucratic system and the Western way of life as basically the same system, based on notions of progess and rationality and not acceptable for Russia. He stresses the sympathy of Western liberals for Stalinism in spite of its cruelty.

Shenkman, Stiv. "The Price of a Jump: Valery Brumel Speaks Up." *Yunost*, no. 4, 1989.

The renowned Soviet athlete discloses the dark side of Soviet sports.

Sidorov, Dmitry, and Piyanykh, Gleb. "Nobody Was Prepared to Concede." *Moskovskie Novosti*, no. 29, July 22, 1990.

A mood of political intolerance was vividly evident at the demonstration of proreform forces on July 15, 1990.

Smirnov, Petr. "Very Naked Screen." *Krokodil*, no. 36, 1988.

An overview of Soviet censorship of sexual material in movies and television: the bigotry and hypocrisy around the film *Little Vera*.

Sokolov, Vladimir. "Monologue or Dialogue." *Literaturnaya Gazeta*, March 21, 1990.

An attempt to understand the new relationship between the Soviet Union and Lithuania.

Solzhenitsyn, Alexander. "How Should We Rearrange Russia? Feasible Reflections." *Komsomolskaya Pravda*, September 18, 1990.

The most renowned Russian writer abroad breaks his silence on the turmoil in the Soviet Union. He unsparingly assesses seventy years of Communist rule, including Gorbachev's *perestroika*, and he blames the Russian people for it. He proposes a "Slavic empire," encompassing Russia, the Ukraine, Byelorussia, and part of Kazakhstan, and he speaks out against Western economic assistance.

Stratanovsky, Sergei. "What Is Russophobia? Reflections on the Article of I. Shafarevich, 'Russophobia'." *Zvezda*, no. 4, 1990.

A penetrating analysis of the philosophy of Russian nationalism and its inclination toward anti-Semitism.

Tsarev, S. "There Is a Need for a Law of de-Zionization." *Molodaya Gvardiya*, no. 3, 1990.

The author, a painter from Rostov-on-Don, states that such a law is needed to defend the Russian people.

Vasilenko, Anatoly. "Readers Speak Up about Their Publication." *Molodaya Gvardiya*, no. 1, 1990.

Conservative issues and positions are described in a fairly intelligent manner.

Vasinsky, Alexander. "The Burning Topics of the Day." *Izvestiya*, March 30, 1990.

Notes on contemporary mores and the sad state of a Soviet society plagued by suspicion, malice, intolerance, and a search for scapegoats.

Volkova, Lyubov. "A Year of the Orange Horse." *Rabochaya Tribuna*, February 21, 1990.

A negative aspect of the legal equality of women in the USSR is the high percentage of women employed in manual jobs and in hazardous industries.

Zhdanov, S. "Anti-Semitism Is a Zionist Scarecrow." *Molodaya Gvardiya*, no. 3, 1990.

A letter from a Moscow professor claiming that there is no anti-Semitism in the USSR and that Jews have more privileges than do Russians.

Zhukhovitsky, Leonid. "The Vagaries of a National Spirit." *Literaturnaya Gazeta*, May 23, 1990.

An attempt to understand the leaders of national movements in the USSR by analyzing their human weaknesses.

Let us be absolutely frank: The party must accept full responsibility for the distortions of the past and the present. Let us acknowledge before our people and before all of mankind that to a greater or lesser degree it is we, the Communists, who are responsible for our current miserable life. And if people judge every one of us according to his merits, we can do nothing but accept our due.

R. Safarov,
delegate to the 28th Congress
of the CPSU, Tashkent

Chapter Two

The Changing Role of the Party

Disarray in the Party

The incessant assault on its power, privileges, and ideology made 1989 and 1990 tough years for the Communist party. The restructuring of the party did not proceed smoothly, and the Communists appear to be the clear losers in the reform process. In the Ukraine, Armenia, Georgia, and the Central Asian republics, the party organizations have devolved into disarray. In ethnic conflicts, the unifying role of the CPSU has not been noticeable at all (see Doc. 9). The leaders of party organizations in the republics are not communicating well with one another or with Moscow. They do not know what to do, what to think, or what will happen next. The uncovering of widespread corruption has considerably weakened the influence of local party leaders, as evidenced by the numerous electoral victories of their nationalist opponents.

The decline of the authority and stature of the party is a deepening and inexorable process. The party's newspaper *Pravda* has admitted losing three million subscribers in 1989 alone. There have been no widespread purges, such as in Stalin's era, but in the last eighteen months four million people—a huge number—have left the party.[1] Its

[1] *Pravda*, November 30, 1989; *Washington Post*, July 27, 1991.

committees are even being expelled from the workplace; during the 1989 miners' strike many party committees were removed from the mines. The crisis has spread to the Komsomol and to trade unions. Recently, the most successful occupation of Komsomol leaders has been the running of video saloons.

The Communist party today seems incapable of advancing any reasonable theory or logical argument for its continued rule or for its political relevance to present-day conditions. The best formulation it has come up with for its present goal is "democratic socialism"—and the word "socialism" has a very low popular rating today in the Soviet Union.[2] Lenin's example is no longer viewed as a theoretical haven or a recipe for all of life's situations; Mikhail Gorbachev rarely quotes him. Even moderates are now treating Lenin's works and actions with more scrutiny and are no longer ready to absolve him for Stalin's rise to power.[3] Nevertheless, in an effort to hold on to at least some of their philosophical basis, even most liberal, reform-minded Soviet thinkers continue to try to prove that Stalin distorted Marxism. In his article (Doc. 11) about the irrelevance of Marxism to past and current Soviet concerns, the philosopher Alexander Tsipko, while displaying a profound knowledge of Marxist theory, despairs that few even among Soviet intellectuals understand that blind faith in Marxism has been the main impediment to their country's development.

Numerous party secretaries and countless instructors are the backbone of the party—not its twenty million enlisted members. The attempts of these party officials to adjust to the new times have mostly been successful. Most of the Gorbachev-era appointments to the Politburo and to the party's Central Committee have been ineffectual. *Plenums* have been called regularly, as usual, but with no results. Constant changes in the party apparatus have only weakened the party's grip on power. The *apparatchiks* who have been fired might have been corrupt, but they possessed a magic power. They knew how to control the local population in the republics and were adept at suppressing the slightest signs of discontent. Their replacements have not been drawn from the progressive elements in the party but rather from among more of the same conservatives. This should not have come as a great surprise, since the man in charge of personnel was conservative Yegor Ligachev.

---

[2]Academician S. Alekseyev has suggested the name "free socialism," as an alternative more closely corresponding to the humanistic understanding of Marxism, in his "The Concept of *Perestroika* and Marxism," ibid., July 25, 1990.

[3]See, for example, Alexei Kiva's "The Myths of the Passing Times," *Izvestiya*, April 2, 1990.

Privileges

The question of party privileges has been hotly debated during the Gorbachev period. Boris Yeltsin was the first to raise the issue persistently, while serving as Moscow party chief, and for this he became known as a populist. The party leadership's refusal to give up its privileges caused the party to lose a considerable amount of influence. The system of privileges was and still is extensive. It shields party leaders and their families from the daily strains of Soviet life and also defines them as a social elite. It is as if, without the privileges, there would be no Communist party. In a speech to the workers of the Izhora plant in Leningrad (Doc. 28), Gorbachev avoided a direct statement on this issue, deliberately confusing privileges with union benefits. Salary increases for party workers, quietly introduced by Gorbachev in the beginning of 1990, infuriated the population and resulted in a further erosion of popularity for Gorbachev and for the CPSU.

Much publicity was given to the revelation that two hundred apartments in one Moscow building in 1990 were allotted to the Central Committee.[4] That the new democrats and established conservatives alike made a grab for these apartments caused a public uproar. New power structures have brought more people into Moscow, where already countless thousands of families have been waiting for more than ten years to get an apartment from the state.

Another source of controversy is party-owned property. The emergence of numerous political parties and the increasing independence of various republics and city councils (each with its own publications) contributed to the struggle in 1990 against party control of buildings and publishing houses. The party apparatus claims that all of its properties were built and maintained with money collected as members' fees. The party used to rule with an iron hand, guided by the principle that everything in the country belonged to the party. Hardly anyone accepts this principle now. Still, even today, many of the party's expenses are paid from the state treasury.

The Party-State Dilemma

One of the often-repeated slogans of *perestroika* recalls the spirit of 1917: "All Power to the Soviets," meaning that the party should return usurped prerogatives to state institutions. This process, called depolitization or departization, would include removing party control of city councils, the economy, the army, the KGB, and the police. Democratic Western countries make use of a nonpartisan civil service. For example, in the United States, although the president is a

---

[4] *Argumenty i Fakty*, no. 44, 1990.

Republican, Republican party officials do not run the FBI, the U.S. armed forces, and other public institutions. Without an independent civil service, together with genuinely competitive elections, there will never be a genuine democratization in the Soviet Union. If the party had allowed the recently elected Soviets to exercise full powers, that would have opened the door to a third option (as opposed to bloody revolt and superficial *perestroika*), the option of a peaceful democratic revolution to a system along the lines of Western democracies (see Doc. 14). The CPSU was not created to compete in free and open elections, and has not done so since its inception. It is not surprising that party functionaries have disliked participating in the recent elections and have frequently lost to their opponents. Party candidates have been soundly defeated in Moscow, Leningrad, and Sverdlovsk.

A significant gap exists in social and political developments between these cities and the rest of the Russian provinces, where the population is less educated and more under the conservative influence. This contrasts with the situation in 1917, when the population in Leningrad (then called St. Petersburg) and Moscow supported the Bolsheviks.[5] After their recent electoral defeats, the conservatives retaliated by cutting the flow of supplies to these two cities. The democratic mayors have tried to get around this virtual blockade by promoting new ties with the republics that are seeking independence from the central government.

A new demarcation of the spheres of power and influence has been taking place in the USSR. It is not along the lines of party-state conflicts but rather between the party and bureaucracy on the one side and the reform and nationalist forces on the other side. Even when losing elections at any level, whether it be in Zhitomir, Moscow, Leningrad, or the Baltic republics, the party does not easily concede any of its power, privilege, or property. By clinging to the same pattern of explicit or tacit rules, the bureaucracy is still obeying only the party, in spite of Gorbachev's promise to give power back to the Soviets. It is a broken promise.

Gorbachev began in 1988 and 1989 to diminish the party's significance, some say in order to change the system of government. The state would be allowed to fulfill its regular obligations, but the party would be restricted to the ideological sphere. The same people, members of the Communist party, would pursue the same goals, but in a different framework. Gorbachev has proceeded in two directions, by introducing institutional changes and by making personnel changes. The 19th Party Conference introduced a new, more democratic election system. It still gave the Communist party numerous advantages, but it also opened a window of opportunity for others. To diminish the party's influence, the September 30, 1988, *plenum* cut in half the personnel in the departments of the Central Committee. If

---

[5] In the elections of June 12, 1991, the voters of Leningrad decided to restore to the old city the name given to it by Peter the Great.

Gorbachev's goal was to remove recalcitrant bureaucrats, supporters of Yegor Ligachev (who opposed his reforms), he hardly achieved the desired results; nobody and nothing could diminish the resistance of the Central Committee to change. A major reshuffling of the Central Committee, resulting in the retirement of 110 members (out of a total of approximately 400), took place at the April 1988 *plenum*. At the September 1989 *plenum*, such hard-line conservatives as Victor Nikonov, Victor Chebrikov, Vladimir Shcherbitsky, and candidate-members Yuri Solovyev and Nikolai Talyzin left the Politburo. Vladimir Kryuchkov and Yuri Maslyukov became members, and Yevgeny Primakov and Boris Pugo were elected candidate-members of the Politburo. Finally, in November 1989, Lev Zaikov was replaced by Yuri Prokofiev as Moscow's first secretary. The consolidation of power in the hands of Gorbachev was complete. But he had spent a good deal of precious time amassing this power. One could argue that the "new" politics of the USSR, with the advent of a multiparty system, has made Gorbachev's Communist party infighting relatively unimportant in the big picture.

The Political Struggle inside the Party

Until recently, party spokesmen denied that an internal struggle was taking place in the Communist party. In a 1988 interview with Princeton University's Professor Stephen Cohen, Alexander Yakovlev (a key Politburo member) denied that there was any opposition to *perestroika*.[6] This statement was difficult to dispute, as the struggle between conservatives and reformers was taking place behind the closed doors of the Politburo. The ratio of forces within the party was overwhelmingly in favor of conservatives, but so much was going on that it took time to sort out the direction of reforms.

The first conservative party leader openly to display rebellious tendencies in November 1989 was Boris Gidaspov, Leningrad's first secretary of the CPSU. He advanced a fairly conservative platform, which called for a retreat on political and economic issues, and he has been supported by the CPSU Central Committee's secretary and chairman of its Military Commission, Oleg Baklanov. Alarmed by devastating electoral defeats in March 1989, conservatives decided to stop relying on the Politburo to look after their interests and came out publicly, and in force, at the February *plenum* of 1990. Obviously, most of the party was nervous about the elections, *glasnost*, and the proposed radical economic reforms. This concern was reflected in the platform of the CPSU for the forthcoming 28th Party Congress, which included nothing revolutionary or radical or exciting. The section on the economy was called "For the Efficient Planned Market Economy," and

---

[6]Stephen F. Cohen and Katrina vanden Heuvel, *Voices of Glasnost* (New York, 1989), p. 60.

it contained nothing new except the use of the word "market." The expression "private property" was not permitted. There was also no change concerning the permissibility of allowing divisions within the party.

The essence of conservative party doctrine is best expressed by Nina Andreyeva, a Leningrad teacher (see Doc. 13). She portrays Mikhail Gorbachev, Alexander Yakovlev, and Eduard Shevardnadze as right-wing opportunists. Her supporters view themselves as the left wing, the true Bolsheviks who defend socialism, even Stalin's socialism. The conservatives still firmly control the instruments of violence: the KGB, the army, and the police. These institutions emerged from the initial reform period essentially unchanged. The KGB remains the party's most important tool of intimidation. For six years, Gorbachev has refrained from any criticism of the KGB and has assured its representatives of a place in the Politburo. He offered Vladimir Kryuchkov, chairman of the KGB, the chance to make a speech at the 72d Anniversary of the October Revolution, in 1989. Such organizations as Pamyat and the conservative ethnic-Russian "international fronts" in the republics show an obvious imprint of KGB involvement. It seems that the KGB is the only Soviet institution that has not been surprised by the reforms, and it is prepared to confront the democratic forces. Widely held suspicions about the KGB were confirmed by the highly unusual statements of a KGB general, a dissenter, Oleg Kalugin, who denounced the conservative nature of the KGB in an interview with the youth newspaper *Komsomolskaya Pravda* (Doc. 12). He was immediately stripped of his rank and pension by Gorbachev.

Russian Party Congress and 28th Party Congress

As he did on previous occasions, Gorbachev tried to placate everyone with promises that the 28th CPSU Congress would resolve all internal party problems. Moderates and radicals hoped that the party, faced with the grim reality of not being relevant to the cause of reform, would have no choice but to move to the center and left. A ferocious struggle within the party between conservatives, moderates, and radicals ensued. The liberal side presented its views in the Democratic platform; the conservatives came up with a Marxist-Leninist platform.[7] However, the Constituent Congress of the Russian Communist party ended the dreams of reformers.

The founding congress of the Russian Communist party, which began on June 19, 1990, turned into a rehearsal for the forthcoming

---

[7]Liberal and moderate CPSU members who left the party because they believed it had exhausted its reform possibilities created a Republican party of Russia, led by Vladimir Lysenko, and the Democratic party of Russia, headed by Nikolai Travkin.

28th Congress of the CPSU (see Doc. 32). Gorbachev was not happy with right-wing conservatives stealing his thunder, even if it showed that there were forces to block Boris Yeltsin within Russia. However, the grim fear of a forthcoming military coup d'état seemed realistic in light of the threatening speech by General Albert Makashov. The party's ideological mood was expressed by V. Golovachev, first secretary of the party's Saratov city committee: "Economic measures suggested by the government are contradicting the ideological concepts of the party. Our ideals are sacrificed for the sake of economic expediency."[8] Gorbachev's performance disappointed his supporters. He appeared to have made no preparations for the congress, and he did not visibly try to influence the choice of delegates. It was as though he wished that the party would simply defeat itself.

Since the majority of the delegates at the Russian congress were also delegates to the 28th Congress of the CPSU, the direction of the second congress was predetermined. Many party moderates, including Alexei Kiva (see Doc. 10), were surprised that Gorbachev was so passive in the spring of 1990, allowing conservatives to capture the majority of delegates' seats for the 28th Party Congress. Deliberations began on July 2, 1990. The first attack was against the Politburo members. The primary targets were Eduard Shevardnadze and Alexander Yakovlev, and each was asked to give an account. Gorbachev might have been next, but he threatened the congress with the possibility of a split in the ranks. Either to his credit, or perhaps because of his weakness, this was the first congress in post-Lenin Soviet history not fully controlled by the general secretary of the CPSU. The documents approved by the congress were more realistic than those of earlier gatherings.

By the end of the 28th Party Congress, the Central Committee and the Politburo were made up of new people, unknown to the party and country. The new Politburo for the first time did not include any members of the government; the number of Politburo members had been increased from twelve to twenty-four, and the most influential former Politburo members—Alexander Yakovlev, Eduard Shevardnadze, and Yegor Ligachev—were not members of the new Politburo. These changes made the Politburo, the party's supreme council, basically irrelevant in the internal politics of Soviet government. Yakovlev interpreted this as a successful separation of party and state.[9] However, it meant only that power from the Politburo was transferred to the holder of the new office of the presidency—Mikhail Gorbachev. One can argue that the general secretary, who became the president without being elected, represents the party and not the entire nation. On the other hand, the introduction of the presidency could portend a new, important, and positive development.

---

[8] *Izvestiya*, June 20, 1990.

[9] Ibid., July 26, 1990.

The delegates found it difficult to accept the necessity of the transition to a market economy. They did not want to hear out Leonid Abalkin, a prominent economist and reform advocate, but they warmly greeted Professor Alexei Sergeyev, who described the current situation: "If a guy's trousers are worn out in some places, he does not take them off until he finds new ones. We took off our economy from its previous management system by force, and who knows when the new clothing will be ready and what there will be instead of old trousers. Until now, nobody has the faintest idea. It might be a Scottish kilt or an Indian sari or only a bow tie." Although he was not even a delegate, Sergeyev was allowed to address the congress because conservatives insisted.[10]

The most important decision, abolition of Article 6 of the Soviet constitution, which mandated the leading role of the Communist party in the USSR, was made at the February 1990 *plenum* of the Central Committee; previously, this suggestion had been defeated in the Congress of People's Deputies at Andrei Sakharov's initiative but was fiercely attacked by Mikhail Gorbachev. However, the sincerity of this gesture is doubtful. Does it mean that a multiparty system is a recognized reality in the Soviet Union? Is the Communist party ready to invite other parties into the government? Would the party concede all power after an electoral defeat? Is it likely that the present party leaders are ready for such a dramatic departure from seven decades of Communist rule?

---

[10]Ibid., July 16, 1990.

9

Looking Around at the Pass

R. Safarov

Pravda
July 28, 1990

The author of this letter, a delegate to the 28th Congress of the CPSU from Tashkent, belongs to a sizable group of moderates whom Mikhail Gorbachev was unable to recruit for leadership positions to replace the rabid conservatives. Safarov gives a colorful and precise picture of the instability and confusion in the country. He then suggests that dialectical analysis would miraculously clarify what is going on. He would like to see his party become more human, take care of the people, and not build castles in the air. It is extremely significant that he rejects the use of totalitarian means of control; his letter provides proof that the past five years have taught many lessons, even to members of the party.

At the present time, the party faces a difficult choice: either to lose its character or to rejuvenate itself in a stronger form. Whether we wanted to or not, it seems to me that at this party congress we bid farewell to many outmoded dogmas and organizational principles that have clearly failed. The old ideas bound us with chains and calcified our hands and hearts. The so-called monolithic unity of the party, which in fact meant the oppression of some members by others, has come irrevocably to an end. We are also finished with the era of endless applause followed by Mephistophelian giggling in the lobby.

We discard old things, and this causes sadness and nostalgia in some people. Others are joyful about the changes, rid themselves of doubts and anxieties, and stubbornly fail to notice that the country is entering thick, noxious layers of the sociopolitical atmosphere. Who can answer the question: "Why is this happening?" Who is bold enough to predict with any degree of accuracy when we shall be able to stabilize the situation and begin to live in a civilized, humane, and democratic society? And finally, who can explain why the path to a rule of law often lies through the jungles of anarchy and lawlessness, shootings and fires, blockades and strikes?

I cannot agree with the assertion that our current difficulties and failures were caused because, at the start of *perestroika,* we underestimated the scope of the aberrations that occurred in the past. What is past is past, but who shall answer for all the mistakes made in the course of *perestroika*? When will concerted actions take place in all sections of the party and in all sectors of the national economy? To this question, it seems to me, the party forum has not given clear answers. Take, for example, the widely extolled independence of industrial enterprises. In the minds of many people a strange thought has found refuge: that being independent means, "Everyone leave me alone. I don't care about you. My welfare is above everything else." The gain from such independence is equal to a kopeck, but it costs us rubles. And the fact that at the present time one ruble is worth no more than a kopeck will not give comfort to anyone.

Life poses many difficult questions. And the most important and seemingly simple question on the tip of many tongues lately is: "To what party do we belong?" The word printed on the membership card is as before: CPSU. The same inscription is printed on the party cards in Moldavia and the Ukraine. But with all respect to Moldavians and Ukrainians, as well as to Communists of other republics, it is difficult to assure myself that we belong to the same party. There are too many party differences and too few similarities.

The Central Committee of our party stands accused of long-term suppression of horizontal connections among people and regions, and support of vertical connections only.[1] Today, it is necessary to weaken vertical connections in favor of horizontal ones. But, in reality, the problems with the party's structural attributes are much more complex. The vertical connections are now considerably weakened. No one listens to anyone nor is anyone willing to obey—this is our pattern today. Unfortunately, the horizontal connections are not getting any stronger, but instead they are weakening. What, then, are we left with? In a critical situation, such as during the events in Osh,[2] the CPSU should have performed a unifying role. It is a real pity that this has not happened.

At the last congress, a lot of words were said about consolidation of all party forces. Party division will make us weaker and undermine our strength. Will the deeds follow

---

[1]The party's policies and structure were and still are based on the theory of "democratic centralism," which mandates tight central control of all activities.

[2]This refers to ethnic disturbances in June and July 1990 between the Uzbeks and the Kirghiz.

the words? I don't have in mind a "reanimation of monolithic unity." In circumstances where powerful pressures against the party have intensified, and many are thirsting for power under cover of ultrapatriotic and democratic slogans, we can bring to bear only one weapon—the weapon of integrity, unity, and ability not only to speak from the rostrum but also to resolve the most arduous political, social, and national problems.

We are fed up with "general euphoria" on soil smelling of gunpowder and stained with blood. Enough of freedom, equality, and fraternity under the muzzle of a gun. Only one method of power struggle is acceptable to the party—the political one. And consequently only one principle of consolidation is acceptable—not the one that says, "think as I do," but the one that says, "let us argue and think together."

Let us at last be honest with ourselves. We must face the fact that not only among the so-called enemy voices from abroad but also in our country *perestroika* is often associated with the disintegration of the federation, with a cavernous economic ulcer, and with diminished safety for both individuals and society as a whole. Let us be absolutely frank (the ability to call things by their real names is a sign of strength). The party must accept full responsibility for the distortions of the past and the present. Let us acknowledge before our people and before all of mankind: To a greater or lesser degree it is we, the Communists, who are responsible for our current miserable life. And if people judge every one of us according to his merits, we can do nothing but accept our due. Open recognition of guilt, relieving the burdens of the soul—with this alone will we gain the confidence of the masses.

I assume that every foreigner would have been curious to gaze into the eyes of the Soviet people as they watched Gorbachev on television in the United States when he received awards for his contributions to international security and to a world without terror and violence. It was nice. However, even as we watched, our eyes reflected the fires in Sumgait and Fergana, Baku and Andizhan, Nagorno-Karabakh and Osh.[3] As we watched, the pain of victims of banditry and extremism and the sufferings of homeless refugees were imprinted in our eyes. And I thought, "Will the

---

[3]Places where ethnic disturbances occurred.

time come when we, the Soviet people, shall present our leader, Communist or not, with the same awards?"

The famous painting by Salvador Dali, *The Premonition of Civil War*, makes any viewer's heart heavy and causes him to shudder. In my opinion, the real indicators of civil war that we are now experiencing are more tragic than the colorful prophecies of Dali. We have already felt this: fires and pogroms, homelessness and murder. There is no time to work. All attention is absorbed by the passions of battle. No one wants to understand anyone else; nobody takes anyone else into consideration. Workers fight with engineers, collectives with their bosses, enterprises with the ministries, ministries with the Council of Ministers, the Council of Ministers with Anatoly Sobchak.[4] It is a kind of mystical train in which every car is attempting to become the engine. Although it is indeed time for each of us to work, it is high time to put an end to the experiments on our own people. The experiments have been going on since 1917! It is enough!

In solving these problems, and other ones, and third ones, and tenth ones, the party should unite and ally with all humanitarian social forces and movements that are emerging and will appear in the future. Because there are people who support the interests of the country in other parties, it is necessary to have a serious dialogue and to collaborate with them.

The most depressing reality is that the problems we have are multiplying like fragments in a devil's kaleidoscope. We are struggling with them, but they are like the heads of the mythological Hydra: As soon as we chop off one head, two others immediately grow up. The essence of our problem is that we are struggling with consequences but have no idea about their true causes. The methodology is outdated. The party scientists are dozing. The cleansing scalpel of dialectics lies abandoned and rusting. No step forward can be made without the most serious dialectical analysis of the current situation as well as identification of the main contradiction of the current epoch. Let us remember, every historical period is characterized by some main contradiction, which determines not only the essence and direction of the society's development but its dialectics as well. Economic crisis, crime, national disarray—all of these are painful but derived contradictions. And who can determine the main one, the

---

[4] Sobchak, a prominent democratic politician, is mayor of Leningrad.

purposeful resolution of which will lead to a natural resolution of our present difficulties? The CPSU is capable of doing this.

The party must prepare a comprehensive analysis and scientific description of the epoch in which we find ourselves. The party must finally determine its own place in this epoch, its character, and its goals, according to contemporary historical necessities.

We no longer have the right, either literally or figuratively, to break people's spines and wings while feeding them wonderful but inaccessible dreams about what can be accomplished under communism. We cannot continue to be the party of the hard-hearted utopia.

Unconditional humanism cannot be a faraway goal; it must be the day-to-day tool of the party. Let us leave the skies to the birds, as Marx often said. We must attend to earthly problems. Flesh-and-blood people are waiting for the advance guard to deliver the real goods. They need it today, tomorrow at the latest, but not in some future historical era. That is how we must view our aims.

The party is at the pass. Where will it go from here? It depends on each Communist, on all of us together. Let us look around and think.

10

Will the Party Catch Up with *Perestroika*?

Alexei Kiva

Izvestiya
July 19, 1990

There are still a few remaining intellectuals who continue to support the party. They generally support Gorbachev and oppose the *apparatchiks* and generals who dominated the July 1990 Russian Communist Party Congress and the 28th CPSU Congress held in June 1991. The 28th Party Congress was characterized by a ferocious debate that laid to rest the myth of the monolithic party. The conservatives fought for their definition of socialism. Kiva is critical of the congress because of its delegates' personal attacks on Gorbachev and their general inability to understand the beneficial character of private property. Many of his talented friends have quit the party, but he has stayed so as not to abandon Gorbachev. He justifies Gorbachev's efforts to steer a middle course which, in his view, is preferable to a popular revolution like the one in Iran. In the end, Gorbachev won this fight against the conservatives in the party. However, since many of his supporters quit the party while the conservatives stayed, it appears that Gorbachev may have won the battle but lost the war. Since then, he has rejected a five-hundred-day plan for transition to a market economy, favored conservatives, and isolated himself from all reformers, moderate as well as radical.

The results of the [CPSU] congress that just ended will be reflected upon in the days to come. Only at first glance does everything seem simple. Here, for example, is what some of my colleagues said about the congress: The uneducated *apparatchiks*, incapable of competing in an open political struggle, wounded by the loss of their monopoly on power and on the absolute truth, nonetheless managed to mobilize and carry out widespread anti-Gorbachev activities among the masses. Encouraged by their first successes, they went to Moscow to take revenge. Not hiding their hatred for democracy, for the multiparty system, for a creative intelligentsia, and toward any carriers of nonstandard original thoughts, toward intellect and intellectuality in general, the conservatives came prepared to "stamp with their feet" and "clap with their hands" in order to drown out the voices of *perestroika*.[1]

I will speak later about "stamping" and "clapping." But how to explain, I asked my colleague, that the delegates of the congress nonetheless elected Mikhail Gorbachev general secretary of the Central Committee, with Vladimir Ivashko as his deputy (a known supporter of substantial reforms), and voted down for this post Yegor Ligachev, a recognized leader of the conservatives? Party documents adopted by the congress corresponded on the whole to the spirit of *perestroika*. Of course, many of these documents are still peppered with revolutionary rhetoric. However, this is, first, a step forward in any case and not a small step for a party so much burdened with conservatism and dogmatism. Second, the realities of life will surely force modifications to the documents, and most likely in the very near future (revolutionary documents quickly get outdated). Third, as the resolutions of the congress are carried out, it will quickly become clear who stands where on the issues.

Even the most favorable observer of the last congress cannot describe it as a forum of like-minded people. This time hardly anyone concealed his views, and a surprisingly wide spectrum of opinions and views was expressed. There were the usual centrists and left-centrists as well as the usual conservatives. However, there were also those who wanted to preserve the totalitarian structure, radical leftists, and Marxist fundamentalists. Clearly, the myth of the monolithic party has been exposed.

And if a split occurs? I do not think it will be a great misfortune. We know of many parties with deep historical roots that have split many times. Each new split has made them more homogeneous and unified and essentially has served as a powerful stimulus for revitalization. As a result, these parties have preserved themselves as influential and even as the most influential political forces in society. This applies, for example, to the Indian National Congress. And, in our case, the exit from the CPSU of some of its members on the left and the right will only contribute to the process of introducing a multiparty system.

---

[1]The conservatives use their numerical superiority to prevent liberals from speaking freely in all settings.

References from the classics often have been introduced to support the correctness of this or that position. However, for the most part, the socioeconomic factors that underlie Marxist-Leninist philosophy are not present in the current situation. Social progress is a historical notion; socialism is a historical notion; the working class is also a historical notion. It is important to see and to understand that each epoch attaches new meanings to old terms, even when it doesn't explicitly reject those terms. We have transformed the word socialism into an incantation. "You are either for socialism or you are against it," is our knee-jerk response to the most complex of life's problems, much like our illiterate fathers and grandfathers.

This is not an exaggeration. There were actually those at the congress who spoke in favor of creating a mass movement in support of socialism. One such initiative came from the indefatigable Yegor Ligachev. The real question is, "What kind of socialism?" The one we wanted and did not get, or the "barracks socialism" with a command-administrative system that has brought us to a historical impasse? Of course, there is no answer, nor should there be one. For many of us, socialism has turned into an abstract slogan or, at best, a symbol of faith.

At the 28th Congress of the CPSU a lot was said about property, but without historical context, without the understanding that the institution of private property was the greatest achievement of human civilization. Several generations of revolutionaries considered private ownership of the means of production as the source of all evils in society. However, as it turned out, its absence created even bigger evils and led to the economic, social, and spiritual degradation of society.

The results of the 28th Congress had a personal meaning for me. After the founding Constituent Congress of the Communist Party of the Russian Republic, I had to decide whether it made sense for me to be in the same party with the Makashovs, Rebrovs, Sergeyevs, and Ligachevs et al.[2] What do I have in common with them? Nothing! Nevertheless, I decided to wait until the 28th Congress of the CPSU. In its first days, the work of the congress was characterized by caddishness, ignorance, feeblemindedness, attacks on the politics of *perestroika*, and personal attacks on

---

[2]Well-known conservatives.

Mikhail Gorbachev; my resolve to quit the party was strengthened. But, toward the middle of the congress, Mikhail Gorbachev and his supporters succeeded in changing the general mood, directing the forum into a radical, creative channel. So I said to myself: "Some of my colleagues, many of them very talented, honest, principled, and socially active, have already left the party. Let's assume I quit and others do as well. Then who will stay with Mikhail Gorbachev and his supporters? At this stage of history, the CPSU is needed for the progress of *perestroika*. But, if it is abandoned by the greater part of the creative intelligentsia and the most politically mature part of the working class, who then will stay in it? And what about the alternative—to radicalize the party, to renovate its cadres and its ideology?"

As it turned out, I was not the only one facing this choice. Many others had the same thoughts. Is it possible that only ignorant *apparatchiks*, bigoted generals, monopolist agrarians, and similar people will represent the party? There is something wrong here. At the present time, the prestige of the bureaucracy is quite low; that of the party *apparat* is even lower. At the same time, these two categories of people comprised two thirds of the congress delegates. How could that happen? Someone had to control the election of delegates to the congress. It became clear to me that the system of elections was faulty. Without question the first days of the 28th Congress of the CPSU left painful impressions. They have not yet gone away. I do not have full confidence that the party with its current personnel is capable of becoming an advance guard, of "catching up" with *perestroika*. People with whom I talk at work and elsewhere also share my lack of confidence. At the same time, I categorically disagree with those who think that the worse the situation is in the CPSU, the better it will be for society. After Ivan Polozkov became the first secretary of the Central Committee of the Russian Communist party, it was widely felt that if Yegor Ligachev had also been elected leader of the CPSU then the question of the party would have been resolved finally and irrevocably; the party would have started falling apart.

Recent events have forced choices, not only for ordinary communists but for our leaders as well. Boris Yeltsin, Gavriil Popov, Anatoly Sobchak, Viacheslav Shostakovsky, and others have already made their choices. Mikhail Gorbachev was forced to make his choice, and not for the first time. "Who are you with—the *apparat* or the people?" someone from the radical left hurled at him. Oh, how our military-Communist education is impeding us!

For us, one is either on the left or on the right, and—even worse—he who is not with us is seen as being against us. But such categorical thinking is inappropriate for the principal leader, especially since he is the leader of a "revolution from above." If anyone prefers a popular revolution instead, I recommend that he refresh his memory about the outcome of the popular revolution in Iran, which came after the "white revolution" of the shah, and then weigh the pros and cons accordingly. But the merger of two revolutions—that is another matter. This, in my view, is what Mikhail Gorbachev is striving to achieve. At the Russian Communist Party Congress he was openly challenged for the first time. The situation changed abruptly. The conservatives who until now were on the defensive resolutely went on the offensive, not against the left, as in their previous efforts, but against the centrist forces led by Mikhail Gorbachev. The *apparatchiks* of the Stalin-Brezhnev stripe, some of the generals (isolated from their junior officers, from their soldiers, and from life itself), workers who do not clearly comprehend on whose behalf they speak, all threw preposterous accusations at Mikhail Gorbachev. They made insulting hints, implying that Gorbachev is acting treacherously, contributing to the disintegration of the Warsaw Pact and the "socialist commonwealth," and so on, and so forth.

And here, it seemed to me, our leader faltered and seemed perplexed. Did he not expect such pressure? Until now he has performed the role of arbiter with relative ease and showed himself capable of reconciling the interests of various political forces. Instead of bringing politically blind and socially shortsighted people to reason, Mikhail Gorbachev in his presentation at the Russian Communist Party Congress began, it seemed to me, by justifying himself. "Is it true, as some affirm, that the leader has exhausted his potential, has so to speak used it up?" I asked myself. Afterward, I got it: Mikhail Gorbachev is intentionally avoiding a confrontation; he is waiting for the CPSU Congress at which he will certainly take up the gauntlet. I shared my thoughts with an acquaintance, a political scientist. "No! You are wrong!" he stated categorically. "The conservatives, certainly, will not remove him but will simply force him to do what they need." I replied, "But what if it happens as in the proverb, 'They went for wool but themselves returned clipped'?"

It seems that I turned out to be right. Mikhail Gorbachev's position has strengthened, both in the party and in the country. First, the general secretary is now elected by the congress. Second, the greater part of power has been transferred from the Politburo to the Presidential Council. Third, the active conservatives have been removed from the Politburo; its present composition is much more desirable. And the way the delegates of the congress interrupted the concluding speech of Mikhail Gorbachev with ovations, the way they stood up after he finished, speaks for itself. Mikhail Gorbachev won the fight with the conservatives.

Mikhail Gorbachev is often reproached both from the left and from the right. Some reproach him for indecisiveness, others for impulsiveness. Some ascribe to him an inability to go beyond the bounds of false Communist rhetoric; others accuse him of retreat, of betrayal of "principles" and abandonment of "values." But he is going his own way. He is capable of changing his views as society becomes more politicized and the mass conscience becomes more radicalized. This is the hallmark of a significant political figure. After all, it is Mikhail Gorbachev who suggested the abolition of Article 6 of the constitution and a transition to market relations.[3] And, in my view, he did not even once attempt to put the brakes on *perestroika*. His fate is inextricably bound to it.

I was thinking during the sessions of the 28th Congress: If it were not for the ability of Mikhail Gorbachev to explain, persuade, and change minds, then it would not have been possible to obtain a change in the mood of the delegates and to direct the work of the congress into a constructive channel.

Is Mikhail Gorbachev an ideal person? No, certainly not, and we well know his shortcomings. He does not foresee everything in advance. Sometimes he lingers in his decision making. At times these decisions are halfway. He is not consistent in everything. I could not understand his Olympian calm during the period of elections of congress delegates when, at the same time, the conservatives were so incredibly active. They were greatly helped by the notorious open letter.[4] "Yeltsin's Syndrome"? A reaction to the provocations of [Telman] Gdlyan, [Nikolai] Ivanov, and

---

[3]Article 6 mandated the leading role of the Communist party in Soviet life.

[4]This refers to "A Letter from Russia's Writers," Document 8.

others?[5] I do not know. But try to find a person without shortcomings! Or, what is no less difficult, to find a person who would have been able to move *perestroika* ahead more skillfully than has Mikhail Gorbachev!

Will the party catch up with *perestroika*? With the "runners" that have dominated the last two congresses, undoubtedly no. However, the party has eighteen million people, and it must advance the most capable and forward-thinking people to leadership posts, those who will lead the revolutionary renovation of society. Only one thing can prevent this—the selfish interests of those who would like to preserve the command-administrative system under the guise of socialism.

---

[5]Gdlyan and Ivanov are state investigators who accused former Politburo member Ligachev of corruption and lost their jobs. They were expelled from the CPSU in February 1990. They had previously exposed massive corruption in Uzbekistan (see *Gorbachev and Glasnost: Viewpoints from the Soviet Press* [Wilmington, DE: Scholarly Resources, 1989], Doc. 21, pp. 208–15).

11

Do We Need Yet Another Experiment? Ideological Paradoxes of Reform

Alexander Tsipko

Rodina
no. 1, January 1990

This is an unusual attempt by a Soviet Marxist philosopher to profoundly analyze and criticize Marx and Lenin. The two fundamental questions addressed here are: (1) Is Marxism relevant to the current period of reform? and (2) Were Stalin's views and the socialism he created in the Soviet Union Marxist in nature? Tsipko's answer to the first question is no. He acknowledges that even many proponents of reform are still attached emotionally to Marxism. But the author considers Marx to be superfluous at this historical stage, no matter if the subject is agriculture or private property, morality or religion. If the USSR continues to be Marxist, its European neighbors will be hesitant in letting it inside the European house. Tsipko's answer to the second question is yes; he does not doubt that Marxism is the source of Stalin's philosophy.

Are Our Principles Good?

The era of reform has been marked by an outburst of spirituality, thought, independent thinking, and remorse for one's silence, toadying, and worship of false idols. It has been a time for cleansing ourselves of the crimes of the Stalinist clique, and it has been cursed by many "patriots" as a spiritual crisis and an era of spiritual degradation of Russia. These people are trampling on the new shoots of an awakened spirituality, spiritual freedom, freedom of thought, economic thinking, and good sense as manifestations of the liberalism they hate. Nevertheless, they are the ones who talk the most about a rebirth of spirituality.

The egalitarians and fighters against privilege and bureaucracy who were swept into the Congress of People's Deputies by a wave of populism are now being replaced by advocates of spirituality and fighters against the shadow economy. But neither the first nor the second group wants to know **why**[1] the Russian people are so poor and why our economy is so helpless, **why** the shadow economy is firmly rooted not only in our country but also in all the socialist countries, **why** people have gotten so lazy, **why** no one keeps his word, or **why** the Russian peasant (who used to get drunk only on holidays) is now prepared to get drunk every day. There are thousands of these "whys" that have not yet been asked. But very few people want to think about them.

We have all kinds of denouncers. We have an abundance of hysterics and advocates. But we have very few analysts who want to know the truth of Russian history and the Russian destiny.

You want to cry when you read certain historical essays in the journal *Nash Sovremennik*. But why are we Russians so strange?! For a long time the contributors to this journal have been writing courageously about the horrors of collectivization and what the Trotskyite communization of Russia cost us, and they agree that the establishment of socialism in Russia was equivalent to pulling a camel through the eye of a needle with all of the attendant destructive consequences. But, as soon as these writers get close to the seemingly inevitable and undeniable philosophical conclusions from all that we know of Russian history after the October Revolution, they suddenly give themselves the command "About face!" and begin to speak the language of their not-so-beloved Trotsky. Having forgotten that the Communist struggle against the Russian petty bourgeoisie and against the so-called philistine private-property way of life turned into a catastrophe and a Russian apocalypse, they start to castigate private property and people's striving for personal benefits and prosperity as the "petty bourgeoisie mentality," "the mercenary spirit," and so forth. Spirituality is opposed to abundance, and moral incentives are opposed to economic incentives.

It's true that, instead of the Marxist concepts of "collectivism" and "socialization," the contributors to *Nash Sovremennik* use the idea of conciliarism.[2] None of them, like the fathers of Marxism, wants to understand that collectivism is a voluntary matter and that no one could turn

---

[1]Passages in boldface, here and below, were marked for emphasis in original.

[2]Conciliarism is an approximate translation of the word *sobornost*; that is, the purported unique ability of Russian people to consult with each other.

a vast country into a network of people who believe in communism or conciliarism. If you truly want a Russian to be spiritual, then leave him the freedom to choose, defend the Russian proprietor, and rehabilitate the Russian merchant and industrialist. That's what good sense tells us. Our reformist attitude toward Marx and Marxism piles absurdity upon absurdity and is driven by absurdity.

It would seem that everyone must understand that the canonization and ideologization of Marxism and its transformation into a "state religion" is one of the most visible and burdensome heritages of the Stalinist era. It would seem that all of our domestic policies (not to mention what's going on in the neighboring countries of Eastern Europe) are a continuous polemic with Marx and a debate with orthodox Marxism. Instead of nationalizing the agrarian sector even more thoroughly and transforming all of our agricultural production into a single gigantic entity, we've taken a step backward toward voluntary cooperation, leasing agreements, and peasant landholdings. Instead of launching further attacks on the market, we are rehabilitating monetary and trade relations and assigning them a leading role in the development and preservation of human civilization. Instead of providing more indoctrination in class struggle and class morality, we are rehabilitating common human morality and returning to the Sermon on the Mount as the foundation of human communal life and as the way to tame the beast within us. Instead of our former emphasis on the revolutionary struggle and the dictatorship of the proletariat, we are now recognizing that violence cannot be the midwife of history.[3]

I could cite scores of examples of how we, as we leave our dead end, are casting aside Marx and his principles. And essentially we have no other choice. There's either dogmatism or survival. But nevertheless here lies the main paradox of our reform ideology and reform consciousness: We've never sworn our fidelity to Marx and his principles as often as we do now. No matter how paradoxical it may seem, it is the best elements of our democratic and reform-minded intelligentsia that are doing this. They are attempting to bring Marx out of the terrible shadows of Stalin's crimes and prove that

---

[3]A paraphrase of Lenin's "Violence is always the midwife of the old society" ("Fright at the Fall of the Old and the Fight for the New," *The Lenin Anthology*, Robert C. Tucker, ed. [New York and London: Norton, 1975], p. 425). Lenin in his turn took it from Marx.

Marxism has absolutely no relation to what happened in our country after the revolution, that Stalin did not build socialism according to Marx, and that Marx is as necessary to reform as air is. Marx's victims pray to him, they use Marx to intimidate others, and they resort to Marx's authority to denigrate their own country and their own history.

So they have proposed building a new socialism on the basis of Marxist principles. But in the process no one can explain how Marxism can help us, what the essence of Marxism is, or what we should take from it. Perhaps the doctrine of class struggle, revolutions, the dictatorship of the proletariat, smashing the bourgeois state? Now nobody wants to clarify the social, political, or humanitarian essence of Marxism, and everyone is simply convinced that the world would collapse without Marx. I believe that many of the philosophers and economists who have recently rushed to save Marx's scholarly authority haven't picked up his books in decades. Associations formed by reading Marx's works a long time ago have very often crowded out his authentic words and texts from scholarly practice.

Never, not even in the era of stagnation, has there been such self-humiliation and self-destruction in Marxism as in our time. There are numerous examples of this. Of the works published in the last two years the orthodox tendency is most clearly evident, in my opinion, in Gennady Lisichkin's article entitled "Myths and Realities: Is Marx Necessary for Reform?" published in the November 1988 issue of *Novy Mir*. In the new year [1990] the author of the article "New Landmarks," S. Chernyshev, astounded everyone with his disheartening faith in Marx's rightness. In the name of saving Marx's authority he accused not only Stalin but also all the Russian Marxists, including Lenin, of an Asiatic inability to think things through. **"Communists,"** he writes, following his teachers, **"can express their theory in terms of a single principle, namely the destruction of private property. In this sacral formula of the Manifesto,"** he suggests, **"lies our curse and our salvation. Marx's words were not interpreted constructively, as the definition of the object of our activity and historical creativity, but Asiatically, as extermination, terror, and a 'Red Guard attack.' "**[4]

---

[4]*Znamya*, January 1990, p. 156 [cited by Tsipko].

Until now in the consciousness of most people the initial postulates, namely the doctrines of classes and class struggle, and the horrors of Stalinism have existed as independent and nonintersecting realities. People not only have preserved but also have reproduced the same mental stereotypes that helped the shamans of Marxism of the 1920s and early 1930s to keep intact their faith in the all-conquering reason of Marx's eternally true and forever-young doctrine and thus to protect themselves from pangs of conscience and thoughts of their personal responsibility for what was done in their terrible era.

People have also resurrected the old interpretation of Stalinism as a departure from correct party policies and, moreover, from Marxism. People have attempted to prove that Stalin was a disappointing exception and that he was the only member of Lenin's guard who was a phony revolutionary from the very beginning. In Igor Klyamkin's opinion, we do not have sufficient grounds to assert that the old party guard dirtied itself in petty politics "while supposedly forgetting about the principles behind it all": **"I am convinced that practically all of them were and continued to be servants and devotees of the idea and belonged to a different category of people in terms of spiritual and moral development than Stalin. The source of the lie was within him. With respect to such figures of the time as [Lev] Kamenev, [Nikolai] Bukharin, and [Alexei] Rykov, the lie was developed and gradually reinforced by the falsehood and ambiguity of the situation in which the old party guard found itself after the end of the civil war."**[5]

It would seem clear that we simply don't have the right today, in the eighth decade of the history of real socialism, to judge Stalin's actions without taking the trouble to make a critical analysis of the principles that guided him. We do not have the right to limit ourselves to a condemnation of the Stalinist clique and its crimes without considering Stalinism—that is, its ideological underpinnings. But despite logic and despite the interests of the truth, the overwhelming majority of the political and social commentators who have denounced Stalin have not decided or are unable to combine two tasks in their research, namely a moral and political

---

[5]"Why It's So Hard to Tell the Truth," *Novy Mir*, February 1989, p. 211 [cited by Tsipko].

condemnation of Stalin's adventurism and the ability critically to go beyond the worldview of his era.

How clever can a person be? Is it worth going to such lengths and going against one's conscience in the face of our falsified history solely for the sake of preserving one's faith in the truth of Marxism, in the possibility of a new Communist offensive against the old world, and in the possibility of building a new life in accordance with Marx's instructions and designs? **"I believe,"** wrote Grigory Vodolazov, **"that Marx and Lenin's doctrine developed creatively for current conditions constitutes the primary and most refined weapon in the fight against all forms and variations of Stalinism."**[6]

My respected colleagues Otto Latsis, Gennady Lisichkin, Grigory Vodolazov, and Anatoly Butenko [scholars and journalists] can't understand that our blind faith in the all-encompassing power of Marx's doctrine was the main impediment to our economic, political, and intellectual development and that a country that has consigned its inalienable right to think to a man who died more than a hundred years ago can never be free. Is Marx's absolute scholarly authority more valuable than the fates of millions of our countrymen who have never learned to think for themselves?

You get confused when you hear the Communist songs of the era of stagnation, which said that as Lenin foresaw we will have to begin everything from the beginning several times; we should not judge modern socialism too harshly, because it is a very young system; we must be steadfast, because the process begun by the October Revolution will inevitably take several centuries. Don't my respected colleagues see that our Russian people have already been exhausted by Marxist and Communist experiments and that they and their children can no longer wait for that happy time when history will begin to travel according to the schedule drawn up by Marx?

A Fruit That Never Ripens

Marx's doctrine is absolutely incapable of helping reform for the simple reason that it contains two mutually

---

[6]"Lenin and Stalin," *Oktyabr*, June 1989, p. 29 [cited by Tsipko].

contradictory answers to the basic questions posed by our life. In Marx's texts one can find justification for any economic or political decision. So, do what you want to do. You can make a sharp turn to the left, or, if you strain yourself, you can find justification for making a right turn.

On the basis of Marx and Engels's texts one can even demonstrate that they were opponents of the class approach and insisted on defending the universal norms and values of bourgeois civil society. They in fact became advocates of common human values and universal morality when they waged a theoretical and political struggle against the anarchists and tried to discredit them and to establish their amorality. In their treatise **"The Alliance and International Association of the Workers"** Marx and Engels sharply criticized the **"all-destructive anarchists who want to make everything amorphous in order to establish anarchy in the realm of morality."** The founders of scientific socialism protested against [the anarchists Sergei] Nechayev and [Mikhail] Bakunin's appeal to sunder "any tie to civil order and the entire educated world, to all the laws, proprieties, conventions, and morality of this world."[7]

But we must remember that there is another Marxism, which taught Communists the same thing that Bakunin preached, namely, that a revolutionary does not have the right to reject any means of achieving his goal. Engels's letter to Gerson Trier dated December 18, 1889, is quite typical in this respect: "To me, as a revolutionary, any means which leads to the end is suitable, be it the most violent or the means which seems to be the most peaceful."[8]

If you rely on the *Economic Manuscripts of 1857–1859* you can prove unmistakably that Marx hypothesized that trade and monetary relations would wither away at a very high level of development of the productive forces, when the economy would cease to depend on the amount of manual labor as the primary wealth of society. There would be no need for the physical labor of workers or their expenditure of muscular energy, and the need for exchange value as a condition and mechanism for disciplining and tying down labor would wither away by itself. But as soon as human

---

[7]Karl Marx and Friedrich Engels, *Collected Works*, vol. 18, pp. 415–16 [cited by Tsipko].

[8]Ibid., vol. 37, p. 275 [cited by Tsipko].

labor loses this quality, **"as soon as . . . work time ceases to be and must cease to be,"** Marx added, **"a measure of wealth and hence exchange value ceases to be a measure of consumer value,"** then "production based on exchange value will break down."[9]

Referring to this manuscript, you can demonstrate quite clearly that Lenin and all the Bolsheviks were total and incurable bunglers, because in Russia in 1917, like Russia in 1990, there isn't or wasn't even a hint of the need for trade mechanisms for enforcing the discipline and quality of labor; that is, there isn't even a hint of the natural and automatic withering away of private property.

Neither Marx nor Engels discerned the motivational and sociopsychological conditions of the actual capitalist socialization of production and did not recognize that Communists would always be condemned to dive into an empty pool. They called for a violent proletarian revolution: "Communists consider it despicable to conceal their views and intentions. They openly announce that their goals can be achieved only by means of the violent overthrow of the existing social structure. Let the ruling classes tremble in the face of the Communist Revolution."[10] In the process they did not take into consideration that this would of necessity lead not to the preparation but to the destruction of the personal preconditions for true socialization, to the destruction of efficient and rational labor, and to a break in the old integrity and interrelatedness of production.

In contrast to capitalism, socialism cannot arise as a qualitative entity in the bowels of a capitalist society. Capitalism does not create either the motives for a new collectivist mode of production or its subjects—that is, people prepared to build a new system of economic relations. The classic treatises of Marxism did not consider the question of who would replace the organizers of capitalist production, with their interest in profits and their material responsibility for their decisions and their concern for maintaining the continuity of skilled management. We also have never managed to resolve this question in practice in more than seventy years of building socialism.

What the theoreticians have called the objective premises for a transition to socialism have in reality proved to be the

---

[9]Ibid., vol. 46, pt. 2, p. 214 [cited by Tsipko].
[10]Ibid., vol. 4, p. 459 [cited by Tsipko].

ruins of the old system of production. As soon as the revolution undermined the right to property and the right to entrepreneurial profit, the old capitalist system of production died out and disintegrated. And in reality the spontaneous movement of scientific and technical progress under the conditions of capitalist competition is one thing, while their movement under the conditions of a monopolistic collective system of production is another thing. It's difficult to determine from Marx and Engels's writings what the motive force for scientific and technical progress would be in a society with no competition, no entrepreneurial profit, and no personal economic responsibility on the part of the organizers and managers of production for the decisions they make.

There is another question that contemporary adherents of Marxism find unpleasant to discuss. Wasn't Marx the author of the theory of permanent revolution, which was so "brilliantly" applied in Russia in 1917? It was Marx and Engels who called on Communists **"to make the revolution continuous until all the more or less wealthy classes have been deprived of hegemony and until the proletariat seizes state power and until the association of the proletarians of not just one country but in all the leading countries of the world has developed to an extent that competition between proletarians in these countries ceases and that at least the decisive productive forces are concentrated in the hands of the proletarians."**[11]

I can't understand why my respected colleagues seem to suffer a loss of memory when the subject of Stalin and his Marxist origins comes up. After all, when we were students we expended a great deal of effort on cramming the ***Communist Manifesto***, the first volume of ***Das Kapital***, ***A Critique of the Gotha Program***, ***The Civil War in France***, and other texts. We practically memorized the well-known letter to Joseph Weidemeyer dated March 5, 1852, in which Marx explained the novelty and originality of his doctrine of classes in the following way: First of all, **"the existence of classes is only associated with certain historical phases of the development of production,"** and, secondly, **"the class struggle necessarily leads to the dictatorship of the proletariat,"** and, thirdly, **"this**

---

[11]Ibid., vol. 7, p. 261 [cited by Tsipko].

dictatorship merely constitutes a transition to the elimination of all classes and to a classless society."[12]

I think there's nothing accidental about the fact that none of the writers who have insisted that Marx is necessary for reform and that only with his help will we be able to overcome the heritage of Stalinism has cited a single idea of his that would help us find a way out of the historical dead end that we are in.

We carried out the nationalization of the land (which the classics insisted on) long ago, in 1917. The fruits of this nationalization are quite well known. A land without an owner is like an orphan whom anyone, no matter how lazy they are, can abuse. The deterioration of the soil—first and foremost our national wealth, the *chernozem*—accompanies the degradation of the peasantry and ultimately of the city dweller, who is compelled to go to any lengths, as far as committing a crime, for the sole purpose of getting his daily bread and a piece of sausage.[13] Marxism has truly proven accurate in that part of the forecast which speaks of the adverse consequences of poverty. Dire need under socialism has led to a struggle for necessary objects, meaning that old abominations must inevitably be resurrected.

In reality Marx and Engels's agrarian program was a program for establishing universal poverty. Their idea of labor obligations and the organization of labor armies on the land compromised itself as early as the period of War Communism.[14] In **"The Transition to Universal Labor Service in Connection with the Militia System,"** Trotsky wrote that **"as long as universal labor service is not the norm and has not been reinforced by habit and has not become indisputable and inalterable for everyone (which will be accomplished by means of social and educational indoctrination and will find its full expression only in the new generation), until then it will inevitably be maintained by measures of compulsion, that is, in the final analysis, the armed might of the proletarian state, for the lengthy transitional period which will precede universal labor**

[12]Ibid., vol. 28, p. 427 [cited by Tsipko].

[13]*Chernozem* is the very rich black topsoil of the regions of southern Russia and the Ukraine.

[14]War Communism was a system of martial law and economic expropriations designed to win the civil war, implemented by Lenin and the Bolsheviks, 1918–1921.

service."[15] But it wasn't Trotsky who dreamed all this up. It was the classical thought of Marxism in the ***Communist Manifesto*** that proclaimed **"identical labor obligations for everyone and the establishment of industrial armies, particularly for agricultural work."**[16] The idea of alternating agricultural and industrial work or, moreover, of assigning secondary and elementary school students to gather the harvest also has never justified itself.

Only a blind man can't see that Marx has become the main weapon of the conservatives in this most dramatic period of the reform process. They have gained confidence from the ideas of the *Communist Manifesto* in their fight to prevent the rebirth of individual and collective entrepreneurship, the denationalization of industry, and the establishment of a mixed economy. And in their own way they're right. Marx and Engels, with their active distaste for the "property-owning trash" and their interpretation of socialism as "the abolition of bourgeois property," are incompatible and irreconcilable with what we now call the renewal of socialism and the democratization of the economy.

Finally, the foreign policy aspect of the problem: By insisting on fidelity to Marxism, we will never be able to get people to trust us or to let us into the European house or to consider us equal neighbors.

Anyone in the West knows that Marxism is primarily a doctrine of the destruction of private property in the means of production—the destruction of the material, legal, and spiritual foundation of Western civilization. No reasonable European politician who has not lost his sense of self-preservation as one who expresses the interests of a bourgeois civil society can avoid reckoning with the fact that by its nature Marxism is an expansionist international doctrine and a doctrine of permanent proletarian revolution. The slogan "Workers of the world, unite" is still alive. Who would want to live in the same house under the same roof with a neighbor who does not conceal his intentions of establishing "his own order" everywhere and subjecting all the dwellers in the house to his own notions of good and evil? Marxist fundamentalism, which has recently resurfaced, is dangerous also because it makes it possible to accuse us of

---

[15]From *How the Revolution Was Armed*, vol. 2, Book 1 (Moscow, 1924), p. 33 [cited by Tsipko].

[16]Marx and Engels, *Collected Works*, vol. 4, p. 447 [cited by Tsipko].

adhering to all the extreme aspects of Marx's doctrine, including his conviction that **"there is only one way to shorten, simplify, and concentrate the bloody agony of the old society and the bloody birth pangs of the new society, only one way, and that is revolutionary terrorism."**[17]

The attempts to combine a program for the creation of the rule of law and a return to the basic political institutions of modern civilization with declarations of the preservation of the vanguard role of the industrial proletariat would astonish any even slightly educated Western politician. The Marxist idea of the decisive role of the industrial proletariat in the progress of human civilization was from the very first an antithesis of a basic principle of political democracy, namely the primordial spiritual equality of all people, regardless of the social stratum to which they belong.

Poor Dühring, Who Has Nothing to Do with It

Not so long ago orthodox Marxists invented a new theory for the gullible reader: that we ended up building socialism not according to Marx and Engels, but according to the leveling ideas of distribution that Stalin took in a ready form from [Eugen] Dühring (Gennady Lisichkin's "Myths and Realities," *Novy Mir*, November 1988). But there was no need for this. Engels, a Marxist and Karl Marx's friend, defended a strictly egalitarian distribution even more passionately than did Dühring. I strongly advise you to open up *Anti-Dühring* and read Part Two, on simple and complex labor, on your own. You'll find a great deal of instructive material there. For example, Engels asserts the following: The attempt to ascribe the idea of possible additional payments for complex labor in the society of the future to Marx **"is simply shameless garbling which one probably encounters only in the work of literary bandits."** Engels insisted that **"the question of higher pay for complex labor"** has absolutely no right to exist within the framework of scientific socialism. **"In a society of private producers,"** he wrote, **"the expenses of training employees are covered by private individuals or their families, and therefore private individuals are the first to get higher prices for trained**

[17] Ibid., vol. 5, p. 494 [cited by Tsipko].

manpower: A skilled slave can be sold at a higher price, and a skilled hired hand gets higher wages. In a society organized on socialist principles these expenses are born by society, and therefore the fruits, that is, the greater values created by complex labor, belong to society."[18]

Honestly, I can't understand why political and social commentators who have sworn fidelity to the initial premise of the article "Myths and Realities" have used *Anti-Dühring* in particular to divorce Stalin from Marxism. In my opinion it would be difficult to think of a more unsuccessful tactic than that. After all, the social utopianism of Marxism is nowhere more openly evident than in this work of Engels, and nowhere is the separation of Marxist economic doctrine from human life and psychology more conspicuous.

And, most important, nowhere are the doctrinal roots of Stalinist administrative state socialism laid more bare than in this work. We're not even talking about details or particulars but about Engels and Stalin's common struggle for universal equality and for public or state property exclusively, of their common distaste for market mechanisms, and of their appeals for the public (that is, camp) upbringing of children and for collective and Communist living.

But enough. One could cite scores of examples of the unity and identity of Engels and Stalin's approaches to the organization of work and life in a collectivist society.

The Lie of Violence and the Violence of the Lie

The basic premises of Marx's worldview and his notions of progress are obsolete and have not withstood the test of time. A doctrine that associates social progress with arson and claims that struggle and social conflicts must be raised "to the highest level of intensity," because only by means of a "total revolution" and a crude "physical clash of people" can we guarantee movement toward freedom and human dignity, is completely incapable of assisting the reform process. It's doubtful that we would now be attracted by Marx's "social science," which in his words denies the possibility of "social evolutions" without "political revolutions" and as its "last word" sets forth George Sand's well-known slogan: **"Battle**

---

[18]Ibid., vol. 20, p. 207 [cited by Tsipko].

or death; bloody conflict or nonexistence. That is the inexorable statement of the question."[19]

Marx and Engels's doctrine of the class origins of morality is even less capable of assisting the reform process. We will be unable to halt the wave of crime, amorality, and cynicism that now afflicts us by convincing our young people that the voice of conscience and the idea of eternal laws of morality are a fabrication of the bourgeoisie, as Marx and Engels believed. Now, in order to save ourselves, we must proceed in spite of Marx and make the old and eternal laws of morality the basis for our new social development. We must argue with rather than agree with Engels, who attacked moral absolutes and the internal moral laws of man. We must object to the classical Marxists who called for the abolition of the bourgeois personality, bourgeois self-reliance, and bourgeois freedoms. Ultimately we should not forget that the doctrine we have worshipped for seventy years created talented but spiritually very unseasoned individuals who have been deprived of a great deal of what our times need both because of their age and because of their character traits. Their ambitious souls contained none of the natural human fear of crime, and they never thought of sin or repentance and didn't particularly like or respect the people they were trying to help.

In Marx and Engels's works and letters we can clearly see intonations of the revolutionary maximalist characteristics of the era of class conflict and the first stirrings of the proletariat. The ideas that we must not be afraid of sacrifices that serve the cause of progress and that we must preserve the revolutionary spirit of the proletarian masses are very characteristic of Marx. For example, he gave a great deal of credit to the Paris communards for not surrendering without a fight. **"The demoralization of the working class,"** he claimed, **"would ultimately have been a much greater misfortune than the death of any number of 'leaders.' "**[20]

We must not forget that in their understanding of the essence of religion and of its place in the spiritual life of man the classic works of scientific socialism held the views of the Enlightenment and of the French materialists of the eighteenth century. Scientific socialism was also unable to

---

[19]Ibid., vol. 4, pp. 184–85 [cited by Tsipko].
[20]Ibid., vol. 33, p. 175 [cited by Tsipko].

overcome the limited framework of vulgar atheism and sociologism.[21] Until their dying days Marx and Engels were convinced that religion and religious philosophy were merely an "opiate," "the sigh of an oppressed creature," and one of the outgrowths of private property. They believed that people could not experience genuine happiness without the abolition of religion. These attitudes explain their contempt for all possible kinds of religious freedom of conscience which, in Marx's opinion, the triumphant proletariat must walk over like anything else that bears the mark of a limited "bourgeois level."

The task of smashing the state was directed not only against the right to private property but also against the inviolability of the home; the principles of the dignity, sovereignty, and independence of every individual; and the right to choose a way of life.

Marx never bothered to conceal that the proletarian revolution would totally do away with all the "old laws" and completely renounce them. The logic of a revolutionary struggle inevitably led Marx and Engels to a decisive rejection of any attempts to bind them to any kind of moral absolutes.

Of course, Marx and Engels were not conscious proponents of barracks communism.[22] And, as G. Vodolazov wrote, one can read about their fidelity to the ideal of the free individual on practically every page. But after all, if we want to think like scholars (and not only as propagandists of the past), we should be interested not in empty phrases but rather in the possibility of preserving the freedom of the individual in the society that the founders of Marxism strived to create. In this society, in accordance with their doctrine of association, all private labor (that is, labor not coordinated by a plan or center) would be eliminated, the slightest manifestations of economic and social self-reliance would be eradicated, and the freedom to select an occupation, a way of life, and a way of supporting one's offspring would be abolished. Doesn't a doctrine of noncommercial production and of the direct socialization of labor lead to the barracks and to a new form of human serfdom, despite the declarations of individual freedom? Is it realistically possible to preserve

---

[21]"Sociologism," a Soviet philosophical term, means the study and explanation of social phenomena by using sociological methods alone.

[22]"Barracks communism" refers to Stalinist-style socialism.

human rights and freedoms in a society in which the possibility of economic and social choice is denied from the very beginning and everything is rigidly determined by creed and the law?

Unfortunately, not one of the writers who has denied the Marxist doctrinal roots of Stalin's barracks socialism has even attempted to begin a discussion of the Marxist doctrine of socialism on an objective and specifically sociological and economic level.

As long as our reformist fundamentalism remains deaf to all of these fundamental structural problems of Marxist theory and to its internal contradictions, it will continue to be an impediment to the movement of our thought and an enemy of the cause of genuine democracy. I believe that the time has come to begin a serious dialogue on the profound and insurmountable contradictions of Marx's doctrine and on the limitations which a largely transitional era imposed on his thinking.

12

The KGB Has Not Changed Its Principles . . . Yet

Oleg Kalugin

Komsomolskaya Pravda
June 20, 1990

Kalugin, a former high KGB official, was recently deprived of his rank of general by Gorbachev's decree. A judicial investigation has been opened to determine if he had leaked any secrets. In this article, Kalugin reveals that the KGB is not dormant and that it is actively serving the conservative forces it has always worked for. With its vast resources and deep penetration of Soviet society, the KGB is a powerful tool in the hands of the party, much stronger than the Romanian Securitate. The KGB keeps close watch on the activities of proreform groups and parties, and it is ready for a crackdown at any time. It seems it was even well prepared for this period of instability. *Perestroika* and *glasnost* have not touched this powerful organization, except for General Kalugin, who has quickly become a democrat. Some reformers are embarrassed that a KGB general is such a prominent member of their movement.

Interviewers: Oleg Danilovich, how does someone get to become a Soviet intelligence resident in the United States?

Kalugin: I graduated from Leningrad University's philology department as an English-language specialist. After graduation, I was recruited to work for the KGB. In 1958, I went on an assignment to Columbia University. It was the first postwar Soviet-U.S. exchange, on the wave of the Khrushchev thaw.

Interviewers: Were you the only KGB associate in that delegation?

Kalugin: Certainly not. But I would like to warn you right now that instances like this are evidently going to arise during our conversation more than once: There are situations in which I cannot give figures, names, or specific circumstances. Despite the fact that I am now in the reserve, I am still a professional intelligence worker and have certain obligations to my country and to the organization in which I worked. I hope you understand me.

So then. On my return from the United States, I was immediately sent to the Committee for Radio Broadcasting.

Then, eight or nine months later, with a Moscow Radio "cover," I went back to New York. For four years, I believe, I successfully combined journalistic and intelligence activity.

Interviewers: Incidentally, do all our journalists working abroad combine these two forms of activity?

Kalugin: Of course not. There are not so many KGB members among journalists. It is another matter that many of them help us by fulfilling some of our requests, so to speak, in an unofficial capacity. Well, in 1964, I returned to the USSR. It had been decided to replace my cover with something more reliable. So, a year later, I returned to the United States with a diplomatic passport as second secretary—and later as first secretary—of the Soviet embassy in Washington. I was the Soviet intelligence deputy resident in the United States, and when the resident left I performed his duties for quite a long time.

Interviewers: What does a Soviet intelligence resident do in the United States?

Kalugin: I hope you will understand that at present I can only talk about this in the most general terms. The responsibilities of a resident include coordinating the work of our agent networks.

Interviewers: You said "networks"?

Kalugin: Yes, there are several of them. The KGB intelligence administration consists of three main subdivisions: political intelligence, scientific and technical intelligence, and external counterintelligence. Each has its own agent network and its own targets. For example, the targets of external counterintelligence include the CIA, the FBI, the National Security Agency, and so forth. Political intelligence is concerned with the State Department. The resident coordinates the work of all these networks and sorts and analyzes information. After all, in principle the gathering of information and the compilation of forecasts on events that could affect our country are the basic tasks of intelligence. Naturally, this information is not culled only from newspapers. We often obtain this information for money. The KGB budget includes the corresponding class of currency expenditure.

Interviewers: Did you never have any doubts about the rightness of the cause you were serving during your time in the KGB?

Kalugin: I must confess that I first had doubts in 1968. I had already become resident by that time. I was sent a telegram from Moscow informing me that Warsaw Pact troops would invade Czechoslovakia the next day. I was directed to prepare for a possible negative reaction, given some minor instruction, and told to inform the ambassador. I was shocked. Our ambassador, Anatoly Dobrynin, reacted in basically the same way. I had in my possession absolutely reliable documents from American intelligence, the Pentagon, and the State Department confirming that neither the CIA nor any other American departments had anything to do with the events in Czechoslovakia. What is more, even they were taken aback by the scale of the events. As resident, I had informed my leadership of this before the invasion. But what shocked me most of all was that, when I went on leave to Moscow a year later, I discovered that the KGB leadership had given instructions that my messages should be destroyed and not shown to anyone.

Interviewers: Judging by the fact that you have agreed to this conversation, that was not the last time you were disillusioned?

Kalugin: After I finished working as chief of the external counterintelligence administration, I was sent as the KGB's first deputy chief to Leningrad, where I built up a fairly full picture of the workings of state security bodies inside the country. And I reached the firm conclusion that if we seriously want to engage in *perestroika*, then we cannot rely on the methods of an organization that has permeated every pore of our social organism and that interferes—at the party's will—in affairs of state and social life, in the economy and culture, in science, sport, and religion. There is not one sphere of life free of the KGB's hand or shadow. As far as I am concerned, all talk of a new face for the KGB is nothing more than camouflage at present. I have every reason to assert that the activity of the state security bodies is based on the old Stalinist training. Their methods have remained largely what they were thirty, even fifty, years ago. From the moment they appeared to the present day, state security bodies have fulfilled the functions of political investigation. Only their targets change. First it was the Mensheviks and Socialist Revolutionaries, then Trotskyites, Zinovyevites, cosmopolitans, nationalists, clerics, Hare Krishna followers, and unofficial movements, and, finally, the strike committees and new political parties.

Interviewers: Can you give us a few more details about the methods used by the KGB within the strike movement, for example?

Kalugin: Well, the methods are the same as those used by police all over the world. They either recruit someone or send their own agents into the organization, discredit the movement's activists, and ultimately cause it to disintegrate from within. After all, we are still actively using the instructions on work with agents that were compiled in the time of [Sergei] Zubatov, chief of the czar's secret police. This is an amazing document, which takes full account of what we now call the human factor. "If you want to have a good agent, you must show concern for his health and family and help him to advance in the service. The police officer must be a substitute mother and father to him."

Interviewers: Could you tell us whether KGB bodies ever have occasion to experience any material difficulties?

Kalugin: No, the KGB has never had those problems. I cannot tell you the size of our budget, but, believe me, we get as many rubles and dollars from the state treasury as we ask for.

Interviewers: And who approves the KGB budget?

Kalugin: The party Central Committee—at the top-leadership level.

Interviewers: Are you also barred from telling us how many people work in KGB bodies?

Kalugin: That is correct, I cannot tell you, but I can say that the KGB is vast and totally out of proportion to the level of external danger or the degree of the threat to state security inside the country. As far as I am aware, far more people work in just the central apparatus in Moscow than in the entire CIA and FBI systems put together.

Interviewers: Is it true that the KGB has compiled dossiers on virtually everyone?

Kalugin: The word dossier is a term used in spy movies. But it is true that there are documents on millions of Soviet and foreign citizens. They are grouped into certain files. I could list a good one hundred people known throughout the country on whom such documents have been compiled. This practice began in 1918.

Interviewers: Does the KGB tap telephone conversations?

Kalugin: That is prohibited by law. But, as first deputy chief of the Leningrad KGB, I could sanction the tapping of any telephone. But I must point out that this is rather a costly undertaking.

Interviewers: But could anyone—an *oblast* party committee, for example—ask the KGB to tap someone's telephone?

Kalugin: The secretary of the Leningrad *oblast* party committee once approached me with that kind of request. I refused at the time. But I cannot rule out the possibility that such steps might be taken in other places.

Interviewers: Does the practice of assassination exist in the KGB?

Kalugin: I do not know how the situation stands now, but the practice still existed a little while ago.

Interviewers: Forgive us for such a direct question, but did you ever have to implement or plan such operations while you were resident?

Kalugin: I just knew about them.

Interviewers: Could you tell us whether there are zones in our country that are closed even to the KGB?

Kalugin: I am aware of only one such zone: The KGB is not permitted to collect and store any negative information on *nomenklatura* personnel. When I was working in Leningrad, for example, I had a special list of these people: the secretaries of the *oblast* party committee, the chairman of the Leningrad city soviet and his deputies, and even the secretaries of the province Komsomol committee appeared to be included. In short, all the ruling elite.

Interviewers: From whom did this ban come?

Kalugin: I think I have already mentioned in our talk that the only organization that can give any instructions to the KGB is the party Central Committee. In this case I do not know the exact name of the relevant document signed on Staraya Square (the Central Committee's headquarters)—a secret instruction or a confidential resolution—but in the KGB it was turned into an official instruction. The document said—I shall try to reproduce this from memory—that it was forbidden to conduct any operational measures against . . . and there followed a list of officials. Then: In the event of receiving adverse materials concerning these people, these materials should be destroyed immediately on the spot. The same was to be done if such material reached us by indirect means. For instance, if a tape of a bugged telephone conversation happened to contain even a mention of such a person, that place on the tape had to be erased immediately.

That is why I was very amused to read a report from the USSR Prosecutor's Office that it had conducted a further check on the statements of [Telman] Gdlyan and [Nikolai] Ivanov about high-ranking bribe takers and had not discovered any corroborating material. In fact, it could not have discovered such material; it simply does not exist in nature. Nikita Khrushchev once stated that the intelligence organs had gotten above the party and that this was intolerable. True, but with one small amplification: Since then, not the party but merely its leading apparatus has been removed from the control of the organs.

Interviewers: Is it true that there is a special subunit in the KGB that engages in the dissemination of disinformation?

Kalugin: Yes, there is indeed such a subunit. This subunit engages in discrediting individual people and organizations and in disseminating anonymous leaflets and false rumors. For instance, materials are collected for a particular story and are leaked to a Western correspondent, and then we read this material in our newspapers, which cite foreign press organs.

Interviewers: In your opinion, how should the KGB be reformed?

Kalugin: First of all, it must be depoliticized. State security must—and will—engage in its own business: defending the constitution and the stability of the state system and citizens' safety. But when the KGB (like, indeed, any other police) begins to worm its way into politics, it invariably becomes an instrument in the hands of various groups and parties.

Interviewers: And, in conclusion, can you predict what the results of this publication will be for you personally?

Kalugin: There is no doubt that unpleasantnesses await me. Of what kind I cannot yet say.

Interviewers: Surely, with your experience, it is not that difficult to predict?

Kalugin: You know, this organization is quite creative and inventive. But I have not exhausted my potential either.

13

The Striving for Truth Has Not Yet Been Suppressed

Nina Andreyeva

Molodaya Gvardiya
no. 2, February 1990

The author of this piece, a lecturer in chemistry at a Leningrad college, was unknown on the Soviet political scene before the publication of her famous March 1988 letter to the editors of *Sovetskaya Rossiya*. The manner in which this letter, a Stalinist and Russian nationalist denunciation of *perestroika* and *glasnost*, was published clearly showed the active involvement of the newspaper's staff and the permission of high party officials, generating widespread fear that the days of *glasnost* were over. This single letter paralyzed political discourse in the Soviet Union for three weeks, until Gorbachev's allies counterattacked in the pages of *Pravda*.

Ms. Andreyeva has continued to participate in the Soviet political debate, with gusto. In the document printed here, she responds to such criticism of her views as an attack by the well-known economist Gennady Lisichkin and an article, "Enraged Critic of Gorbachev," published in the liberal journal *Ogonyok*.

Everyone in our country now, from the general secretary to the secretary of a grass-roots party organization, from the minister down to the worker, from the academician to the laboratory assistant, is privately taking a test of his fidelity to Marxism-Leninism. Far from all of the holders of high positions, scholarly degrees and titles, and national honors are successfully passing this exam. Many of them, who have become accustomed to swearing their fidelity to a scientific and proletarian worldview in vain, are quite often objectively on the opposite side of the historical barricade that separates the worker and the drone. There are also quite a few who have looked for socialism in Denmark and Sweden and who have tried to make nazism look good by equating nazism with "feudal socialism." Far-from-socialist pluralism has opened floodgates through which ideological and political ideas of destruction fraught with disaster for working people are pouring.

A great many Soviet people, some of whom have written to me, are seriously concerned about the destiny of the motherland. Being unable to answer everyone (although I've tried to do so), I was compelled to write a letter to the magazine *Molodaya Gvardiya* in April 1989, which was published in the July issue of this publication. I was completely prepared for the editors of this young people's journal to refuse to publish the letter, in light of the experience of the newspaper *Sovetskaya Rossiya*.[1] The editors of *Ogonyok* and *Moskovskie Novosti*, the [U.S.-sponsored] radio station Liberty, and a number of Western media outlets didn't make me wait too long. I consider it my duty as a citizen and a party member to respond to their criticisms.

People's Deputy and Doctor of Economics Gennady Lisichkin, a prominent architect of the current economic reform, was one of the first to comment on the publication of my letter in *Molodaya Gvardiya*. In his article entitled "Nina Andreyeva: Pro and Contra," published in the August 13, 1989, issue of *Moskovskie Novosti*, this critic made what was in many respects an interesting attempt to analyze the reasons for the "innocence of optimism" of the people who hold my views. Unfortunately, this prominent scholar did not refrain from statements that in no way make him look good.

I can understand the distaste of a creator of the model of "market socialism" for the traditionalism of the "antimarketeers." Now that the latter are not allowed in the mass media, it is safe to accuse them of wage leveling, groundless criticism of leasing and cooperatives, and a great deal else that is incompatible with a "lofty science" which in four years has done a great deal to turn the "scattered crisis phenomena" of the era of stagnation into the profound economic, social, political, and ideological crisis of today.

The People's Deputy also accused me of painting not only the past but also the present in rosy hues, citing an excerpt from my letter to *Molodaya Gvardiya* after first abridging it. In particular, passages pertaining to my characterization of certain features of the "national revolution" in Hungary in 1956 and the Prague Spring in Czechoslovakia in 1968 were shortened. Here is some of the text that was omitted:

> As in the aforementioned countries, extremely exaggerated economic difficulties and the inability of the leaders of these countries to cope effectively and in a timely manner with

[1]This journal printed Nina Andreyeva's letter entitled "Polemics: I Cannot Waive Principles" in 1988. A translation of it is included in *Gorbachev and Glasnost* (Scholarly Resources, 1989), pp. 277–90.

> the problems which are emerging have served as pretexts and starting points for attacks on socialism. Anti-Soviet groups, which had created the nuclei of political parties and took advantage of aid from abroad and the support of revisionist and unstable elements in the party and governmental apparatus, became the motive forces of the processes in these countries. The role of a "strike force" was assigned to inexperienced and politically immature youths and students in these countries. Literary circles and writers' conventions and the activation of pro-Zionist elements (which had infiltrated the mass media and were oriented toward manipulating public opinion, deceiving the public, and distracting the workers from resolving the important problems of socioeconomic renewal and socialist development) became the reference point and "starting point" for these processes. They took extensive advantage of nationalist tendencies and prejudices.

You'll agree that there is a great deal of similarity between this and the crisis afflicting our country today.

This ardent "point man for reform" clearly went too far by saying that I had suggested that there was no need to exaggerate the current economic crisis. At the same time, by himself skillfully exaggerating the economic situation, Lisichkin asked the readers to understand that "all of these shortcomings are not the result of reform but are the heritage of preceding decades." But what about his statement that "if we choose the proper economic development strategy and tactics, the results will make themselves known very soon"? Now we're in the fifth year of reform! This is why he tries to deflect criticism of his fellow economists, whose recommendations have supposedly "not been carried out or have been carried out in such a way as to discredit the idea itself." In other words, it's all the fault of the Council of Ministers, the State Planning Agency, the ministries, and the economic agencies who are supposedly not hurrying to implement [Nikolai] Shmelyov, [Leonid] Abalkin, and [Tatyana] Zaslavskaya's designs.[2] But perhaps the managers of industry, agriculture, science, and administrative agencies who have not lost their sense of responsibility for the destiny of the socialist fatherland and who in fact have realized the fatality for the country of the projects of the current reform economists—perhaps they are not allowing these sorry

---

[2]Well-known reformist economists and sociologists.

excuses for experimenters to destroy everything altogether and to bury the country's economy once and for all along with the hopes of the people for socialist reform.

With a great deal of interest the readers of *Moskovskie Novosti* learned from Lisichkin's article that at present our national debt is 312 billion rubles(!), but unfortunately the author did not mention that one third of this gigantic sum is the "achievement" of the last year of reform and that the annual budget began to run a deficit only in the early 1980s. This respected scholar's attempt to defend the honor of the uniform of the representatives of a "market economy" by referring to the repressions of the 1930s is quite amusing. He emphasizes that market economics "was persecuted in the same way that genetics and cybernetics" were in their time because "bureaucrats need not scholars or scientists but obsequious lackeys from science." However, half a century has gone by since then, and don't our glorious professors and academic economists resemble the old woman in the folk proverb who called herself an orphan until she was eighty years old?

The article "Gorbachev's Infuriated Critic," published in issue no. 33 of *Ogonyok* [August 1989], is quite different in nature. After proclaiming his noble purpose of "preventing false interpretations and ad-libbing," S. Lyamkin, who prepared this article for publication, very humbly thanks the correspondent of the *Washington Post*, David Remnick, for "providing the text of the aforementioned conversation."[3] It's still difficult to judge who the cowboy is here, the interviewer himself or the translators and editors of *Ogonyok*. It's hard to say who borrowed from whom the endless fantasies, which distort everything, starting with my biographical information, and on the whole reduce a serious conversation to the level of sordid sensations and attribute to me all sorts of unusual and unseemly opinions, which in fact are quite widespread in the American press. In my opinion there was only one possible purpose for such an article, namely to crush the morale of and to destroy an individual.

However, in order to keep the reader of *Ogonyok* from getting the impression that the interview covered only rock and roll, cooking, "cosmopolitan spies," the secret views of the

---

[3]Andreyeva is accusing Lyamkin and the popular magazine *Ogonyok* of distorting her interview with David Remnick of the *Washington Post*. The *Ogonyok* article presents Andreyeva as the antihero of our time.

"Kremlin leaders," the sexual bestiality of men, or the notorious "European issue" in the USSR, and that the most "lofty topic" covered was supposedly the issue that "the state is first of all order," I now believe it is necessary to familiarize the reader with several of my answers to questions I was asked recently by American correspondents on the telephone. My answers were tape-recorded. Familiarity with them will make it possible for any reader who so desires to form his own opinion on the content of the article in *Ogonyok* and to judge its objectivity for himself. So here are the questions and the answers.

How would you evaluate the situation in the country and the results of the 1st Congress of People's Deputies of the USSR? Could the current progress of reform be considered an acceleration of the development of Soviet society?[4]

I think not. It's more likely the reverse. Our successes in reform are so modest and miserable that practically none of the deputies mentioned them in their speeches. However, failures and mistakes and the problems they caused were discussed on all sides, quite often with glee.

In fact, how could we help but be disappointed by the further lag in the development of the material and technical infrastructure; in the introduction of new equipment and technology; in the growth of the "shadow economy," the "black market," and speculation; in the expansion of the scope of unearned income; in the perversions in the development of cooperatives; in the national budget deficit and foreign debt, which were unheard of even during the war; in the galloping inflation, the devaluation of the ruble, and the fall in the real standard of living of the Soviet people, forty-three million of whom are living below the poverty line; and in the legalization of so-called socialist millionaires and wheelers and dealers, whose liquid capital, by invading the realm of national priorities, is deforming the economy?

A political structure for such antisocialist forces as "democratic alliances" and "popular fronts" is developing, and the number of environmental disasters and difficulties is growing. I am disheartened by the decline in morality and behavior, particularly among the young, by the rampant crime, the cult of profit, the rise of nationalism, which has given rise to centrifugal separatist tendencies, and a great

---

[4]Emphasis here, and in other boldface passages, was in original.

deal else. And in my opinion what's most frightening is that the prestige of honest productive labor has been undermined.

In recent years we clearly have facilitated a crisis in the international labor and Communist movement, and we have complicated the situation in the socialist commonwealth. Poland and Hungary (which, as the secretary of the Central Committee of the Czechoslovak Communist party, Jan Fojtik, has rightly noted, has buried not only Imre Nagy[5] but also communism) are in the grip of a profound crisis and are running ahead of us to the abyss. In reality we are also hurrying to push East Germany, Czechoslovakia, and Bulgaria toward this kind of phony reform. But, as you can see, we still have not managed to do this.[6]

All of this has led to a situation in which the Communist party of the Soviet Union is gradually losing its vanguard role in the global revolutionary and Communist movement and is apparently intent on turning it over to the Communist party of China, whose leaders have claimed this role for a long time. It seems to me that their resolute—perhaps cruel—crushing of the counterrevolutionary uprisings in Beijing, the changes in the Chinese leadership, and the condemnation of the persons who indulged in the illegal subversive activity on Tiananmen Square constituted a kind of statement of this claim.

The situation prevailing in our country has confirmed the misgivings I stated with respect to the meaning of Mikhail Gorbachev's assertion that in the reform process we must first "cut down the old tree, then uproot it, grow new trees, and harvest the fruits" (*Pravda*, September 25, 1988). Such references to cutting down and uprooting socialism obviously impelled the American sociologist [Theodore] Shabad to say, at a roundtable discussion sponsored by *Ogonyok*, that "if Gorbachev wins, capitalism will triumph in the USSR." And the editor of the journal and his colleagues didn't even try to object to this interpretation of reform, which apparently is all right with them.

Thus in the reform process we have seen two processes with opposite and mutually exclusive contents. The confrontation between these processes is determining the

---

[5]Nagy, leader of the Hungarian revolution of 1956 and executed after Soviet intervention, was recently given an honorable reburial.

[6]Gorbachev did pressure these countries to switch to less rigid, more moderate methods. Since this article was written, of course, the situation in these countries has changed dramatically.

nature of and prospects for the socioeconomic and political situation in the country. And not just in our own country.

I'll repeat: It is conflict, not convergence, not consolidation, not harmony, and not "mutual enrichment," as our bourgeois neoliberals have claimed. Our "foremen of the spirit" have also emphasized the contradictory nature of the processes and trends of reform. In the process they have tried to conceal and disguise forces that are in genuine conflict, to obscure their class content, and falsely to substitute for them the opposition of Stalinists and anti-Stalinists, Zionists and anti-Zionists, Russophobes and Russophiles, conservatives and revolutionaries, democrats and bureaucrats, right-wingers and left-wingers, nationalists and chauvinists, and so forth.

In reality, in the arena of contemporary sociopolitical struggle in this country there are two conflicting sides: On one side are comparatively small but well-organized antisocialist forces, which are skilled in demagoguery and which have support from abroad and from revisionist elements at all levels of the party and governmental apparatus. On the other side are the broad masses of people who hold dear the country's choice of socialism and a Communist future.

The latter constitute an absolute majority, but they are disengaged and unorganized and subjected to ideological pressure from the propagandists of the anti-Communist platform, who have seized a large percentage of the mass media outlets. They are also disoriented by the inconsistent stance of a demoralized party and government apparatus. Not only the mass demonstrations against the owners of cooperatives but also the numerous strikes in practically all areas of the country, which have quite often turned into political strikes (this has been particularly evident in the Baltic republics, in the coal-mining areas of the country, and in the activities of the international fronts)—all of these have constituted a spontaneous protest on the part of the silent majority.

The antagonistic tendencies in reform processes, which have been distorted by the mass media, were reflected in just as distorted a manner in the debates at the 1st Congress of People's Deputies of the USSR. The so-called strongly democratic minority, consisting of about 20 percent of all deputies, formulated and worked on its program during the preparations for this congress. This minority consisted predominantly of deputies from Moscow, Leningrad, the Baltic republics, Moldavia, and several other regions. In order to gain experience in bourgeois parliamentarism, several of them managed to go abroad before the congress, where they received the appropriate "good wishes" from the West. Not without success, they tried to take the initiative in their own hands as soon as the congress began. They managed to swallow up more than 60 percent of the floor time, which obviously was far out of proportion to their numbers at the congress and to the social base they represented.

An irony of fate lies in the fact that for some reason our mass media began to call the ideologues of the strongly democratic minority "leftists." However, we know that in the international workers' and Communist movement individuals who have betrayed their class and who have slithered away from scientific proletarian positions and advocated a bourgeois way of life and relations have always been described as right-wing opportunists and revisionists. We have also classified those leaders who in one way or another pander to such renegades by their wavering stances as rightist opportunists and revisionists.

For example, what kind of a "right-winger" is People's Deputy Sergei Chervonopisky, a veteran of the war in Afghanistan and a secretary of the Cherkassy city Komsomol committee, whose main principles are "power, motherland, and communism"! On the other hand, Boris Yeltsin could quite properly be classified as right-wing, as could the so-called Yeltsinism, the adventurist and demagogic authoritarian political intrigue which he gave rise to.

Which of the two opposing tendencies won out at the 1st Congress of People's Deputies?

I think that no one won a total victory. At first glance the "strongly democratic minority" was quite successful. They successfully made use of the highest tribune in the land to propagate their restorationist ideas. Several political formulations shifted "right" under their pressure, and they won posts in the Supreme Soviet and on its commissions and in the government. However, they clearly lacked the kinetic energy required for the major move to the right that they had planned. On the whole, the potential energy of socialism among the masses proved to be insurmountable for these point men. And this was no accident. Despite all the costs, the seventy years after October have created a new kind of mass which cannot be immediately overcome by manipulating the consciousness of working people.

Historical experience has revealed that the transition from private property in the means of production to public property is possible only by means of the dictatorship of the proletariat, a workers and peasants' state, which has operated, is operating, and will operate in the most diverse ways. It would be naive to think that a reverse transition of property to private hands would be possible without political structures that would essentially constitute a dictatorship of the neobourgeoisie, that very same homespun neobourgeoisie which is now developing successfully in our country. The "foremen of the spirit" are now refining an ideological platform for a new political system, after first anathematizing the very concept of ideology. Apparently they figured that the Congress of People's Deputies would mark the transition to their dictatorship, which might have taken either a bourgeois-democratic or an authoritarian form. The latter frightens them not only because it could take on extreme forms but also because of the uncertainty of the answer to the question of who might gain power. This fear was quite often evident in their speeches. (It has also come up at later overblown rallies held by the "popular fronts" and "democratic alliances.")

In other words, at first glance the "liberal minority" seemingly won, but it did not achieve its main strategic goal, which its representatives now so emotionally bewail. I'll allow myself to draw a historical analogy with the Battle of Borodino in 1812, which was ultimately a victory for the Russian army, despite their retreat and the surrender of Moscow. I think that the Congress of People's Deputies, in which victory remained with the healthy socialist forces of society and which was not subjugated to so-called neoliberal conceptions of the restoration of capitalism, could be evaluated in the same way. Moreover, in the public consciousness of the Soviet people there was a universal and explicit turn in the direction of recognizing the danger hanging over socialism and over the Communist prospects for human development.

One could first discern this in the Moscow intelligentsia, which was sensitive to the situation and which began to coin phrases such as the "Abalkinization" and "G. Popovization" of the economy and the "Gelmanization" and "Grossmanization" of culture.[7] Many government and party employees have awakened from their lethargy, and the theoreticians of antimarket economics who are not published in the press have become more active. But, most important, broad segments of the public have come to understand that the struggle in the country is again following the principle, "Who does what to whom?," as was the case in the first decades of Soviet power. Because of this, the questions asked at lectures, the assessments of political figures, and the kind of letters written to the editors are changing. New organizations such as the United Front of Workers and the all-union society called Unity for Leninism and Communist Ideals are emerging.[8] Patriotic societies and organizations are ridding themselves of infantile disorders, are reforming themselves, and are gaining maturity.

This and a great deal else make it possible now to say: There will be no restoration of capitalism in the Soviet Union, and creeping counterrevolution shall not pass!

On what basis did I decide to talk about all of this to my "guest," the Moscow correspondent of an influential American newspaper, David Remnick, with whom I agreed to meet after his fourth persistent request? I proceeded primarily on the basis of the feverish growth of the political consciousness of the workers, who are now seriously pondering the long-term and short-term prospects for the development of their country. As Maxim Gorky loved to say, "If only people start to think, they will always get to the truth."

---

[7]Derived from the names Leonid Abalkin, Gavriil Popov, Alexander Gelman, and Vasily Grossman, all of whom are associated with the Soviet reform movement.

[8]Andreyeva founded Unity for Leninism and Communist Ideals in May 1989, aiming to transform it eventually into a Communist Party of Bolshevik-Leninists. This aim was made moot by the establishment of the conservative-dominated Communist Party of Russia in June 1990 (see Doc. 32).

14

Enough Talk! Let's Get to Work!

Ilya Zaslavsky

Demokraticheskaya Rossiya
no. 4, October 1990

This article, by People's Deputy Ilya Zaslavsky, contains a brilliant and penetrating description of the role of the Communist party in the reform process and the party's struggle against the new structures dominated by democratic and nationalist forces. Zaslavsky is a remarkable example of how even a restricted democratic process can uncover new leaders with fresh ideas. Handicapped from childhood, she fearlessly fought in election battles and won the admiration of Muscovites.

Why Improve the Party?

As our president has rightly observed, *perestroika* has its opponents. And they constitute the primary reason for all the difficulties that reform has encountered on its journey, a journey which has already lasted several years. Now even the very term "opponent of reform" has become a kind of cuss-word. As I understand it, opponents of reform are, first of all, those who in the president's opinion want to leave everything just the way it was, and also those who in the president's opinion want to destroy everything. It's true that the president has not specified exactly what it is they want to destroy. Hence, I would like to take a brief look at what our reform is.

Obviously, in attempting to define what reform is, there is no need to put too much faith in the pronouncements of specific individuals. Instead we should look at what exactly is the process that has been unfolding in our country in recent years under the influence of the most diverse forces. And then it becomes clear that reform is a unique process of social restructuring that perhaps has no counterparts in the past, a process which involves the creation of new structures that take something from the old structures and have partially incorporated new ideas and new people, a process which involves constant administrative changes in both the old and new structures, reorganization of these structures, and so forth. But what's most important in this process is that this restructuring is taking place within the framework of a definite system that emerged a long time ago.

After all, the essence of reform is improvement and liberalization, the production of a new, improved version of the same old model. In contrast, the path of social self-development leads to the creation of a stable system. The system in which we live is unstable and is capable of existing only under conditions of firm pressure, when society is led where someone wants to lead it. The entire world considers this system undemocratic and amoral. It represses the individual and, in addition to everything else, is quite inefficient, because the more complex an economy is, the more difficult it is to administer from a single point, regardless of whether this administration involves the release of several tons of sulfuric acid with Comrade Stalin's personal approval or regulation of the market. Of course, the market could be regulated by taxation or by a certain amount of government purchases, but after all we have been offered a system that clearly doesn't work, in the guise of a regulated market.

So why do we need this kind of market? If the party can't regulate the market, how could it have a vanguard role? What would happen to the party if it did not direct public life and did not do anything it wanted as long as it was put within the framework of "a socialist choice and a Communist future"? Reform implies the domination of a single ideology and a single methodology, in this instance the ideology and methodology of the Communist party. Everyone else has the right to provide constructive criticism.

This is under a liberal regime. In a totalitarian regime people who don't please the authorities are eliminated, but essentially it's all the same: Some people, the good vanguard, have the right to exert influence, while others do not. The principle itself is vicious. And the group of inefficient and bumbling administrators who hold power in the role of a vanguard will continue to lead us in the wrong direction and will continue to wreak havoc. Of course, this in no way means that a different group would work well in the place of this group of bumblers, because there is always risk involved when you pick something new to replace the old. But, if we replace what we already know doesn't work, we at least have a chance.

When Mikhail Gorbachev began *perestroika*, our avant-garde unofficial society, a society which had been deprived of non-Bolshevik structures, had in reality only two choices, namely revolt or reform. Gorbachev didn't have this first choice, because revolt would have been too bold for him. He intelligently chose reform, and this was good for the country. Because revolt would have meant blood and the destruction of the economy, and this would have been bad from every vantage point.

Around 1988 and 1989 there began to appear new, previously unheard-of democratic structures in our society, and then a third one was added to the two paths of social development (reform, or restructuring of the system, and revolt, or the explosive destruction of the existing structures). This third one was the path of creating new structures that would be capable of taking on tasks that the old structures, although restructured but still subordinate to the same old idea, could not accomplish.

The difference between reform and democratic development is that reform constitutes a change in the old system accompanied by the preservation of its specific features. This is the reform of a system in which a certain party claims a special role, even if it is not spelled out by the constitution; let us remember the documents that the Central Committee of the Communist party submitted to the 28th Party Congress.[1]

The draft of the program of the Central Committee contains an abundance of pretty words but no clear-cut plan for achieving its objectives. The draft speaks of financial and monetary recovery, of a radical rise in the rate of housing construction, of emergency aid to areas affected by natural disasters, of guaranteed housing, and of free medical care. Everything will be improved and put in order. But where is the money coming from? How are the improvements to be made? Well, perhaps by a reasonable reduction in expenditures for defense, for inefficient capital investment, and for the bureaucracy—in other words, everything the opposition had been advocating all along. But, if the same inefficient system remains in place, we'll at best be able to add another patch to it. What we need is quite different: We need to use our last remaining resources in order to break out

---

[1]Zaslavsky refers here to the abolition of Article 6 of the Soviet constitution, which mandated the leading role of the Communist party.

of this vicious circle, and this in effect has not been mentioned.

Why should a party that needs an ideology and a methodology even exist? There's only one answer: for power. By the way, this kind of structure is nothing new, and the whole world calls it the Mafia. And this structure and party, which claims eternal power and justifies this in terms of a socialist choice which was made for once and for all (it's true that we don't know when the referendum was held) and some misty Communist future by which we, regardless of whether we want to or not, must proceed in order to justify our past—this same party is now intent on improving and modernizing itself. That's what's called reform!

But, we might ask, what's the point in improving the party? Why improve that which is already so bad to begin with? It would be better to create something new, for after all a great deal of effort has already been expended on overcoming the innate conservatism of the existing structure, effort which would not have to be continued if we were to create a new structure in a new place.

This obvious truth is understood not only by democrats but also by the most reform-minded reformers. In speaking to the 28th Party Congress, Alexander Yakovlev in fact bemoaned socialism and the still-living Communist party.

"Yes," he said, "it's time to operate in a new way, for otherwise we might have to talk about the party's inability to respond to the challenge of the times. Essentially this congress will not decide the fate of reform but will go further and decide the fate of the party itself. If the party cannot find the strength within it to renew itself in the spirit of reform, the new difficulties may prove to be insurmountable, and life will pass us by."

In giving these warnings, this realistic and intelligent man could not help but understand that the party is already incapable of renewing itself, even in the spirit of reform, that life "passed it by" a long time ago, and that the party is not undergoing a crisis but an agony.

But what sort of salvation does he see in this for himself and for other "quality" reformers? "We must bring the machinery of presidential power up to full capacity more quickly." In other words, while the party's vanguard role might not be too avant-garde after all, those at the head of the vanguard must change seats as quickly as possible, getting rid of certain comrades they've grown tired of on the way. Said and done! Yakovlev immediately set an example: Without waiting until the congress was over, he moved to the Presidential Council. And this is also a kind of reform: from the Politburo to the Presidential Council.[2]

The Right Takes Hold of the Center

In contrast to the *perestroika* path, the third path that opened up with the emergence of structures parallel to the Soviet Communist party is the path to democracy without any vanguard, the path of peaceful, democratic revolution. That these structures are much more viable than is the Soviet Communist party is evidenced by their popularity among the public.

Therefore it is not surprising that the new structures have become more successful than the Communist party and are beginning to take real power at the district, city, and republic levels.

The new structures include a wide variety of people, including people who were quite recently members of the *nomenklatura*. However, in contrast to the "vanguard formations," these structures make no claim to exclusivity and are not working to preserve the old system. They are pursuing quite different goals and are intent on finally building a normal society from a pathological society.

In this light it would be interesting to examine how the political disposition of forces changed from 1985 to 1990. In 1985, when the choice was between revolt and reform (that is, liberalization of the system), there emerged an explicit alliance between the center and left-wing Communists and all the democratic forces. This coalition was based on the temporary coincidence of the strategic interests of the democrats and the reform-minded Communists. This alliance was clearly evident in the telephone conversation between Gorbachev and [Andrei] Sakharov and Sakharov's return to Moscow, and so forth [see Chapter 5]. It seems to me that one of the last echoes of this alliance was Sakharov's [May 1989] speech to the 1st Congress of People's Deputies, in which he spoke of the possibility of conditional support for Gorbachev

---

[2]That is, moving the center of power from the party to Gorbachev personally.

as a candidate for chairman of the Supreme Soviet of the USSR, taking into consideration the position that Gorbachev himself would take. This was the last accord of the alliance between the democrats and reform-minded Communists and a harbinger of future changes in the disposition of political forces.

As we remember, Andrei Sakharov stated after the congress that his support was conditional in nature and that, insofar as Gorbachev had taken undemocratic positions, it was already incorrect to speak of conditional support and that the new watchword was "opposition." Immediately after the congress Sakharov raised the issue of the need for democrats to form a parliamentary opposition. Unfortunately, this formation occurred only after his death, because the interregional group organized in the summer of 1989 could not be called an opposition. These people, with their own special positions, did not raise the issue of opposing the majority, let alone Gorbachev. The opposition that emerged after Andrei Sakharov's death only supported Gorbachev if their viewpoints agreed and proclaimed that it would oppose him if their views did not coincide. Finally, the "Democratic Russia" group openly proclaimed its own policies.

People began to be aware of the possibility of a different path, not of reform but of democratic revolution, which would involve the creation of new structures, the assumption of power by the new structures, and the removal of the Bolsheviks from power. Not liberalization but removal, because liberalization, as our history has demonstrated, is always reversible. And it is quite frequently followed by the most heavy-handed reaction, if the system is liberalized but not changed.

At the same time, a close alliance between the center and the right, and between Gorbachev and the [Boris] Gidaspovs and [Ivan] Polozkovs and people who openly support hard-line Bolshevik policies, has begun to emerge.

All of us remember how the congress went. When the Russian Communists proclaimed their own party, the liberals began to panic, fearing that droves of Bolshevik reactionaries would go to the congress, topple Gorbachev, and thus deprive us of our only light at the end of the tunnel. And at first that's what it looked like. The right-wingers let loose with furious and hateful attacks aimed at Gorbachev.

Let me remind you that the delegates of the Constituent Congress of Russian Communists also made up the overwhelming majority of delegates at the 28th Party Congress [see Doc. 32].

So what happened? They amiably and unanimously elected Mikhail Sergeyevich Gorbachev general secretary of the party, steamrollered Yegor Kuzmich Ligachev in his desperate attempt to become the number-two man in the party, and elected Comrade Vladimir Ivashko, whom Gorbachev supported.

A paradox to beat all paradoxes! What should we call it? Did they undergo a drastic change of heart there? No way. This is merely a typical example of the alliance between the right and the center. The right gave up on "their" man, Ligachev, and supported the centrist Gorbachev, because they understood that this was their only chance of saving anything.

Now the idea of an alliance between the left and the center in the name of a market economy and progress and national salvation has once again become popular. The Gorbachev-Yeltsin [500-day] economic program has become a unique symbol of the anticipated alliance.

At the same time, we cannot help but note that the appeals for an alliance between the center and the left have primarily originated from the leaders of the left. Gorbachev at one time has agreed to negotiations with [Boris] Yeltsin and at another has renounced the Gorbachev-Yeltsin program, calling for a compromise between the adherents of this program and the adherents of [Nikolai] Ryzhkov's program, thus coming out in favor of crossbreeding a cow and a horse.

These kinds of vacillations on the president's part are not surprising. Obviously the interests of the center and the left, which partially coincide with respect to tactics, are strategically divergent.

The center, or "enlightened elite," is working for privatization in its own interests, for a change from the collective management of property by the bureaucratic class to private ownership of property by members of the same class. On the other hand, democrats are working for privatization in the interests of the people. From this we can put together a forecast of the future of the left-center coalition. Our partner is unreliable, so let's stay alert!

Now we can clearly see two struggles in the country: a struggle between the republics and Moscow for sovereignty and a struggle between Communists and non-Communists.

These two struggles have been uniquely superimposed on one another as a result of a purely temporal factor. The Communists have managed to seize the commanding heights in the union, while democrats have taken power in many of the republics. Thus, the struggle for sovereignty is simultaneously a struggle against a Communist and totalitarian system.

By the way, this is not fully understood in the West. People there quite frequently say: "Well, listen, how could, for example, the state of Texas leave America? Isn't this the same thing as the sovereignty of Russia?" No, it's not! Texas is an integral part of the United States: It has the same system as the United States and practically the same ideology and same political parties. We are talking not only about a republic's right to sovereignty, which it has constitutionally, but also about the realization of the right of the democratic forces, who won democratic elections, to build their own, different system. After they have freed themselves from the yoke of a strong Communist center, the republics will be able to sort things out among themselves. We cannot rule out the possibility that many of them will enter into new relationships and organize a federation in which they will put an end to both the dictatorship of Moscow over the republics and the dictatorship of the Communists over other ideologies and other social forces.

What ways do we have to eliminate the Communist central authority? There are only two. The first involves the voluntary elimination of union-wide power structures, while the second involves the elimination of the Communist central authority by means of concluding a new treaty of union between the republics. The central authority, be it Communist or non-Communist, would only be a product of this union treaty and could not exist without the agreement of the republics. This change could take different forms, ranging from the actual elimination of the existing power structures of the central authority to drastic curtailment of their powers in order to make these structures purely symbolic and incapable of having a detrimental effect on the country's destiny.

I will allow myself to disagree with the idea of dissolving the union from above. It's a splendid idea, but the structures that are in power now will not dissolve the union by themselves. They won't even reorganize it. Moscow would take this step only under strong pressure from the republics, which once again implies initiative on the part of the latter.

First Let's Switch Bands

True to his eclectic tactics, Mikhail Gorbachev is now appealing for the consolidation of everyone and everything. The absurdity of this appeal, which is perhaps capable of persuading only a complete idiot, is obvious: A team consisting of an executioner and a victim works as a team only as long as the axe is in the hands of the executioner, and let us remember that it usually takes a lot more than exhortations to make the victim enter into such an alliance. However, the other extreme, namely the complete fragmentation of social factions, is no less ridiculous and dangerous.

Fragmentation is even more dangerous, because there have only been appeals for consolidation, while fragmentation already exists in reality. New political parties are now forming in large numbers. Some of them are more serious, while some are less serious. This depends, first of all, on the party's ability to attract experts, and second, on its ability to attract ordinary people. As a rule, our parties are only successful in attracting one or the other and quite often do not have a clear ideological program for leading the country out of the impasse it finds itself in.

These parties are constantly squabbling. Some say that we must choose a course and proceed to social democracy. Others prefer Thatcherism, while still others prefer Christian democracy, and so on. I am quite convinced that this will accomplish nothing.

In principle there are two types of systems, rigid and self-regulating. Systems of the first type, which are governed or very strongly influenced from a single point, have a power structure which oppresses everyone and everything and have a dominant or even single, in our case the Communist, political party. In structures of the second type different parties with their own ideologies and methodologies compete on an equal footing for power. Of course each party considers its own ideology to be the best, but it acknowledges that the public might have a different opinion. These systems are characterized by a steady natural circulation and turnover of methods and ideologies. And the public, as a rule, chooses those methods that are best suited for a given situation and given conditions. In one case the social democrats' methods are more suitable (for example, in Finland, where the economy is stable but problems of social protection and of lessening the large gap between high and low incomes are urgent). In another case (for example, Great Britain), the situation is the opposite. Britain was faced with a problem of correcting its economy and leading itself out of an economic crisis, and the Conservatives, headed by [Margaret] Thatcher, immediately came to power. They introduced "more market" into the economy. The economy righted itself, but at the same time a large gap emerged between higher and lower standards of living, although in principle the lower classes in Britain don't live too badly. In any case the condition of recognizing the rights of others to exist is indispensable. There's no such thing as a vanguard role!

When our social democrats or liberals appeal to Western experience, they forget that they are appealing to a different system, where a certain situation has stabilized at a given moment and the conditions for certain economic relationships have emerged and which is characterized by swings from social democrats to conservatives (in the Western sense of the word) and vice versa.

However, we, to use the language of systems analysis, are in a situation of transition from one system to another. And in this case it is impossible to proclaim the superiority of social democrats over Thatcherite conservatives or vice versa without providing any kind of proof. In general, transitional methods are for the most part terra incognita, and the examples of this kind of transition can be counted on one hand. A transition from a totalitarian system that managed to subordinate completely the entire economy to itself, which never happened elsewhere, even in Germany, is even more unprecedented.

We need to find methods that will enable a transition between two quite dissimilar systems. One system, the totalitarian system, is stable only with the complete suppression of all "nonvanguard" structures, while the second is stable when all structures can coexist on an equal footing. As soon as liberalization took place in our country, the totalitarian system quickly began to lose stability. Very soon it must either disintegrate (and this would be bad, because nothing will emerge in its place except for the threat of economic collapse) or transform itself into something different.

This must be understood by everyone who is now debating the subject of who's best: the social democrats, the liberals, or someone else. Because the main point is first to make the transition to a self-regulating, self-developing system. The point on the path of the pendulum at which we find ourselves after the transition is made is not important, because we can always make adjustments then. But there's no point in tuning a radio to the required frequency by means of the fine-tuning knob if we haven't switched bands yet.

It is here, on the development of a program for "switching bands," that we should all concentrate our efforts. It seems to me that this is where all the democratic parties could unite or, in Gorbachev's term, "consolidate."

Of course, in this case it would be very important to organize interparty think tanks—groups of experts who would devise a quite unprecedented but completely possible (in principle) program of transition from a rigid system to a flexible system, from a regulated system to a self-regulated system, from an inefficient system to an efficient system, and from a totalitarian system to a democratic system.

When We Say "Party" We Mean "Mafia"

Obviously, the program for "switching bands" could not help but be directed against the Communist party. Any alliance or compromise with the Communist party alone would be unthinkable. We cannot compromise with the Communists if only for the reason that the ideology of the Communists is uncompromising. Compromise with them is impossible, like a compromise with the devil; after all, a compromise is always a deal, and everyone knows the price of a deal with the devil.

When the public prosecutor in the Ostashvili trial mentioned that the Pamyat organization had met at the Sverdlovsk district committee headquarters of the Communist party before the provocation in the Moscow Writers' Club, I wasn't particularly surprised.[3] Why should I

---

[3]On January 18, 1990, a group of Pamyat members led by Konstantin Smirnov-Ostashvili disrupted a meeting held at the Union Writers' Club, in Moscow, of the writers' organization called April. Pamyat hoodlums

have been surprised, when a similar, if not "harder," action had been planned on June 18 against the Oktyabr District Council in Moscow, where I work? This action had been organized by General Yu. Votintsev, a delegate to the 28th Party Congress of the Soviet Communist party and chairman of the District Veterans' Council, "in the presence of" (as it was so shamefully formulated afterwards) the chief of the organizational department of the Oktyabr District Committee of the Communist party, V. Rodin, who is subordinate to yet another delegate to the 28th Congress, V. Kubrin.

By the way, judging by the information available to us, one of the slogans shouted at the meeting was "Down with the Israeli Council." Why our district council is called the Israeli Council is hard to explain, but most probably it's for the purpose of cursing it. But the fact that in this instance party members worked under the auspices of Pamyat (to be able to blame everything on "patriots" if excesses occurred, as happened in the Writers' Club incident) was so clear to me that I even issued a brief statement in defense of Pamyat, saying that this society was unimportant but had absolutely nothing to do with this particular provocation.

I could go on and on with such examples, but our people are quite familiar with the tactics of our "vanguard" without them. During the consumer panic in Moscow, one could immediately hear people in the colossal lines snarling "Sabotage! Damned Communists!" The chairman of a miners' strike committee was killed under mysterious circumstances. An accident had happened to someone the authorities didn't like at just the right time, and although there were no legal grounds to suspect anyone, people asserted without a shadow of a doubt that "it was the work of their hands."

Let me emphasize that I in no way wish to accuse Communists of all unsolved crimes—let everyone take responsibility for his own actions—but I can only say for sure that for many people they are always prime suspects. Particularly now, when such barbarities have become more frequent. Investigative agencies and the courts should investigate and establish the guilt of the particular individuals responsible for each crime.

---

shouted anti-Semitic slogans and beat up several writers. As a result of the public outcry, Ostashvili was tried and sentenced to two years in prison. In April 1991 he committed suicide.

The historical guilt of the Communist party is obvious. Over the course of seven decades it has instilled the ideas of implacable cruelty and disrespect for the individual in society. Now the spiritual heritage of Bolshevism is nurturing the most diverse currents and movements with totalitarian tendencies regardless of their ideologies, whether they be Marxist or Fascist.

I remember the words of the exiled poet Joseph Brodsky: "If there's a murder on the wedding day, the milk will be red."

Bolshevik-minded people are actively migrating from the Communist party to new totalitarian structures, and this process is moving faster the more their old "roof" leaks.

Transitional Tactics

We are faced with the question of how the quite poorly organized democratic forces can compete effectively with the Communist party. How can they take power away from the party and its props, the military, KGB, and Ministry of the Interior? Of course there is no real question here. Taking power away from monsters requires technology. And, by the way, the monsters will partially move into the new system. Their agencies are necessary in any society. But their punitive functions will obviously have to be eliminated.

It seems to me that we could rightly call Gavriil Popov one of the most outstanding practical, and not theoretical, experts on transitional techniques. He has a good feel for the specific characteristics of a transitional situation. Let us say, for example, that according to the works of the classic free-market economists, markets are unconditionally good and rationing is unconditionally bad. The problem is that their arguments are valid for a stable regime, when the system has stabilized both economically and politically. But now we have a system that is unstable both politically and economically. And in this case what is absolutely absurd for a stable system may prove to be good for several months.

A typical example is allowing out-of-towners to purchase goods only with visitors' passes. From the vantage point of free-market economics this is a blatant outrage which is absolutely unacceptable in a free-market society. But this is reasonable and necessary for us, if it is introduced for a short period in order to halt the panic, which is completely natural under conditions when sabotage has been committed and when the government is terrorizing the public with its idiotic program.

Our transitional tactics must also take into consideration that the natural economic and social burdens of introducing a market economy in the Soviet Union will be compounded by difficulties caused by the blatantly antisoviet, wrecking activity of the Bolsheviks (I think that these ancient epithets are more appropriate in this case than they ever were before).[4] We should anticipate that at some time in the future, when the country is ready to get out of its crisis and when it can finally see the light at the end of the tunnel, the advocates of a totalitarian system will launch their main attack.

They will have more than enough pretexts and opportunities for this, if only the very same difficulties of life. No doubt the existing form of government, the councils, will also disappoint and irritate the public.

The system of councils created before the October Revolution had quite a few shortcomings associated with its combination of executive, legislative, and judicial powers. Subsequently the system was made even more complicated by the addition of executive committees. Now, before the [March 1990] elections, yet another agency, the Presidential Council, has been added. As a result we have a system which might often be democratically elected but is clearly ineffective.

By all appearances this suits the president, because as he moved from seat to seat he clearly counted on arranging it so that the new system of power would be just as rigidly centralized as before, which would make it possible for him to govern without paying any attention to the councils. By the way, an article written by Andranik Migranyan and Igor Klyamkin a year ago, entitled "We Need an Iron Hand," is quite typical in this respect. When articles of this type appear, it's usually because someone needs them. At one point Nina Andreyeva's outpourings in *Sovetskaya Rossiya* were necessary for Ligachev (see Doc. 13). Honestly, I wouldn't be surprised if subsequently it turns out that our

---

[4]In this context the author uses antisoviet to refer to actions directed against popularly elected local councils, or soviets, rather than against the Soviet Union as a whole.

president had needed this article by Migranyan and Klyamkin a year ago.

Despite the expectations of the "higher ups," they never got their "iron hand." The councils have continued to take power into their own hands, the republics have gotten out of control, and a power has emerged which is still not effective enough, despite all its efforts, a power tormented by contradictions and disputes between the republics and the cities, between the cities and the districts, and most importantly within the agencies of power themselves. Jabbering councils are not only ineffective, they're dangerous. When D-day comes, the Bolsheviks will hardly pass up the chance to take advantage of the council's mistakes and shortcomings in their next attempt to install an "iron hand," even if the outward appearance of the system has changed. In the final analysis, the Mafia possesses the ability to transform itself and migrate from one structure to another.

A recent article in *Ogonyok* provided an account of one district party committee secretary who moved from his seat to the seat of chairman of the district council. This situation is quite typical these days. This is the way in which the forces who in the future may try to attack and introduce an "iron hand" are preserving themselves.

We have only one way to repel an attack on this flank. Without dissolving the councils (absolutely not!), we must gradually reorganize them in order to preserve the unique human material gathered in them by the will of the voters and gradually restructure them in order ultimately to create a system of power that will be effective at all levels, from top to bottom. The basic purpose of this power will be to facilitate the growth of a self-developing society rather than endlessly interfere in its affairs. At the same time, and this is very important, we will have to create mass media capable of reforming people and independent of both the new power and the old totalitarian system.

We must reorganize the councils so as to eliminate the bicentricity between the presidium and the executive committee and to obtain a simple and effective authority that reflects the public interest, is elected for a definite term, and has clearly defined powers. I believe that we could use the electoral model provided by the United States, with its governors and president and the legislatures and Congress which counterbalance them.

A jabbering democracy is a step toward dictatorship. Perhaps the only slogan it would make sense for us to borrow from the conservatives now is "Enough talk! Let's get to work!"

Bibliography

Alekseyev, S. "The Concept of *Perestroika* and Marxism." *Pravda*, July 25, 1990.

According to Academician Alekseyev, Marxism by its humanistic nature is in harmony with such concepts of *perestroika* as pluralism, a multiparty system, the market, and freedom.

Bogomolov, G. "By Slow Step, by Shy Zigzag." *Ogonyok*, no. 44, 1989.

Workers conflict with a plant's party leadership.

Dolganov, Viacheslav. "Justice or *Uravnilovka*." *Izvestiya*, December 10, 1989.

A struggle against the privileges of the party elite is the most popular cause in the Soviet Union at this time.

Glotov, Vladimir. "The Hot and Cold December." *Ogonyok*, no. 51, 1989.

Describes the demonstration of December 6, 1989, against Leningrad's conservative party leadership.

Kiva, Alexei. "The Myths of the Passing Times." *Izvestiya*, April 2, 1990.

A reply to the leftist and rightist critics of the party platform of the 28th Party Congress.

Kiva, Alexei, and Petrov, A. "The Third Force." *Izvestiya*, September 28, 1990.

Discusses the possibility of the military seizing power in alliance with Russian nationalists at a time when many democrats are unnecessarily provocative (especially concerning the destruction of monuments). A transition period is taking place in an atmosphere of general crisis.

Konovalova, Irina. "The Last Hope." *Ogonyok*, no. 51, 1989.

A dialogue between two deputies of the Supreme Soviet reflecting opposite points of view.

Mostovshchikov, S. "Xerox: Above Suspicion?" *Izvestiya*, October 4, 1989.

The Ministry of Internal Affairs is about to renounce its control over printing and copying equipment.

Ovidiyev, Alexander. "KGB and *Glasnost*." *Molodaya Gvardiya*, no. 1, 1990.

A conservative line is obviously preferred by the KGB.

Solomenko, Yevgeny. "The Hero at the Crossroads." *Pravda*, December 31, 1989.

A bitter recollection of the party's shortcomings in carrying out *perestroika*, written by a "nonformal" Communist.

Volkogonov, Dmitry. "Trotsky Looked in the Mirror of History for a Long Time." *Kommunist Vooruzhennykh Sil*, no. 19, 1989.

A full rehabilitation of Leon Trotsky, a sensation for the Soviet Union, from an unexpected corner—the author is a former chief of the Red Army's Propaganda Directorate. Emphasizes Trotsky's closeness to Lenin, his role in defeating the White armies, and his personal courage. This is the most sympathetic account of Trotsky's role in the Russian Revolution published heretofore in the USSR.

Yakovlev, Alexander. "The Answer Is in Ourselves." *Voprosy Economiki*, no. 2, 1989.

An intelligent criticism of the past and of conservative trends in Soviet society by the only member of the Politburo who can likely provide the theoretical foundation for reforms. Socialism and Lenin are considered as the basis for change.

> I am sure that Gorbachev deserves the Nobel Peace Prize, but I wouldn't think that he deserves the prize for economics.
>
> Georgy Arbatov,
> director of the U.S.
> and Canada Institute

Chapter Three

The Economy

The Economy Spirals Downward

We are witnessing the collapse of the Soviet socialist economy. The hallmark of its disarray is the widespread introduction of rationing forty-five years after the Allied victory in World War II, at a time when Germany and Japan, defeated in the war, have now become the world's leading economic powers.[1] Pouring salt on old wounds, German citizens have enthusiastically and wholeheartedly donated food parcels to the former victors. Food assistance is also coming from such countries as India, China, Pakistan, and Turkey. Soviet economist Vasily Selyunin correctly assesses the current state of the Soviet economy: "The so-called *perestroika* has replaced the inhuman and wasteful command management system with an even less efficient one. The latter combines the irremovable vices of command planning with an absence of any responsibility on the part of producers. The result is economic chaos."[2]

Economic travails have bred political discontent. A sharp deterioration in their living standards drove coal miners to strike in the summer of 1989. Thus a new phenomenon, absent for seventy years, was successfully introduced into Gorbachev's Russia: a mass, well-organized strike with political overtones (see Doc. 15). (There had been a number of spontaneous strikes previously, but never on such a scale.) The strikers mistrusted local authorities and said they would negotiate only with the party's leadership. The miners also put forward

---

[1]The negative and humiliating symbolism of rationing might not have been understood by Anatoly Sobchak, the democratic mayor of Leningrad, who suggested that it be introduced together with a customs-free zone in an effort to develop free enterprise and attract Western capital. *Izvestiya*, October 5, 1990.

[2]Lev Timofeyev, ed., *The Anti-Communist Manifesto* (Bellevue, WA: Free Enterprise Press, 1990), pp. 31–32.

a political demand—removal of Article 6 from the Soviet constitution, which proclaimed the leading role of the Communist party in Soviet society. Political strikes have since become a common event, especially strikes by Russian workers in the Baltic republics, supported by the conservative forces. In Armenia and Azerbaijan, strikes have been so frequent as to make normalcy seem like an exception.

Simple people, reformers, and even Gorbachev himself believe that from the very beginning of the reforms there has been a widespread bureaucratic plot to strangle and defeat any movement toward meaningful changes. The bureaucracy resists any changes and sees that its privileges will be threatened if the reforms are carried out. The Soviet bureaucracy is highly organized and sophisticated in its ability to operate in a coordinated manner and without any command to defend its power and privileges. The "cigarette riots" of September 1990 were a classic case of the bureaucracy deliberately sabotaging reforms to foment popular discontent. Twenty-four cigarette plants were closed for summer repairs, and nothing was done to meet the voracious Soviet appetite for tobacco. Once the public realized that a shortage was imminent, frantic hoarding took place. After that, no matter what the government tried, the shortage persisted. Suddenly, the government "found" money to buy American Marlboros and specialized equipment for cigarette manufacture. The big question many observers asked is: "Where were all the bureaucrats before the crisis erupted?"

The Disintegration of the Distribution System

The biggest misfortune afflicting the population of almost three hundred million in the Soviet Union is the disintegration of their country's distribution system. It means that foreign aid coming into the country cannot be distributed justly or evenly, almost no matter what effort is mounted. Furthermore, it also means that, no matter how much is available in the warehouses, food cannot be delivered. There are several reasons for this predicament: 1) The Soviet distribution system for food and consumer goods is the most complex in the world, designed to reward the party and state bureaucracy and a small group of workers in key enterprises; 2) The Leonid Brezhnev era was a golden period for a flourishing of corruption throughout the distribution system; 3) Gorbachev has continued the tradition of parallel distribution systems (separate from the distribution system for the general public) for the privileged, for war veterans, and for invalids; 4) Food and consumer items are sold at the enterprises that produce them, bypassing the distribution system; 5) Paper money has been printed indiscriminately; 6) All the republics and localities have introduced by now rationing systems and coupons (see Doc. 17); and 7) Hoarding has become a universal phenomenon, challenging any reason and self-defeating.

Infrastructure

One of the least discussed but most serious problems in the USSR today is the country's weak and rapidly deteriorating infrastructure. In the last few years the performance of the railroads and the condition of the highways have declined. It is presumed that more food spoils in Soviet warehouses than is preserved, making this the weakest link in the food distribution system. The equipment in light industry is hopelessly outmoded; for example, of the country's 318 sugar refineries, 166 were built under the czars.[3] Power stations do not have reserve capabilities, which is especially dangerous given the harsh Russian winter. Equipment is worn out and outmoded, and the legacy of Chernobyl has curtailed nuclear power production.[4] Russian technicians are quitting the utilities in the republics of Transcaucasia and Central Asia because of the ethnic disturbances, and this reduces output.[5] Cities are falling into disrepair. Sewage and heating systems, roads, and housing are decaying, especially in the industrial cities, which were hurriedly built. The list could go on and on. Winter is always a particularly trying time for Soviet cities.

To indicate how much it will cost to improve the infrastructure of the USSR, it suffices to say that the government of West Germany is allocating $100 billion to upgrade the infrastructure of what used to be East Germany in 1991 and will spend more than $1 trillion over the next decade. And East Germany is thought to be in much better shape than is the Soviet Union.

The Soviet Union is considered to be one of the richest countries in the world in terms of natural resources. At the same time, the most remarkable features of the Soviet economy are waste and mismanagement. These are intrinsic attributes of the socialist system, but many believe that they are also a result of the country's abundance of natural resources. According to Alexander Yakovlev, a leading reform theoretician, "Mismanagement is a true national scourge. If we were not so rich, we might have been more organized. Natural resources corrupt many people and engender laziness and irresponsibility."[6] The newspaper *Izvestiya* (October 15, 1990) notes that at least 30 to 40 percent of the harvest of potatoes, fruits, and vegetables, 15 to 20 percent of the grain, 5 to 7 million tons of bread and baked goods, 2 to 2.5 million tons of meat, and many other foods spoil annually before they can be brought to market. Twelve billion

---

[3] *Izvestiya*, September 28, 1990.

[4] Exaggerated Soviet hopes for increasing the production of nuclear energy have collapsed in the wake of Chernobyl: Sixty nuclear power plants either have been shut down or have had their construction canceled (ibid., March 23, 1991).

[5] Ibid., October 4, 1990.

[6] "The Answer Is in Ourselves," in *Perestroika and the Contemporary World* (Moscow, 1989), pp. 8–9.

rubles are lost in revenues every year because of railroad malfunctions. One million drivers of official cars are cut off from the productive sphere. And who can count how much construction material, consumer goods, and food are stolen from state enterprises?

Projects such as the economic and military development of the north and the construction of nuclear icebreakers are extremely costly but are never subject to the judgment of the people or even given any public discussion. A fascination with such giant projects as hydroelectric stations brought about a "bulldozer economy."[7] There is no bigger symbol of waste than Minvodkhoz, an irrigation ministry employing almost two million people. Critics charge that the ministry has engaged in gigantic useless projects, such as diverting Siberian rivers and the Volga-Chograi Canal.[8]

New factors straining the Soviet economy are natural disasters and national disorders. Localism and separatism are not always along ethnic lines, as we can see in the "food blockade" of Moscow and Leningrad. Once democratic forces won elections in these two cities, other Russian provinces cut their food deliveries to them. The fight to keep food for local use and the erection of customs barriers everywhere in the country are in striking contrast to the ongoing removal of trade barriers in the European Economic Community (EEC).

Industry has suffered from ill-conceived reforms, half-measures, ethnic unrest, and general lack of discipline. The attempt to decentralize has led to problems with honoring past obligations undertaken by the enterprises, and the considerable depreciation of the ruble has weakened the fear of sanctions and fines. The centralized economy means that civil strife even in an area as small as Nagorno-Karabakh disrupts the work of plants thousands of miles away, in Russia proper and in other republics, by interrupting deliveries. Maintaining ties between enterprises in various republics and regions is becoming virtually impossible; the imperial economy, in the absence of either a strong authority or a market system, is disintegrating rapidly, and productivity is decreasing accordingly.

Soviet workers seem unprepared to accept the changes necessary to bring about a viable economy (see Docs. 18 and 21). Laziness, negligence, and the preference given to quantity over quality of goods produced are at the heart of this problem. The remarkably low quality and incompetence of Soviet managers is appalling, above and beyond the counterproductivity of the system and the laziness of the workers.

---

[7]To produce huge quantities of all kinds of minerals a great amount of heavy equipment is necessary, which requires in turn lots of iron ore. Thus a closed circle is created from which the interests of the consumer are excluded.

[8]Both projects were canceled under public pressure before actual construction began. *Kommunist Vooruzhennykh Sil*, no. 19, 1989. pp. 56–62. Nonetheless, another "project of the century" has proceeded—the costly Baikal-Amur main line.

"The Russians cannot work well," said Deputy Prime Minister Leonid Abalkin. There is no bigger symbol of the shoddy Soviet attitude toward quality strangely intertwined with a naive belief in technology than Chernobyl—perhaps the most important single event in the USSR over the last decade. The Chernobyl nuclear disaster has discredited the leadership, discouraged peaceful use of nuclear energy, influenced military doctrine, and inflicted staggering economic losses. Chernobyl forced a rude awakening to the true state of Soviet technological backwardness. It continues to figure prominently in the news; radiation levels are still very high in parts of the Ukraine, Byelorussia, and Russia, and the damage continues.

The financial system is also in a disastrous state, largely due to the absence of an independent fiscal body like the Federal Reserve in the United States. Numerous economic policy mistakes have been committed by Mikhail Gorbachev. The convertibility of the ruble, foreign trade, and hard currency repatriation are long-standing issues that have yet to be resolved. The improvident policies of Gorbachev and Nikolai Ryzhkov brought the printing of rubles to 14 percent above the yearly growth of the economy as a result of unstoppable inflation and what many consider to be irresponsible salary raises. In addition, the scrip of various enterprises (*beznalichnye*) found its way into the system and contributed to the havoc. All this paper money should be taken out of circulation as part of a currency reform. Should this occur, the savings of some "honest workers" would greatly diminish. But unfortunately, within the framework of the inefficient Soviet economy, these workers have not been producing any real wealth.

Agriculture

The Soviet system is unable to produce enough food to feed its people. Countries such as China and India, with populations many times that of the Soviet Union, have succeeded in resolving their food problems. The list of failures in Soviet agriculture is nearly endless, covering a period of seventy years. In 1989, for example, the USSR produced more than twice the amount of mineral fertilizers as did the United States, but with no corresponding increase in agricultural output and with a negative impact on the environment.[9] Huge subsidies to collective and state farms to produce meat have not resulted in any overall growth of production. The farm officials have simply purchased meat from the population. Instead of performing major surgery by disbanding collective and state farms, Gorbachev has tried various palliatives such as collective, group, and family contracts and leases. Considering that he grew up in a village, was party secretary in an agricultural area, and then was responsible for agriculture at the national level for fourteen years, it is surprising that Mikhail Gorbachev

---

[9] *Izvestiya*, June 20, 1990.

does not exhibit any innovative approaches in this arena—he scarcely measures up to Czar Alexander II's handling of land reform. For conservatives it is the same old game; if only the state will increase the subsidies to collective farms and build them roads, schools, and houses, then maybe they will farm better. Of course, the urban population, students, and soldiers will still be needed to help with the harvest. It is beyond most people's imagination in the USSR that such help would not be needed—a typical Soviet economic aberration.

For any fundamental questions to be resolved in agriculture, the question of who should own the land must be settled (see Doc. 19). Historically there has always been a problem with private property in Russia, especially concerning land. Although no one doubted the supreme authority and property rights of the czars, peasants did not accept the land rights of the nobility, and the peasant community (*mir*) rather than individual peasants was the collective owner of lands belonging to peasants.

Thus, the Soviet Union is the only major European power in which the ownership of land remains unresolved five hundred years after a centralized state established itself in Europe. On this difficult question, the views of Gorbachev and Yegor Ligachev have been remarkably similar: Collective and state farms should be preserved and protected under the demagogic slogan "Let All Types of Property Flourish." While some land would be given to peasants and citizens who would like to farm, the proposed changes in the law would not permit its sale. Both leaders have wanted to have a referendum on land before a unionwide law would be enacted. But such a referendum would offer a clear choice between socialism and capitalism. The relatively liberal Law on Land adopted by the Russian Republic on November 22, 1990, allows the sale of land, but only ten years after the prospective owner receives the plot. An often-cited concern about land privatization is that the Soviet *kolkhozniks* (collective farm workers) have forgotten how to farm land independently. And as long as the collective and state farms and local bureaucracies are in charge, no laws or other measures will resolve the problem of feeding the country.

Cooperatives and Joint Ventures

The introduction of cooperatives is one of the most controversial issues of the last several years. The cooperative is a new business entity with a considerable degree of entrepreneurial freedom from the control of the centralized Soviet bureaucracy. Cooperatives are disliked by the public, primarily because of their high prices. Riots at cooperative stores in Novy Uzen and the Turkmen Republic in 1989 were a vivid expression of these feelings. Conservatives use such violent events as an excuse to close down cooperatives. For example, local authorities in Krasnodar Territory, led by the infamous Ivan Polozkov, ultraconservative first secretary of the Russian Communist party, ordered the closing of 323 cooperatives.[10] In the confused legal atmosphere of the country, it is impossible to administer the cooperative movement with steadying regulations, so control is accomplished mostly by prohibitions. Nevertheless, the cooperative movement is getting stronger, according to the participants in the June 1990 Congress of Leaseholders and Entrepreneurs, held in Moscow.

A new type of Soviet entrepreneur is slowly emerging, typified by people such as Artem Tarasov, a self-proclaimed millionaire and member of the party, and Mikhail Bocharov, president of Butek, a construction company owned by its employees.[11] Income taxes from cooperatives are quickly becoming an important item in local and national budgets. For 1990 this has amounted to 1.5 billion rubles, compared to 3 billion rubles from the salaries of the more than one hundred million state employees. Gorbachev has grown more defensive about cooperatives, suggesting that local authorities, which are on the whole relatively conservative, should decide whether such measures should be taken as reregistration and closing down of cooperatives engaged in price gouging.

Permission to organize joint ventures between Soviet enterprises and Western corporations is open recognition that Soviet reforms cannot succeed without Western help. It has been very difficult for Soviet leaders, including Mikhail Gorbachev, to admit openly that they need all the Western economic assistance they can get. To do this is to admit a most painful failure of the Soviet system, the failure to create a viable economy based on socialism. China is often cited (with envy, disbelief, and irritation) by Soviet experts as an example of significant achievement in forming joint ventures. Distrust and inertia are two dangers associated with joint ventures; the Soviets often invite foreigners to do tasks that could or should have been done by themselves.[12] But Russian suspicions that the Westerners are getting good deals at their expense can be an obstacle in this sphere of cooperation. Misguided patriots on the one hand complain about shortages while on the other hand loudly protest against Western investment (see Doc. 20). Objections of nationalists in Leningrad led to the cancellation of a $5-billion investment in a recreational complex at Lisiy Nos, which potentially meant thirty thousand jobs and an influx of hard currency for the city. There is corruption and incompetence on the Soviet side. Faced with a tangle of contradictory legislation crowned by the KGB's legal right to review and control documentation, it is doubtful that the joint venture form will survive. The Supreme Soviet's decree

---

[10] *Moskovskie Novosti*, no. 39, 1989.

[11] Tarasov's Moscow premises were searched in March 1991 by the KGB under the pretext of investigating financial improprieties.

[12] In an extensive article on joint ventures, *Izvestiya* (December 13, 1990) reported that Sakhalin Sealines invited Chinese construction workers to repair their club, for which the Chinese were paid several million Swiss francs.

empowering the KGB to combat "economic sabotage" was compounded by a presidential decree creating "workers' control organs." Both measures signify the authorities' growing helplessness to stop the deterioration of the economy, and they have only accelerated the ongoing economic and political disarray. A deputy of the KGB's chairman has claimed, without naming names, that some Western business interests have asked that the KGB handle Western humanitarian assistance, since the KGB is less demoralized than other Soviet institutions.[13]

Concessions, a type of foreign investment in which it is not necessary to have a Soviet partner, have better chances for success than do joint ventures. Although there is now a general trend of reorientation toward West Germany and toward Europe in general, there are many questions that must be resolved before Western assistance to modernize the Soviet Union can reach major proportions. These questions include whether this assistance is in the West's best interests, where to obtain the huge resources needed, and whether investment is practically feasible in a country experiencing profound political turmoil.

Privatization and the Market

Privatization and the market—frightening words for most Soviet citizens—are tied to the unresolved dilemma of property. Should most property be held by the state or be privately held? Leasing, introduced in 1988, was intended to offer some remedy for the centralized economy and possibly to facilitate a transition to privatization. There are no clear legal and financial frameworks for the existence of other forms of property. However, all attempts under *perestroika* to introduce leasing have failed, largely because factory workers cannot feel free if the ministries are still in control, just as individual rural leaseholders cannot survive if collective and state farms and rural *apparatchiks* retain power.

Many people in the Soviet Union do not have a clear understanding of what private property means. The most common Soviet perception of private property is exploitation of someone else's labor, putting someone's personal interest above social and state interests. But, as Document 16 points out, government-owned enterprises also can exploit workers. That private property involves persistent efforts, risk taking, and the interest in productivity needed to create abundance is rarely discussed. The Soviet administrative-industrial complex, which resists privatization, is even more powerful than the military-industrial complex. Pavel Bunich, president of the Union of Leaseholders and Entrepreneurs, stated at its congress in

---

[13] *Nedelya*, no. 1, 1991. Humanitarian aid from the West is now handled by military detachments (*Izvestiya*, March 18, 1991).

June 1990 that "the economic part of the government is still resisting the privatization of the economy and the leaseholders' movement." Although Soviet privatization has been more modest than has Polish privatization, it may yet become an intermediary stage in the Soviet economy's transformation.

2,000 Days

The Gorbachev-Ryzhkov team had 2,000 days, between when they assumed power and when Ryzhkov resigned, to implement their economic policies. Certainly the current economic crunch is the product of the general direction the Soviet economy has taken since 1917. However, beginning with the policy of acceleration and the antialcohol policies of 1985, there has not been even one sensible and successful economic undertaking by the Soviet leadership in the past six-year period. The country never recuperated from the antialcohol measures, which undermined Soviet finances and did not solve the alcoholism problem. This was one of the gravest of Gorbachev's mistakes, and he has tried to attribute it to Mikhail Solomentsev and Yegor Ligachev. *Gospriemka*, state quality control, was likewise an ill-conceived solution to a pressing problem.

Most reform measures introduced by the government have been counterproductive. However, the biggest mistake was to increase the rights of enterprises without making other necessary changes. The result has been a rise in group egoism; the narrowly understood interests of enterprises and their collectives have easily taken precedence over national goals. What was supposed to be a decentralization measure designed to work miracles in the quality and quantity of produced goods (and basically to cure the economy of all ills) instead has contributed to the present disastrous situation. Another step Gorbachev believed was necessary was to improve the machine-building industry.[14] Instead of buying consumer goods from the West, would it not be better to buy equipment and produce them on the spot? The Soviet performance in buying and using Western equipment has been abysmal in the past. There are now mountains of unopened boxes of equipment imported for the equivalent of more than five billion rubles in hard currency. It would have been much better to have followed the advice of Soviet economist Nikolai Shmelyov to purchase consumer goods directly in the West and resell them for rubles. This would have helped to remove extra rubles from circulation and to raise the spirits of the public. But small, insignificant measures cannot

---

[14]It could be that the traditional dominance of industrial leaders in the USSR and their influence on Gorbachev was a main reason for these policies. See Anders Aslund, *Gorbachev's Struggle for Economic Reform* (Ithaca, NY: Cornell University Press, 1989), p. 181.

improve the economy; a revolutionary breakup of the socialist system might.

500 Days

The 500-day economic reform plan, drafted in the fall of 1990, could have been a heaven-sent salvation for the country and for Mikhail Gorbachev. For a very short time, everyone again believed that there was reason to hope for improvement. The plan was timely, especially in view of the scandalous and sad predicament of the 1990 harvest, which happened to be a record harvest but was accompanied by record purchases of grain from the United States and by an inability to provide the cities, in particular Moscow and Leningrad, with potatoes. Television images of Soviet citizens and soldiers digging potatoes by hand in the rain did not help the USSR's image as the world's second superpower. The 500-day plan was mostly associated with Academician Stanislav Shatalin, the latest of Gorbachev's economic advisers. The plan was conservative enough to win Gorbachev's support, and it contained enough new elements to win Yeltsin's. But according to Alec Nove, a well-known expert on the Soviet economy, it would have taken a miracle to accomplish all of the stipulations of this plan even in two years.[15] Nevertheless, had it been implemented it could have been at the very least a step in the right direction.

Under conservative pressure, especially from leaders of heavy and military industries, Gorbachev withdrew his support for the plan in October 1990 and moved the country closer to the abyss. He announced a compromise program, the third since 1985, which, like the others, was quickly abandoned and forgotten. Eight months later the main provisions of the 500-day plan were incorporated into a new ambitious project, "Grand Design." It was prepared by one of the authors of the 500-day plan, Grigory Yavlinsky, in cooperation with Harvard University political scientists. It envisions a switch to the market economy in six years with assistance from the West of $120 billion. However, the Soviet leadership and the country are not prepared for such a drastic concept.

At the same time, it was a political mistake on the part of President George Bush at the London summit of the G-7 industrialized countries in July 1991 not to go along with the European proposal to offer Gorbachev $10 billion to achieve the internal convertibility of the ruble. The decision to let Gorbachev leave empty handed would make him a subject of derision by the conservatives and deprive him of his biggest political advantage: an ability to deliver the West's loans.

The conservative point of view on the economy is often dismissed without serious consideration; however, not all of it is nonsense. The conservatives are right to cite the public's lack of enthusiasm, the

---

[15] Alec Nove, "Reforming the Soviet Economy," *Dissent*, Winter 1991, p. 9.

absence of any reform successes, and *perestroika*'s many unfulfilled promises, even though their intent is to discredit reform. A case in point is the incident of the twelve new T-72 tanks discovered in Novorossiysk Harbor ready to be shipped abroad, which has provided the conservatives with an opportunity to make an enormous fuss about the sellout of the country by the cooperatives. (Conservatives portrayed selling the USSR's best tanks abroad as a betrayal of Soviet defenses.) The guilty party in this case was the organization called ANT (from the Russian words for automation, science, and technology), a state cooperative created with the participation of Prime Minister Ryzhkov himself. It was intended to sell military hardware and materials abroad for billions of dollars, which would have permitted the purchase of consumer goods to resell in the Soviet Union for tens of billions of rubles. In the end, Ryzhkov had to justify his actions and refute his participation, thereby demonstrating the strength of the conservatives and the Soviet military-industrial complex. Everyone seems afraid to speak up against the conservative clichés about undermining Soviet military might, and conversion of military industry to bring in hard currency has so far not produced any spectacular results.

The Soviet economy is in complete disarray, and nothing effective is being done to reform or to modernize it. Marshall Goldman wrongly attributes this situation to Gorbachev's efforts to dismantle the centralized system.[16] What Gorbachev has been trying to do is to preserve the essential attributes of the Soviet system by slightly modernizing them. Nor can it be said that since Gorbachev's turn to the right in October 1990 radical economic reform has ended, because it never took off in the first place. Gorbachev has been a great procrastinator about serious economic reform.

The Soviets are afraid of switching to a free market economy. Their fears, because they have never experienced capitalism, are speculations based on ideology, especially on the philosophical identification of private property with capitalism. They are afraid of the exploitation of man by man, of unjustified income differentiation and unearned income, of unemployment, and of the threat to the environment. All of these concerns are rooted in decades of a hostile attitude toward the capitalist system, a hostility that greatly exaggerates its shortcomings and hides its successes. There is also an understandable fear of the unknown.

Are Soviet economists at fault for not being able to come up with workable solutions? Having been educated and brought up under the Soviet system, they are not necessarily familiar with the subtleties of a market system. But even if they were experts on the market, they have been given an impossible assignment by their economically incompetent leaders: to design a regulated market economy that will preserve Soviet socialism. And this must be completely blueprinted, with nothing left to be modernized as you go. The Soviet leaders do not

---

[16]"Moscow's Money Troubles," *World Monitor*, October 1990.

appear to understand that by trying to preserve a primitive equality scheme they are excluding private enterprise. They are used to resolving everything through centralized commands, and they do not appear to possess the necessary qualities to proceed with revolutionary reforms.

Why have all the attempts to improve the condition of the economy brought negative results, while in the area of foreign policy there have been so many successes? Why has the Soviet Union failed where China, India, and South Korea have succeeded under much more adverse conditions? The essential reason is that the deideologization of the economy did not fully take place. The Communist party continues to hold the economy under its sway.

15

The Strike: Sketches for a Portrait of a Phenomenon

Nina Maksimova

Eko
no. 11, November 1989

This miners' strike of the summer of 1989 was a totally new phenomenon for the Soviet Union; its scale and level of organization surprised and shocked everyone. Even party members participated. It was an inevitable and spontaneous explosion of the workers' wrath. A new type of power emerged in the form of strike committees, which were later transformed into workers' committees with courageous, talented, and energetic leaders. The strikers maintained an iron discipline, with no drunkenness, crime, or anarchy. The workers changed from slaves to free people, and a high level of solidarity among workers in different trades was achieved. The "crowd on the square" became a symbol of collective will and wisdom. Nonetheless, the workers and their leaders could not match the Byzantine skills of the party and government leaders. It is hard to say whether the miners ever had any reasonable hope of having their demands satisfied on the first try. What is more important is that the self-confidence and experience they acquired will stay with the workers for a long time. This strike taught many Soviet workers a valuable lesson.

Less than two years later, on March 4, 1991, the miners struck again. This time, their main demand was for the resignation of Mikhail Gorbachev.

After all the strike was preceded by a series of events and actions of a preventive nature. It was predicted ahead of time, and people tried to prevent it, consciously or unconsciously. Steps were taken. But could they have changed anything?

In the spring of 1989, four months before the strike, the chairman of the Council of Ministers of the USSR visited the Kuznetsk Coal Region. He also spent some time in Prokopyevsk, which subsequently became the "capital" of the strike. He was taken on a preplanned route. The local authorities even built Potemkin villages underground. Reliable people who would say all the right words were sent to work a shift at a mine prepared for the visit of the dignitary. Everything that could catch the eye of the great leader was torn out and put in order. They say that they even managed to paint the coal cutter loader. But nevertheless the chairman of the Council of Ministers said that he'd never seen a town as bad as that and was surprised that people were living there. He promised to help the Kuznetsk Coal Region in the near future. Subsequently many miners remembered Nikolai Ryzhkov's visit and his unkept promises.

Miner shifts and teams went on strike in the spring in Kemerovo, Mezhdurechensk, and other towns in the Kuznetsk Coal Region. In response, the bureau of the Kemerovo regional committee of the Communist party adopted a resolution condemning this form of protest. They even suggested expelling Communists who had taken part in the strike from the party. If the resolution had been adopted for enforcement after the events of July, the ranks of the Kuznetsk Coal Region party organization would have grown much thinner. But afterward the committee decided that the participation in the strike of party members had been justified.

About ten days before the national strike, the miners of Mezhdurechensk presented their demands to the local authorities. But the authorities didn't respond.

When the strike in Mezhdurechensk began, the directors of the Prokopyevsk Hydraulic Coal Mining Amalgamation tried to prevent it from spreading to their own town. They immediately held meetings at the mines, informed everyone about the strike, and said that they would try to improve the miners' working and living conditions. They ordered every mine to send representatives to the amalgamation. There they read to the representatives a program of demands which the directors of the mines had written themselves and had decided to send to the ministry and the Council of Ministers on behalf of the Prokopyevsk miners. The representatives unanimously approved both the program and the proposal not to strike. But several hours later the strike began in Prokopyevsk and received support in other towns of the Kuznetsk Coal Region, with echoes in the Donets Coal Region, the western Ukraine, Karaganda, and Vorkuta.

And all of this couldn't have been otherwise. The people couldn't get anything except for speeches, resolutions, programs written in their name, threats, and vague promises—or, at best, sympathy. The workers, like Atlas, had grown tired of holding a talkative administrative system on their shoulders. A social explosion was inevitable.

Democracy Day

Western observers had anticipated this in the fall. There were reports that the Prokopyevsk miners were preparing to strike in December. But they went on strike at the hottest time of the year. The miners said that it all happened spontaneously, without leaders. They hadn't agreed to do anything beforehand.

In the evening of July 12, the day after the strike in Mezhdurechensk began, the third shift at the Kalinin mine changed into their work clothes and refused to go into the mine. They sat on the lawn near Lenin's monument. The fourth shift arrived. "What are you sitting here for?" "In support of Mezhdurechensk." "We'll change clothes and come too."

Shortly before dawn a KamAZ truck stopped next to the miners.[1] "Are you on strike?" the driver asked. "Should I block off the road?" And he parked his truck across the road. Buses stopped and discharged the workers they were carrying to other mines. The workers said that they also would go on strike. The Kalinin miners asked the truck driver to leave, in order to keep from being accused of fomenting disorder. But this incident gave them a hint of what to do next. Buses were carrying workers to all the other mines except for two mines near Kalinin. The Kalinin miners stopped the buses and walked into the trolley cars: "Are you miners? We're on strike. Will you support us?" No one had to be talked into it. In the morning only the workers whose mines were on different routes went to work. After they learned about the strike, they immediately stopped working.

By noon the anarchy had begun to organize itself. The miners had elected strike committees. Messengers from the "central" mine and the Kalinin mine went to all the mines and urged the miners to unite. Workers from the central mine, followed by workers from other mines, moved toward Victory Square, the city's main square, where holiday demonstrations were usually held. Here the strikers joined together and apparently felt like a force for the first time: "We were born on this day." Their first common decision was also born, namely to celebrate July 13 of every year as Democracy Day, a day to hold rallies for the residents of the

---

[1]KamAZ trucks are produced at the Kama Truck Plant, the largest such plant in the USSR.

city and to hear reports from the city authorities and mine directors.

Four days later almost all the miners of the Kuznetsk Coal Region were on strike. And in Prokopyevsk practically the entire city had gone on strike with the miners. A regional strike committee (elected by the representatives of the city strike committees) was organized in Prokopyevsk. The committees included many "natural talents" (as the miner Dobrynkin called them) and rare individuals for whom the interests of society are more important than personal interests. This is what people say of Teymuraz Avaliani, a People's Deputy and deputy director in charge of major construction of the Kiselevsk Coal Amalgamation, who was elected chairman of the regional strike committee. Everyone knows from the newspapers and the radio that he wrote a letter to Brezhnev asking him to resign from the leadership and was almost locked up in a mental hospital for his undertaking. Yury Rudolf, a highly qualified miner, was one of the organizers of the strike that had been planned for the fall in Prokopyevsk.

Naturally, he first headed the Prokopyevsk city strike committee and then became deputy chairman of the regional committee. This is what he said in an interview with the city paper: "My task is to do what has to be done in order to make people believe in a bright future again." The coal-face hewer Vladimir Makhanov (deputy chairman and subsequently chairman of the city strike committee) has a wealth of life experience for his twenty-nine years. He attended a mining school, worked on a Komsomol construction project, was a team leader of the housing cooperative for young families, and has traveled abroad, which disposed him toward independent thinking. He is not only capable of understanding complex economic nuances and bureaucratic casuistry but is also capable of explaining it to everyone else. Mikhail Anokhin, a housing construction worker, was in the hospital when the miners' strike broke out. He was discharged in time and became involved. He possesses oratorical and literary talents. The Altai Publishing House is publishing a collection of his poetry. The spontaneity of the strike put leaders such as these in the forefront.

Many people didn't believe that the miners themselves had figured out such reasonable organizational solutions as closing up the liquor stores and preventing vitally essential activities from going on strike. Supposedly someone gave them a hint. But in Prokopyevsk these decisions were made by the city strike committee, the absolute majority of which consisted of workers. They had taken into consideration the experience of the Mezhdurechensk strikers, who sealed up the liquor stores when drunks appeared among the strikers (and then the Donets miners borrowed the experience of the Kuznetsk miners from the newspapers). And they had the sense to avoid risking lives in the city when the workers of many organizations wanted to join them. They authorized the electrical goods and electrical machinery plants to go on strike. They asked the bus drivers, housing construction workers, and other people to express their solidarity in a different way (and in their free time these workers came to the rallies, included their demands in the strike program, and sent money in support of the strikers). And the directors asked the miners to do the work required to keep the mine faces from collapsing. The miners agreed.

The government commission went to meet the people at the square. They were followed by the city fathers, the public servants, and the directors, who had lost their air of power and had become as timid as schoolchildren who have not done their homework. And there they went through a kind of public certification. The workers reproached the general director of the Prokopyevsk Hydraulic Coal Mining Amalgamation for his abruptness and rudeness. They advised the minister not to deceive himself or others with unkept promises. They told a secretary from the Central Committee of the Communist party, "Don't try to put all the blame for the city's miserable situation on your predecessors. You, the current leaders of the country, are also at fault."

Why Are They Always Trying to Trick Us?!

Most of my time I spent at the podium, which had become both the "office" of the city strike committee and a "gallows"—not a place where people were executed, but a place where officials and orators talked to the people. And the people talked with them and with each other. There were so many people at the rallies that it was impossible to sit down. People stood for hours as if they were unaware of the scorching sun or the rain. Only the ambulance would leave from time to time, carrying off people who had fainted.

I didn't recognize the workers whose houses I had gone to so many times in preparing my articles. At that time I had been struck by the subdued manner with which they automatically accepted the regular revisions of their quotas, which made their work cheaper and sweated more and more out of them (I still wasn't prepared to call it by its exact name: exploitation). They accepted the notorious "correlation between labor productivity growth and wage hikes," a reform-era invention of nameless economists, which at times made it impossible for the workers to get their full wages. The workers had been controlled and manipulated by pitting them one against another, which technique, according to Engels, the capitalists had employed early in the nineteenth century for the same purpose. I can't understand by what miracle workers' solidarity had survived and brought them to the square. People who had resigned themselves to violence and arbitrariness as if to fate and whom a quota setter could sidetrack were now presenting demands to the government.

This is how they understand their situation now:

"Every worker feeds five to seven administrators."

"We're niggers! We have a slave-owning system. No one respects us."

In their eyes there is no longer any hopeless submission. And this is not the crowd about whom [Alexander] Solzhenitsyn wrote in *The Red Wheel*[2] and which, in Academician [Vladimir] Bekhterev's opinion, combines and aggravates all the worst traits of humanity. At this time I almost believed in the possibility of collective reason and even of the dictatorship of the proletariat. Sometimes it seemed that all those at the square already constituted a single entity. Anokhin, the aforementioned member of the city strike committee, said that the square reminded him of the science-fiction Solaris (the "thinking ocean," from Lem's novel).[3]

And this made the moments of disunity even more tormenting. A barrier of alienation arose between the strike committees and the strikers, the podium and the square. The other towns didn't avoid this. Even exchanges of experiences

---

[2]After his expulsion from the Soviet Union, Solzhenitsyn undertook the gigantic task of rewriting Russian history, in a series of novels, to prove that the evil doctrine of Marxism came from the West. *The Red Wheel* is one of these huge historical novels.

[3]*Solaris* is the name of a novel by Polish science-fiction writer Stanislaw Lem.

didn't help. A representative from Mezhdurechensk who had come to Prokopyevsk appealed to the miners "not to repeat the mistakes" made by the miners in Mezhdurechensk and cautioned them against schisms and mistrust in the strike committee. He was jeered as a strikebreaker: Mezhdurechensk was no longer on strike. People didn't want to listen to him. And soon Prokopyevsk repeated Mezhdurechensk's "mistakes," for which one could discern natural and common causes.

The democracy of the strike gradually faded. People stopped passing the microphone from hand to hand freely in the square and it became moored to its traditional spot at the podium. Obviously one couldn't just go up to the podium and say anything. Sometimes only members of the strike committees and the press were allowed onto the podium. And not everyone could get into the building where the regional strike committee and the government commission were located. People were admitted only with credentials, and only members of the strike committees were issued credentials, the same kind of "red covers"[4] that the rank-and-file strikers so disliked.

The entire committee spent more time with the authorities. They made an effort for the people and stood up for the interests of the strikers. But they consulted less and less with the square, although they promised to "consult with everyone." There was more and more silence and secrecy. And the square sensed this.

On July 18, in the daytime, the Kuznetsk Coal Region radio broadcast a speech by Avaliani, the chairman of the regional strike committee. He read and commented on a "Report on Steps to Correct the Situation in the Kuznetsk Coal Region," which had been signed by the strike committee and the government commission. He tried to convince the audience that a great deal had already been accomplished (first and foremost, there was an agreement to give the miners economic independence). But the people at Victory Square didn't listen to this speech. The strikers demanded that the regional strike committee come to the square rather than talk to them on the radio. The strike committee referred to technical difficulties. But in the old days radio reports of the holiday demonstrations were broadcast all the time from

---

[4]Communist party membership cards.

Victory Square! As a symbol of protest the Prokopyevsk miners turned off the radio. And now no one knew anything more about the "Report" or about the appeal to stop the strike.

Three hours after Avaliani's appeal to the strikers, Vladimir Makhanov, the chairman of the Prokopyevsk strike committee, signed a resolution to temporarily halt the strike. Seven hours later he went to the podium. Perhaps he wanted to prepare people for a message concerning the document he had signed? He read it slowly, explaining every point and translating mysterious jargon into the plain language of the workers.

Makhanov would call the following day, July 19, the most difficult. On that morning, when the members of the strike committee appeared on the podium the square was already in an uproar. The crowd had received its first information on what had been reported about Prokopyevsk to the entire country and to the strikers in the towns of the Kuznetsk Coal Region.

An agitated resident of Novokuznetsk said that in his city they had received a telegram supposedly sent by the Prokopyevsk city strike committee. It stated that the strike should be stopped and that the strike committees should be converted into workers' committees. It had been signed by Makhanov and Naydov, the general director of the Prokopyevsk Hydraulic Coal Mining Amalgamation. Afterward, the Novokuznetsk strike committees resigned their commissions, and the miners didn't know what to do.

The miners of Kiselevsk had been informed that Prokopyevsk was already back at work. But they checked and sent a messenger. The factories in Prokopyevsk had also sent confused messengers. They had also been told that the miners had decided to stop the strike.

The members of the strike committee were summoned to give a reply. Makhanov walked up to the barrier.

"I didn't give anyone a telegram. And I signed a resolution to halt the strike, but it was merely a recommendation. You are the only ones with the right to continue or to stop the strike."

"Did they put pressure on you? Did they buy you off? Did you sell out? They greased them there."

"Guys, don't get scared. No one put any pressure on me. The committee adopted the resolution on its own, without the authorities."

The microphone and telephone on the podium went dead "on their own." A message arrived indicating that the trade union committees no longer had a way to feed the strikers (although all of them, with the exception of the trade union committee at the Kalinin mine, were still bringing food at the time). The resolution of the city strike committee to temporarily halt the strike was read several times over the radio, accompanied by appropriate speeches by a prosecutor, a doctor, and a schoolteacher. A nameless voice on the radio said: "We request that you immediately clear the square and go back to work." Apparently the authorities were trying to "speed up the conclusion of the strike" by confusing the strikers with disinformation and prodding them from behind. But these administrative maneuvers had the opposite effect.

People muttered, "For decades they've been herding us into a stall."

The square expressed its mistrust for all the strike committees, trade union committees, amalgamation directors, and city authorities and demanded their removal and new elections. People were already disbelieving the authorities, the party, the mass media, and each other. People said that there was no need to go to the mines to walk the picket line and change shifts. All the shifts should gather on the square to form a "united fist" and "stand up to the end." At the peak of the fervor, the square decided that the whole city would go on strike. Even several vitally essential organizations came to a halt. From time to time, miners from Kiselevsk came to Prokopyevsk, and on one occasion several hundred came. They exchanged information and encouraged one another: "Hold on! Don't give in to provocations! We're with you!"

The miners stubbornly refused to "clear" the square. No matter how rough they had it (they slept right on the asphalt and didn't always eat on time), they experienced moments of unity, cleansing, and enthusiasm. But what would happen if they were to go back to the mines? This is what the strikers said: "If we go now without getting everything, we won't rise up again." "The bosses will strangle all of us one by one." "They'll put the most active people behind bars, and intimidate everyone else." "They'll pass a law on strikes which will be so tough that no one will even dare raise his head. And if you complain, you'll be an 'enemy of the people,' just like in 1937." They didn't believe the prosecutor when he tried to convince them that a law would not be passed without discussion by all the people. They were afraid to leave. And they were afraid to stay: Why had policemen been sent to Prokopyevsk from Novokuznetsk? The miners demanded that Gorbachev and Ryzhkov come. They demanded that the members of the government commission come back to the square as they had promised.

But the government commission didn't come back to the square. They negotiated only with the strike committee. I was present at their meeting in the conference hall of the city party committee when they signed the next "Report on Steps" (for Prokopyevsk). Initially, Nikolai Slyunkov, the Central Committee secretary and chairman of the government commission, uttered the familiar words that everything must be done for the sake of man and in the name of man, that the Kuznetsk Coal Region would get help and that a comprehensive development program for the region was in the works. (What kind of a program? I've lived in the area for more than ten years, and I've heard of all kinds of "comprehensive programs.") Then he read aloud a draft of the agreement, which had been handed to him, and issued orders concerning every point, indicating the times and "persons responsible for implementation." There was something fascinating about the way in which the "waving of a powerful hand" made it possible to build power and heating plants, hog farms, and water systems, to provide scores of buses, road maintenance machinery, and street sweepers, and to lend millions of rubles to the miners for garden cottages.

But the fairy tale was ruined by a question from a member of the strike committee: Where had several of the miners' demands gone? "I don't know," the chairman shrugged his shoulders, without demonstrating any interest in their disappearance.

Afterward, when I compared the "Report on Steps" and the strikers' program of demands, I made a discovery. The program had not just been abridged. It had been almost completely ignored. The report had been fabricated, judging by all appearances, out of whole cloth by a bureaucrat who knew what "facilities" the city was lacking but who did not include all the complaints of the miners against the authorities. There was no demand to reexamine the issue of the allocation of apartments in a twelve-story prestige building. There were no "expressions of mistrust" in officials. There was no demand to "keep from harassing the strikers." It was all quite different. Does that mean that once again someone else was doing the workers' thinking for them?

When Slyunkov concluded his speech almost all the members of the strike committee raised their hands to ask questions.

"No," Slyunkov said, firmly putting a period at the end. "Today I'll be talking to the entire region on the radio."

For fifteen minutes there was shouting in the conference hall. The members of the strike committee, as if they had regained consciousness, said over and over again with dismay: "How can we go out onto the square? What will we tell the people?" One of them asked the first secretary of the city party committee: Who had given the order to "cut off" the strike committee's telephone? The first secretary swore up and down in fear that he had had nothing to do with it (but later, when he talked to me, he didn't deny his part in it). Another member shouted at the petrified mayor: "You have to be decent! Honest!" And a delegate from Nizhny Tagil walked between one group and another in confusion, asking for coal for his steel mill. His blast furnace had already shut down, soon the coke ovens would begin to fall apart, and the steelworkers wouldn't get paid.

Legachev, the deputy chairman of the strike committee, called for a vote: "Should we start shipping or not?"

No one voted: "How can we authorize any shipments without consulting with everyone?"

The mayor, having recovered from his shock, gave some advice: "But you can handle them. Why are you letting the square lead you? They trusted you, so you decide. Otherwise you're taking on government responsibilities."

Legachev once again called for a vote. The vote was unanimous in favor of allowing shipments. Evidently the mention of "government responsibilities" persuaded them. The strike committee already knew that it couldn't "get involved in politics." In the early days of the strike they had been reminded of this by the head of the local office of the KGB.

The square greeted the committee with whistles and shouts. "Tell us everything!"

Makhanov began to read and explain the "Report on Steps for Prokopyevsk" (but not all the way through). He had no microphone. The square couldn't hear him. Somebody figured out what was going on and brought his personal tape recorder with a microphone up to the podium. Makhanov informed the crowd of the strike committee's decision to "ship a minimum amount of coal" to Nizhny Tagil. He reminded them of the strike committee's decision to temporarily halt the strike. He asked everyone on the square to gather with the workers from his own mine and discuss the decision. There was more whistling and shouting. But Makhanov didn't come unhinged. He remained calm, saying, "Comrades, comrades, we have to listen to one another." Ultimately he managed to round up and convince the workers from his own central mine that the government commission "had made major concessions." But no one had yet convinced the whole square of this. And the square remained steadfast and insisted on continuing the strike and on not shipping any coal. Makhanov didn't even talk the miners into allowing shipments to defense plants, although with a knowing tone of voice he reminded them that in this case the strikers "were getting mixed up in politics."

Opinions are opinions, but in real life everything happens the way it happens. And there was the perception that there was no longer any chance to change anything. The workers, who were not in the least embarrassed by the presence of women, cursed the bosses, the strike committee members, and each other at the top of their lungs. There was irritation, hostility, and rudeness. Solaris had turned into a mob.

And suddenly it became calm. And for the hundredth time I was surprised at how much and how little people need in order to become human beings again. It turned out that a woman's words were needed, words from Makhanov's mother, who came to the square every evening. She didn't give a clue of how the shattered hopes would be restored or how the relationships between the strikers and their committee should be in the future. Her words contained nothing but compassion: "Guys, don't be cannibals."

People, voices, and words became less harsh. And from the square one could hear like a moan the words: "Why are they always trying to trick us?"

The strike committee was left "in power." The chairman was sent home to get some sleep. ("He's tired. It's hard to walk among generals.") Twelve hours later the strike was temporarily halted. The miners left Victory Square.

"The miners are walking away. Was it a victory or a defeat?" was the question the *Shakhterskaya Pravda* [Miner's Truth] newspaper of Prokopyevsk asked itself and its readers. I myself don't know.

16

Property and Freedom

Boris Pinsker and Larisa Piyasheva

Novy Mir
no. 11, November 1989

According to this article, one of the best of 1989 delineating problems with the economy, it is hard to carry out economic reform while using fuzzy political and economic concepts. Since the 1960s the centralized system has shown signs of bankruptcy, which had been only forestalled by huge oil and arms sales profits and by sacrificing urgent social needs for the sake of capital investment. Standing in the way of successful reforms is the party *apparat*, which will lose its significance with the transition to a market system. The *apparat*, in an attempt to cling to power, has imposed a series of ideological taboos. For example, no unemployment is acceptable in a socialist country, so no statistics are kept, and no assistance is given to people out of work. The unemployment problem is compounded by political and economic crises taking place at the same time. It is significant that Gorbachev is not mentioned by name in this article, mainly because he has not influenced the economy to the extent that he has influenced foreign policy.

"The policies of today are determined by what university professors of economics were teaching thirty years ago."

Friedrich von Hayek, winner of the Nobel Prize for Economics in 1974

The Concept of Acceleration: Hope and Disappointment

The fact that basic political and theoretical issues are unresolved has made any discussions of specific economic policies fruitless and has consequently led to the perpetuation of economic and social stagnation. The so-called concept of acceleration, which to a large extent has aggravated our country's economic crisis, could serve as a convincing example of this.

The idea of accelerating economic growth entered the public consciousness in 1985 and 1986 along with the proposition of the need for radical economic reform.

"Acceleration and reform" has been the slogan from the very beginning. The unity is obvious and natural: Economic reform became indispensable due to a prolonged and natural process of reductions in the rates of economic growth and the deterioration of its quantitative and qualitative indicators. The fundamental unsuitability of the centralized planning system became increasingly obvious since the late 1960s as the momentum provided by Kosygin's unsuccessful reforms petered out.[1] Over the course of three five-year plans, growth in the country's gross national product (GNP) slowed by a factor of 2.5 and became practically negligible from 1979 to 1983. The only reason the economy remained static instead of shrinking was the major income derived from energy exports. Without energy exports the real per capita GNP would have dropped.

The economy's leaders tried to maintain the fading process of updating and modernizing fixed industrial capital by reallocating funds intended for social purposes to capital investment. This did not lead to an improvement in the situation in industry, but it did lead to the accumulation of a heavy burden of social problems. Our traditional problems, namely shortages of housing, kindergartens, nurseries, schools, and hospitals, were compounded by a rise in infant mortality, a reduction in the average life expectancy, the spread of genetic abnormalities in a number of regions (due to the unjustified and uncontrolled application of fertilizers and toxic chemicals in agriculture, the insufficient capacity and low quality of water treatment facilities in industry, and other similar reasons), the emergence of pockets of poverty and underdevelopment, and widespread alcohol and drug abuse. This is a far-from-complete list of the social problems that have accumulated over the course of decades of unbalanced economic development. A unique economic indicator of the aggravation of these problems was a drastic reduction in expenditures for education, public health, and culture, a reduction which was unprecedented in peacetime.

We need medicine to eliminate the aforementioned problems and to cure our society, and thus we need to make the economy more efficient. That is why the choice of the basic priorities of the new policy made at the 27th Party

---

[1]Economic reform was attempted under Soviet Prime Minister Alexei Kosygin in 1965.

Congress, namely the change from quantitative and extensive economic growth to intensive development, was so obvious.

Some economists, politicians, ideologues, and managers of the economy (the supporters of radical reform) have understood the party's new policies to be a call for profound economic and political transformations and for reforms for the sake of subsequently accelerating economic growth. Others have understood what is transpiring in a traditional way: We must work harder, intensify our efforts, and move faster, and this will constitute acceleration. They see the prospects of reform not in the radical reform of the entire economic and political system but in stronger administration and tighter discipline. (The police roundups of job truants during Andropov's reign is a classic and sad example of this kind of reform.)[2]

The leadership's inability or unwillingness to see inevitable and vital solutions indicates a basic impediment and obstacle to reform, namely group, class, and caste interest.

Now let us imagine that the problem of the optimal functioning of our economy has already been resolved. The consumer has become king in all of the country's major markets. There is no longer any thought of shortages. The quality of a product is determined solely by its price and by consumer demand. So what would this mean? The party *apparat* in its current form and with its current functions would be useless.

No one has ever surrendered commanding heights or the accompanying privileges voluntarily and naturally.

One of the most proven and effective weapons that the administrative system uses in its fight against changes that will kill it is an unspoken and tacit list of all kinds of ideological taboos and sacred and decrepit postulates and dogmas which cannot be subjected to an uncompromising discussion. Now the bureaucracy is using this weapon, this list to successfully impede a forthright and honest examination of the issues and problems that are key to economic reorganization. It is thus slowly but surely nullifying reforms and the reform process as a whole.

For example, let's take one of the most important subjects for a society entering an era of radical socioeconomic changes:

---

[2]Yuri Andropov led the Soviet Union for less than two years, between 1982 and 1984.

the subject of unemployment. Until now representatives of the highest echelons of authority and official scholarship and propaganda have employed the old incantations that there is no unemployment under socialism, nor could there be. But as the Central Statistics Agency's data indicate, the lack of unemployment in the Soviet Union is not the accomplishment of an advanced economy; it is merely an "achievement" of our accountants and statisticians, an "achievement" for which we have eliminated the opportunity for an individual to be unemployed and the right to receive aid and have made the status of involuntary unemployment a crime or a matter for administrative sanctions.

The question of whether unemployment is compatible with the Soviet version of socialism is not a topic for scholarly research but an ideological and political issue. Neither economists nor life itself have the right yet to answer it; only the supreme political leaders do. The lack of academic freedom and genuine openness in this area has condemned scholars to ambiguous and inconsistent analyses, politicians to hasty and knowingly mistaken decisions, and society to stagnation.

But the command-administrative system is interfering with a sober and scholarly analysis not only of this issue but also of all the other fundamental issues of economic reform. Let us examine them in order.

Prices

We have been discussing the issue of prices, which is so fundamental for reform, for four years already. Its resolution will determine the practical implementation of self-support relations in our country and the true possibility of a transition to the self-financing and self-sustenance of state enterprises.[3] The transition to wholesale trade[4] is both a condition and a result of resolving the problem of prices. The fate of reform is highly dependent on it. Until now we have only been asked to take part in a discussion of the question of whether or not to raise meat prices or to slash them, to make

---

[3]The author is referring to economic rather than command methods of management, by which an enterprise's losses would not be covered by the state.

[4]"Wholesale trade" means the right of enterprises to sell unnecessary equipment and supplies.

prices proportional to prices in foreign markets, or to leave everything the way it is.

A change in the existing pricing mechanism would require a redistribution of both rights and responsibilities and a change in the system of incentives and sanctions. But while the topic of incentives has at least been considered, albeit superficially, the problem of sanctions is completely unclear. Who would be responsible and in what way for the consequences of bad economic decisions? A worker responsible for defective products is fined. And this is reasonable, particularly when the losses that result from these defective products are comparable to his wages. But how and with what could employees of the State Planning Agency and ministries and business directors be held responsible for decisions (or indecisiveness) that result in the loss of millions or billions of rubles?

No one has ever entrusted a hired office worker or shop assistant with complete economic independence, including the freedom to set prices, because he would utterly ruin the business. (If there is a need for an outsider to play a direct role in a business, he is taken on board and made a co-owner. This is how joint stock companies operate on a day-to-day basis. At one time this practice gave rise to the belief among the founders of Marxism that stock property constitutes a "negation of bourgeois property.") The illusion of the possibility of completely divorcing the right to own property from the right to be freely in charge of it has been triumphant in our country for seventy years. So what's become of it? The hope of making a bureaucrat feel like a proprietor proved to be just as utopian as the once-popular idea of turning a wolf into a vegetarian.

The main issue in pricing reform is not whether to raise or lower prices but on what items to raise them and by how much. The main issue is property: the motivation of the producer and the trader, and the legal and political foundations of the economic self-reliance of businesses.

For now the very statement of these issues has been postponed indefinitely because several political and ideological issues have not been resolved. For example, is socialism compatible with personal wealth? If so, then to what degree? Could personal wealth take the form of productive capital? Could the owner of a piece of jewelry worth a hundred thousand rubles (and more expensive stones have been sold) exchange it for, let's say, a tractor with a price of ten thousand rubles or a truck? Why can a Volga, a passenger car, be private property, but a ZIL-111, a luxury official limousine, can't? Why is it permissible to earn extra money for transporting people by taxis but not freight by trucks? A private individual is now allowed to have his own personal computer, which is as powerful as the mainframe computers of the 1960s and 1970s. But the minicomputer of tomorrow, which of course will be superior to today's government hardware in all respects—could it be in private hands from the time it is produced? Or will we, as we did before, fundamentally insist that all the most up-to-date and productive goods must belong to the government alone (as in ancient China, where only members of the imperial family could wear sable coats)?

The laws on cooperatives and individual labor legalized, to a certain extent, the right to own the means of production.[5] But it's another matter how guaranteed and how consistent this right is. It's permissible to own a watchmaker's lathe. But what about a modern machining center? If not, then what is the upper limit for private capital? Is this limit based on logic, or is it solely dependent on the level of public prejudices and determined by some kind of intuitive perception by a philistine who is oriented toward "a medium level of well-being"?

In contrast to the subject of the propriety of the existence of individual property and individual labor, the subject of hired labor remains closed. One can hire a man to chop wood or to dig up a potato garden for personal consumption, but if you're planning to sell this wood or these potatoes, don't even think of hiring anyone. A group of three officially registered cooperative businessmen can contract employees, but each of them individually doesn't have the right to do so. After all, this would be the exploitation of man by man!

But what is the sense of this battle against exploitation, in the name of which we've shed so much blood and committed so many crimes? After all, exploitation in the original sense of the word means "the use of natural wealth and the derivation of benefits from this use."

For many years we've been assured that the market has always and everywhere led to the restoration of capitalism.

---

[5]New laws in these areas took effect in 1987, and since then many additional changes have been made.

We memorized the appropriate excerpts from Lenin at school, and apparently they've been a part of our collective subconsciousness for a long time. It's true that now our subconsciousness has undergone certain changes. Now that we have learned—as a result of the endless shortages, the growing gap between our standard of living and that of the developed Western countries, and the fact that our basic social and economic problems are unresolved—we have grabbed onto the hope that a change from administrative to market relations will help us to overcome a crisis that has lasted for decades. The market will feed, clothe, and save us. In principle it's impossible to object to this, because in fact the market is feeding, clothing, and putting shoes on billions of inhabitants of the earth. It is already pulling humanity through a fourth scientific and technical revolution, and it is quite effectively resolving the basic economic problems of the most diverse societies. The only trouble that I can see is that we always use the combination "socialist market" to describe the future economic system that must replace the administrative mode of production, planning, and distribution. Apparently we understand that a socialist market would be a market in which the institution of private property would not exist, or more precisely that kind of private property which presupposes the possibility of utilizing hired labor would not exist. The following questions are inevitable: Could the market be efficiently financed without the institution of private property? Would a combination of the three basic "socialist" forms, namely state, cooperative, and lease property, be sufficient for full-fledged economic development?

Leasing in Agriculture and Industry

Certain politicians and legislators consider leasing within collective or state farms and leased farms to be an acceptable way of resolving our long-term agricultural crisis, which is an economic, cultural, and social crisis. Thus, they propose, putting it crudely, to preserve our virginity and to derive pleasure at the same time by maintaining the monopolistic system of nationalized property in land while simultaneously creating conditions for the development of market systems for regulating agricultural production. Putting it mildly, this is a dubious project. After all, what do all of the many centuries of experience in other countries tell us (leasing or renting land was widespread in the Roman Empire and in medieval Europe, and renting is still common in all of the developed countries)? They tell us that short-term and medium-term leases are socially destructive and dangerous.

Long-term leasing with the right of inheritance is supposedly free of the basic disadvantages of the preceding version, because it guarantees sufficient economic interest in improving the land and creates incentives for a reasonable and long-term intensification of farming. At the same time, long-term leasing contains the seeds of major social and economic conflicts between the tenants and the owners of the land—in our case, the representatives of the government. (Problems of this kind have been studied quite well by experts using appropriate examples from medieval Europe.) From the vantage points of the interests of the lessees and of the economy as a whole, the best kind of leasing is that in which the rent is fixed by custom or by law. The lessees then will naturally invest more of their own resources and labor in improving the land and the farm. However, during periods of rapid inflationary devaluation of the currency, fixed lease payments lead to the impoverishment of the landowners.

According to statistics for 1987, 5.5 million persons were employed in producers' cooperatives in the entire nonsocialist world, a figure which accounts for less than 2 percent of the total number of persons employed in production. This is the case even when the commercial prosperity of cooperatives is maintained by hefty tax privileges, in the countries with the most successful cooperative sectors (the Scandinavian countries, France, Spain, and Italy). But despite all their privileges, including tax benefits and technical and commercial services from government agents at the taxpayers' expense, cooperatives have demonstrated no capacity for growth. The difficulties are the same as they were at the beginning of the century: inadequacy of capital formation and lack of skilled commercial and technical management. It's quite interesting that cooperative members are always and everywhere more inclined to consume income than to save it. In this respect the collective will is clearly inferior to the will of an individual owner.

Won't we in the future need to establish legally a percentage of funds for investment purposes in order to stimulate savings in cooperatives? Even now we're ready to answer yes. This will be followed by the needs for strengthening the system of supervision and for new edicts and administrative regulations to keep money from leaking out of investment accounts. All of this will inevitably end in the complete nationalization of cooperative businesses. So with these kinds of prospects is it worth going to all the trouble? Wouldn't it be better to admit right off that only government property and administrative power are possible in Russia? (In general, as the saying goes, "Don't waste your efforts, just sink to the bottom.")

Perhaps it would make sense to remind the reader that free individual and entrepreneurial farming has emerged victorious in the historical competition and that many centuries of human experience have convincingly demonstrated that freedom of the individual is not only the highest spiritual value but also the foundation of the most profitable way of organizing social life. If we ignore this, we are condemned to relive human history.

The State Planning Agency and the Stock Market

One more fact indicates that cooperative and lease property are completely inadequate for the full-fledged operation of the market. A very important element of any economic system is its mechanism for making decisions concerning the direction of investment. This mechanism determines future national economic proportions and whether an economy prospers or declines. In countries with a market economy this function is performed by stock and commodity markets, which set prices for the basic factors of production, including raw materials, processed materials, and equipment.

Could a market exist without this central mechanism determining the direction of economic growth? Yes, it could, but only as a secondary market and as an appendage to the world economic system. Moreover, if there is to be no stock market—that is, a mechanism for reallocating resources among industries and regions—we would need some kind of planning mechanism to take on the same functions. (And we know how well such administrative mechanisms work from the example of our own State Planning Agency.) In essence this is also a market, only poorly managed, practically unpredictable, and extremely inefficient because it considers "incoming factors" (such as the influence of different political and business figures and organizations on the allocation of capital investments, the personal and subjective opinions and prejudices of high-placed party and government bureaucrats in selecting future directions for economic development, and so forth) more than it considers immediate economic factors. Because of these characteristics of our present system for allocating investment funds, every fifteen or twenty years we make attempts at a general adjustment of basic economic proportions, and in the process we are guided not by the needs and requirements of our own economic and social development but rather by information twenty to twenty-five years out of date on the optimal proportions of the capitalist market.

At one time hopes for a rapid growth in national well-being were associated with the idea of rejecting private property in favor of state and public property. Now it seems that these hopes have been dashed. Over the last seventy years we've had the opportunity to see that the exploitation of labor by government-owned businesses usually looks less attractive and pays much less than it does in privately owned industries. It seems that the time has come to draw a conclusion from this indubitable fact for once and for all.

Property and National Economic Policy

As we know, not one of the socialist countries which have set out on the path of reform by development of economistic models of economic management has been able to avoid the high inflation characteristic of the experience of Yugoslavia, Hungary, China, and Poland. Not one of the developed capitalist countries which tried to guarantee stable economic development and full employment in the 1950s and 1960s avoided the troubles associated with inflation.

Friedrich von Hayek, the prominent theorist of monetary circulation, has claimed that inflation in the twentieth century has been purely political. The right of the government to create money from thin air is too great a temptation for politicians, who are thus able to resolve their problems of the moment while avoiding long-term and difficult decisions. Soviet scholars have always suggested that this interpretation of inflation is applicable exclusively to the economies of the state monopoly capitalist period. They believed that the socialist countries (those adhering to state monopoly socialism) were protected from these kinds of disasters for once and for all.

It's difficult not to agree with von Hayek's conclusion that the persistence in resorting to inflationary methods (both here and in the West) is a consequence of internal defects in the political system and evidence of the undemocratic nature and arbitrariness of power and may be corrected only by changing the political system. Critics of inflationary policies (von Hayek, [Milton] Friedman, and others) associate the tendency to resort to inflationary measures with the shortcomings of representative democracy. The drive for popularity compels elected representatives to demand higher spending from the government. And the government meets these demands even though at times it realizes that these policies are harmful. Friedman believes that the problem of inflation could be solved by limiting the rate of growth of the money supply to 3 to 5 percent per annum by law—that is, to a rate proportional to the growth in the GNP. What's important to us in these discussions is the certainty of the diagnosis that long-term political solutions are required for the resolution of economic problems. Libertine financial policies destroy the economy.

In general, judging by all appearances, the country is entering a period of faster inflation of the Polish or Yugoslavian type, in which the attention of the government toward the needs of different segments of the population, industries, and regions is primarily expressed by printing new money faster, which correspondingly leads to a rise in prices, pensions, and wages. As global experience has shown, the best-off workers will be those who are able to get their demands met every time prices and wages rise. In our case these would be the miners, steelworkers, chemical workers, oil workers, power plant operators, and railroad men. Comparatively small but very cohesive and organized ethnic groups, such as the Balts and the peoples of Transcaucasia, will also be in an advantageous position.

We are alarmed that economic conflicts which are in general normal for a civilized society will become increasingly politicized as the struggle for a slice of the budget pie heats up and will take on the characteristics of a power struggle.

In our society any economic conflict is clearly universal and is to an equal extent economic and political. And this is natural; after all, any manager or director of any business acts as an agent of the government and is incapable of making any decision on his own. No matter what the subject is—be it the supply of soap and sausage in the stores, the quality of protective coveralls, or the operation of kindergartens and dining halls—only the central leadership is expected to make decisions, be it the Politburo, or the Council of Ministers, or now the Supreme Soviet. The miners' strikes in July shed a clear light on the situation: Getting adequate supplies of goods of prime necessity to the workers' neighborhoods required the intervention of the head of the government. And as soon as the employees in other industries understand (and they understood immediately!) what's required to get better supplies and more economic independence, they'll do it. The strike pistol is too tempting a weapon not to use.

The situation is complicated even more: Along with its economic crisis, the country is clearly faced with a political crisis aggravated and intensified by the operation of the Congress of People's Deputies of the USSR and by the policy of separating legislative and executive powers. This separation still has not become a fact of life, but it has become a factor for undermining the old system of administration. We could only hail such a result if it were not that the perplexity and helplessness of the national and local administrative agencies, who timidly await decisions from the Supreme Soviet, have quickly worsened the chaos and paralyzed the economic and political systems.

Bureaucratic willfulness and the celebrated passion to issue all kinds of edicts, orders, and administrative regulations did not spring up by themselves but were called to life by the needs of a centralized, nationalized economy. Because it is not directly subject to the laws of the marketplace, this economy requires detailed administrative regulation to keep moving.

Could a modern democratic parliament, with its inevitably slow and compromising procedures and long debates, manage a gigantic centralized economy? Of course not. After all, the sine qua non of economic management is competence, timeliness, calculated risk, and an orientation toward profit. All of this sits very poorly with the rules of parliamentary politics, with deliberateness, thoroughness, and an orientation toward balanced decisions. And this means that either our parliament will turn into an appendage of the authorities and a discussion club under an all-powerful Council of Ministers or we will make a transition to a market economy, which is the natural and sole basis for political democracy.

17

To Heaven on Ration Cards

Yuri Orlik

Izvestiya
March 30, 1990

To a certain degree, rationing has always been a symbol of the socialist system. There have always been items in short supply, available only to *apparatchiks*, retail employees, and other influential groups. Nonetheless, the introduction of ration coupons forty-five years after World War II is a most distressing and vivid illustration of Gorbachev's bungling of the economy. It is hard to understand why the democratic mayors of Moscow and Leningrad were among the first to adopt rationing. Ration cards will further undermine any desire on the part of the workers to improve their productivity. Rationing will contribute to the flourishing of the black market, and it will impede economic reforms.

Each province and republic has its own rationing rules. In Moscow monthly ration cards issued to each person are worth thirty-one rubles, which permit the purchase of four pounds of meat, half a pound of butter, and one pound of flour. In Kiev, 70 percent of salaries are given in coupons, and stores will not accept rubles anymore; people without jobs are allowed only a minimum of coupons. The authorities of Kalinin have gone further than anyone else; there one cannot obtain a burial permit until the ration cards belonging to the dead person are turned in.

I cannot stop thinking about the letters from defenders of rationing. Yes, of course, a minimum amount of material goods must be guaranteed to everyone. But this minimum is like a death sentence to our system, which for decades taught people to be satisfied with the smallest amounts of goods, but then couldn't provide even that. Here are the arguments in favor of rationing in the letter from T. Sharkovoi, an engineer in the city of Novomichurinsk, Ryazan province: "You come here, and you will see for yourself that you do not have to stand in lines because there is nothing to wait for. When a consignment of shoes does arrive, then the waiting line is such that you must register yourself several times a day. During the sale, the counters crack and the walls shudder. Speculation [resale at black market prices] starts right at the cash register. And when, do you suppose, was the last time I bought a good pair of shoes? You will never guess—it was eight years ago. So, I am speaking up for my right to have a guaranteed minimum." A citizen of Kharkov, Ms. L. Bondarenko, proposes to introduce rations for "all that is absent—that is, for shoes, clothes, shampoo, meat." She suggests "that each person be given one ration card for summer shoes, one for winter shoes, and one for fall/spring shoes; the same system should be used for clothing." A. Pivovarov from Nizhny Tagil reckons that "the rations must be supplied preferentially to those who work well." Proposing "to divide all according to the rules of justice," V. Kuzemka from Ust-Labinsk questions the wisdom of giving an equal amount of rations to those who are "striking, agitating, and killing each other." In his view, rations should be regarded as a means of encouragement or punishment.

Reading these letters, I imagine some mysterious editorial board deciding whether to reward me or not with a ration card for fall shoes or for a piece of soap for the holiday. I want to exclaim, as did A. Rudkovskaya from Khmelnitsky, "I don't want rations! God save us from them. I am seventy-two now. I've had enough of all this rationing."

I have few supporters, but they nevertheless exist. "Distribution of goods through rations is the dream of the destitute. And it seems that we are accomplishing it," bitterly notes S. Krasin, an engineer from Irkutsk. "In our Academgorodok (part of Novosibirsk, a city of 1.5 million people) distribution through rationing has already been going on for a long time," L. Mironov writes. "And the people who distribute, of course, have everything they need. Rations are sold, exchanged, or presented as gifts to 'useful' people from other city districts. Single women are redeeming size-45 winter boots [the largest in the USSR] and are selling them on the used-clothing market. Ration cards mean a life of despair and create a siege mentality. With rations you cannot feed all. With rations there is no need to produce above quotas."

Muscovite E. Belyaev believes that deficits of many goods are created artificially. "Suddenly, salt disappeared from the stores. What happened? Have Lakes Elton and Baskunchak vanished from the face of the earth without a trace? Or was the salt bought up in one hour by shrewd old women while the rest of us were working? Later, salt reappeared in the stores, but by then people were already agitated, suspicious, and dissatisfied. Maybe that was the goal?"

It is doubtful that someone's ill will could create a deficit on all consumer goods. The problem lies not with the manager of the vegetable warehouse, nor with the chairman of the provincial soviet. If only it were so! It is, however, beyond doubt that the rationing system "strengthens the power of the bureaucrats," in the words of V. Akimov, Moscow, and that "it is reinforcing the dependence of the workers on the authorities," according to G. Shragin, Penza. This relationship reinforces the instinctive hostility of the bureaucracy to market relations.

It is absolutely obvious that one should sell to those who have money and not just to those who have achieved higher productivity or who are active in public life. In these cases, money loses its role as a measure of labor and consumption. Why do we need to work hard and to earn a lot if the number of ration cards we can obtain, not our salary, determines our life-style? Ms. D. Tomkina, an electrician from the collective farm Druzhba in the Chervonoarmeysky district of Rovno province, is indignant: "Everywhere are ration cards, coupons, and passports—you cannot buy anything. I question the value of breeding cattle for sale. You invest your labor, but you can buy nothing for the money you earn. And a cotton jacket and tarpaulin boots can be bought for a salary, too."[1]

V. Dovbenko, an assistant professor from Lvov Polytechnic Institute, develops the same idea: "Yes, it is hard to be poor. I feel it myself, not just when money is needed, but—as one of my colleagues said—when big money is needed. However, my point of view is that people should not be discouraged (through the persecution of cooperatives, etc.) from pursuing their natural interest in becoming rich."

There are many letters in the editorial mail about such "forms of trade" unknown abroad as making the sale of consumer goods contingent on a show of passport or visit card [a form of identification]. The introduction of this novelty in Leningrad, the "second city" of the country, caused an especially wide response. L. Smolianinov from Smolensk evaluates the decision of the Leningrad City Council: "It is a blow to the reputation of Leningrad." The decisions of Leningrad and other cities to introduce trade restrictions on commuters are labeled "serfdom" by Y. Mushkov, a

---

[1]A cotton jacket and tarpaulin boots may well be the only clothing that the woman quoted can find in the stores—they are virtually the uniform of low-class Soviet workers.

serviceman from Kalinin, because the province pays its taxes by laboring for the city, but it is still mistreated and not permitted to sit at the table.

Ms. L. Selivanova, from Chudovo in Novgorod province, writes: "I don't know why we are showing off by supplying the capital and Leningrad while depriving small towns and villages of their share and humiliating them. In our nation of 'social equality' people are divided into two kinds. My children and I are of the lower kind."

It is necessary to mention the reaction of Leningraders themselves to the introduction of visit cards. "In the days of the [German] blockade, help came to our besieged city from all over the country," remembers L. Alberg, a survivor of the siege, speaking on behalf of a group of Leningraders. "In April 1942, inhabitants from the liberated districts of Bolebelkovo (in Novgorod province) and Dedovichi (in Pskov province) walked over three hundred kilometers through the occupied territories and front lines, and delivered 223 carts of food to the starving city. And now we are depriving them of a piece of sausage made from meat that they themselves have produced! No words can be found to justify this. We, the authors of this letter, are ordinary Leningraders. We stand in lines; rarely eat cheese and sausages; cannot buy the shoes, fabrics, and other deficit goods that we need. But we do not want to have advantages at the expense of our fellow citizens. We want to be able to look in their eyes honestly."

"Who benefits when Leningraders are set against our province, ours—not an American one? Who profits from embittering and causing a quarrel among our people?" asks D. Belgov, who then tries to answer himself. "A suspicion is growing that, in the first place, representatives of the power structure and *apparat* are benefiting from this. When people quarrel and whole regions are at war with one another, then fewer conflicts with the authorities occur. And it is much easier for the City Council to introduce visit cards or rations than to conduct effective and planned activities aimed at creating and developing markets and market relations. I am ashamed, my God, really ashamed for my own city."

18

Why They Work Better Than We Do

M. Lapitsky

SSHA
no. 2, February 1990

Who does better work than the Russians? The list is long: West Europeans, Japanese, South Koreans, Americans. Somehow it is the Americans that attract the greatest attention. The work ethic is considered to be one of the most important attributes of capitalism, yet there have not been many articles examining the factors that influence this phenomenon. Examining the case of the United States, the author of this article emphasizes the Protestant work ethic and the human factor—that is, managers who treat their subordinates with attention and understanding. One shining example cited is that of the visiting American scholars in the USSR, who seem to personify hard work and efficiency.

One can hardly find a reader who hasn't pondered this question, in the same way that one can hardly find anyone who would claim the opposite, because it's so obvious that they work better than we do.

Since childhood we've been taught and have learned stereotypes which only now we are beginning to go beyond, in a cleansing process of reevaluating established notions. When we defend one such stereotype—namely, our notion of capitalism as some sort of pit of vices—we forget its strong points and the elementary truths of its superiority over feudalism. Every history teacher in elementary school talks about this when he explains the progression from one formation to another, but what conclusions have we drawn from this for ourselves?

When we look at capitalism as a long-past phase and evaluate the capitalist stage of social development condescendingly, we rarely ponder the facts that "capitalism in Russia failed to perform a number of its most important historical functions" and that "we did not inherit its contribution to our historical progress in the form of mechanisms for the self-development and regulation of economic and social life, and this might constitute the basic reason why a number of our problems have mysteriously remained unchanged for decades."[1]

Of the "unlearned lessons" that we have not inherited from capitalism, we should first mention an attitude toward work. Having condemned and discarded the mechanism of the direct dependence of an individual's standard of living on the results of his labor worked out by this mode of production (and capitalism, by the way, has refined this mechanism to the hilt) and the interest in quality that comes from hard (even cruel) competition in the labor market, we, without wanting to, of course, have taught people not to work conscientiously and well and have replaced true love of work and enthusiasm with make-believe slogans and appeals.

Yes, we didn't have enough time after the abolition of serfdom to teach people how to work well during the relatively brief period of development of Russian capitalism, which preserved the rural commune in its early feudal form. Neither a better attitude on the part of society toward the human personality nor a sense of pride on the part of everyone in his work managed to take root. Russia was always full of "lefties," of unique miracle-working craftsmen, but bourgeois democratic traditions never developed stable habits of quality work, self-reliance, or collective as well as individual responsibility among the masses.

In comparing "our" and "Western" systems in his essay "Abroad," Mikhail Saltykov-Shchedrin noted that "they" "have one very important advantage, namely the general acknowledgment that the human is characteristic of human beings." From this acknowledgment "should follow everything reasonable and good on which social stability is based. Only then when this acknowledgment becomes an accomplished fact will our manners become better, will human savagery become tamed, will the plunderers disappear, will the sciences and arts prosper, and will even the 'wild oats' begin to thrive."[2]

Forced labor has more than once demonstrated both its inefficiency and its incompatibility with love for work. Capitalism ultimately rose to the top because slave and serf

---

[1] I. Ariyevich, "Unlearned Lessons," *Novoye Vremya*, 1988, no. 39, p. 24 [cited by Lapitsky].

[2] Mikhail Saltykov-Shchedrin [a noted nineteenth-century Russian satirist], *Selected Works*, vol. 5 of 7 (Moscow, 1948), p. 145 [cited by Lapitsky].

dependence proved to be inefficient. Command-administrative methods of managing people have been discarded, but our society is far behind and is close to precapitalist relations. The acknowledgment of "the human in humans" of which the great writer spoke is the way that leads to love for work, conscientiousness, entrepreneurship, and thrift.

In our eyes the enthusiasm and hopes of the first prewar years were replaced by a general lack of faith and loss of ideals. For many people the country has essentially turned into no one's. The loss of prestige of work has been tragically reflected in society. Sayings thought up by wags, such as "It doesn't matter where I work, it only matters that I don't work," "He who doesn't work eats, and he who works drinks," and "If vodka interferes with your work, quit working," did not come from nowhere. The lack of incentives, the firmly rooted wage leveling, and low wages have infected many, as the political and social commentator Gennady Lisichkin put it so accurately, with "a grabbing mania." But money grubbing and greed, as one can quite easily see, do not make enthusiasm for work possible.

Not so long ago we rarely took a critical look at ourselves and never related our domestic problems to global problems, and we erected a brick wall in front of ourselves to shut ourselves off from the rest of the world. We flattered ourselves, exalting everything that was ours and cursing everything that transpired in the capitalist world. Our ideology considered it a given that "our" individual was a "head above" anyone from "over there." And the same applied to work. But reality proved to be quite different.

Soviet commentators have written quite a bit about "the American dream," a specific notion of an individual's success in life. This notion grew out of the tradition of individualist ideology and psychology that emerged as capitalism developed in the United States. This dream, although it may be unattainable to many people, still remains a bright star and an attractive incentive for all of one's life and a goal which one must do everything one can to achieve. Yesterday's downtrodden "little man" soon became an independent farmer, while yesterday's unskilled worker became a wealthy entrepreneur. Sociologists call this "upward mobility."

We cannot help but mention the influence of Protestantism as a very important factor inclining Americans toward entrepreneurship and pragmatism. Alexis de

Tocqueville, a keen observer of America in the nineteenth century, wrote that the entire destiny of America was contained in the first Puritan who landed on these shores. The Protestants worked out their own system of values, traditions, style, philosophy, and rhetoric: simplicity to the point of asceticism; faith which became inner experience; life which became realized duty; and work, saving, and exactness which became benefactors.

Protestant dogmas condemned shiftless poverty and submission to it, comparing it to a disease and a surrender to fate. They considered the indicators of true faith to be not so much zeal in carrying out religious prescriptions and serving the heavens but rather the honest fulfillment of one's obligations on earth, which involved increasing abundance by means of tireless work. They believed that this made a person more pleasing to God than anything else. It's not surprising that the Protestant immigrants to the United States were subsequently called "the pioneers of skilled labor."

But one doesn't even have to cross the ocean; it is sufficient to meet with American scholars in our own country. This writer has more than once been astounded by the capacity for work of visiting scholars in our country, who efficiently utilize any free time they have (when they are not attending conferences, symposia, and meetings or excursions) for their work. Some scholars select material for their next articles or monographs and at times carry quite weighty books with them in their suitcases across the ocean (it would seem that they're going back to build houses), while others prepare for forthcoming lectures which they will deliver at their universities upon their arrival from the Soviet Union, while still others don't waste any time although they've only come for a week! And, as they take an active part in conferences and in other numerous activities and work in the intervals between them in the rooms and halls of their hotels, they seem never to suffer any fatigue and always look hearty and fresh.

A work ethic is not something that is frozen and handed down for all time. It must be constantly stimulated. Any regression inevitably entails the attenuation of work skills and traditions. To a certain extent this has also taken place in the United States and in particular is reflected in the quality of American goods. This has become one of the most important national problems faced by the United States.

Previously, American producers set the tone in the world arena with essentially no competition. In today's conditions of intense rivalry with Japanese and West European companies, American companies are compelled to operate in different circumstances where what's called the "human factor" comes to the forefront.

The best companies combine an interest in satisfying the customer in the best way possible with a respectful attitude toward their own employees, a democratic style of management, trust in the abilities of blue- and white-collar workers, and efforts to make their work easier and to inspire them to greater achievements. The American researchers Tom Peters and R. Waterman have called this "productivity from the person."

Treat people like adults and partners, respect their dignity, and be attentive to them. Look at them and not at capital investment as the primary source of industrial growth. These are the kinds of appeals made by exemplary companies. Researchers have focused special attention on the fact that the companies that are successful treat people with dignity.

A key image of RMI (a subsidiary of U.S. Steel and National Distillers), like that of many other companies, is a smiling face, which can be seen on company forms, over factory gates, on the company's advertising logos, and on workers' hard hats. "As many smiles as possible, as many handshakes as possible, know everybody and call them by name" are well-known characteristics of the American political and business establishment. This is a splendidly formulated technique for stimulating work activity at factories and shops.

Daniel, who goes by the nickname of Big Jim and is the chief executive officer of the aforementioned company, is constantly side by side with the workers, exchanging jokes with them, knowing every one of two thousand workers, and paying quite a bit of attention to the trade union. The chairman of a union local gave him the following praise: "He invites us to his meetings and keeps us up to date, which never happened at other plants."

Of course, it's not the case that Big Jim is a great friend of the workers: His interest in human relations is in no way altruism and is dictated by his conviction that the company's profits will grow with this kind of approach to business. But at the same time we cannot help but admit that humane relations in industry are much better than inhumane relations.

First of all, the incentives are quite diverse and are not only material: Morale incentives are also extensively practiced. In the lobby of IBM's finance office in New York there is no "Board of Honor" like we are accustomed to seeing, but there is a glass display case with photographs of all the office's employees over which there is a sign that reads: "It's All Up to People." V. Magun has rightly observed in this regard that the point is "not the best people," and "not the real people," but all the people and every employee in an office, factory, or any undertaking.

Although today people speak much less often about the traditional American love for work than about the Japanese love for work, for example, the Americans' attitude toward work could serve as an example for many people.

The fact that many Americans are now working not only better but also more than they did before is to a great extent due to the problem of unemployment, which got worse in the 1980s and threatened many people with the loss of their jobs. *Time* magazine has written that wage workers are constantly saying that they would prefer an even longer workday and even greater income to more leisure time and lower wages.

One TV viewer asked our international correspondents the question: "Why is there an abundance of goods in many countries but not in ours?" Alexander Bovin, a political correspondent for the newspaper *Izvestiya*, responded briefly: "Because we don't work as well."

In order to work better, we will have to study both our own experience and accomplishments and the accomplishments of other countries. The businesslike style, skills, and efficient organization of labor—everything positive created on American soil—could and should be applied on a new basis in our country.

19

Finding a Steward for the Land

Georgy Podlesskikh

Moskva
no. 10, October 1989

This round table discussion sponsored by the journal *Moskva* explores the complexities surrounding the questions of land, land use, and property rights in Soviet agriculture and reveals the wide gap between the views of conservatives and liberals. It appears that these issues are even more complicated now than they were in czarist Russia. The participants agree on one thing: The village needs vital assistance with social problems.

Arkady Veprev (chairman of the Supreme Soviet Committee on Agrarian Issues and Food, and director of the Nazarov State Farm): Our paramount task is to prepare a law on land and land use. In our opinion, our country's major misfortunes are due to a devil-may-care attitude toward the land. Only fly-by-nighters could act this way, thinking, "After me, the deluge." But who will think of our children and our grandchildren? Without any concern for or ability to care for the land, we've been grabbing it from the peasants. To convince yourself of this, all you have to do is look at two statistics. Just twenty years ago there was more than a hectare [2.47 acres] of farmland for every inhabitant of the country. But now we've reached a point where there are only eighty hundredths of a hectare per person. In the last few years, due to our shameless mismanagement of the land, our waste of water, and our destruction of thousands and thousands of so-called unpromising villages, the country has lost about twenty-five million hectares of farmland, which has become overgrown with scrub and has practically disappeared from agricultural use.

Another distress and concern of ours is the peasantry, which is completely and utterly socially defenseless. Nobody lives worse than the peasant. When I met with the constituents of my territorial district before the elections, I found out that we have about one doctor for every five thousand residents in our rural areas. But the picture is quite different in any former district seat, which produces absolutely nothing but has a district committee, a district council, and the institutions and agencies that service them. For example, the town of Nazarov has sixty thousand residents, and there are about three hundred doctors there.

Alexei Yemelyanov (People's Deputy of the USSR and department chairman at Moscow State University): There are two basic things that agriculture cannot live without, namely the peasant and the land, and we have put both of them in the emergency room. How can we save them? What can we do with our legislative authority and our right to monitor the enforcement of the laws we make?

First of all we must legally define the right of property and the conditions under which the land is provided to the person who tills it. Only then will leasing agreements begin to function properly to resolve the main problem of making a man the proprietor of his land. And this means that the land will not be thrown into the common pot. Within collective farms and state farms any form of management should require that the land have an owner and be assigned to small groups, although this still doesn't constitute a true leasing agreement whereby individual peasants would manage farms outside the collective farms and state farms.

The question is usually posed this way: Who's the lessee and who's the lessor? The lessee could be a collective farm or a state farm, or individual peasant farms within them, taking technology into consideration.

But who could be the lessor? It's our job to give this its first genuine legal basis. At present the Lease Law, which was first adopted a year ago, and the decree of April 7 supposedly indicate very clearly that a collective farm, state farm, or local agencies of Soviet power may be lessors. Theoretically this is the case. But in most areas of the country local agencies of Soviet power have no free land in the national land accounts. This means that for all intents and purposes the land is assigned to collective farms and state farms, and only they can lease it. Consequently, the decision to lease land or not depends on the farm or, more bluntly, on the director of the particular collective farm or state farm. And this is a violation of common sense.

Another issue that deserves attention is the issue of lease payments. Once we permit individual peasant farming, the economic conditions, including land use conditions, should be the same for everyone. But in reality we encounter scandals everywhere we turn. For example, let's say that a collective farm or a state farm gets practically nothing per hectare. If a lessee were to lease this land, the collective farm would drive up his rent until he screamed. And the price he paid for equipment would be just as bad. But legally everything would seem OK—land would be provided—but in fact it would be the same old recipe: the economic repression and ruin of substantial peasant farms. Could we really reconcile ourselves to such a situation out there? After all, if we would look at the situation soberly, we would see that in our dying nonblack-soil region we should give away land at no cost or even pay anyone willing to take it.[1] There's no one tilling it now, and entire farms are becoming overgrown with weeds and shrubs.

In reality the problem is that nobody particularly wants to take the land and work it. And that's why I wouldn't even begin to raise the issue of private property on land. Now we are faced with the much more important issue of property in the form of resources, buildings, tractors, farm products, and everything else.

Ivar Rayg (People's Deputy of the USSR and senior scholar at the Institute of Economics of the Estonian Academy of Sciences): The basic problem in the countryside is the problem of power. How can we free the rural worker from the exploitation of the central authorities? A certain contingent of any bureaucracy may be considered exploiters. A special policy has been implemented by which surplus value was almost completely confiscated and turned over to other sectors of the economy. This constitutes exploitation of the countryside in its purest form. In order to put an end to it, we must carry out land reform. The power of the bureaucracies and monopolies must be replaced by genuine popular power, by the power of local agencies of self-government. The economic basis for this should be the transfer of land ownership to the agencies of local government and the creation of a system of peasant farms, associations, cooperatives, and combinations of all of the above. We need a new model, a fundamentally new model.

With respect to the private peasant farm, it in no way contradicts socialism and Leninist views. We must not go against life's truth. At one session of the Supreme Soviet, Comrade Victor Nikonov cited statistics on the growth in

---

[1]Nonblack soil refers to regions of European Russia with mediocre or very poor topsoil, in contrast to the black-soil region of very rich topsoil encompassing the south of European Russia and the Ukraine.

agricultural yields over the past twenty-five years in different countries. In countries with private property, yields have risen 100 to 200 percent over the past quarter of a century. In socialist countries with cooperative property, yields have risen 50 percent. But we haven't improved our yields in twenty-five years. After all, these are facts which are impossible to dispute! We need to approach obsolete dogmas creatively and to develop Leninist views. In my opinion we must now adopt a land decree and turn over land to local agencies of self-government. This decree could be prepared very quickly so that it could go into effect in the fall. But a law would take much longer to prepare. It will take years, because there are so many fine points that would have to be coordinated with different agencies such as the State Committee on Nature and other organizations. But a land decree could be adopted immediately as a political act, and we could change to a new system for managing agriculture. We've been trying for fifty, sixty, seventy years and haven't gotten anywhere, so how much longer will we have to wait? The old system's not working. We have to rebuild everything from the bottom up.

Peasant farms are not just economics, as some people have said. Peasant farms constitute a culture of labor, the way of life of the rural population—their way of thinking, communing with nature, ethics, everything. We must rebuild a system of private peasant farms, while of course making the necessary compromises with reality. Not everyone can be a proprietor. This would be utopia. Human qualities in and of themselves make it impossible for everyone to be an owner. That's why we'll have to combine different forms. We could have state and cooperative farms, and if particular collective farms are good, collective farms. I'm very much in favor of communes, or soviet farms. Sweden has the kind of communes that we imagine as socialism. In Sweden, 80 percent of the income the peasants receive is distributed on a centralized basis. But in our country we simply have hired hands, hired workers.

Vasily Boyev (general director of the Lenin Academy of Agricultural Sciences' Scientific Center): For sixty years in a row we've said that agriculture is the foundation of the economy and that the party and the state must pay more attention to it. Delegates to the 27th Party Congress talked about this, and all the subsequent plenary sessions of the party's Central Committee gave priority to agricultural development.

From the audience: In words.

Boyev: Yes, unfortunately, on too many occasions our deeds have not matched our words. And today we are once again encountering a complete misunderstanding of the main problems of economic development. We are painting ourselves into a corner because of our complete ignorance of the laws of expanded production, the advantages of a socialist economy, and scientific and technical advances.

We must face the facts honestly. So, Comrade Rayg, how can you say the things you've been saying? You've said that we have a socialist system, large collective farms and state farms, and that's why everything's so bad. But in the West, where they have small peasant farms, it's OK.

Well, just compare the statistics, and if you don't have them, come to me and I'll show you the dynamics. In Yugoslavia, Poland, Hungary, Czechoslovakia, and East Germany, the best figures do not pertain just to an increase in production, but rather to efficiency and the solution of social problems. East Germany and Czechoslovakia—that is, countries that have truly made use of the objective advantages of large-scale socialist production—have agricultures at a very high level of development. So why are you obscuring our understanding of the problem? You're cutting yourself off from a realistic understanding of things.

Just take the Nazarov State Farm, directed by Arkady Filimonovich Veprev. Was his farm really in a better position than the others? His land isn't any better and his funds aren't any bigger than any of the other state farms in Krasnoyarsk Territory; in fact, they're even smaller. If all of our agriculture had reached the level of the Nazarov State Farm, we would have completely resolved all of our food problems. Instead of purchasing forty million tons of grain, we would have been able to supply the world market with sixty-five million tons of grain per year. Can you imagine what the global situation would be now?

Now I would like to turn to Alexei Yemelyanov. You're a living witness, so to speak, and you and I have taken part in devising splendid solutions for the problems of agriculture. But all of them either became hopelessly entangled in red tape or were carried out enthusiastically but stupidly. As the proverb says: "Make a fool pray to God." If a directive were put out, people would plant corn close to the North Pole and would either eliminate all the fallow land or restore all of it, whether it was necessary or not. And if you tried to avoid carrying out the order, you'd have to turn over your party card immediately. After all, there was a political emphasis placed on these activities.

But now everything's crystal clear: leasing. Let's have leasing everywhere. But if somebody were to tell me of just one farm that was operating efficiently on a lease, I would drop everything immediately and go there.

Veprev: Everything that the mass media is talking about is not leasing, but a parody of it.

Boyev: But just try to explain it to the hot-to-trot innovators who only consider their own opinions. And a lessee steps forward in a collective farm and demands, "Give me this plot, I'll take it." And they tell him, "Listen, there'll be a problem with crop rotation." "Crop rotation! So that means you're against leasing? But what did Gorbachev say? And what did Yemelyanov say?" That's how elementary good sense is betrayed by the political situation.

In my opinion, the time has come to define all our priorities clearly. We've prepared a memorandum to the government which demonstrates the impossibility of setting up leaseholder farms on abandoned land. Any attempts to do so would be condemned to failure if fifty-thousand-ruble cottages were not built, if roads were not built, if medical services and telephone lines were not provided, or if all the children's needs were not taken care of. In the United States, for example, 120,000 school buses take farmers' children every morning to places where they are fed, looked after, and amused, and in the evenings they take them back home. In this case American farmers have no problems whatsoever. We have to know and understand this and be basically honest about it.

But in our country a lessee who's decided to run his own farm outside a collective farm or state farm and thus outside its infrastructure has knowingly taken on a hopeless task. For example, we set up a special lease subdivision in Pytalovo. Gorbachev gave it a good word, which is why we gave it the appropriate certificate. But now fifteen of our scientists are tearing their hair out in Pytalovo trying to get this leasing arrangement to work out.

There's no doubt in my mind that the socialist system of managing the economy has colossal advantages over any other system. The problem is that for many long years we've bound it hand and foot with innumerable decrees, guidelines, and instructions. And instead of untying all these knots, we've suddenly tried to pull agriculture back into the past without any understanding of the essence of scientific and technical progress.

And here Comrade Rayg says that large farms have not proven themselves and that highly productive agricultural machinery is unnecessary. But, Ivar Helmutovich [Rayg], take a look at the American farmer. He has 300 acres of soybeans, 370 acres of corn, 80 head of cattle, and 5 tractors, ranging from twenty to three hundred horsepower. Isn't that a large-scale operation? And, I might add, an efficient operation?

Veprev: It seems that no one was ready to change anything. What was important was to open up the valve a bit so that the peasants could blow off the dissatisfaction that they'd stored up.

Yemelyanov: But no farms, be they peasant farms, collective and state farms, or leasing within the collective farm, will work unless we scrap the current economic system. The starting point is the economic system. Here's a question: Why can we literally count such farms as Veprev's in this country on our fingers? Why can't the other farms operate in the same way?

Boyev: Well, you answer the question, and then everything will become clear.

Yemelyanov: I'll say again that the whole business lies in the economic system. Academician Leonid Abalkin has said that we live no worse than we work. Of course, that's true. But we must put a different emphasis on it: Why have we reduced the people to a condition in which they work so poorly and don't make enough to live on? That's the question.

Veprev: I think this lack of self-reliance has led us to these kinds of outrages. We're incapable of figuring out what democracy is and what anarchy is. But we clearly like anarchy better, so that's what we're involved in. Our native anarchy and our obsession with gross output has led us to uncompleted construction projects.

Rayg: I would like to answer Vasily Romanovich Boyev, who asked me a question. First of all I must say that no one in Estonia is proposing to eliminate collective and state farms by some sort of overnight decree. This would be unthinkable. But we must set our sights on what will be in the future.

Boyev: Even here in Moscow, Central Television is broadcasting appeals to eliminate collective farms and state farms.

Rayg: But where I'm from we haven't. That's just a fact. Let's go on. You cited statistics. But I can't understand why you dwelled on Yugoslavia, East Germany, and Poland. After all, they are also relatively underdeveloped countries. Why not take, for example, Austria, Sweden, Finland, Denmark, and West Germany?

And here's what's fundamentally important. In 1940 the agriculture of Finland and the agriculture of Estonia were at the same stage of development. Estonia exported half of its agricultural production—half! Estonia's products were competitive in London, in Paris, and in any country. Now they aren't competitive anywhere, and there's nothing to export. Economic indicators in Estonia are much worse than are those of all its close neighbors.

It would probably be methodologically improper to generalize from a specific example. You've referred to Veprev's farm. But Arkady Filimonovich [Veprev] is a phenomenon, a hero. Not everyone can be a hero, in the same way that not everyone can be a proprietor. There are very few farms like Veprev's. They are the exceptions. But we're talking about the rule. It's been pointed out that we have collective and state farms that have high crop and milk yields. But our record for the amount of milk per cow is ten thousand, while in the United States the record is fifteen thousand. And the United States doesn't buy grain from us, we buy grain from it. So how could you say that the American farming system is in a crisis?

Boyev: You completely misunderstood me. The farmer system is flourishing, but due to the elimination of unproductive small farmers, which account for only 30 percent of all American farmers.

Rayg: But the American agricultural industry has developed on the basis of individual farms.

Boyev: But there's something else you must understand. Small farms are going under. Large and very large farms are flourishing.

Rayg: There are other countries besides the United States. Why do you use only America as an example? We're not Americans. And one mustn't conclude that if small farmers are going under in America they would be uncompetitive here. One more thing: I was very fond of your idea that we must eliminate the dictatorship over the producer. But after all the producer is the peasant. This means that we have to give the peasant freedom.

Boyev: So, what's a peasant? The chairman of a collective farm's a peasant, his leading specialists are peasants, and his rank-and-file machinery operators are also peasants.

Rayg: Then I'll elaborate. A producer is someone who produces a product and works in the production of material goods. And a producer should not have some agency over him or any kind of boss at all.

Boyev: If that's your opinion of agricultural development, the only thing I can do is spread my hands in dismay. In essence you want to pull us down the path of total anarchy.

Rayg: You're confused because you're unwilling and unable to renounce bureaucratic methods of running the economy.

Boyev: When necessary, the United States has employed centralized and rigid planning. But they know when to stop. Without rejecting a planned centralized system, the Americans have gotten far, far away from having their president travel around the country and teach farmers how to plant corn. We must clearly see the advantages and the shortcomings of planned and unplanned farming and of large- and small-scale farming. Then we'll be able to talk specifics.

Rayg: The advantages of the small farm are particularly obvious in raising livestock. This has been demonstrated by global experience.

Boyev: If we take the agro-industrial complex as a whole, small farms could have no advantages. This would be objectively impossible.

Rayg: I have to disagree with you. The argument that small farms are incapable of resolving the social problems of the countryside is also groundless. For example, there are no large farms in Finland or Sweden, but the peasants in these countries live in a way that we can only dream of.

Boyev: We must go from words to deeds and try to do something. Let me cite an example. Last year eleven American states were struck by drought. While the drought was still going on and before the farm economy fell apart, [President Ronald] Reagan ordered the allocation of $4.6 billion worth of assistance. The money was found. Businesslike people got together and solved the problem.

Veprev: Vasily Romanovich! Why are we comparing ourselves to America? We should be comparing ourselves to Ethiopia!

Rayg: Our cashbox is empty. Where did these billions come from? The cashbox is empty.

Veprev: We won't budge an inch if we don't make substantial investments in agriculture. There won't be any farmers under leaky roofs. They just won't stay! That's why our state farm has proceeded to build two or three farms, to spend five to six hundred thousand rubles, and to create the kind of conditions that a farmer in the West has.

Another very important matter. Everyone knows that garden plots are used more efficiently than publicly farmed land—some people say ten to twelve times more efficiently, and others say four to five times. That is why we should provide city dwellers with as much land as they want to take and are able to work. And the land should be in a place near the city, not where garden plots are now, 100 to 150 kilometers away in a place that's impossible to get to. If we do this, we'll have enough potatoes, vegetables, and even fruits and berries. It looks now like someone needs us to suffer from shortages of these commodities. This is even truer, I believe, of meat, a problem to which a great deal of thought has been given. In all the small towns, which are not too different from villages, people could keep broilers, pigs, and cows. We must provide plots to all who want them and improve them by providing water and roads and by posting security guards. If we didn't post security guards, of course, everything would be hauled away. And I must tell you that the shortages of potatoes, vegetables, and meat would be eliminated overnight. I tried to push for a resolution of this problem in my territory and district but without any success. People tried to convince me that the workers didn't want it. But if you meet with the workers they'll tell you that they haven't been given any land. And if they have gotten it, they've had to haul truckloads of humus there. Well, who would agree to that?

Hence our most important task today is to find proprietors in the village, in the factory, and at the collective farm. In the final analysis, we must find individual proprietors. If we don't, we won't resolve anything. But why couldn't there be a collective proprietor within the structure in which he works, such as the state farm? And as soon as a market appears in the country any operation, be it a factory or a collective farm or a state farm, must be divided up into shares of stock which would be sold to the employees of the operation. Vasily Romanovich, you haven't said a word about American businesses. In America practically all businesses have been sold to their employees in the form of shares of stock. And there every worker is a proprietor, more of a proprietor than we are. We know that the mere conversion of a business into a joint stock company leads to a 15 to 20 percent improvement in labor productivity. But we are simply hired hands at our own businesses.

And I'd also like to say: Comrades, could any country live without working? The folk saying is right: By your labor is your honor. And there's no need for us to make endless references to Karl Marx. That won't fill our wallets. Our only salvation is work and more work. We must establish a six-day work week and an eight-hour day. We are also competing with someone. Perhaps there are international treaties. Perhaps. But international treaties are for the well fed and the well clothed. And we have a long way to go before we get there.

20

Help! The Dollars Are Coming!

Sergei Novikov

The Literary Gazette International
no. 1, August 1990

Sergei Novikov, an economist at Moscow University, delivers here a sermon to the Soviet public, which often objects to the free enterprise zones and to joint ventures with Western capitalists. The information in this article was kept secret from the public for years. In a historical sketch, he emphasizes the crucial role foreign investment played in the industrial development of Russia, especially during the first years after the revolution. (However, Novikov could have cited many more positive current examples of foreign investment in his country.) The conservatives, who are largely responsible for the sad state of the Soviet economy, have been especially vigorous in mobilizing public opinion against Western assistance. Novikov urges Soviet citizens and the authorities to change their attitudes.

The ancients were right: "Sometimes there's nothing more harmful than public opinion."

The election program of the bloc of Russian socio-patriotic movements published in the *Literaturnaya Rossiya* weekly contains calls for an end to the economic occupation of our country by foreign companies and for opposing economic concessions and zones of free trade and enterprise. These "patriotic" sentiments were expressed at the Congress of People's Deputies by the celebrated Russophile writers Vasily Belov and Valentin Rasputin, who demanded the stemming of the "pernicious economic and cultural influence of the West on our multiethnic Russia."

These calls have already had their effect. Plans for the first free economic zone in this country, to be set up in Novgorod Region, have been turned down by the public, as represented by Novgorod's branch of the United Working People's Front.

What's happening to us, dear fellow countrymen?

On all sides we hear complaints, screams, and moans: "Life's becoming unbearable! Out of compassion, do something!" But as soon as there appears a radical recipe for improving the economic situation, we reject it out of hand.

Judge for yourselves. The Novgorod free economic zone project provides for massive foreign investment in three basic fields: (1) development of foreign and domestic tourism; (2) manufacture and sale of videocassettes, videodisks, holograms, and albums of masterpieces of domestic and foreign art; (3) large-scale manufacture, sale, rental, and servicing of videos and other electronic equipment. The plan provides not just for the construction of industrial facilities based on state-of-the-art technology. It also envisions expanded food production and construction of housing and of cultural and consumer service establishments.

Who could have anything against such a plan? But here is what we read in a leaflet of the Novgorod branch of the United Working People's Front: If such a zone is opened, they claim, "the city and region will be inundated with profiteers and prostitutes; Novgorod's plants and factories within the consortium will be bossed around by transnational corporations; in the event of economic disaster Novgorod Region will be racked by social upheavals; next to foreigners, local Novgorod residents will be in the position of second-class citizens; there will be growing inequality and suppression of patriotic feelings." Such are the arguments.

There is no disputing, of course, that profiteering and prostitution are social ills that must be combatted. But just imagine what would happen if we decided to wall ourselves in: Would we have no profiteering and prostitution? Alas, these ills don't come from the West. They are engendered by our internal social and economic problems.

What we are being offered is a new lease on life for a backward part of Russia that could be turned into a major tourist and industrial center with a developed infrastructure. But no, we're too proud to accept it.

Let our economy be a shambles, let the natural environment be on the brink of disaster, "We won't give up a single inch of Russian land!" This is Novgorod's motto. Won't give it up to whom? Who wants to have it, our long-suffering, ruined land? And yet xenophobia is gathering speed. Moscow residents have already turned down plans to build a second complex of the Sovincenter, which could give the Soviet state an annual revenue of twenty million American dollars.

Actually, we economists are also to blame for the public's phobia of foreign capital. Wasn't it us who drummed into people's heads that Western capital is the source of all socioeconomic problems, polarization of society, brutal exploitation of the local labor force, and export of superprofits? No wonder the man in the street is panicking: "They want to put the yoke of foreign exploitation on us! They are threatening to restore capitalism in our country!"

Let me remind the zealots for preserving Great Russia's purity that in the past this country had a rich history of economic contacts with the West.

Let's take a look at Russia's prerevolutionary experience. By 1913, more than four billion rubles had been invested in Russia by foreign companies, which made more than 40 percent of all investment in our economy. A mammoth sum at the time. Almost half the investment in industry had come from abroad. Most of the railroads in Russia had been built on foreign loans. Perhaps not everyone knows that the development of the iron-and-coal production area in the south of Russia (now the Donets Coal Basin, or Donbass) was started by an Englishman, John Ewes. In 1869 he signed an agreement with the Russian government to build a large rail manufacturing plant that would use iron ore from Krivoy Rog and coal from the Donets Basin. He invested three million rubles in it. British capital, combined with the huge demand for railroads, worked a miracle: By 1890, Donbass plants produced about half the iron and steel made in the whole of Russia. Russia's iron production jumped from seventh place on world charts to fourth, leaving behind Austria-Hungary, France, and Belgium.

Russia's entire power industry was in effect built on foreign capital. Russian affiliates of German, American, and British companies manufactured the entire range of products for the power industry, from wires to generators. Moreover, foreign investors not only built and equipped large modern factories but also developed the social sphere.

What has foreign capital given Russia? Between 1890 and 1913, industrial production in Russia increased fourfold! Foreign capital acted as the locomotive of industry, encouraging Russian entrepreneurs to invest. Russia started manufacturing its own locomotives, rails, harvesters, and high-grade iron and steel.

After the Bolshevik Revolution of 1917, the Soviet government started establishing new contacts with foreign companies. As early as the spring of 1918, the 1st Congress of Economic Councils of the Russian Federation set forth the basic principles of Soviet concession policy, and in November

1920 the Council of People's Commissars passed a decree on the general economic and legal terms of concessions.

At the time, the granting of concessions to Western companies did not constitute a concession to capitalism as such or a step toward restoration of capitalism in Russia. On the contrary, Lenin saw it as an economically expedient measure planned to last for thirty to sixty years.

In 1921 to 1928 (the period when the Soviet economy developed most dynamically) Western companies had more than 160 concessions and joint ventures in Russia in mining, forestry, chemicals, electrical engineering, and trade. Foreign-owned factories also manufactured consumer goods. Although the number of foreign factories was small compared to the whole of Russia's economy, they had a tangible impact in certain key areas of the economy. The famous Swedish joint-stock company SKF alone contributed 30 percent of all the roller and ball bearings manufactured in Russia. Another Swedish company, Erickson, which supplied telephones to the whole of Russia before the First World War, helped set up automatic telephone exchanges in Moscow, Leningrad, Kiev, and Kharkov, while the German company Telefunken furnished the equipment and know-how to develop television in this country.

In general, foreign concessions and joint ventures in Russia brought about a dramatic increase in industrial production. This gave rise to healthy competition between concessional and Soviet state-owned enterprises, forcing the latter to keep up with Western standards.

But, alas, the concessions boom was short-lived. When Stalin came to power and started phasing out Lenin's New Economic Policy, he anathematized all the progressive forms of involvement with foreign resources. And for many decades economic relations with the West were reduced to trade alone.

Even today, after the government has permitted the establishment of joint ventures in the USSR, the contribution of foreign capital to the Soviet economy is negligible by world standards—a mere $1.5 billion annually. (Compare this with the annual $200 billion invested by foreign firms in the U.S. economy.)

Having made a number of decisions on the development of foreign economic contacts, we decided that foreign capital and technology would immediately flood the Soviet market. But this has not happened.

Foreign companies are holding back from large investments in our economy. How come?

From the viewpoint of the needs of our Western partners, the USSR is of limited practical interest (except, perhaps, as a source of raw materials and fuel). The promise of an unlimited Soviet market has not so far attracted too many foreign partners, because they find they cannot take their profits out of the country because the ruble is not a convertible currency. Another advantage of investing in the USSR—cheap labor—often comes to nothing, because our workers and engineers lack the qualifications, the discipline, and the proper respect for another's work and property. We can hardly expect Western capital to flood our economy if our government doesn't adopt an intelligent policy to stimulate foreign investment. And if the local authorities in this country block those few projects that have got off the ground, even this trickle of investment will dry up.

What we need are serious, innovative, creative decisions. In my view, the first thing we should do is return to the practice (time-tested in the 1920s) of concessions—in other words, of setting up foreign-owned capitalist plants and factories in this country. After all, when the Soviet state takes Western loans and credits to build its own enterprises here, it must pay high interest, while concession companies, constituting an oasis of modern production methods and efficiency in a desert of our slovenliness, could become an example to emulate. At the same time, the Soviet state could get considerable revenues in the form of taxes and rent. We should encourage the establishment of such Western enterprises, especially in science-intensive industries and in those manufacturing food and consumer goods.

In the second place, we must expedite the adoption of legislation on foreign investment. Today virtually every country has such legislation. Western companies will invest in our economy only if they are confident that their activities will be protected by Soviet law and will not be influenced by fickle party policy.

It goes without saying that foreign investments won't be a cure-all for the sick Soviet economy. And Western companies, after their previous bitter experience of dealing with us, will be very cautious before investing here again. There is no question, therefore, that we must first of all learn to use our own resources efficiently. At the same time, we cannot expect to turn the Soviet Union into a modern industrialized power (this is not exclusively the dream of the bloc of socio-patriotic movements of Russia—it is the dream of every Soviet citizen) without the capital and experience of Western companies. Our common objective, therefore, should be to convince our public that sweeping bans will lead us nowhere. We've had our fill of extremes.

21

The Risk of Going Over to a Market Economy Is Less Than the Cost of Marking Time

Stanislav Shatalin

Izvestiya
April 22, 1990

Academician Shatalin is one of the few widely respected Soviet economists. He follows in the footsteps of Abel Aganbegyan, Leonid Abalkin, and Nikolai Petrakov as the most important economic adviser to Gorbachev (who, in desperation, changes his advisers frequently). In this interview with Alexander Voznesensky of *Izvestiya*, he unsparingly depicts the sad state of the Soviet economy and the blunders made during the first years of *perestroika*. He defends here a gradual transition to the free market, a point of view he would abandon two months later in favor of a quicker transition.

Voznesensky: Stanislav Sergeyevich, the question submitted to the joint session of the Federation Council and the USSR Presidential Council is very topical. Our economy is "suspended" in the transitional, interim state characterized as a crisis state. There is still no wholesale market, and the retail market has long since ceased to exist. On the other hand, there is a market for coupons, of coupons for coupons, as well as workplace merchandise sales, etc. It seems that soon we, like semiprimitive commodity producers, will go over to simply bartering the products of labor. Why have we come to this stage? Certain countries have begun transformations later than ours but have achieved far more.

Shatalin: It is difficult to answer unequivocally. I am certainly not saying this to avoid giving a direct answer. When people compare our reform with the transformations in the German Democratic Republic or in Hungary, for example, where more has been done in two or three months than we have done in five years of *perestroika*, it is understandable and explicable on an emotional level. But from the viewpoint of a professional economist such conclusions sound flippant, to say the least. This is, above all, because these countries (and I could extend the list of them) are at the center of Europe, where social democratic, economic, and market traditions have long existed, without interruption. Although they have lost something in recent years, the skills and culture of each nation and of their working people have nonetheless been preserved.

Voznesensky: And yet five years have already passed, a considerable time at today's pace of sociopolitical and socioeconomic development.

Shatalin: Forgive me, but once again this is a dilettante approach. Let us be honest and objective. *Perestroika* is into its fifth year. But we formulated the ideas of economic reform only in June 1987, and the first steps were taken only at the beginning of 1988. It is, in my opinion, premature to speak of the failure of a reform that has been under way for just two years. In addition, today it is possible to state almost with confidence that the economic transformations are receiving ever-greater political support. Consequently, the five years of *perestroika* have not been wasted.

Furthermore, throughout the previous decades we gave up a mass of the concepts and virtually destroyed the institutions inherent in a normal market economy. What are prices, inflation, credit, currency exchange rates, and interest rates? You will find few specialists today who have a full grasp of these terms, for generations of Soviet economists have been brought up on quite different concepts. Therefore, before looking for the forces that are slowing down *perestroika* in the Central Committee or in the government (I am not saying that such forces do not exist there), I would suggest that critics—economists in particular—should think about their own competence. The overwhelming majority of them do not understand what a modern market economy is or how to build it. And this is a fact, another of the reasons for the economic reform's slow progress.

I have recently been accused of becoming almost an apologist for Gorbachev, [Nikolai] Ryzhkov, and their program.[1] This is quite wrong. But I realize that even they, who began *perestroika*, cannot—or, if you like, are biologically unable to—instantly change their philosophy and switch from the established way of thinking to the new realities. They, like everyone else, spent decades absorbing the ideas of a

[1]Nikolai Ryzhkov, chairman of the Council of Ministers of the USSR, has been widely blamed for the current economic crisis because of his conservative, centralist positions.

rigid plan and a technocratic approach to resolving economic questions. In criticizing them, we forget about this.

In complaining of the reform's sluggishness we fail to account for one more factor: A large section of the working people is not prepared to accept new technologies and an entire new economic structure as a whole. Our people are talented, but they have forgotten how to work and have grown accustomed to freeloading.

Voznesensky: Does this mean that you disagree with selling everything at free market prices and with the radical economists' proposal to introduce real market relations without delay?

Shatalin: Absolutely, since this would be more terrible than the great crisis of the late twenties and early thirties. What is needed above all is preparation of a well-considered market infrastructure: new financial-credit, monetary, currency, price, and fiscal policies, a banking system (including a reserve system); a social protection mechanism; and much besides. Without all this, only kamikazes seeking simultaneously to destroy the country would introduce a market today.

Voznesensky: The conditions necessary for a switch to a new economy, which you have enumerated, are in fact levers for state regulation of the market.

Shatalin: Naturally. And the degree of state influence on the market in our country must initially be greater than it is in countries that have already traveled this path. For the market has taken shape over millennia before us.

It is, of course, possible to act according to Napoleon's principle: The chief thing is to go into battle, and then we shall see. This sounds fine, and he undoubtedly was a talented military leader. But he battled Russia and got bogged down.

Voznesensky: So, maybe the deterioration in the economy over the past few years is connected with our acting according to the Napoleonic principle: We introduced some elements of the market mechanism, but we failed to create state regulation mechanisms consonant with them, did we not?

Shatalin: We not only failed to create them but also strengthened (I do not know whether intentionally or not) the former management mechanism. We left the majority of ministries, enlarged some of them by merging them, and said: Just coordinate your sector's activity now, and nothing more. But we left all material resources at their disposal; that is, we created still more gigantic monopolies capable of living without any technical progress just by raising prices. At the same time we urged them to struggle against the monopolism of their own enterprises. In my opinion the Soviet economy is the most monopolized economy in the world. This means that we must also think about how to overcome the long-standing monopoly on decision making of the state and its organs.

We have created a totally abnormal *nomenklatura* economy with enterprises under union jurisdiction, union-republic jurisdiction, republic jurisdiction, etc.[2] Today all republics are hampered by enterprises under union jurisdiction. OK, let us hand over the enterprises to the republics. What will change? Nothing! They will simply get new chiefs. To whom are Mitsubishi or General Motors subordinate? The president? Some state or prefecture? No, they are subordinate only to the economic and juridical laws of the state in question.

Therefore, for the time being, the Ukraine, Kirghizia, Lithuania, the Russian Republic, and all the other republics should act as constituent parts of one state; business on their territory has nothing to do with them. Businesses should be governed only by the economy, by the market. The local authority—I repeat—should intervene only when juridical norms are violated. And it should support business if there is an interest in developing it. The basic function of the authority is to tackle social questions—to build roads, to feed the unemployed, to improve medical services and trade.

Voznesensky: Theoretically, the thesis that the overwhelming mass of enterprises should belong exclusively to the economy seems very attractive. But you will agree that, like any theory, it is somewhat abstract. It is still easy to hitch to it the equally theoretically abstract thesis of the entire people's ownership of the means of production. In real life and in economic practice we have to find if not the owners then at least the proprietors of these enterprises. Who are they?

Shatalin: If we were to arrive at normal (from an economic, not an ideological viewpoint) enterprises, I am sure that shared ownership would be the optimum for us.

---

[2]Enterprises under union jurisdiction are directly subordinate to the USSR ministries in Moscow; those under union-republic jurisdiction take orders from both the Moscow ministries and the ministries of the republic in which they are located; enterprises under republic jurisdiction report to their republic's ministries only.

Consequently, the proprietors of enterprises would be shareholders, although this does not sound absolutely correct from the position of pure science. However, there is an invisible obstacle here to our thinking today. By buying shares in the Norilsk combine, for example, I automatically would become a private owner exploiting someone else's labor. And I must not engage in self-deception. No one is opposed to people getting interest on honestly earned money invested in a savings bank. And yet interest is private property just the same.

Voznesensky: The possibility cannot be ruled out that, given their absolutely free sale, shares would be bought up by the representatives of the "shadow economy" [black market]. What about social justice then?

Shatalin: There are many antimonopoly and other measures being applied successfully in many countries. I believe that part of this arsenal could suit us too.

As for the shadow economy, I have my own viewpoint on this. In our present economic situation many of its representatives are clever, businesslike people who profit from the slow and sluggish nature of the socioeconomic system. While this system is still thinking, they are already acting and responding to buyers' needs. The state economy cannot compete with them, but it can suppress them administratively, juridically, with its monopoly on resources, and so forth. This will always be so until we create a normal economy. Of course, the representatives of the shadow economy also include many out-and-out thieves and scoundrels who must be combated. But this is a job for the special units and the law. Catch them, put them behind bars, but remember the Russian saying: "If he has not been caught, he is not a thief." And do not tar everyone with the same brush.

Voznesensky: What is your attitude toward the government's program? Is it possible within its framework to arrive at normal economic relations?

Shatalin: The program approved by the 2nd Congress of People's Deputies suffered from a number of shortcomings: (1) it relied too heavily on the effectiveness of command-administrative methods, which are no longer capable of managing the economy at all successfully; (2) it contained too much unwarranted optimism and too many poorly substantiated macroeconomic and sectoral indicators of the efficiency and use of production resources; and (3) the program contained virtually no realistic market economy methods for enhancing the balanced nature of socioeconomic development.

In the first quarter of 1990 the national economy is not developing as the government program intended. The consumer market is collapsing still further. The chances of increasing the state budget deficit are growing, and living standards are falling.

In this situation the country's leadership has made the important political decision to radicalize the course of the reform and to take more decisive steps toward a regulated, socially protected market.

Voznesensky: Well, what must be done to ensure that the "baby" is not stillborn nonetheless?

Shatalin: What is needed is quick and comprehensive, yet minutely considered, action. At the session everyone spoke of the need for social protection, primarily for the badly off and average-to-well-off sections of the population, and of minimizing the social cost of the economy's radical *perestroika*, although I believe it is still necessary to demonstrate whether this cost must be paid and who must pay it. In any case, to argue professionally, the risk of going over to a regulated market is far less than the cost of marking time.

One of the hardest problems of an efficient transitional period consists—I emphasize—of simultaneously creating a balance in the national economy, improving the economy's financial health by reducing the abnormally large state budget deficit, setting up an anti-inflation mechanism, and giving the economy a dynamic boost on the basis of real pluralism of all ownership institutions (including private ownership in all its forms) by encouraging free enterprise in every possible way. The sectoral production ministries (which are, as we have already said, one of the chief factors of inefficient monopoly development) must be eliminated as quickly as possible. Many people at the session emphasized the needs to "tie up hot money," to increase sharply the issue of shares and bonds, and to sell enterprises' above-normative stocks.

I agree with those who believe that we will not build a modern, efficient economy without large-scale cooperation with the West in various forms: importing consumer goods and capital, and exporting and importing "brains," which unfortunately are now "draining" out of our country without payment. It is necessary to encourage not only the creation of joint ventures but also direct foreign investments on USSR territory. We have had enough of bewailing the government's sale of natural resources with no concern for our grandchildren. It is not this but something else that is terrible: We make rapacious use of these resources, cast them to the winds, and live—unlike the whole civilized world—according to the "dog in the manger" principle and the idea that "if things are going to be bad, then they must be bad for everyone."

Of course, the deficit of consumer goods is terrible, and price formation is wild. But, however concerned I am for the people's lot, a reform of retail prices must be implemented. Probably not this year, but certainly in 1991.[3] Of course, I would like the whole population to be compensated for the expense, but I will say as an economist and a mathematician that this is practically impossible. So I believe that the most highly paid sectors of the population must be excluded from the program to compensate for the growth in prices.

And finally, in my view, we must arrange for the optimum correlation between the results of labor and incomes without ruining—and even by strengthening—the mechanisms to motivate labor and the efficient use of resources. I assert this as a professional: Practically the entire increase in the population's monetary income over the past two years, this entire avalanche-like growth, has not been earned. Hence the growth in the budget deficit and the impoverishment of the consumer market. The reason for this is, on the one hand, the shortsightedness of the economic policy of a leadership which "forgot" that several mechanisms exist for turning cashless money into ready cash.[4] On the other hand, it is also the fault of the enterprises themselves, which fail to display proper economic ethics and live the life of economic timeservers. If I were the head of government, I would say to enterprise leaders and workers today: You accuse us of working badly and of not giving you economic freedom. Well, to some extent you are right. But you, too, work to such low professional standards. You cannot be relied upon, and you have no business ethics.

---

[3]Prices of most consumer goods were raised dramatically on April 2, 1991.

[4]Shatalin is criticizing Gorbachev for allowing the "cashless money," or scrip, that enterprises use for internal exchanges to break into the consumer market.

Voznesensky: And yet, from the position of the worker it is possible to reply: I have been underpaid for decades, and, although I am not producing more output today, for the first time there is a hope of getting as much as I should have been getting all these years.

Shatalin: Yes, it is necessary to increase the wages of many categories of working people even if they have not formally increased their contribution to the national income. This must be done professionally, yet we opened the monetary floodgates for everyone at once in an economically incompetent manner, regardless of even the most immediate consequences. I repeat: The enterprises themselves bear an equal share of the responsibility for the situation that has been created. They used the proclaimed principle of socialist enterprise to enact the worst version of a market economy.

As a result, the situation is as follows: Like it or not, we must limit monetary incomes without, as has been already stated, undermining the mechanisms for motivating labor. More output or services should correspond to more (with no farfetched limitations) pay. For the time being this will have to be done to a considerable extent administratively; in the future the functions of a regulator will inevitably pass to the market.

Voznesensky: How is all that you have said to be viewed: As your personal viewpoint? Or as the opinion of several members of the Presidential Council? Or as a specific program of measures approved by the president?

Shatalin: Beyond a doubt this is not my viewpoint alone. But I think the USSR's president will himself tell the people what he will do.

Voznesensky: Your prognosis for 1990?

Shatalin: **I hope that we will acquire the momentum.**[5]

---

[5]Boldface indicates emphasis in original document.

Bibliography

Antonov, Mikhail. "There Is a Solution!" *Nash Sovremennik*, nos. 8 and 9, 1989.

A conservative political and economic manifesto with a criticism of the reform economists.

Braginsky, Lev. "Where to Take a Bag with Money." *Ogonyok*, no. 42, 1989.

Discusses the Soviet Union's financial system, the most troubled part of its economy.

Bunich, Pavel. "Emergency Measures in Extreme Circumstances." *Ogonyok*, no. 47, 1989.

Suggests the introduction of "leasing" instead of the more radical measure of private property. According to Bunich the worse the current situation is, the greater will be the incentives to carry out radical reforms.

Dyatlov, Andrei. "Tanks Did Not Advance. And It Is regrettable . . . ." *Komsomolskaya Pravda*, June 16, 1990.

A true-life detective story about the cooperative ANT and its unsuccessful attempt to sell the newest Soviet tanks abroad in exchange for consumer goods, a move that prompted one of the most vociferous conservative attacks on reforms.

Gurov, Alexander, and Shchekochikhin, Yuri. "Lion Hunting, or the Fight with a Shadow (Is the Mafia Also Getting Ready for Reform?)" *Literaturnaya Gazeta*, May 23, 1990.

The authors state that the reasons for the mafia's existence are rooted in the Soviet economic and political system and in its connections with the old command system.

Kasatonov, Valentin. "Merchants: What We Are Selling and Trading." *Priroda i Nauka*, no. 9, 1989.

Kasatonov is critical of extensive business relations with the West. He believes that Soviet scientists readily give away significant military secrets and that the West is trying to sell the USSR outdated technology. KGB chief Vladimir Kryuchkov repeated the main arguments of this article in his television appearance on December 22, 1990.

Kostikov, Viacheslav. "In Crowd and Above Crowd." *Izvestiya*, May 28, 1990.

Discusses the artificial relationship between power and the people. Empty slogans lauding workers and peasants have only succeeded in corrupting them.

Likhanov, Dmitry. "People Zan Den." *Ogonyok*, no. 47, 1989.

Reveals the plight of Vietnamese workers in the Soviet Union.

Rytov, Yuri. "A Critique of Reform and the 'Critical Mass' of Its Successes." *Pravitelstvennyi Vestnik*, no. 13, 1990.

In this interview, Leonid Abalkin defends the need to introduce a market economy and discusses the preconditions for its functioning.

Selyunin, Vasily. "The Burden of Actions." *Novy Mir*, no. 5, 1989.
Discusses the ecological catastrophe in the Aral Sea brought about by efforts to increase cotton harvests and resulting in the undermined health of thousands and a children's mortality rate of 100 per 1000. The author argues that the four people who signed for the project bear primary responsibility—not the system and the ministries.

———. "Planned Anarchy or a Balance of Interests?" *Znamya*, no. 11, 1989.
On Soviet bureaucracy and the planned economy.

Sharyi, Grigory. "Peasants Do Not Have Time for Meetings." *Molodaya Gvardiya*, no. 1, 1990.
A People's Deputy's defense of collective farms.

Spandaryan, Victor, and Shmelyov, Nikolai. "On Expanding Reform in the Area of External Trade." *Mirovaya ekonomika i mezhdunarodnye otnosheniya*, no. 9, 1989.
A discussion of the importance of improving and developing foreign economic ties.

Tikhonov, Vladimir. "To Live without Illusions." *Ogonyok*, no. 36, 1989.
Academician Tikhonov suggests the denationalization of state property in cities and villages as the only solution to the current economic problems.

Tiksin, V. "Let's Be Frank." *Molodaya Gvardiya*, no. 3, 1990.
A strong warning to those reformers who would like to see private property introduced in the USSR. For the militia, the KGB, and conservatives, this signifies the restoration of bourgeois ideology.

Tsvetov, Vladimir. "When the Dead Grab the Living." *Ogonyok*, no. 49, 1989.
The party *apparat* cannot shed their ideological encasement, which prevents the success of economic reforms.

Vinogradov, Boris. "Nature Asks for Protection." *Kommunist Vooruzhennykh Sil*, no. 19, 1989.
Discusses Soviet ecological problems associated with the irrigation agency Minvodkhoz.

Zhuk, Viktor, and Shteinbok, Mark. "The Compatibility Test." *Ogonyok*, no. 21, 1989.
A vivid comparison between the operations of an Austrian firm in Byelorussia and similar Soviet enterprises.

We are looking for a more realistic, indeed, a modest place in the world, without opposing the West but joining efforts together in recognition of the ideals of civilization. This is the path that we are attracted to by the common sense and a feeling of realism which cost us dearly.

Izvestiya, April 20, 1990

Chapter Four

Foreign Policy and the Military

Foreign Policy

The "new thinking" in Soviet foreign policy has brought about the shattering of almost all socialist myths and perceptions about the world. As a result, foreign policy has turned out to be a major asset of Gorbachev's rule. Mikhail Gorbachev was first among heads of state to begin speaking about a new world order. However, only future historians will be in a position to assess the role of Gorbachev, versus the roles of Anatoly Dobrynin and Eduard Shevardnadze, in the actual conduct of foreign affairs.

Beneath the lofty rhetoric lies the bitter truth of a Soviet economy gravely undermined by socialist planning. For several decades the USSR militarily challenged Western Europe, the United States, and China weapon for weapon, decimating the Soviet economy. It became urgent to retreat from this policy as gracefully as possible. The main burden of implementing this retreat fell on the man from Georgia, Eduard Shevardnadze. An appropriate heading for the new foreign policy, "deideologization," was first elaborated in Gorbachev's address to the United Nations, on December 7, 1988.

Glasnost was an important foundation of the new foreign policy. Broader and more accurate news coverage made it more difficult to frighten the Soviet people with the military threat of the United States and Western Europe. *Glasnost* also made it impossible to continue to pretend that the Soviet army did not fight in Afghanistan. During that war, Stanislav Kondrashov points out (Doc. 24), the Supreme Soviet did not make a single inquiry of the government concerning the Soviet military presence there.

A new and more conciliatory foreign policy necessitated the replacement of Foreign Minister Andrei Gromyko, known to the West as the "*nyet* man." So, Shevardnadze, a party boss in Georgia, suddenly became foreign minister in July 1985 without any previous foreign policy experience. He quickly learned the ropes and, with his open and pleasant disposition, was readily accepted in European capitals and in Washington. His role in bringing about an agreement on Afghanistan cannot be overestimated. In arms control negotiations, he succeeded in pressuring the Soviet military to accept disproportionate cuts in the disproportionately massive Soviet armed forces. And he sincerely believed that the Soviet Union should not interfere militarily in support of the East European regimes, which had completely lost the trust of their populations. It is ironic that what one man from Georgia—Joseph Stalin—created, another Georgian—Eduard Shevardnadze—put asunder.

Shevardnadze's special role in Soviet-American relations can hardly be overestimated. He met with Secretary of State George Shultz thirty times and established a good relationship with him. His Wyoming meeting with Secretary of State James Baker in September 1989 greatly improved mutual understanding between the two countries and was considered a breakthrough in Soviet dealings with the George Bush administration. Shevardnadze resigned in December 1990 after harsh criticism from military officers and Gorbachev's political move to the right. In his emotional resignation speech before a stunned Congress of People's Deputies, Shevardnadze warned of the imminent danger of dictatorship. The timeliness of this warning was confirmed by the bloody events in the Baltic republics soon thereafter.

Relations between the two superpowers to a large degree determine the international climate. With Gorbachev coming to power, a warming in relations started slowly. In 1985 and 1986 the atmosphere was darkened by the killing of Major Arthur Nickolson and the arrest of Nicholas Daniloff.[1] Only after the December 1987 Washington summit did relations between the two countries begin to change. Summits, a relatively modern form of diplomacy, with their publicity and pressure to produce results, acquired considerable attractiveness. The fourth Moscow summit, in May–June 1988, which featured Gorbachev and President Ronald Reagan walking in Red Square, was a giant step toward the new relationship.

The Malta summit in December 1989 focused on the upheaval in Eastern Europe, and President Bush, for the first time, promised to assist the USSR. This meeting helped bring an end to the feeling that the countries were enemies. An accumulated effect of all high-level Soviet-American encounters made the sixth summit, held in the

[1]Nickolson, a U.S. Army intelligence officer, was killed while trying to take a picture of a new Soviet tank. American journalist Daniloff was arrested by the Soviet authorities and accused of spying shortly after the FBI arrested a Soviet UN employee, Gennady Zakharov, for spying.

summer of 1990 in Washington, a personal triumph for Gorbachev, who traveled around the country meeting Americans.

Soviet policies toward Western Europe and Japan continued to improve with the resolution of Soviet-American discord. In 1989, Gorbachev made an effort to visit many European countries and to invite European leaders to the Soviet Union. Although the official Soviet goal was to build a "common European home," Gorbachev never returned home empty-handed. For its new peaceful posture the Soviet Union was generously rewarded with credits, loans, and technological projects.

As a result of the generous attitude for years patiently exercised by West German Chancellor Helmut Kohl, a crucial new development occurred; Soviet foreign policy in Europe, traditionally oriented toward France, was now putting Germany ahead of all other European countries. This change necessitated a rethinking of the old Soviet-Russian attitudes toward Germany and the Germans. In the last few months of 1990 the Germans seemingly became the USSR's best friends. Germany, with the help of its economic power and generosity, acquired what it could not achieve by any other means—the friendship of Russia. After some prodding and some new economic assistance, on July 16, 1990, Gorbachev changed his mind to favor permitting a united Germany to become part of NATO, an enormous concession that made possible a new European environment. In forty-five years, Europe has gone from Yalta to Paris, from a Europe split into two opposing blocs to a more peaceful continent. How stable this arrangement will be depends to a great extent on whether Eastern Europe again becomes balkanized and on whether the Soviet Union will be satisfied with a much more modest role in Eastern Europe than it has played in the past.

The end of 1989 witnessed the unexpected and spectacular collapse of the old socialist order in Eastern Europe. In the space of just a few months, one by one the outmoded Communist regimes fell like dominoes under the nonviolent but ferocious assault of liberal democratic forces. There was no attempt to apply the doctrine of Leonid Brezhnev, which had led the Soviet Union to interfere in the internal affairs of other East European countries if their adherence to socialism was threatened, as it was in Hungary in 1956 and in Czechoslovakia in 1968. The Gorbachev reforms helped to inspire the forces of change. Moreover, initially, the Soviet Union helped to put reformist pressure on the most conservative regimes, those in Czechoslovakia and East Germany. Gorbachev's intention was to create reform-minded regimes similar to his own, in an attempt to prevent the fall of socialism, but the speed and the extent of change surpassed everyone's imagination. This was made possible in part by the political and economic crises within the Warsaw Pact and by the mutual disappointment of the Soviet Union and its East European satellites. The primary reason, however, was that the Soviet Union could no longer sustain the economic costs of its empire. The Soviet

Union and its East European satellites had begun to compete with each other for economic assistance from the more advanced Western countries and from Japan. This new and more relaxed climate in Europe and in Soviet-American relations also made military intervention a risky proposition. In addition, for the previous decade, the Soviet military had been distracted from East European affairs by the war in Afghanistan.

New relations in the former socialist camp led to the dissolution of the Warsaw Pact, although NATO remains as strong today as ever. As a consequence, there are two new foreign policy concerns in the Soviet Union. The ideologues are afraid that the collapse of the East European regimes means the victory of capitalism over socialism, and the Russian nationalists worry that the results of World War II are being undone and that now Russia is being pushed out of Eastern Europe with its security compromised. Even what to call these new countries is not clear; one suggestion is to call their condition "postsocialist state capitalism."[2] Certainly, Soviet-East European relationships will have to be renewed on a more equitable basis. Many in the USSR are belatedly acknowledging that the nations of Eastern Europe have always tended to look to the West, rather than the East, politically and economically (see Doc. 25). Others blame the Communists in Eastern Europe for becoming bureaucratically isolated from the working class, thus causing the social and economic crises that led to the collapse of their own regimes (see Doc. 26). Undoubtedly, if the Soviet Union had an opportunity to influence events in Eastern Europe, it might even attempt a comeback in some of these countries. On the other hand, liberal-minded Soviet people envy the East Europeans, who used to be several years behind the Soviet Union in political reforms but now, after only a few crucial months, are several decades ahead of them.

The Soviet Union has gradually adopted a new and less ideological attitude toward its allies among the developing nations of the Third World. In a sharp departure from past policies, friendly relations with Israel, South Korea, and South Africa have been actively sought. The June 1990 San Francisco meeting between Mikhail Gorbachev and President Roh Tae-Woo of South Korea was a bold step, even if based on pure economic need rather than on "new thinking" in Soviet foreign policy. Precautions have been taken not to alarm excessively the Soviet conservatives or to injure the sensitivity of the USSR's Third World allies. For example, numerous exchanges with the Republic of South Africa have been made secretly and have not been reported in the Western or South African press.[3] On September 30, 1990, a true

---

[2] Aleksei Pushkov, "Eastern Europe: Societies without Analogs?" *Moskovskie Novosti*, no. 46, 1990.

[3] One such exchange, which I witnessed, was a visit to South Africa by the first deputy of the Soviet minister responsible for the gold and diamond industry in October and November 1990.

foreign policy revolution occurred with the establishment of diplomatic ties with South Korea and consular ties with Israel.

The Soviet Union's lofty policy of new thinking has turned into a more down-to-earth policy of "new realism." However, Soviet policy toward the 1991 war against Iraq showed that the Soviet Union did not yet completely, and may never, renounce all of its imperial ambitions. Regardless of the future political system and ideology of the Soviet Union or Russia, it will remain a great power with national interests that may clash with American and Western goals. At the September 9, 1990, Helsinki summit between Gorbachev and Bush, the Soviet Union approved U.S. steps to contain Saddam Hussein's Iraq but also asked that the allies not destroy it. The subsequent belated Soviet attempt to save the ruthless Iraqi dictator by imposing a cease-fire was intended to please Soviet conservatives and the military, and perhaps to please a broader constituency as well: Document 27 argues that there was widespread Soviet sympathy for Iraq, indicating a lingering Soviet superpower complex and inclination to resolve conflicts by military means.

Who won the Cold War? Gorbachev, or Ronald Reagan? The Cold War was not ended by the policies of Republican or Democratic administrations, nor was its end a result of a "hot" war on the fields of Germany and Eastern Europe, nor a result of the arms race. One might say that the Soviet Union was successful in the arms race and in the Cold War, in that it created a powerful war machine equal or superior to that of the rest of the world combined, an amazing accomplishment based on a clearly inferior economy. The Soviet political system flourished in times of stress and Cold War. However, that system as well as the Soviet economic system finally is collapsing as a result of seventy years of misguided attempts to centralize and militarize. The expansionist policies of the Soviet leadership have been a continuation of the empire building pursued for the last five centuries by the Russian state. When the threat of nuclear war between the Soviet Union and the United States and its allies finally recedes completely, and a stable political system prevails on the territory of the USSR, then everyone will have won.

Military Issues

The process of lowering the status of the Soviet military began with the surprise May 1987 landing of West German teenager Mathias Rust's Cessna 172 airplane in Red Square and has continued with the final withdrawal from Afghanistan in 1989 and the withdrawal from Eastern Europe in 1990 and 1991. The military has tried to defend itself from charges of inefficiency and excess in the press.[4] New Soviet

---

[4]See especially the four-part article by A. Dokuchaev, "Boeings, Cessnas, and Others" (*Krasnaya Zvezda*, March 13, 14, 15, and 20, 1991),

foreign policy has forced many painful material and psychological changes on the military. The historic retreat from Eastern Europe seems to many Soviet generals like a rewriting of the results of World War II, with the USSR once again pushed back to its borders. Withdrawal of Soviet troops and the hasty reunification of Germany have caused imperial misgivings among the many Russians who have taken seriously previous Soviet assertions about security concerns.

A profound change in the role of the Soviet armed forces has taken place over the last six years, a transition from defending Soviet interests all over the globe to policing the country itself—in essence, a fundamental change from an external to an internal function. In an effort to explain the shift, Minister of Defense (and, since 1989, Marshal of the Soviet Union) Dmitry Yazov has claimed that the national republics have disbanded their militias, forcing the army to take over their job.[5]

The approximately three hundred thousand troops of the Ministry of the Interior, commanded by Colonel General Yuri Shatalin, have been the main instrument for internal suppression. Their primary duties are to quell domestic discord and to police the prison system. The Soviet government recently decided to increase their numerical strength, equipment, and salaries. They are now supplied with air force transport planes and helicopters. In addition, General Boris Gromov, formerly the commander of Soviet troops in Afghanistan and well known for his conservative views, was appointed a deputy minister for internal affairs of the USSR in the summer of 1990.

The army's use of shovels and poison gas against demonstrators, including women and children, in Tbilisi dishonored the army in the eyes of many people. There are twenty-five hundred deserters per year—ten times more than as recently as 1987 and 1988. Discipline is at an extremely low level, and there are numerous cases of troops stealing weapons and selling them to the public and to armed groups in the republics. On December 13, 1990, *Izvestiya* reported that a soldier in Irkutsk sold a bullet-proof vest for five cigarettes. The military draft in the national republics is a complete disaster, especially in the Baltic republics and in the Caucasus. In the fall of 1990 the draft was practically derailed in the Baltic and Transcaucasia republics; with the assistance of the local authorities, young men refused to serve in the Red Army. According to Colonel General Dmitry Grinkevich, the Soviet army is short four hundred thousand men.[6]

The extremely high number of draftees killed during military service has received enormous public attention, thanks largely to the efforts of an organization formed by soldiers' mothers. In December 1990 a

---

which uses new material concerning the KAL 007 and Cessna 172 incidents.

[5] *Argumenty i Fakty*, no. 41, 1990.

[6] *Izvestiya*, October 4, 1990.

Congress of Soldiers' Mothers, in Moscow, demanded from the military a full accounting of the circumstances of their sons' deaths.

The military has begun to worry about its low public standing. As a goodwill gesture toward its critics among the intelligentsia, for example, all students were demobilized before their fall deadline. In August 1989 the General Staff of the armed forces organized its first public affairs section, with Major General Yury Markelov at its head.

The January 1990 disclosure by General V. Babiev in Vienna of the real size of the military budget attracted widespread attention for the first time; the budget turned out to be four times larger than the size that has been normally reported—70.9 billion rubles for 1990. It is interesting that U.S. expenditures for the procurement of armaments closely approximate expenditures for manpower, whereas in the Soviet budget spending for armaments is listed at three times that for manpower. According to NATO experts, the Soviet Union spent 130 to 150 billion rubles in 1988, almost twice what has been openly budgeted for 1990.[7] It is likely that the true budget is more than what has been proclaimed. The new Congress of People's Deputies does not yet exercise any supervisory or budgetary role concerning military expenditures. According to Soviet sources, the country's military arsenal includes 10,000 strategic nuclear devices, 8,200 frontline aircraft, and 64,000 tanks. This is clearly far in excess of what is reasonably needed for defense, especially for a country in dire economic straits.[8] In the absence of internal or external pressures, the Soviet military-industrial complex finds it very difficult to decrease its own appetite. General Yuri Lyubimov's reply (Doc. 23) to Alexei Arbatov's accusations concerning the overabundance of Soviet armaments (Doc. 22) reveals how difficult it is for the Soviet military leaders to acknowledge their past excesses.

A new phenomenon, free elections to the Soviet parliament, has resulted in some cases in which young officers who ran against generals won in the elections of March 25, 1989. Liberal officers, led by Colonel Vladimir Lopatin, have formed an organization called Shield to further their views.[9] Conservative generals are trying to purge those who dare to express liberal positions or who criticize Gorbachev. One victim turned out to be General Dmitry Volkogonov, who expressed support for Boris Yeltsin and criticized Gorbachev.

Minister of Defense Dmitry Yazov and the leadership of the army are essentially conservative. General Colonel Igor Rodionov, head of the Academy of General Staff, called the "executioner of Tbilisi" and

---

[7]Yuri Kornilov, "Secrets of Parity," *Ogonyok*, no. 15, 1990.

[8]*Argumenty i Fakty*, no. 43, 1990.

[9]Shield claims twenty thousand members in five hundred cells in the military (*Argumenty i Fakty*, no. 50, December 1990). Thirty-year-old Lopatin has been appointed minister of defense for the Russian Republic and has retired from the army.

also considered a possible future Kornilov,[10] was found in possession of leaflets containing a faked speech of Alexander Yakovlev, faked so as to cast aspersions on the liberal former Politburo member. General Albert Makashov, commander of the Volga-Urals military district and former commander of the Soviet troops in Yerevan, who paid a visit to Iraq in 1990, is an undaunted and aggressive conservative.[11] The army's role in politics is indicated by the special position of Marshal Sergei Akhromeyev, a close personal adviser to Mikhail Gorbachev and a man of the past and defender of the empire. But despite all of this military influence, the army's transport battalions are being sent to help with the country's harvest. Indeed, majors and colonels who survived Afghanistan are now sorting out rotten potatoes in the vegetable warehouses of Moscow.

Because of its inherent conservatism, the military is not trusted by the democratic forces. There are incessant rumors about coups d'état. (For example, the movement of paratroop detachments toward Moscow on September 9, 1990, was widely interpreted as an attempted military coup.) *Krasnaya Zvezda* and other military publications write about the Baltic republics on their front pages in a threatening tone similar to that which preceded the 1968 invasion of Czechoslovakia. This attention to the Baltic republics is especially frightening to liberals and is perhaps designed to intimidate the opponents of Soviet military control.

If the country is to become a democratic state and turn into a nation ruled by laws and not men, then the military must be depoliticized. This would require the removal of the CPSU's control of the military and a change in the role of political officers, who are the ideological and political watchdogs of the party. Even now, however, the party's influence on the military is dwindling, as it is in the rest of Soviet society. A clear indicator of this is that, in 1990, 41,000 military personnel joined the party but 34,000 left it.[12] It is also obvious that a professional army must be substituted for the present draft system. Given the resistance to the draft in non-Russian areas of the USSR, there should be no particular military objection to this idea. But to forgo imperial ambitions might be a more difficult policy for the Soviet military to accept.

---

[10] General Rodionov gave orders to disperse the demonstration in Tbilisi, a move that led to the killing of twenty people, mostly women and children. General Lavr Kornilov led a rebellion against the provisional government in September 1917.

[11] The Soviet military has an ambivalent attitude toward the American pounding of Iraqi troops, who were former Soviet pupils.

[12] *Izvestiya*, March 11, 1991.

22

How Much Defense Is Sufficient?

Alexei Arbatov

International Affairs
April 1989

The Soviet military is not accustomed to criticism, no matter how constructive or polite it may be, particularly with respect to fundamental issues of strategic planning and force structure. Nor is it accustomed to informing and consulting its own people. Soviet generals have always greatly exaggerated their needs, and this in turn has influenced the military policies of the United States and the other North Atlantic Treaty Organization (NATO) countries. All recent military agreements require the Soviets to destroy or to disarm at least two or three times the number of weapons required of NATO.

Alexei Arbatov, a senior researcher at the Institute of World Economy and International Relations, delivered this speech at a January 1989 meeting of members of the Soviet scientific and cultural communities. In Arbatov's view, thoughtless miscalculations by the military have undermined the Soviet economy. He feels that certain advanced types of aircraft, such as the American B-1B and "Stealth" bombers, were introduced solely for the purpose of exhausting the USSR economically. The Soviet air defense forces provide a glaring example of military waste. They are half a million strong, with thousands of aircraft and missile sites, yet there is no Western opponent with a comparable force.

It is likely that not all of what Arbatov writes is a persuasive argument from a strictly military point of view (and see Doc. 23 for a rebuttal), but the very fact that such a debate is taking place is significant. His proposals deserve full attention in light of the severe predicament of the Soviet economy at this time.

The plans we announced for a unilateral reduction in Soviet armed forces[1] showed that the adoption of a defensive military doctrine and *perestroika* in the armed forces are not merely declarations, as the West has alleged, but a practical policy of the Soviet Union and its allies.

---

[1]Mikhail Gorbachev announced these plans in his speech to the United Nations on December 7, 1988 (reprinted in *Gorbachev and Glasnost: Viewpoints from the Soviet Press* [Wilmington, DE: Scholarly Resources, 1989], pp. 329–52).

It is clear, however, that we have only just set out on a long and arduous journey to reshape our doctrine, strategy, and operational plans, the quantitative levels and structure of our armed forces, their deployment and training system, and programs for modernizing their armament and combat equipment. The army is part of the state and society. The negative processes and phenomena that became deeply rooted in every sphere in the decades of stagnation and put our huge country on the brink of national crisis could not have bypassed the army as a kind of nature sanctuary. Naturally the problem goes far beyond mere breaches of regulations by privates. The army is the component most marked with all the attributes of the command-administrative system: a rigid hierarchy, departmental interests, and the absence of *glasnost* under cover of all-embracing secrecy. This is explicable in part, for no army can exist without discipline, nor can it do without guarding secrets against a probable enemy. But under an overall command system these natural peculiarities took extreme forms, and defense has become largely exempt from control by society, whose interests it must serve.

Soviet Foreign Minister Eduard Shevardnadze, speaking to the Foreign Ministry's Scientific and Practical Conference in July 1988, said: "Any carelessness in the military sphere, which in the past was devoid of democratic control, can, in the context of acute mistrust and universal suspicion, cost the country a great deal and have most severe economic side effects. Many losses of this kind could have been averted if interpretation of national security interests had not become the exclusive province of several departments, the Ministry of Foreign Affairs included, which, moreover, were shielded from criticism, as was the case in the past."[2]

The problem can be found mostly in the lack of *glasnost* and unclassified information on military matters. Surely the fact that the Soviet public generally learns something about the country's armed forces only as a result of the Soviet side supplying the West with relevant information during talks cannot be regarded as normal. And surely the Soviet people need this information much more than does the West. After all, it is primarily a question of our security, of using our people's resources (and what resources!) for defense. This

---

[2]*International Affairs*, no. 10, 1988, pp. 19–21 (cited by Arbatov in original document).

raises the question: From whom is all that information really concealed, and to what end, since the West has long freely used an immense amount of data on both its own military potential and ours? The problem is also that of the lack of the democratic procedures, which in the past made it impossible to discuss and oversee defense measures.

Profound reform is already under way in the Soviet economy and foreign policy, and military policy must not impede these processes but become actively involved in them. The country's defenses must certainly not be impaired in the process. Thus there is a need to take a fresh look at established directive principles and narrow bureaucratic approaches and to bring military theory and practice into greater harmony with the economic, foreign policy, and military strategic realities of today. The economy being a subject for a separate talk, we shall confine ourselves to the last two points.

Foreign Political Realities

The buildup of the Soviet Union's military potential at home and abroad was undoubtedly justified and necessary in many cases but unwarranted in others. At present a system that embodies the confrontation and rivalry of the more than three decades of the Cold War prevents us from reducing our direct military and political overinvolvement in international conflicts, putting an excessive strain on our economy, handicapping our diplomatic flexibility (despite the efforts of our diplomats), and holding up the progress of Soviet initiatives aimed at forming a comprehensive system of international security.

It is on this point that considerations and objectives of military policy and military programs often enter into conflict with the diplomatic dialogue. Unfortunately, this applies to both our negotiating partners and ourselves. Suffice it to say that in the early 1980s our defense requirements were estimated to include the need to keep at all costs a considerable number of intermediate-range missiles in the western and eastern parts of Soviet territory. As for the "zero option," we saw in it a bid to assure NATO double superiority in delivery vehicles and triple superiority in nuclear warheads. Among the barriers to negotiations raised by our military policy were: our traditional objections to on-site inspection and to forms of control other than such means as satellites and radars, the inviolability of the structure of the nuclear triad, and so on.

A historic breakthrough in this respect came with the signing of the Intermediate-range Nuclear Forces (INF) Treaty, whose significance therefore goes much further than simply scrapping part of the world's nuclear armory, including two classes of Soviet and U.S. nuclear weapons.

Military Strategic Realities

Official documents adopted by the Soviet Union and the Warsaw Treaty Organization (WTO) in recent years (as well as statements by political and military leaders) contain key provisions offering a starting point for a revision of military doctrine and strategy. I refer, first of all, to the recognition that victory in a world nuclear war is impossible (because the damage it would cause could not be limited to an acceptable level), as is the waging of either a limited or a protracted nuclear war. Victory would also be out of the question in a large-scale conventional war in Europe between the WTO and NATO because of the disastrous consequences which even conventional hostilities would have for the population, economy, and environment of the continent and in view of the practically inevitable nuclear escalation of such a conflict.

Apart from the foreign-policy and moral aspects of the problem, this leads even from the purely military point of view to the fundamental conclusion that it is necessary to regard the prevention of nuclear and conventional war as the chief task of the armed forces, to pledge "no first use" of either nuclear or conventional weapons, and to revise strategy, operational plans, and military capability based on the principles of defense.

We can infer from the foregoing some further and more specific amendments to the strategy of defensive sufficiency, without forgetting, of course, that generalizations of this nature are relative and inevitably open to question:

—until such time as all nuclear weapons are eliminated under relevant agreements, the combat task of offensive and defensive strategic forces will be not to limit damage in the event of nuclear war (which is impossible in any circumstances), nor to defeat the aggressor's armed forces, but to deliver a crushing blow against its life centers;

—the task of the armed forces and of conventional armaments is not to conduct offensive strategic operations in the main European and Asian theaters of war, but to engage in defensive operations to frustrate offensive operations by the enemy;

—a protracted conventional war is impossible, and the task of the armed forces is to prevent the enemy from winning the upper hand in intensive short-term combat operations and from resorting to nuclear escalation with impunity;

—a war on two fronts simultaneously (that is, against the United States and its allies and against China) is very unlikely in the foreseeable future;

—no future use of limited Soviet forces in international conflicts or in internal conflicts in developing countries shall be envisaged.

Such analogies, although artificial, may be described in simplified terms as a transition from the strategy of two-and-a-half wars to a strategy of one war, or rather to the ability to stave it off on the basis of a reliable defense potential.

I can list another three general principles. First, the emphasis must be shifted from extensive to intensive means of ensuring defense. Second, the development of the military potential of our probable adversaries is not only an objective reality for our planning but also a process directly influenced by our measures. Our activity is likely to lead to an intensification and extension of their programs or, on the contrary, to these programs being slowed and wound down. Third, disarmament talks offer ample additional opportunities to strengthen our security at lower cost.

Thus what we mean by reasonable or defensive sufficiency is not simply a reduction in troops and armaments but a thorough revision of strategy, operational plans, and armed forces, in part by reducing them, revising modernization programs, and redeploying forces, primarily with the aim of greatly strengthening the country's defenses on a long-term basis.

Strategic Offensive and Defensive Weapons

Strategic nuclear forces and conventional armed forces differ fundamentally in tasks, in their patterns of financing, and in what they require for keeping up an acceptable military balance. Hence there can be no standard approach to assessing their sufficiency or to cutting the costs involved.

The greater part of spending on strategic armaments, with rare exceptions, goes toward their development and testing and toward investments in production capacities. This spending depends to a lesser degree on the amount of serial production (that is, on the number of produced models) and on the maintenance costs of deployed forces. This is why expenditures for strategic offensive forces (SOFs) depend chiefly on the diversity of new systems put into service in place of or in addition to existing ones and not on the quantity of delivery vehicles or warheads.

The strategic and military-technological reality now is the following: It is impossible to reduce one's damage in a nuclear war by hitting the aggressor's strategic forces. Indeed, this implies delivering a first strike—that is, assuming the role of aggressor and responsibility for a holocaust. This is unacceptable politically (in light of our commitment to no first use of nuclear weapons) as well as technically (since from 30 to 70 percent of U.S. weapons, such as those carried by submarines and bombers, are invulnerable to attack).

The idea of striking back at U.S. SOFs is evidently strategic nonsense, too. Why should the United States leave part of its forces as targets after it has delivered a first strike? In terms of reasonable sufficiency, targets suitable for retaliation are the aggressor's economic facilities. A mere four hundred nuclear warheads of the megaton class could destroy up to 70 percent of the U.S. potential. This number of warheads hardly exceeds 10 to 15 percent of the Soviet Union's present strategic forces. Defense will be ensured if this many of them survive any attack and reach their targets. All further weapons and operations involving the use of SOFs would be doubtful in any respect and evidently unnecessary in terms of sufficiency.

Our current military programs therefore raise certain questions concerning the declared principle of reasonable sufficiency. To judge by the information published in foreign sources, we have responded to each SOF system deployed by the United States at this stage in the arms race with two new systems of our own simultaneously. We counter intercontinental ballistic missiles (ICBMs) of the MX type with land-mobile SS-25 and SS-24 ICBM systems (we call these missiles RS-12M and RS-22); to submarines of the Ohio type and Trident 1 submarine-launched ballistic missiles

(SLBMs), with new systems of the Typhoon type and what the West calls Delta-4s plus two corresponding types of SS-N-20 and SS-N-23 SLBMs; to B-1B bombers, with TU-160 bombers and a new modification of TU-95; to sea-based Tomahawk cruise missiles (SLCMs) carrying nuclear warheads, with SS-N-21 and SS-N-24 SLCMs. It is only air-launched cruise missiles that we counter 1:1.[3]

Aren't quantity-oriented mechanisms typical of other echelons of the command-administrative system at work here? Are such asymmetric responses inevitable? They suit those Americans who advocate wearing out the Soviet Union economically, encouraging them to carry on talks from "positions of strength." This is all the more so because countermeasures in the ratio of 2:1 will be even harder for us to adopt if we sign a treaty on a 50 percent reduction in SOFs and on a drastic lowering of strategic force levels and sublevels. We could probably effect a serious reduction in economic expenditures without undermining our security, while strengthening and not weakening our negotiating positions, if we followed a ratio of 1:1 or, better still, 1:2, with emphasis on the qualitative aspect of new strategic systems and on the high efficiency of their command-control communication and early warning system.

To reinforce land-based missile forces, it would apparently be enough for us to have one new long-range submarine missile system capable of hitting targets from near the Soviet coast and hence making it unnecessary to venture onto the high seas through enemy antisubmarine barriers. In the case of lower SOF levels the Delta-4 submarine, which carries sixteen SS-N-23 missiles tipped with sixty-four warheads in all, would apparently be more attractive than the Typhoon, with its two hundred warheads mounted on twenty SS-N-20 missiles. The former makes it possible within the limits of the same number of warheads to distribute forces over a greater number of launching positions than does the latter, thereby adding to the survivability of our missile-carrying submarine fleet. In light of the expected lowering of SOF ceilings by treaty, parallel construction of two new types of submarines seems all the more questionable (the nuclear-powered missile submarine is the costliest single SOF system).

With regard to strategic defensive weapons, it is time to reconsider at long last our apparently very costly air defenses

---

[3]*The Military Balance*, 1988–89, pp. 18, 33–34 (cited by Arbatov).

deployed several lines deep. According to foreign sources, our air defense system comprises 8,600 antiaircraft missile launching sites and 2,300 interceptor fighters. The United States has 290 fighters (including the National Guard forces), but no antiaircraft missiles.[4]

The country's system of air defense against strategic weapons is doubtful for at least three reasons. First, it could hardly intercept all U.S. airborne strategic weapons, especially with the deployment of cruise missiles on heavy bombers—that is, many thousands of "Rusts" carrying 200-kiloton warheads.[5] After all, to intercept 60, 70 or 80 percent of them would not mean more than intercepting none. The 20 or even 10 percent of heavy bombers and cruise missiles that could break through, carrying 800 or 400 nuclear warheads with yields ranging from 200 kilotons to 9 megatons, would be able just the same to inflict disastrous, unsustainable damage. It is like a bridge reaching to the middle or spanning two thirds of a river: No matter how wide, solid, or fine, no matter how expensive, it would be as useless as if it had not been there at all. Nor is that all.

Second, radars, the launch sites of air defense missiles, and the airfields of interceptors are themselves entirely vulnerable to ballistic missiles. Incidentally, the United States actually plans in the event of war a "precursor" strike with sea-based missiles, to open "corridors" for its bombers in air-defense zones.

Third, land- and sea-based ballistic missiles (some eight thousand warheads in all) could, if necessary, hit practically all targets by themselves, without the aid of heavy bombers. The chief reason now given for preserving and renewing them in the United States (B-1B, Stealth) is that the Soviet Union will have to spend many times more on modernizing its air defenses, which means that this is seen as one of the most advantageous lines of economically exhausting the Soviet Union.

An argument put forward occasionally is that we could use our air defenses in a conventional if not in a nuclear war. But this is more like justifying a system that is already there than it is defining its real task. Is a conventional war

---

[4]*The Military Balance,* 1988–89, pp. 19, 35 (cited by Arbatov).

[5]A West German teenager, Mathias Rust, successfully penetrated Soviet airspace and landed his Cessna 172 on Red Square in Moscow on May 28, 1987.

between the Soviet Union and the United States—a war involving massive mutual air raids without using nuclear weapons—conceivable at all? If so, does this imply that the huge WTO and NATO forces in Europe and the Soviet Union and the U.S. forces in the Far East would stay out, doing nothing? It is very hard to imagine such a thing. However, we admit at the official level—and it is part of our doctrine—that a wide-ranging war in Europe, even one fought with conventional arms, would lead to a catastrophe and would develop almost inevitably into a nuclear holocaust. It follows that a conventional air war is less likely still.

A far more modest air defense system is certainly necessary for an early warning of attack, for controlling airspace in peacetime, and for safeguarding the country against possible terrorists. Certain events have suggested that this is something to work on. We also need an air defense system at a nonnuclear operational and tactical level to shield troops from air strikes. As for the doctrine of averting nuclear war, military-technological and strategic realities demand that we admit explicitly and without qualification that the concepts of "repulsing missile space attack" and "destroying the armed forces and military potential of the enemy" are hopelessly outdated. These concepts are typical instances of projecting prenuclear military thinking into the solution of the historically unprecedented problem of security in the nuclear and space age, which calls for fundamentally new approaches.

It would be useful to think once again whether it is advisable to maintain and modernize the anti-ballistic missile (ABM) complex around Moscow. The one hundred antimissiles allowed under the ABM Treaty are clearly insufficient for defense against a dedicated strike by major U.S., British, and French forces. Defense against strikes by terrorists or by other nuclear powers as well as against unauthorized and accidental missile launches necessitates coverage, if only a "thin layer" of it, for the whole territory of the country, and this is something the Moscow ABM complex cannot provide in any circumstances. The defense of Moscow hardly justifies the expenditures it entails, since foreign ballistic missiles would still hold hostage Leningrad, Kiev, Tbilisi, Sverdlovsk, Novosibirsk, and other cities, not to mention the fact that for terrorists ballistic missiles are the most inconvenient system of delivering nuclear weapons and the hardest to acquire.

Preventing a "decapitating" strike against the military and political leadership—a threat coming from the United States and from third nuclear powers, not from terrorists—would probably cost less if we diverted at least part of the resources saved to raising the survivability, efficiency, and quality of our underground and air command and communications systems. Needless to say, Soviet-U.S. agreements must guarantee the inviolability of the ABM Treaty and the prevention of an arms race in space.

Conventional Armaments

In the area of armed forces and conventional armaments, as distinct from SOFs, substantial cuts could be made in spending by lowering quantitative levels and reducing the series of weapons and combat equipment put out. As in the case of strategic forces, great savings can be achieved by building and modifying fewer types of systems while accentuating the qualitative aspect. According to foreign sources, Soviet ground troops total about one hundred eighty divisions equipped with and having reserves of, among others, fifty-three thousand tanks. Ninety-nine of these divisions (55 percent) are stationed in Europe and oriented to the European theater of war, twenty-four (13 percent) to the southern theater (Turkey, Iran, Afghanistan), and forty-six (26 percent) to China and Japan; eleven divisions form the central reserve.[6] Roughly 50 percent of these divisions have only about 20 percent of statutory personnel and obsolete equipment, and it would take a long time for them to acquire combat readiness by drawing on reserves. One half of our tank fleet—the backbone of the combat power of our ground troops—is made up of tanks (T-54/55, T-62) designed in the fifties and early sixties.[7]

We declare officially that a protracted large-scale conventional war with NATO in Europe is impossible and unacceptable. This presumably applies also to the United States and to Japan and, in still greater measure, to China, a great Asian socialist power. In line with our new doctrine and

---

[6]J. Steinbrunner and L. Sigal, *Alliance Security: NATO and the No-First-Use Question* (Washington, DC, 1983), pp. 52–53 (cited by Arbatov).

[7]Vitaly Shlykov, "Tank Asymmetry and Real Security," *International Affairs*, no. 12, 1988 (in Russian) (cited by Arbatov).

strategy, we apparently could disband without detriment to our defenses all divisions whose combat readiness is low, scrap the enormous stockpiles of obsolete arms and equipment, and abolish the unwieldy system of mobilizing industry for war with due regard to the realities of the quick pace and supertechnologization of modern warfare. The new doctrine calls for a more compact, more combat-ready, and well-paid army having the latest equipment.

How many divisions would be enough for defense, with the NATO forces unchanged? On the main front, in Central Europe, the West permanently keeps about thirty divisions whose number could be increased to some fifty in the event of mobilization. Throughout the European zone NATO has about one hundred divisions. To close the 800-kilometer Central European front, the WTO needs from twenty to thirty divisions. Defense echeloned in depth (including the troops stationed in the European part of Soviet territory, some of which are intended to close the southern and northern flanks) evidently could be ensured with the aid of fifty to sixty WTO divisions. This is organizationally roughly one third of the forces now deployed on the extensive basis.

This approach could be applied also to air forces in view of their high mobility and multipurpose character. It is hardly advisable to have about eight thousand tactical aircraft, most of which are obsolete.

The accomplishment by 1991 of the unilateral cuts of Soviet armed forces in Europe as announced by Mikhail Gorbachev will in itself mark a big advance toward restructuring our ground troops and air forces. Still deeper reductions are possible on a reciprocal basis in the context of the WTO-NATO talks on armed forces and conventional armaments from the Atlantic to the Urals.

Military Production

According to foreign sources, Soviet ground troops today deploy three types of tanks and three types of combat vehicles and armored carriers simultaneously (against one of each in the United States); nonstrategic air and naval forces deploy seven models of fighters, strike planes and bombers (against three in the United States); naval forces deploy five different classes of warships and three multipurpose submarines (against four and one, respectively, in the United States). The same sources claim (while ours are silent) that from 1977 to 1986 the Soviet Union produced twice as many fighters and submarines as did the United States, three times as many tanks and combat helicopters, and nine times as many artillery pieces and antiaircraft missiles. It was only in the construction of large warships that the United States found itself ahead of us, by 10 percent. Concerning nuclear weapons the USSR produced four times as many ballistic missiles and thirteen times as many heavy and medium bombers.[8]

These data cannot be taken at face value.[9] But if they reflect the actual state of affairs at least to some degree, then *perestroika* in this field should include a whole set of measures, such as broader discussion of key programs from the standpoint of defense sufficiency and stricter selection of programs on the principle of comparing cost and effectiveness. It is also necessary to end superfluous duplication, introduce healthy competition between construction bureaus and in industry, limit output series, and effect renewal at longer intervals while taking bigger leaps in quality.

With the acute deficit of information on our armed forces and military budget, it is very difficult to estimate the likely economic effect of the proposals I have set out. However, tentative calculations indicate that their implementation in the next five-year plan period could reduce our defense spending by 40 to 50 percent, and this, most important, would not weaken but would strengthen the country's defense, to say nothing of other aspects of security, both economic and political.

It is occasionally said that the military has "no stake" in cutting armaments expenditures or in extending military *glasnost*. It is hard to accept this view. There is no reason to deny that in this area as in other spheres of our society and state there are sincere supporters of *perestroika*, just as there are staunch opponents and those who preach *perestroika* yet would like to reduce it to cosmetic adjustments.

---

[8] *Soviet Military Power, 1987*, p. 121 (cited by Arbatov).

[9] Nevertheless, they do reflect the Soviet military's propensity to outdo itself in the arms race. According to the START agreement signed on July 31, 1991, in Moscow by Presidents Bush and Gorbachev, the Soviets would have to cut their long-range nuclear weapons by one third more than the Americans. If it had been signed two years ago, the agreement would have been a genuine triumph. Now, however, in the post-Chernobyl era when even Caspar Weinberger might have reconsidered the wisdom of multiple nuclear exchanges, it has lost much of its significance.

23

Enough Defense, Not Enough Competence

Yuri Lyubimov

Kommunist Vooruzhennykh Sil
no. 16, August 1989

This is a reply by the military to the liberal position on excessive military expenditures, as expressed in Alexei Arbatov's article in *International Affairs* (Doc. 22). Lyubimov finds Arbatov's article prejudicial to the military and uninformed about military matters. According to Lyubimov, all is well in the Soviet armed forces during this period of reform, and he maintains that no mistakes were made in the past. He defends the army against the accusation that it is the most conservative element in the Soviet system. Major General Lyubimov is still tilted toward achieving equal status with the United States rather than toward the doctrine of reasonable sufficiency. The dispute over this issue reflects the deep rift between the Soviet military and the Ministry of Foreign Affairs, a factor that led to Eduard Shevardnadze's resignation, in December 1990, as minister of foreign affairs.

Recently our country has been undergoing a reform process based on the principles of democratization, *glasnost*, and greater openness. This process is also under way in the Soviet armed forces. The military is a part of society that cannot be divorced from the people. *Perestroika* benefits the armed forces, and it is inspiring not only political activity among the rank and file but also a growth in their skills and an improvement in the combat readiness of the army and the navy.

Military life has been extensively discussed in the press. At a meeting with the directors of media outlets, ideological agencies, and literary and artistic unions, Mikhail Gorbachev remarked that *perestroika* is a "creative process with its own dialectics, own contradictions, and own dramas. There is no sense in trying to conceal that one encounters confusion in analysis and evaluations in the press and in society as a whole." Hasty analyses and superfluous evaluations have not bypassed military life. And in this case we must be particularly attentive toward discussions of the issues in the mass media, because they touch on the interests of the country's defense capabilities.

First of all we should mention that the problem of reasonable defensive sufficiency has been examined by different organizations of the Soviet Ministry of Defense and by a number of other agencies. As we know, the countries of the Warsaw Pact have agreed on, adopted, and published a defensive doctrine which now serves as the guidelines for the fraternal countries in the development of their armed forces.[1] The Soviet Union has made very important unilateral decisions not to be the first to employ nuclear weapons, to renounce tests of antisatellite weapons, and to reduce its armed forces significantly. A Soviet-American treaty to eliminate medium- and short-range missiles is now in effect. The Soviet Union has introduced far-reaching proposals at negotiations on nuclear weapons, space weapons, and conventional armed forces. A great deal of analytical work stands behind all of this.

It's hard not to see the consequences of this work, namely a general relaxation of international tensions, the softening of the "image of the enemy," a process of gradual resolution of prolonged regional conflicts, and a growth in mutual trust. The red light has come on for the arms race. And the entire world is becoming more firmly convinced that any further arms race would be extremely dangerous.

We must not ignore another issue: We now have the opportunity to devote a major portion of our resources to resolving the food problem and social issues and increasing the production of high-quality consumer goods. Of course the starting point for such decisions is a profound and comprehensive understanding of the problem of defensive sufficiency.

Unfortunately, the article "How Much Defense Is Sufficient?" [Doc. 22] in my opinion has not moved us toward an understanding of the principles of the new defensive developments or toward realistic proposals concerning necessary weapons expenditures. It does not answer the question of how much defense is enough.

I'll start by saying that this article, which claims to be a critical assessment of the principles of Soviet military doctrine, is clearly confusing to experts. It's hard to imagine that the author has not been informed that our army is already practically carrying out radical structural

---

[1]Since this article was written, in March 1991, the Warsaw Pact was formally dissolved as a military organization.

transformations on the basis of the new military doctrine. Strategic views of the use of the armed forces and their role in preventing possible military conflicts are changing. The ways in which troops are employed in operations are also undergoing changes. New combat tactics are being developed for the defensive doctrine. This is a major research process which relies on the creativity of our commanders and political officers. Military academies, staffs, and military institutes are involved in it. Finally we cannot help but mention the democratization of the entire way of military life and the emerging *glasnost* and openness. Despite all of this, our army is cited in this article as "the component most marked with all the attributes of the command-administrative system." If the author is adequately informed or competent in military matters, he must know that a large number of scientists, designers, and researchers from widely different agencies, including the Soviet Academy of Sciences, have always been involved in working out the future of our military development. (I hope that the editors of *International Affairs* and the author of the article will not take my comment as an attempt to put any area off-limits to criticism.)

I must also disagree with the leitmotiv of the article, that reform and *glasnost* are bypassing our defense policies. The author writes that "Profound reform is already under way in the Soviet economy and foreign policy, and military policy must not impede these processes but become actively involved in them." But, after all, our most weighty initiatives in foreign policy have had a military side. And if we speak of economic reform as profound and already under way, the conversion of a large portion of the defense industry constitutes a very quick and noticeable contribution to economic reform.

As the starting point for his assertions the author took the proposition that "defense has become largely exempt from control by society, whose interests it must serve." Therefore he suggests that we "take a fresh look at established directive principles and narrow bureaucratic approaches and . . . bring military theory and practice into greater harmony with the economic, foreign policy, and military strategic realities of our day." I cannot help but agree with the author that the conditions of reform in our country have required more openness in all fields, including the military field. An intelligent discussion would undoubtedly make it possible to avoid mistakes we may have committed in the past, including in the development of the military. But any opinions must be substantiated, which unfortunately the author doesn't do. The article does not contain any serious attempt to persuade the reader. Instead of this, he presents a system of ready-made and supposedly completely obvious guidelines.

For example, in the article he mentions the idea of the contradictions between the goals of military policy and diplomatic dialogue. Supposedly our military programs rigidly constrain the efforts of our diplomats, so that the people, agencies, and scientific centers that are directly responsible for these negotiations and interrelations are simply obliged to insert their point of view into the making of our military policy. Otherwise they will be condemned to simply chew on the consequences of decisions which they had no part in making. The article asserts that we must eliminate the conflict between foreign policy plans and military activities. Currently, the author subsequently claims in the article, "a system that embodies the confrontation and rivalry of the more than three decades of the Cold War prevents us from reducing our direct military and political overinvolvement in international conflicts," ties down "diplomatic flexibility (despite the efforts of our diplomats)," and impedes "the progress of Soviet initiatives aimed at forming a comprehensive system of international security."

I believe that all of these opinions are far from the truth. It is doubtful that our diplomats, society, or government could make such irresponsible evaluations. And this is why: Doesn't the author know that decisions on all the most important issues of defense policy are carefully examined by the Defense Council of the Soviet Union and are made by the government? The area of disarmament negotiations is also constantly under consideration by our party's leadership. And before any decision is made, these issues are carefully worked out with all concerned agencies and organizations, including scientists.

The section of the article concerning military strategic realities demonstrates that the author is quite remote from these realities and from an understanding of strategy. The section provides "specific amendments to the strategy of defensive sufficiency" under new conditions. The author's guidelines can be summarized as follows: As long as nuclear weapons have not been eliminated, the mission of the strategic forces is not to defeat the armed forces of an aggressor but to launch a crushing counterstrike on vitally important centers; a prolonged conventional war is impossible, and hence our main mission is to prevent an enemy victory in brief combat operations; and a two-front war is highly improbable. There follows the caution that our actions should not cause the opposing side to intensify its programs. In the process Alexei Arbatov tries to convince the readers that our measures have had a very immediate effect on "the development of the military potential of our probable adversaries."

But the reality is that **our policy in the field of defense, our strategy, and our practical actions continue to be aimed at preventing both nuclear and conventional wars.**[2] This is the core of Soviet military doctrine. This is the purpose of all of the Soviet Union's peace initiatives. With respect to the author's opinion on the immediate effect of our activities on the development of the military potential of our probable adversaries, this either voluntarily or involuntarily leads to the idea that our practical actions were supposedly the cause of the arms race. It is absolutely impossible to agree with this.

Undeniable facts in the past and in the present indicate otherwise. For example, let us refer to a recent programmatic address by the new U.S. secretary of defense, Richard Cheney. In his words, the United States of America should maintain a "position of strength" at negotiations on both conventional and strategic weapons. Cheney is opposed to reducing the military budget, he supports the continuation of Strategic Defense Initiative research, and he opposes any unilateral steps by the United States to reduce armaments. He is "comforted" only by the continuation of the Soviet Union's self-disarmament. He also interprets our major unilateral reductions in armed forces and armaments as not being a "significant reduction in Soviet potential." The United States of America has continued its policy of achieving unilateral advantages in negotiations after the latest Soviet peace initiatives.

The American "conception of rivalry" calls for giving priority to those projects in planning long-term weapons development that should enable not only the achievement of U.S. military superiority but also the profound economic exhaustion of the Soviet Union (while keeping the U.S. military budget stable and fixed). According to the Pentagon's

---

[2]Boldface here indicates emphasis in original.

plans, this should lead to a reduction in the Soviet Union's ability to take countermeasures to ensure its own security in a flexible and timely manner.

In comparing the strategic resources of the two opposing countries, Alexei Arbatov employs the thesis associated with Western information sources of the "inadequacy" of the Soviet Union's countermeasures in the arms race imposed on it. In supporting this thesis, the author of the article in *International Affairs* understandably arrives at the wrong conclusions concerning the balance of new strategic offensive weapons systems introduced recently by the Soviet Union and the United States, counting our modernized version of the RS-12 intercontinental ballistic missile and the TU-95 bomber while for some reason ignoring such American systems as the Trident-2 nuclear missile submarine, the B-2 strategic bomber, and modifications of the B-52 bomber for cruise missiles.

In pointing out these glaring inaccuracies, it is important to emphasize that the Soviet Union has opposed the deployment of new strategic resources such as the B-1, the Trident, the Ohio submarine, and all kinds of cruise missiles and other systems at all stages of the arms race imposed on it. Hence it's hardly right to accuse the Soviet Union of an "immoderate" reaction to U.S. actions. Our reactions have always been counterreactions necessitated by the U.S. leadership's refusal to accept our proposals to prohibit new systems.

Both new and long-known general principles of nuclear deterrence figure in Arbatov's article. But by all appearances the author does not have a clear idea of what "deterrence" is. He suggests that all we need is one mobile ground-based intercontinental ballistic missile system and for "insurance," one new long-range submarine-based missile system, or we could keep four hundred one-megaton nuclear warheads under any conditions for a counterstrike, and our defensive capabilities would be ensured. I'll say forthrightly that this is too superficial an approach to answer the difficult question of "How much defense is enough?" But this doesn't embarrass the author a bit. He recommends a 1:2 ratio for Soviet weapons to U.S. weapons. And, by his reasoning, peace would be assured. That's how simply he resolves the issue of defensive sufficiency!

The author almost completely denies the need for an air defense system. He explains the advisability of an air defense system in conventional warfare as "shutting the barn door after the horse has left." He proposes replacing the existing air defense system with a "modest air defense system" for early warning, for protecting the skies in peacetime from terrorists, and for defending ground forces at "a nonnuclear operational and tactical level." In order to reinforce his conclusions Arbatov cites several statistics on Soviet and American air defense systems. In the process he completely ignores the main point—the difference between the geostrategic situations of the Soviet Union and the United States. He does not take into account that American planes, and only American planes, are based at numerous military facilities located along practically the entire perimeter of the Soviet Union. The Soviet Union and its allies have no military air bases near U.S. territory.

Let the innocent reader just try to figure out what he's saying! But the author himself is the first one who should try. Currently the United States has a strategic air force of approximately six hundred planes which can be armed with both nuclear and conventional weapons. And the Pentagon has no plans to reduce it. Calculations have indicated that, in terms of the bombs that this kind of force could deliver to the territory of the other side in one mission, the United States has at least tenfold superiority. We might ask if we can afford not to take this into consideration.

There's more. Instead of the one antimissile system approved by the antimissile defense treaty, the author believes that "thin" coverage of the entire territory of the country to protect "against strikes by terrorists or by other nuclear powers as well as against unauthorized and accidental missile launches" would be advisable. But in fact this would mean abrogating the permanent antimissile defense treaty. The Soviet Union is resolutely opposed to such a stance, and the author supposedly advocates the permanence of this principle. But in this case the ends clearly don't meet. This is the first problem.

Second, the creation of even a very "thin layer" of antimissile defense for the country would evoke a counterreaction by the other side and lead to a strategic offensive arms race. Do we really need to set forth such careless proposals?

In the passages on conventional weapons the author boldly designs a system for guaranteeing security based on "intensive" principles. In our view, this is so indicative of the author's point of view that we would like to cite his basic premises. In Arbatov's opinion, an in-depth defense covering the European portion of the USSR could be reliably provided by fifty to sixty Warsaw Pact divisions, including coverage of the southern and northern flanks. They could successfully stand up to one hundred North Atlantic Treaty Organization (NATO) divisions. The Warsaw Pact would need twenty to thirty divisions to cover the 800-kilometer central European front. The cumbersome system of industrial mobilization would be eliminated. Stockpiles of obsolete weapons and equipment would be eliminated. A war would be quick and highly technological. In accordance with our defensive strategy, the air force would reduce its resources for attacking the other side's rear-area objectives and airfields. The navy's mission would be limited to defending the coastline and to providing security for submarines with long-range missiles in coastal waters. All of NATO's aircraft carriers would be sunk near our coasts. Missile-carrying aircraft would be employed only within the operational radius of escort fighters.

I believe that these citations are sufficient without any commentary. Don't these proposals remind you of the projects of one of Gogol's heroes?[3]

[3]Manilov, one of the heroes of Nikolai Gogol's novel *Dead Souls*, often indulges in unsubstantiated lazy dreams.

24

From the Shadows of the Unknown: Flashes of Openness in the Realm of Military Secrets

Stanislav Kondrashov

Novy Mir
no. 8, August 1989

This article discusses the consequences of not informing the nation about crucial military decisions. Kondrashov begins with the Cuban missile crisis of 1962, during which Nikita Khrushchev recklessly plunged into confrontation in spite of the obvious American superiority in nuclear missiles. Soviet missiles were transported secretly to Cuba, while the Soviet people were kept in the dark as to what was going on. The Cuban missile episode provides an excellent case study of the differences in approach between a democratic and an authoritarian state to decision making at a time of crisis. The questionable war in Afghanistan is another case in which neither the Soviet people nor the Supreme Soviet were ever consulted. In spite of *glasnost,* openness in military matters has still not been achieved.

The second issue addressed in this article is the attempt by the Soviet Union to attain strategic parity not only with the United States but also with all of the Western countries combined. In giving priority to perceived military needs, the USSR neglected agriculture and consumer needs, and turned itself into a backward country. To justify their policies, the Soviet leaders greatly exaggerated the military threat from the United States and the West.

In late January of this year, an unusual international group, namely a group of veterans of a catastrophic war that fortunately never took place, gathered at a private residence far from downtown Moscow. The official title of this meeting was "The Soviet-American-Cuban Symposium on the Problems of the Caribbean Missile Crisis of October 1962." At that time, it is believed, humanity moved closer to the edge of the nuclear abyss than it ever had. Since then, after learning the lessons of the Caribbean well, humanity has not come any closer.

Two of the leading figures—the people who created and took part in the crisis, namely Nikita Khrushchev and John Kennedy, who led us to the brink of the abyss and then, thank God, jumped away from it—have not been alive for a long time. But many other important personages are alive and well, although they've aged twenty-six years since then. Let me list the names of the participants in the symposium and their positions in October 1962: Andrei Gromyko, Soviet minister of foreign affairs; Anatoly Dobrynin, the Soviet ambassador in Washington; A. Alekseyev, the Soviet ambassador in Havana; Robert McNamara, the U.S. secretary of defense; McGeorge Bundy, assistant to the U.S. president for national security affairs; Theodore Sorensen, special assistant to the U.S. president; Deputy Chairman of the Joint Chiefs of Staff of the U.S. Armed Forces General W. Smith; and others. On the Soviet side a unique family element was a sign of the new times. Nikita Khrushchev was in a way represented by his son, Sergei Khrushchev, who remembered that time well and referred to his father's memoirs (which, by the way, have not been published in the Soviet Union), while the late Anastas Mikoyan's place was taken by his son, Sergei Mikoyan, a prominent expert on Latin America.

The most important crisis of the nuclear age has provided steady food for scholarly research, which is why scholars were authoritatively represented on both the American and Soviet sides.

The idea of deploying missiles in Cuba was put forth by Nikita Khrushchev personally. It was approved in Moscow in the summer of 1962 after a visit to Havana by a Soviet delegation which included Marshal Sergei Biryuzov, the commander in chief of the Strategic Missile Forces, who traveled under the alias of "Engineer Petrov." Both ground-to-air defensive missiles and ground-to-ground missiles with nuclear warheads were placed in Cuba at the disposal of Soviet military personnel and under their command. The missiles were to be launched only in the event of an American attack and only on orders from Moscow.

Moscow considered its missiles in Cuba to be defensive weapons, and in fact a means of nuclear deterrence and a way of slightly correcting the strategic imbalance. According to McNamara, the United States at that time had seventeen times more strategic nuclear warheads than did the USSR, five thousand as opposed to three hundred. Washington considered the missiles in Cuba to be offensive weapons which could not be tolerated near the territory of the United States not only because of immediate national security considerations but also because of considerations of global prestige (although at that time U.S. nuclear missiles were deployed in Turkey and were “tolerated” by the Soviet Union). Moscow and Havana proceeded on the assumption that the American military threat to Cuba had not only remained after the Bay of Pigs but also had grown.[1] Washington stated that it had no intention of invading Cuba before the Caribbean crisis, and McNamara resolutely reaffirmed this at the Moscow symposium.

Thus, the two sides didn't understand or accept one another, and these disagreements in interpreting motives and intentions have not been overcome in twenty-six years. The disagreements may now be polite and somewhat subdued, but they still persist because they are rooted in the differences between two systems and how their politics operate.

However, at one key point the assessments, if not the interpretations, converged. They could not help but converge: The Soviet missiles had been transported to Cuba **secretly**.[2]

The secrecy of this action evoked particularly great displeasure on the part of the Kennedy administration, reinforcing the impression that the action was provocatively anti-American and aggressive in nature. As one of the American participants observed, “the severity of our reaction could be explained in particular by the fact that we had been deceived and that this constituted a known and conscious deception.” Another participant reminded the symposium that no secret had been made of the deployment of American missiles in Turkey and that the American and world public knew of them. Perceptions of deception and treachery did not arise merely because the opposing side could not agree with the Soviet interpretation of the defensive nature of the missiles. Another aspect of the situation was that early in September 1962, when the first doubts as to what kind of weapons were being shipped to Cuba had arisen but while there was still no photographic evidence, Nikita Khrushchev stated bluntly in a personal message to Kennedy sent through the Soviet ambassador that the Soviet Union had such powerful missiles that there was no need to look for them outside of Soviet territory, for example in Cuba.[3]

---

[1]“Bay of Pigs” refers to a failed attempt in 1961 to oust Fidel Castro's government made by Cuban exiles, backed by the U.S. government.

[2]Boldface passages here and below indicate emphasis in original.

[3]This information was taken from Arthur Schlesinger's book *The Thousand Days: John F. Kennedy in the White House*. This book has not

Judging by the testimony of the Soviet participants in the symposium, the issue of deploying missiles in Cuba had been pondered quite thoroughly and collectively by the Soviet leaders, and the decision took several months to carry out. But the symbolic essence of this step—its riskiness, its adventurism, or, putting it in complimentary terms, its "revolutionary romanticism"—is in my opinion best expressed by words attributed to Nikita Khrushchev. He said that "we had to put a porcupine in the Americans' pants." (This version is confirmed by Khrushchev's memoirs, which state that the "imperialist beast" had to be compelled to swallow a porcupine which it would be unable to digest.) Said and done. And the people who put it there, who in the Russian way focused their imagination only on how ticklish and terrible it would be for the person who had the porcupine in his pants, didn't take the trouble to think that the object of the experiment might not just get agitated but could become infuriated at the "revolutionary romantic."

Gromyko knew about the missiles. But Ambassador Dobrynin (as he once again confirmed at the symposium) didn't know. He didn't know in the sense that he hadn't been officially informed by Moscow or personally informed by Gromyko, who had come to a session of the United Nations. Our diplomats, journalists, and other employees in Washington also didn't officially know about them, although they could have guessed unofficially, on the basis of suggestions and reports in the American press, that where there was smoke there was fire. In Moscow this was a well-guarded secret which continued to be kept from our own people, as is our custom, even after other people, in Washington, had discovered it. Reconnaissance photographs had already appeared in American newspapers and on American television screens, but Soviet diplomats had to deny or to reject these facts or even to expose them as falsehoods by attempting to "prove" to Americans that there were no missile bases under construction at all and that the whole business was a falsification and a provocation.

These were the kinds of torments faced by Soviet diplomats and correspondents at the time. But this is only a small part of the picture compared to a gigantic fact that has never been given the requisite attention: **Our entire**

---

been published in the Soviet Union. (Cited by Kondrashov in original document.)

country was drawn to the brink of the nuclear abyss without knowing about it, being incapable of understanding from the Soviet mass media what kind of spark was setting the forest on fire. This was truly a dark epitome of **secrecy**.

From an objective point of view this could quite rightly be called deceiving the people, or in any case a complete disregard for the people's right to know about matters that may determine their destiny and that raise the issue of life or death. And only after October 28, when in an emergency exchange of messages Khrushchev and Kennedy worked out the conditions of a compromise and the tension was greatly diminished, did our press (and even then not immediately) begin hesitantly to mention the key word "missiles." Only after the people had walked away from the brink of the abyss did they begin to realize how close they had been. And only afterward were they taken aback, with the exception, of course, of those who listened to "the voices of the enemy."

My assertion may seem extreme. But just leaf through the newspapers of those days. Never once was there a word of explanation or a word of acknowledgment. The Americans knew, the Cubans knew, but our people didn't know.

In 1962, Khrushchev was just not faced with the question of whether he and the other leaders had the right to risk the fate of their own people for the sake of helping another people, the Cuban people. This right and other authoritarian rights in the field of foreign and domestic policy were understood. And they worried and frightened the bourgeois democratic governments of the West, which had no such rights, because their actions are restrained by parliaments. By the way, these discrepancies in methods of governmental administration, even without taking the other factors into account, have aggravated mistrust and have hindered the practice of cooperation, even when there has been agreement on the general principles of the peaceful coexistence of the two systems. The institution of the rule of law in the Soviet Union will eliminate many of the obstacles that feed the suspicions of our Western (and Far Eastern) partners. Democracy is a complex concept which varies for different countries, and moreover for different systems, but any effective democracy that is not just window dressing means politics out in the open, politics that can be seen by one's own people and by the entire world. The actions of a government of laws are open and more predictable than the actions of an authoritarian government, and this in itself facilitates dialogue and cooperation in the international arena.

During the Caribbean crisis, President Kennedy consulted not only with his own cabinet members and closest advisers but also with congressional leaders from both parties, he took into consideration the opinions of moderates and hard-liners, and he maneuvered under increasing pressure from the advocates of immediate military action. All of this is described in detail in American writings on the subject. From the press and from officials, Americans knew how the crisis was developing and were subjected to ideological influence from different directions.

Now, albeit much later, we have our first opportunity to publicly ask the questions that could not be asked before. These questions are not idle, because today we are haunted by the past. Did we draw the proper lessons from the Caribbean crisis? In a narrow sense, yes, because we've never taken nuclear missiles outside our country since then. But what about in the broad sense, in the sense of informing the people and enlightening the public, in the sense of public participation of one kind or another in making very important foreign policy decisions that are fraught with the risk of war or of a drastic rise in international tension and that could lead to the loss of life or the senseless expenditure of billions and billions of rubles? In the broad sense we have never posed the question of drawing lessons, in the same way that we have never posed the question of democratizing the country's foreign and military policies. Under [Leonid] Brezhnev we moved in the opposite direction, toward more bureaucratization.

As before, the most important decisions continued to be made behind the scenes, and they are still concealed, as the saying goes, in the shadows of the unknown. In the critical field where foreign policy issues touch on military issues, only documents of a general, often declarative nature have been available until now, but not concerning the specific strategic decisions that have determined the course of our military development (if, of course, it hasn't proceeded by inertia). Were these decisions thought out years and years ahead of time in light of their burden on the nation, possible countermeasures by the other side, or their possible consequences for East-West international relations?

Let's take an issue of historical significance, specifically how and at what price we acquired strategic parity with the

United States by the early 1970s. In looking at the last third of our century from the vantage point of the twenty-first century, historians of international relations might single out the following as a key point: how the Soviet Union sought military equality not just with the United States, but with practically the entire West, and how it subsequently, under the burden of unbearable military expenditures and after a sober analysis of the situation in the period of reform, withdrew to more modest and much more reasonable and responsible positions of defensive sufficiency. Parity was a historical achievement: This is what we heard from [Yuri] Andropov during his brief stay at the top, which coincided (the second half of 1983) with an extreme deterioration in Soviet-American relations.[4] And it was an achievement. But wasn't it a kind of Pyrrhic victory? What did we pay for parity at any cost? What is the flip side of this coin in the nuclear missile pocket of a superpower? While spending endless resources on the military and on space (another unexplored topic for research pertaining to the financially reckless "revolutionary romanticism" of unaccountable leaders) for the purpose of achieving parity in the Brezhnev era, we abandoned the peaceful industrial sectors which produce consumer goods, and we also abandoned agriculture, so that the process of transforming peasants into modern agriculturalists came to an end. And we were completely incapable of developing both one and the other.

The task of achieving parity at any cost inevitably posed a question of national priorities, and it seems that priority was given not to raising the people's standard of living, which is natural for peacetime, but to developing the military, which was never denied anything. Priority was given to military superpower status. And the best proof of this lies in the contrast that very few people saw before but which under *glasnost* everyone sees: a superpower in terms of military might and a third-rate country in terms of meeting the daily needs of its own people. Isn't it time to say that the flip side of the drive for military parity was domestic economic stagnation? Moreover (another unexplored subject), in addition to more intensive military competition with the West, relations with China remained tense in the 1960s and 1970s, which led to a buildup, once again excessive, of our

---

[4]In September 1983 the USSR shot down the Korean airliner KAL 007, killing all who were aboard.

armed forces in the East, which in turn, until the recent major steps to normalize the relations between the two socialist powers and to ease the military tension on the Soviet-Chinese border, fed Beijing's suspicions.

Another general and important question is that of the necessity and expedience of all these efforts—in other words, of the true aggressiveness of the United States and the West. I am profoundly convinced that our Stalinist heritage led us to underestimate the bourgeois democratic character of the United States and Western Europe and to exaggerate the military threat from them. Our thinking and actions were based on the "besieged fortress" complex handed down by Stalin which, as we know, he employed to justify the concept of "intensifying" the class struggle and to find more and more "enemies of the people." In this case we have been slow to part with Stalin, and the genes of our father and teacher are still having an effect. The new political thinking means speeding up this departure. In Eduard Shevardnadze's words, by undertaking the recent major unilateral reductions in our armed forces, the Soviet Union and its allies have sent a "political signal" to the other side, and this signal gives evidence "primarily of a new approach to assessing the probability and extent of the military threat from the West" and also "of our growing confidence that security can be assured to a greater degree by nonmilitary means."

Another very topical example of an expensive policy and of the reality in which the bureaucratic norm has triumphed over the democratic norm is Afghanistan, our nine-year war, which ended in February of this year to the great relief of the country. Let us put the question of whose fault it was, how we got there, and why we spent so much time in senseless bloodshed and the destruction of a foreign land off to the side and leave it open. Let's take another question, which could only be raised in the context of the extraordinary apathy of a society oppressed by total ideological and other control. The state and the authorities, the Ministry of Defense in particular, had the right (?!) to send young people to fight and die in a foreign land in peacetime (after all, we never declared war!), and society, the country, and the parents of these young people were even denied the right to ask publicly how many of them were fighting there and how many were dead and wounded. Every one of these soldiers truly died alone, and every family bore its grief alone. Of course, people would write to different agencies and to the press, which wouldn't publish their letters, and they would ask questions of lecturers, but a country that was officially living under developed socialism was "officially" silent. In nine years our highest constitutional body, the Supreme Soviet of the USSR, never made a single inquiry to the government concerning Afghanistan and our military presence there. From the point of view of any citizen of the United States, Great Britain, West Germany, France, Japan, India, or many other countries this would be unimaginable, but before reform and *glasnost* we couldn't imagine anything different.

How can we explain all this? We can explain it by the lack of a legal obligation for the authorities to account for their actions to citizens, even when the most important subject—human life—hangs in the balance. But I think there is also a more specific reason: the lack of an efficient system of public information which would operate almost automatically. Perhaps because we have been accustomed to the rigid old ways, we just haven't thought of new ways, although everyone is hearing the rehabilitated word "charity." Perhaps no one has gone to the authorities with a proposal for the systematic publication of information on Soviet casualties in Afghanistan. Perhaps. But, after all, no one has ever mentioned this "omission." In the era of ***glasnost***. Does this mean we're not supposed to?

In this regard it would be appropriate to mention that a figure for the casualties we suffered in the Great Patriotic War,[5] a figure which was cruelly rounded off and very approximate (twenty million dead), was first published not in 1945, under Stalin, to whom the question of casualties was not important, but only several years after his death, under Khrushchev. But there is no such approximation in other countries' count of the victims of the Second World War. For example, 292,131 Americans died directly in combat operations and another 115,185 died from wounds and other war-related causes.

A count to the closest million, and a count that is accurate to the individual. The difference not only indicates differences in the scale of the war and in the countries' parts in it but also speaks of the different historical phases which the two countries are passing through, different levels of development, different obligations by the state to its citizens,

---

[5]The Soviet name for World War II.

and ultimately of different degrees of human dignity and different values placed on human life.

Without a fundamentally new level of openness and truth in military affairs, we cannot count on stable trust in our policies in the world around us. But the primary responsibility of the authorities is to their own people. We cannot speak of the triumph of new political thinking as long as this pillar of the old thinking, our irrational obsession with secrecy, is still standing. We also cannot speak of the rational management of affairs in the country or of the rational mobilization of manpower and resources for reform. If the people are truly the owners of their country, we ought to confirm the people as true owners and to confirm their right to verify how the economy is being managed, where the wealth they produce is going, and what the true expenditures on defense are through the agency of their duly elected representatives. We are not just talking about thrift but about the people's right to democratically determine national priorities to suit popular and social priorities.

25

Russia: The Earth's Heartland

Igor Malashenko

International Affairs
no. 7, July 1990

Discussion in the USSR of the notion of a "Soviet empire" reflects a newly acquired freedom to criticize official policy. On the other hand, a reiteration of the old thesis that the Russian empire was defensive in nature is treated skeptically by the rest of the world. Nonetheless, Malashenko, a senior consultant to the International Department of the Central Committee, rightly refers to the geopolitical aspects of the Soviet-American rivalry. He points out that the Soviets imposed Stalinist socialism on Eastern Europe, although he claims that the Soviet armies were trying to prevent a repeat of the 1941 invasion. The "loss" of Eastern Europe arouses groundless fears among hardened conservatives. To calm them down, Malashenko advances the interesting theory that it would be wise for the far-flung Soviet forces to retreat from their precariously dangerous deployment.

Geopolitical Alignment

Geopolitics, as the term suggests, is the politics of a country as determined by its geographical features.[1] Russia, as one of the founding fathers of geopolitics, Sir Halford John MacKinder, held in his day, occupies a central position on the world's map and lies in its key region, the Heartland, a giant quadrangle bordering on the Caspian Sea and Lake Baikal in the south and the Arctic seas in the north.

Relative though such realities are, this region does bring, as if in focus, all lines of force of the great continent that constitutes the greater part of the Earth's land surface and contains most of its manpower and economic resources. A classic postulate of geopolitics, as MacKinder formulated it, is: Those who control Eastern Europe dominate the Heartland; those who rule the Heartland dominate the World Island (that is, Eurasia); those who rule the World Island dominate the world. Zbigniew Brzezinski, dismissing the

[1]Boldface, here and below, indicates emphasis in original document.

Heartland as an archaic notion, "straightens" this geopolitical syllogism: Those who control Eurasia dominate the world.

The confrontation of the continental power that controls the heart of Eurasia and the coalition opposing it is by no means confined, geopolitically, to a contest between East and West, between socialism and capitalism (or between "totalitarianism" and "liberal democracy," in Western parlance), as has quite often been said over the last few decades. It is an element of genuinely global politics. Properly speaking, the very terms "East" and "West" also reflect in a way, if inadequately, that it is not only an ideological rivalry, or even a clash of sociopolitical systems, but also a "deideologized" geopolitical confrontation.

Of course, genuinely global politics is a historically recent phenomenon. However, attempts at establishing control over the whole world were made more than once in ancient times as well.

For centuries Russia beat off the West's numerous attempts at establishing control over Eastern Europe, as through the expansionism of Lithuania, Poland, France, and Germany. There appeared to be only one way to ensure the security of Russia and the key region belonging to it: to raise a well-defended geopolitical barrier around it, brick by brick, block by block. This task arose over and over again before various rulers, dynasties, and even political systems. The creation of the empire was a response to the geopolitical challenge of the West.

By the turn of the century, the imperial idea whose legitimacy had not been called into question for ages had ceased to serve as the raison d'être of polyethnic states. Traditional empires began to crumble, and Russia seemed destined to have the same fate. However, the revolution gave a fresh and powerful impulse to reinforcing the state, which possessed a machinery of violence of unprecedented proportions, and—what is particularly important—a new source of legitimacy for its power over vast territories of Eurasia.

Revolutionary ideology became an invisible yet powerful force linking up the parts of the former empire, which disintegrating trends seemed certain to detach from each other. Whenever it was necessary, the instrument used to preserve the unity of the state or to build it up was armed force, which seemed to be a quite lawful continuation of revolutionary violence. There emerged a new political body, a revolutionary empire actually based not on the discredited imperial idea and the nominal "democratic expression of the will" of the peoples in favor of a federation, but instead a revolution which had welded together its power, on the verge of disintegration, by iron, blood, and ideology.

The strength of the Soviet state was clearly underestimated by the Third Reich, whose strategists understood well that domination in the heart of Eurasia was the key to world supremacy. Nazi Germany's geopolitical challenge, monstrous in its scale and power, united the Soviet Union (for which World War II was a struggle for survival) and the Western powers which sought to prevent key geostrategic positions from being seized by an avowedly aggressive state.

After the defeat of the Axis powers there was a sweeping realignment of forces which grouped the Soviet Union's wartime allies with its recent opponents. The international order based on a balance of forces in Europe crumbled during the war, and a power vacuum arose on the European continent. The interests of the two mightiest powers, the Soviet Union and the United States, which became geopolitical rivals, were bound to clash. The USSR and the United States have become the main poles of the international system, and relations between them have become the main axis of world politics.

The geopolitical division of Europe was maintained by a high level of military-political opposition (which froze the development of traditional contradictions and problems on the continent) and supplemented by a separation due to ideological and sociopolitical considerations. But, while the "threat from the East" (or at least the belief in it) and an organically "Western" identity constituted a fairly solid base for the unity of the NATO countries, the nations of Eastern Europe for the most part found Stalinist "socialism," imposed on them, obviously trying. In those circumstances, ideological opposition to the West was largely no more than a "transformed" geopolitical confrontation.

What Moscow saw as the main threat to the nation's security was the prospect of a repetition of what had happened in 1941—that is, yet another attempt by a hostile coalition to launch a massive invasion of the territory of the USSR and to destroy it as a sovereign state. It was the top priority of national security policy to avert that threat. One way to deter possible aspirants to domination of Eurasia was to make a "buffer zone" of the states of central and southeastern Europe under the direct military and political control of the USSR and to keep mammoth ground forces, with their most efficient units advanced well to the west, at the line of contact with a potential enemy.

During the Cold War, however, the Soviet Union's main opponent was a naval power which, considering the postwar alignment of forces and the strengthened positions of the Soviet Union, could not count on establishing direct control over the heart of Eurasia. It was the founder of the American school of geopolitics, Admiral Alfred Mahan, who first warned that the center of Russia could not be broken and called for her to be "contained" by strong pressure on the flanks. This idea formed the basis of the United States' postwar "grand strategy."

In the early postwar years American strategists may have thought that the U.S. monopoly on atomic weapons and strategic delivery vehicles deprived the Heartland of its traditional defensibility and allowed Washington to hope for the acquisition of a global position of strength. However, with the Soviet Union developing a modern nuclear potential which would make the mainland United States no longer invulnerable, there was no more ground left for any expectations about "breaking the center of Russia."

In an attempt to counter the pressure on the flanks, the Soviet Union strove not only to keep all of its postwar gains but also to increase its security and to extend its sphere of influence. It could do so mostly in distant regions of little geopolitical importance. Yet control over them was, on the one hand, extremely dear to achieve and, on the other, of practically no use in resolving the key objective of ensuring national security. Besides, the traditional methods of military-political control over peripheral territories proved increasingly ineffective as time went on.

For instance the attempt to solve the Afghan problem by armed force, far from adding to the security of the USSR, created a seat of instability across its southern border. Meanwhile, military aid to a number of Third World regimes turned out to be just an extra economic burden as well as damaging to this country's political reputation.

The colossal Soviet military buildup on the territory of the Warsaw Pact countries did not prevent the social and political trends that ended Soviet political control, if not yet influence, over them. While the Warsaw Treaty Organization is fast breaking up, the North Atlantic Treaty Organization (NATO), although undergoing some change as well, stands united and capable. The weakening of the political positions of the USSR in central Europe is accompanied by a reduction of its military presence in that region. In the meantime, the unification of Germany is going on by leaps and bounds. Sooner or later, that country will succeed in translating its enormous economic strength into political influence, acquiring the status of a European superpower.

The opponents of the Soviet Union have enough reason to speak of their success: The USSR has to relinquish its military-political control over Eastern Europe. It is no longer seeking to prevent another center of force from emerging on the European continent. Only a few rudiments remain of its "sphere of influence" in the Third World. To cap it all, threatening seats of instability have arisen within its own national frontiers. In Washington's opinion, one of the objectives of the postwar U.S. strategy, which George Kennan once described as the "gradual mellowing of Soviet power," has been achieved. It is not surprising that, in the new circumstances, President [George] Bush should have declared his intention of going beyond the framework of deterrence, inasmuch as its objectives have been achieved. The point is, however, not just whether to concede the victory of the United States or the defeat of the Soviet Union, but to consider the significance of the present geopolitical shifts from the standpoint of national security.

The Post-Postwar Period

The end of the Cold War has produced not only a feeling of relief in Soviet society over the winding-up of the long-drawn-out confrontation but also fresh fears over our security and dissatisfaction with the results of years of efforts. Amid apprehensions over the erosion of this country's international positions, it is often asked whether we did the right thing by allowing Eastern Europe to slip out of Soviet control or by reducing our military potential there. Some are urging us to "remember 1941." It would, however, have been far more appropriate to have reminded us of the blitzkrieg (which caught us napping) in the years during which we created and maintained a state of our own vulnerability. For, in fear of a NATO invasion, the USSR deployed its crack divisions in such a way that it would inevitably have lost them, as it did in 1941, in the event of a surprise enemy attack.

Of course, neither the United States nor NATO as a whole has hardly ever contemplated a lasting war against the Soviet Union in the European theater of operations: That would be too much for either the political or the economic system of the West to sustain. But the "probable adversary" has, apparently, succeeded in using its technological edge to create a military potential capable of breaking down Soviet advanced forces by using a wide range of superior hardware, by blocking the reserves, and—thanks to naval supremacy and a ramified system of bases—by striking at the Heartland from all directions.

This probability did not develop into a reality, both because of the common determination of the contending parties to avoid an armed confrontation and because of the existence of the nuclear factor, which keeps even dramatic crises and conflicts from escalating into a war. Today the probability of war is drastically reduced by a new quality of political relations between all parties to the Cold War. But however small the danger may be of a direct confrontation between the East (the Soviet Union, to be exact) and the West, it is still there, and therefore any change of the international order that means lessening the vulnerability of the Soviet armed forces means enhancing our national security.

The withdrawal of most (and possibly all) Soviet forces from the territory of the Warsaw Pact countries will greatly reduce the danger arising from their forward deployment. Of course, this pullout must be accompanied by certain guarantees of the Soviet Union's security and by maintenance of a wide disengagement zone established along the perimeter of its Western frontier. This will not ward off any further attempts at exerting pressure, but it will conjure away the specter of yet another blitzkrieg.

There is, in point of fact, a dismantling of our system of military and political control going on over vast areas that have been traditionally considered crucial to this country's security. This in turn creates the possibility of transforming the cumbersome, vulnerable, and extremely expensive military machine, which is still best suited—despite all readjustments to meet the challenges of the day—for enacting the battles of World War II. It has to be replaced by truly modern armed forces, militarily and technologically upgraded and geared to resisting not even so much the present war danger as the future one.

The Soviet Union's ability to influence its international environment and, in the long run, the strength of its geopolitical positions will depend in large measure on whether or not this country succeeds in embracing a new model of economic, social, and political development. Relative "demilitarization" and "economization" of international relations do not mean that a geopolitical realignment is impossible. It cannot be achieved (at least in the foreseeable future) by military means. The Soviet Union still holds the key geopolitical positions. If it grows so weak that a power vacuum appears in the middle of Eurasia, the vacuum will inevitably be filled by one or several contiguous powers greatly augmenting their specific weight and influence.

Why is it, then, that today, when many find the Soviet Union slipping downhill, Western leaders (above all, those of the United States), far from trying to speed up this process, are speaking of their "support for *perestroika*" and not going into raptures over the prospect of some republics leaving the USSR, let alone of it breaking up?

Successive American administrations never tire of making the point that it is in the vital interest of the United States to "prevent any hostile power or group of powers from dominating the Eurasian land mass." It should be added that any state aiming to achieve this—whatever its ideology or sociopolitical system—would surely be viewed by Washington as hostile by definition, so to speak. Practical geopoliticians prefer, I think, to see the Heartland of Eurasia still controlled by a Soviet Union worn down in the Cold War and, in their opinion, growing weaker still, rather than to face new "troublemakers" and the threat of a succession of crises and conflicts.

What is happening today, both because of the weakening of the Soviet Union and as a result of the emergence of new centers of power in Eurasia, is an erosion of the postwar structure of bipolar confrontation. This is being replaced by a multipolar system of international relations built largely on a balance of forces—and not only and not so much military force, in the present circumstances.

Beyond Geopolitics

The central political issue of *perestroika* is the problem of the legitimacy of power, of its "lawfulness" in the full sense of the term, not only and not so much in legal as in sociopolitical and historical respects. With over seven decades gone since the revolution, one shouldn't be surprised at the gradual weakening of the role of revolutionary legacy as the source of the legitimacy of power and the cementing force in the polyethnic state. Remembering the historical fate of other revolutions, it is rather more surprising that this weakening process should not have begun much earlier. The future of this polyethnic state depends, to a certain extent, on the results of the search for a new framework of legitimacy through democratic development.

The gradual dismantling of the structures of totalitarianism and the natural process of the extension and consolidation of democracy spotlight the imperial origin of the present federation, in which disintegrating trends are gaining momentum. The idea of democracy and its political "materialization" can hardly by themselves serve as a sufficiently solid "backbone" for an updated federation. As one can see, for instance, from the record of Yugoslavia's democratic process after Marshal Tito, a stronger antidote is needed to neutralize nationalism.

An overall reform of the economy and the progress toward economic integration which it is quite likely to stimulate can set off centripetal trends. The present state of the Soviet economy is actually fueling the separatist trends: Just about every republic or region is dissatisfied with its place in the system of the division of labor and, still more so, with its share of the economic pie. So long as the economic system ensured extensive growth, at least, with the political system blocking outbreaks of nationalism and regionalism, the status quo was somehow tolerated. The crisis in the economy and political democratization made a recasting of the economic system imperative.

Another central question—from the standpoint of the union's future and geopolitics—is that of the future of Russia, which has historically occupied the key region of Eurasia. It was largely for the sake of its security that an empire was built. It is this circumstance, incidentally, that Zbigniew Brzezinski wanted to have taken into consideration in making American plans for a nuclear strike at the USSR to hit "notably on its imperial Great Russian component."[2] The concept of "ethnic targeting" (as this principle of nuclear genocide came to be called) was simple: The Russians had created the empire, so wiping them out would hasten its collapse. This is no longer a case of geopolitics, nor even of geostrategy (an alloy of strategy and geography), but of ethnopolitics, so to speak.

Russia is by no means an imperial state only, having mechanically united an incredibly multifarious conglomerate of lands. It is an ethnically and culturally unique country (a "superethnos," as Lev Gumilev called it), lying in Europe and Asia—that is, a Eurasian country in the true sense of the word—which was not only an instrument of expansionism but also a powerful center of attraction for numerous ethnoses.

There is, however, a diametrically opposite view, widespread in the West, that Russia has no "cultural magnetism" at all and that therefore nobody will ever willingly stay within its fold. Well, the West (that is, much of Europe and the United States) is an entirely different ethnocultural entity, an older and more mature superethnos which in itself creates a very strong field of gravitation. (Witness, at least, the countless articles in our press on "how to go European.")

The zone of superethnic contact is a likely arena for the appearance of geopolitical complications. Above all, a number of countries of central (Eastern) Europe have constituted such a zone throughout the postwar period. "This region has always looked West, not East," said George Bush in 1983, being then vice president. He made a point of stressing the historical and cultural orientation of that part of Europe. This argument, although it was backed up in that speech with rather incorrect reasoning, is more difficult to challenge today than it was seven years ago.

Of course, Russian history is far from a tinsel picture of a voluntary union of peoples. Many of its peoples were incorporated as a result of wars and conquests. Those territories of the former empire that have never become integral to the fabric of Russia and that irresistibly gravitate toward other superethnoses (not necessarily Western, but Muslim as well) are most likely to strive consistently for secession. However painful this process might be, the

---

[2]Zbigniew Brzezinski, *Game Plan*, 1986, p. 192 (cited by Malashenko).

strength and security of a reborn federation will hardly suffer, in the end.

For centuries, the vast diversity of the various parts of Russia has served not so much as a threat to her integrity as a condition for her preservation as an ethnocultural system. Official Russification and imperial depersonalization, although they provoked natural rejection in the provinces, still did not create anything like a real danger to the very survival of ethnoses and to their distinctive development. This system would certainly have become so complex and even unwieldy as to require alteration and simplification at the turn of the century. The disintegration of the empire, with some "blocks" breaking away, would quite likely have given rise to a more integral and compact entity capable of evolution. What happened instead was an oversimplification of the internal structure, the removal of the partitions that separated the various ethnocultural elements, and the "straightening" of connections between them. It was like a giant steamroller passing over the surface of this Eurasian country, leveling the distinctions between the various ethnoses and cultures.

For a time, the dismantling of this structure, which had taken a tremendous effort to maintain, generated a vast amount of energy to use outside national frontiers—for example, for establishing the direct military-political control of the state over new vast territories, advancing far to the West. But the same process of dismantling undermined the nation's major internal source of strength and viability and condemned it to stagnation.

One cannot, unfortunately, rule out the possibility that the decades of coercion by the state, deportation of ethnic communities, and destruction of culture might have reduced to nothing the forces of ethnocultural attraction which made Russia what it was, rather than just a "Russian empire." If confidence between our ethnic communities turns out to have been irreparably damaged, and if the repulsive forces prevail in relations between them, we will have only one prospect in store—that of a nationalistic upheaval in the Heartland of Eurasia, beside which even the most macabre variations of the German question pale into insignificance.

Today, however, we have far less ground for pessimism than we had just a few years ago when this country floundered in the deadening grip of immobility. This hope for the better comes largely, strange though it might be, from the same drive for independence and regionalism which in their extreme manifestation beget outbreaks of violence and militant separatism. The pressure of some regions, whether the national republics as such or the Russian Federation and its individual components, for secession and their pursuit of a form of autonomy spring not only from their economic interests (these are easy to see) but also from intensified ethnocultural processes without which you cannot imagine the rebirth of Russia as a "nation of nations." And if Russia should still remain a symbiosis of various ethnoses and cultures, her rebirth will be a natural and powerful process, and we shall beyond question come to occupy a worthy place in Eurasia and, hence, in the world.

Russia and the empire have different lots in store for them. The Cold War ended with the defeat of the empire. And this defeat of the empire has been the starting point for the regeneration of Russia and a new geopolitical round.

26

A Time to Learn What the Events in Eastern Europe Are Telling Us

Anatoly Butenko

Nedelya
no. 11, 1990

Butenko, a senior researcher at the Institute of Economics of the World System, analyzes Eastern Europe's rejection of socialism and why the Communist parties lost power. It is important, he says, for the Soviet people and the Communists to know why the Soviet Union is lagging behind. Why should Communists initiate reforms if it is clear that they will be the losers? The Communist parties that imposed "barracks socialism" became bureaucratized and alienated from the workers. They are now giving way to new "elites," who are restoring capitalism. Nevertheless, according to Butenko, if you believe in the ideas of social justice, then reforms must be initiated, and the sooner the better. In his view, the restoration of capitalism will be attempted "furtively." He doubts that workers will agree to the presence of capitalists in their countries, even if it will improve their material well-being. Lazy workers, in particular, will be unhappy with capitalism. Butenko justifies Gorbachev's inaction in Eastern Europe. Delaying change could have only led to bloody upheavals like the one in Romania. From this angle, Butenko views a multiparty system as being preferable to a one-party system.

It is doubtful that anyone would deny that almost every Soviet person is attentively following the events in the fraternal European countries and is trying to make sense of them in some way.

The processes under way in these countries are outwardly dressed in the quite decent clothes of a democratic transition from the power monopoly of a single Marxist-Leninist party to a system of parliamentary democracy involving not the rule of one party but the competition of several parties, which will struggle with one another for political power and for the trust and support of the electorate. But this, I repeat, is only the shell of what is transpiring. More important is that this transition has been stimulated by the collapse of the former authorities—the parties that once ruled and had become bureaucratized and divorced from the workers, and had led their countries into socioeconomic crises and dead ends which evoked the dissatisfaction and anger of millions. And once again this statement of the situation does not completely characterize the transition that is under way. It is much more important to expose its inner essence and to clarify whether this constitutes a rejection of the socialist path of development and the confirmation of a new "elite" in power which wants to gradually reimpose capitalism on the people who have risen up. Who in this process will safeguard the interests of the overwhelming majority of the population, namely the workers, and how?

No doubt the complex and contradictory events currently under way in central and southeastern Europe, where powerful Communist parties which existed and ruled for decades are breaking up, losing members, and disappearing from the political arena, will be studied for a long time to come, and not just by the parties associated with the ideals of socialism. Even now it is important to derive certain lessons, at least for those Communists whom the bitter cup has bypassed for the time being and who are prepared to acquire intelligence and reason in order to keep from disappearing once and for all under the implacable grindstones of history.

It is even more important for us Soviet Communists and for all Soviet people to ponder these lessons now, after the February plenary session of the Communist party's Central Committee, which has opened up the prospect of a multiparty system to Soviet society. A new approach to complex problems that have long required unique solutions is now emerging.

Our country is a vast nation which extends over two continents. Events in our country are developing, and this could not be otherwise, at a different and slower pace than they are in the relatively small countries of central and southeastern Europe. It's easier to get a small rowboat going than a huge barge. Only naive people or tricksters pretending to be fools would bemoan the fact that we are once again lagging behind our neighbors after beginning before they did. But how are we lagging? Because we are not conducting the witch-hunt and Communist hunt that has already begun in some places? Because we are lagging behind in the restoration of capitalism and in the rise in unemployment? Or in the number of suicides? Or what else? And why is it so bad to be lagging behind? Isn't it because we are used to "being first," "going ahead," and teaching others? And perhaps all of this is even better? Perhaps hasn't fate finally given us the chance to learn from the experience of others? To ponder the lessons of history and where their essence lies?

Lesson One.[1] When Communist authorities face the task of renewing the socialism created under their aegis, the prestige of Communists will not increase because of this. In a number of cases it will decline so catastrophically that only with a full accounting of such grave consequences and with improbable efforts will they be able to remain "afloat" without completely losing their authority and remain in power.

Obviously the conclusion that follows from this is clear to everyone: In order to keep such situations from arising, we should not lead the development of our society into such crises, and we should not lead our countries into socioeconomic dead ends. But I think that just saying this is not enough. Because only a person who doesn't do anything doesn't make any mistakes. But how should we proceed if mistakes have already been made and society is in a crisis or at a dead end? Is it worth it at all for Communists to attempt to reform or renew socialism if their results in this situation are so miserable, first of all, for the Communists themselves?

Does the Communist party of the Soviet Union or its leaders need to take on the initiative of reform now that bloody clashes in Transcaucasia have occurred, separatist attitudes in the Baltic republics are growing, and the economic crisis is growing graver and threatens an explosion of dissatisfaction and general civil war everywhere? Should the Polish Communist party have offered a seat at the discussion table to the opposition, only to suffer a crushing defeat in the elections for the Polish parliament after legalizing it and to become a semioppositional party which terminated its existence at its 11th Congress?

Let us be open: These or similar questions have come into the mind of every Communist who is troubled by the fate of the entire Communist movement, and they have gnawed at the souls of the sponsors of reform and renewal. What is worse is the fact that halfhearted doubts have crept in; to wit, aren't we by our own actions creating such grave situations for ourselves and driving ourselves into a corner? Could it be that admitting errors, repenting, and going back to the sources aren't for us?

It is quite obvious that, for everyone who thinks that socialism is a stillborn idea imposed by Communists on their

---

[1]Boldface here and below indicates emphasis in original.

countries, the answer to this question presents no difficulties and is quite clear and extremely simple: Sooner or later, but inevitably, people must recognize their error and thus reject the idea of socialism and the Communists and return to the bosom of capitalism.

But for the people who believe that social justice is an everlasting idea, which neither the crimes of Stalin and the Stalinists nor the very gross errors and perversions of the Communists who tried to realize this idea by means of bureaucratic "barracks socialism" could kill, the answer is also clear, but different. If it was the trampled ideal of social justice that inspired millions of people in central and southeastern Europe, and if under its banner these people are so resolutely sweeping the bastions of neo-Stalinism and the injustice of "barracks socialism" off the European stage, only naive fools could think that these millions of people would tomorrow easily agree to put on the yoke of the social injustices of capitalism, injustices whose existence has never been disputed by anyone.

If we answer the general question that's been posed forthrightly, then our answer is: Communists have sworn their fidelity not to their leaders but to their countries and have promised to wage an uncompromising struggle for social justice. If Communist leaders have deceived them in this respect, and if "real socialism" has in fact turned out to be Stalin's "barracks socialism," then, in remaining true to their oath to be faithful to the people, Communists not only must sooner or later part with this system but also are obligated to prevent its consolidation and dominance.

This explains why the very task of renewing socialism means admitting mistakes and therefore doesn't add to the authority of party members. For the same reason, Communists should have no problem answering whether reforms should be initiated or not. This is a problem not for honest Communist politicians but for political intriguers and for everyone who believes that if Gorbachev had not begun the reform process in the mid-1980s the parasites could have sat on the necks of the people for another five or ten years! Perhaps they could have! But then could Communists like that have even considered themselves Communists?

Lesson Two. The longer it takes a ruling Communist party to recognize the social injustice of the social orders created under its leadership, and the longer it tries to hold onto power that has lost authority among the people, the stronger and deeper will be the schism between the party and the people, and the more difficult it will be to bridge with good intentions the gap separating the party and the workers.

All is well for a time, but in politics this is like postponing death; in this case, any delay and any inconsistency can lead to incalculable disasters. Everything that transpired late in 1989 in central and southeastern Europe gives evidence that the faster and more resolutely Communists themselves deal with the mistakes, miscalculations, and distortions in their own party and in its leadership, the less the party and socialism will be discredited in the country, and the less the anger felt by the people against the party and its members will be.

I would like to remind the people who are now trying to blame reform and its initiator, Mikhail Gorbachev, for the bloody events in Transcaucasia (and to blame those who began discussions and negotiations for the defeat of the Polish Communists in the elections to the Polish parliament) that the development of socioeconomic systems has its own logic, which is independent of the nobility or baseness of the Communists in power, and that a system that is rotting alive is always and inevitably condemned to death. However its fall may occur, be it in bloody fighting, in an uncontrolled rebellion, or in a "gentle revolution," and whether it will crush its creators under its own ruins or not—all of this depends on many factors, primarily on the actions of party members and on their effectiveness and decisiveness.

The development of events in the Soviet Union, Romania, and Poland clearly confirms the differences here. An administrative-bureaucratic system that was incompatible with socialist principles existed in the Soviet Union for a longer period than in the other countries. And the revolutionary reform of this system began as early as 1985—that is, earlier than in the other fraternal countries. Vadim Medvedev, a secretary of the Central Committee of the Soviet Communist party, stated at the February plenary session that

> such a critical mass of explosive material had accumulated over decades of deformation and stagnation that if there was any further delay it could cause an upheaval of unbelievable force. Now we can see this even more clearly in the example of the East European countries. I am profoundly convinced that reform, and the fact that it has

> made it possible to get to the roots of many problems and proceed to the development of new democratic mechanisms and structures, allowed us to prevent a very grave turn of events and avoid a catastrophe.

Does this mean that Soviet society has already passed the danger point? No! "We've gotten the opportunity to convert this explosion into a controlled reaction, although this is only an opportunity," Medvedev said in the same speech, "and how we take advantage of this opportunity depends on our decisions and actions today."

As we know, the criminal policies of Nicolae Ceausescu and his cohorts made it impossible to avoid such an explosion in Romania, and transformations in other countries also began too late, which led to an incredible loss of authority on the part of Communists and their parties.

The events in Poland developed quite dramatically. The first secretary of the Polish Communist party, Mieczyslaw Rakowski, was asked whether it wouldn't have been better for the party and its leaders not to have proposed discussions and acknowledge the opposition as a real political force. He answered in the following way:

> I am profoundly convinced and will say that sooner or later, but probably sooner, the situation would have proceeded to the same kind of anarchy as in Berlin or in Prague. Knowing the temperament of my countrymen, one could have guessed that in Warsaw we would have had "two Pragues" or "three Berlins." In my opinion we selected the only right course.
>
> I am the last person who would want to blame the Soviet Union for our own failures and mistakes. However, there is still no doubt that in past decades our party was heavily influenced by the programs and plans carried out by the Communist party of the Soviet Union. This is a truth that is impossible to deny.[2]

Let us add for ourselves that if the Stalinists and neo-Stalinists had not removed Nikita Khrushchev from the leadership of the party and the country in 1964, and if the reforms had continued, we could hypothesize that Soviet society would have overcome a great deal of what became

---

[2]"The Goal: Democratic Socialism," an interview with the first secretary of the Polish Communist party, Mieczyslaw Rakowski (*Pravda*, January 24, 1990). (Cited by Butenko.)

burdensome for the country in the 1970s and 1980s. A great deal of precious time was lost.

Lesson Three. A multiparty system, even if it is inefficient, is a firmer guarantee of peaceful social transformation than is a one-party system. The feverish events of 1989 gave evidence that in the countries where a multiparty system had been preserved (Poland, East Germany, Bulgaria, and Czechoslovakia) the loss of reputation of Communists and their parties, although it involved the collapse of the old political structure of society, did not have catastrophic consequences. A number of socially important functions, which made it possible to control the development and to keep it from becoming anarchically confrontational and bloody, passed to other parties and organizations ("The Popular Forum," "The Civil Initiative," and so forth).

Where a one-party system existed, as in Romania, the disgrace of the supreme leadership, whose despotic power rested on the party apparatus, was transferred by the masses to the party itself (hence the demands to disband and ban the Romanian Communist party). Under these conditions society, which had created a National Salvation Front supported by the army and which had proceeded to the gradual development of a multiparty system, was in reality deprived of the necessary political structures that would make it possible to come to grips with an extraordinary situation which proved to be quite dangerous. During practically all of January 1990, Romanian society was threatened with the real danger of becoming a toy in the hands of irresponsible social forces (such as effusive youths and students, hooligan elements, and so forth) who were then still capable of imposing their own will on the still-shaky new authorities. The intensification of these processes, which compelled the National Salvation Front to appeal to the working class for support, almost led to a direct clash between the opposing forces.

The bloody events in Timisoara and Bucharest revealed the sinister face of Stalinism in its modern form: Neither material difficulties nor the lack of civil rights are capable of keeping Stalinists from defending their barren power and privileges. Moreover, no kind of sufferings on the part of the populace, not even the blood of hundreds and thousands of people, can stop Stalinists in their fight for the power they have usurped from the people and their desire to defend their illegal domination with the support of the party and government bureaucracy and armed force, or their readiness to use tanks to crush the desires of their peoples and their fellow citizens for freedom.

Lesson Four. The greater the efforts, difficulties, and sacrifices involved in establishing new arrangements in one country or another, the more noticeable the positive changes that "socialist power" has brought to these countries. And the more organic and thus stronger they are for the people of the country, the more difficult it will be for antisocialist forces to turn these countries back toward the restoration of capitalism.

In order to be convinced of the major differences here, all one has to do is compare, on one hand, the strength of the revolutionary gains of the Soviet Union, China, and Vietnam (where the consolidation of the new power was accompanied by a very bloody battle by their peoples for freedom and independence) with, on the other hand, the strength of the new power and the new orders in Hungary, Czechoslovakia, Poland, Bulgaria, Romania, and East Germany, where a beachhead for the establishment of a "noncapitalist system" was cleared by the victories of the Red Army.

Who said that only successes on the common socialist path have national peculiarities? The disasters and failures on the as-yet-inchoate common high road to socialism also have specific national traits!

Lesson Five. The modern adherents of capitalism in central and southeastern Europe are not so primitive as to appeal openly to the workers to reject socialism and to "struggle" for capitalism in all cases. Under the current conditions, and in light of the prolonged dominance of certain ideological stereotypes and the psychology of the citizens, there are grounds to assume that the capitalist restoration will as a rule proceed furtively and gradually.

Of course, in some countries socialist development has become quite profoundly discredited in the eyes of the workers. For example, in Poland people are openly proclaiming the sunset of the era of "real socialism" in the Polish republic and exhibiting the unconcealed desire to restore capitalism in Poland in its old nineteenth-century clothes.

However, in other countries, as is quite obvious to everyone already, the policy of restoring capitalism cannot be so open. First of all, not every worker and every toiler, who knows quite well that capitalism in any form means the exploitation of the workers, is prepared to agree to the presence of capitalists and of exploitation in his country for the sake of improving his own material situation. Second, the improvement in material well-being anticipated as the restoration of capitalism progresses will not happen overnight and will require a difficult transition with a rise in prices, unemployment, and so forth; a lack of social protection; labor conflicts; and hard-to-predict changes in the consciousness and actions of the workers. It would be ridiculous to think that the hope of realizing the formula "Work like we do, and get paid like they do" will disappear very rapidly and painlessly.

Not so long ago the newspaper *Washington Post* rightly wrote that "the main issue now facing Eastern Europe and the Soviet Union is whether people will be able to begin working in a different way. East Europeans have not worked very hard, because for forty years working hard hasn't made much sense. Hence in the years ahead it is not only the politicians who will have to work harder if they want democracy to have a chance to survive."

Third, the old maxim of "What we have we don't take care of, but once we've lost it we cry over it" could also play quite a cruel joke on the current apologists for capitalism who are counting on a painless turn toward the restoration of capitalism in their own countries. Even now one can hardly find jokers who would believe that the workers of central and southeastern Europe, who have to a large extent been corrupted by wage leveling, drunkenness, and endless idle time and "smoke breaks," and who have still not tasted labor in the capitalist way and have been accustomed to looking at the state as an almshouse and the administration as a milk cow, will immediately become model workers and toilers without resisting or putting up a fight. This is how we'll have to answer all of today's boasters who have portrayed rivers overflowing with milk and honey. Once everyone realizes that the capitalist paradise will require endless sweat, which our workers forgot about a long time ago, up close it will look quite different than it does in the fantasies of its current apologists.

These are several lessons from the current events in Eastern Europe.

27

Nation on the Eve of War: Subjective Notes on the Margins of Letters from Strangers

Irina Lagutina

New Times
no. 3, January 1991

Thousands of letters pouring into Iraq's embassy in Moscow with expressions of support for Saddam Hussein testify to the serious political malaise of the Soviet people. Morality has not yet become a criterion for Soviet actions and thinking because of the well-established spirit of totalitarianism and a strong belief in the use of force. The Soviet Union, according to journalist Lagutina, is called a superpower only because of its military might. That is why only one prominent politician, Eduard Shevardnadze, has been bold enough to call Iraq an aggressor.

The Persian Gulf: "Please Consider Me as a Volunteer"

These letters came to the Iraqi embassy and to the Soviet Ministry of Defense. They are from Soviet volunteers who want to fight in the Persian Gulf on different sides of the conflict. At the request of the Iraqi embassy, we are publishing letters addressed to Saddam Hussein without the authors' signatures.

> I am a citizen of the USSR. I am thirty-four years old, have a college education, and live in Tbilisi.
>
> I was greatly agitated and depressed when I heard of the beginning of the blockade against the Republic of Iraq, in which my country has taken part. I can't understand how we could betray a friend and country with which we've had very warm relations for eighteen years, since April 9, 1972. Although, of course, it would be hard to expect anything different from the Soviet government. On April 9, 1989, the Soviet leadership opened fire on a peaceful demonstration in Tbilisi, betraying its own people. As a symbol of protest against the actions of the Soviet government with respect to the Republic of Iraq, as

a symbol of protest against the actions of the Soviet government in the events of April 9, 1989, in the city of Tbilisi, and as a sign of support for my idol Saddam Hussein, I would like to enlist as a volunteer in the army of the Republic of Iraq. I am healthy and have previously served in the Soviet army.

Tbilisi, Georgia

I am thirty-three years old. I served as a warrant officer in the Soviet army for nine years. As a result of the reduction in the armed forces I am now a civilian. I was a tank company technician and worked on T-72 and T-64 tanks.

I would like to express my total solidarity with the people of Iraq. You are the only genuine and sober force in the Middle East and, most importantly, the only force for justice. You should unite as many Arab countries as possible around you, and then you will be invincible in your struggle for your just cause.

I am prepared to fight personally in the ranks of the Iraqi army against American imperialism and Israeli Zionism. Everything you are doing is right. I support you completely.

I know what war is. I fought for two years in Afghanistan. But I ask you to help me get to Iraq. I am prepared to fight even as a simple tank driver and mechanic.

Novocherkassk, Russia

I would like to convey my words of support through you to my Moslem brothers in Iraq and to its heroic army. Don't despair, and don't give up. Hold on tighter to your weapons, brothers. Carry the sacred banner of Islam with pride. You are setting an example for the entire Moslem East.

And I would also like you to send me as a volunteer to the armed forces of the Republic of Iraq. I am seventeen years old, but I can handle a Kalashnikov [machine gun] as well as any soldier; that is, I have a certain amount of experience in handling it. I as a Moslem am intent on fighting the brazen infidels in the Holy Land of the East to the bitter end and defending the Moslem holy places from their dirty paws.

I am convinced that victory will be ours.

Dushanbe, Tadzhik Republic

In the difficult times that Iraq is now living through, I would like to give my energy, my experience, and if necessary my life to the just struggle of the Iraqi people against imperialism.

I am thirty-four years old, a former athlete (boxer), and single.

Kiev, Russia

Please send me as a volunteer to Iraq. I am ready to fight American imperialism without any regard for my own life. I believe that the Iraqi and Soviet peoples have common enemies, the United States and Israel. The United States declares any region of the world its sphere of interest and sends its troops there. Grenada, Panama, and now Saudi Arabia. Someone must stop the United States. Therefore I ask you to send me as a volunteer to Iraq.

Leningrad, Russia

Although I am not a politician, I can say with confidence that the Americans and other Western powers do not need Kuwait but do need the cheap "black gold" produced in this small, defenseless country. The leader of Iraq, Saddam Hussein, was one of the first to understand this, could not tolerate it, and took heroic measures. And now this issue should be resolved at the conference table by the Arab and entire Moslem world and not by the Western powers, bristling with weapons and trampling on the sacred Arab lands. At one time America came to the Korean peninsula as the same kind of "protector." And the fruits of this are well known to everyone by now.

I as a Moslem demand condemnation of the behavior of the rulers of Saudi Arabia by the Arab League for allowing infidels to trample on the holiest of holy lands of the Arab and Moslem world.

It seems to me that, as long as Iraq is under blockade, we in the Soviet Union should open a special account for providing aid to the Iraqi people. I am personally prepared to contribute a large sum of money from my wages to an Iraqi aid fund, although I have a big family.

Makhachkala, Dagestan

I would like to take up permanent residence in the Republic of Iraq because I wholeheartedly disagree with the policies of the Soviet leadership with respect to Iraq and its people.

I wholeheartedly support the actions of President Saddam Hussein in annexing Iraq's old nineteenth province to Iraq. About a month ago I applied to join the Iraqi People's Army, but as yet I've received no reply. Three months from now I will be summoned to the draft board for service in the Soviet armed forces. I don't want to serve in the Soviet army because of my convictions, but citizens of the Soviet Union are punished with rather lengthy prison terms for refusing to serve in the military.

Moscow, Russia

This letter is written by a reserve warrant officer who was born in 1948.

I fully approve of and support the policy of the president of the United States in the Persian Gulf and would like to take part in Operation Desert Shield with American soldiers. I have already mastered many Soviet weapons. I have also studied American, British, and West German weapons on my own and in the service. I took part in the events in Czechoslovakia in 1968. I ask you to send me as a volunteer to the Persian Gulf.

Andrei Nikolayev
Berkakit, Yakutia

I always believed that the friendship between the American and Soviet peoples, which was born in the difficult years of the Second World War and which has passed all the tests of time, would once again emerge triumphant. And I beg you to consider my request seriously.

At a time when the dictator of Iraq is gathering his forces under the "green flag" of Islam and is threatening the world with chemical and, perhaps very soon, nuclear weapons, which in the hands of such a figure as Saddam Hussein could trigger a nuclear conflict, I consider it my duty as a man and a citizen to join the multinational forces in the Persian Gulf as a volunteer.

Andrei Shcherbakov
Arkhangel'sk, Russia

If we have decided to build a democratic society, then let's build it wide awake, not sound asleep. And if I decide to give my life so that others might live, it's my right, and no one can tell me not to do this. Therefore I ask you to send me to the Persian Gulf to help Kuwait repel Iraqi aggression.

Nikolai Prikhodko
Poltava, Ukrainian Republic

This letter is written by a former internationalist soldier who served in Afghanistan in 1981 and 1982.

I was a private in the border guard. I am troubled by the situation in the Persian Gulf and the lives of our countrymen in Iraq. I understand the "Afghan syndrome," which is alive and well in our country, but I cannot condemn the decision to send our troops to Afghanistan. I believe that our troops were needed there.

And if we are now faced with the question of sending Soviet troops to the Persian Gulf, please send me there. I have experience, and, if I have to, I can and will keep my mouth shut.

Anatoly Simoshenko
Dzhezkazgan, Kazakhstan

Something's missing in the reports from Iraq. Saddam Hussein's position is well known. But what do the Iraqi people think?

In fact, what are the Iraqi people thinking of? Did they really spend the whole time before January 15 calmly waiting for the chance to fight the multinational forces? They hoarded food and amassed "strategic" family stockpiles, and as a result the price of rice increased twenty-six times and the price of tea increased twenty-five times. They bought cars, even used cars (the price for them jumped 40 percent last week), in order to take their families to a safe place a bit farther from Baghdad. Old men who had gone through the eight-year war with Iran breathed uneasily. But everyone was counting on the ruler not to give up Kuwait and not to start a world war.

This is what I didn't get from the reports from Iraq: an analysis of the mental state of the nation before the war.

I'll try to describe it from here in Moscow.

Now the saying "We won't allow our soldiers in the Persian Gulf, Afghanistan was enough" is in vogue. So I'll start with Afghanistan.

It seems to me that we are very much in error when we try to find the people who signed the order committing Soviet troops to Afghanistan and condemn them. It wasn't just [Leonid] Brezhnev and his chronies who started the war in Afghanistan. And it wasn't just the totalitarian regime. Wars can start regardless of whether a country is totalitarian or democratic. The White House wasn't exactly known as a dictatorship when it sent troops to Vietnam. No matter who gives the final order to start a war, the blame for war lies with the entire society and the entire nation. What do I have in mind?

One Western reporter asked a mother who had lost a son in Afghanistan the following question: "But why are you now accusing the Soviet government of taking your son away from you? Why didn't you protest? You knew where they were sending him in 1987. You yourself are to blame for his death." The mother fainted. The cruelest part of the question was its truth. How corrupt must the conscience of a mother be for her to make her son carry out the expansionist plans of the state without a murmur of protest?

No matter who signed the order starting the armed intervention, it's more important that the nation knew and didn't say anything. The nation remained silent. And when people tried to explain to the nation that it was the aggressor, the nation didn't want to listen and persecuted the lovers of the truth. And the nation didn't even think that it was aggressive. Undoubtedly, before the war and in order for it to begin, the public must have become conscious of its status as the population of a superpower. The chauvinism of a supernation must have thrived among the public. The form in which this psychology of national superiority is expressed is unimportant, whether it be advocacy of the American way of life, Communist ideology, or Aryan supremacy. Or in the desire to annex a "land that has belonged to it from time immemorial" to its territory. It's important that the entire nation believe that it can dictate its conditions to others.

But I'm afraid that we've surpassed everybody. We've not only fostered this dictatorial spirit in ourselves, we've also learned how to export it, in addition to weapons and in addition to our ideology, which we made warlike. And in addition to raw materials. When Kuwait was seized, we blamed ourselves for supplying military equipment to Iraq. Of course not everyone repented, but a segment of our society undoubtedly did. But there's nothing to repent and nothing to upbraid ourselves for. After all, we have always tried to create our own image and likeness everywhere. Or we have looked for "kindred spirits" and pandered to them.

But we haven't upbraided ourselves enough for invading Afghanistan. I believe that a nation heals itself by repentance. But we haven't succeeded in healing ourselves, and we continue to throw rocks at those who dare to hint at our aggressiveness, at what is deeply rooted within us.

The letters to the Iraqi embassy . . . from more than ten thousand volunteers. I'll put aside the letters written by Moslems. They constitute a special case. I'll also put aside the letters written by veterans of Afghanistan and other veterans of foreign wars, because they were written by sick hands. Veterans who still want to fight are gravely ill. The Americans already know about this, but we still don't. No problem, we'll learn.

Letters were written by militant anti-Semites, who (fortunately) can't find the support they need in the Soviet socialist society. Letters were written by military men. Times are hard for them: The army fighting in Afghanistan did not justify the expectations of our warlike nation and inflicted on it the humiliation of defeat. The military is trying hard to recover its reputation and its authority and at the same time its martial ardor. Even if it is reproduced in one single individual, it must be manifested in some way. A military man can demonstrate it only in battle, as he was taught.

What is left are several thousand letters signed by ordinary Soviet citizens whose mentality and psychology have not been disfigured by anything besides indoctrination in the spirit of dictatorship. These people are aggressive by nature, and mere statements to the effect that aggression against another country is immoral and is condemned by international law and the international community are incapable of convincing them. They attempt to justify aggression from the very beginning. This kind of psychic deformation has its own history.

What we now so elegantly call "political force"—the Russian language is so rich that sometimes I wish that it were poorer, because there would be fewer euphemisms—is in reality nothing more than aggressive policy, because force relies solely on the military and because a power becomes a "superpower" only because of its military. This has also been reflected in [our] military doctrine, which is exclusively defensive. The sense of this "defense doctrine" since the 1930s may be summarized as follows: If the homeland is attacked, the army concentrated at the border will launch a counterattack, expel the enemy to his own territory, and defeat the enemy there. Gradually we came to the conclusion that a potential enemy could also be defeated on foreign territory. Afghanistan is an example of this, and our military men still say that if the USSR had not committed troops there, American missiles would have been installed on the Afghan-Soviet border. The concept of aggression does not exist [in our military doctrine]. War on foreign territory meets the requirements of defending national and state interests. Military aggression against another people is permitted as the simplest way of defending these interests, one which requires no mental effort. In part this is why it is so difficult now to discuss the subjects of aggression and morality. Not to mention Iraq, which we considered our friend for so many years. It is typical that in the letters of the volunteers wanting to fight against Iraq, I only encountered one letter which indicated the desire to fight against an aggressor.

Now for more on mothers. In the Iraqi embassy I read a letter (which for some reason they didn't give to me for publication) from an ordinary Russian woman, who was apparently from Voronezh. She wholeheartedly supported Iraq. But I was struck by something else. I had two sons die in Afghanistan, she wrote, but if I had a third I would send him to Iraq without giving it a second thought. This mother, what is she, a monster? Is she sick? How can we understand her in human terms? I myself can't understand how it would be possible to cure her and those like her of their narcotic intoxication with superforce. Because I don't know how we managed to achieve such an impressive effect, namely a total immunity to immoral actions and a consciousness of our own complete innocence.

We have not healed ourselves, so at any minute we might expect that someone will express support for Iraq.

Sometimes people say pointlessly that our parliament does not reflect the attitudes of the public. But it does, and sometimes it even anticipates them. One could hardly have been surprised after reading the letters to the Iraqi ambassador. But the Supreme Soviet of the USSR surpassed all expectations. I made a special point of listening and wondered who would have called Iraq the aggressor after hearing the Supreme Soviet's half-hour discussion of a resolution concerning the actions of our country with respect to the Persian Gulf situation, a discussion which took place three days before the announced deadline of January 15. No one [called Iraq an aggressor]. Only Eduard Shevardnadze could permit himself to do so. But the public and the deputies, who claim to express public opinion, obviously think otherwise. Consider Yevgeny Kogan, who demanded that the minister of foreign affairs [Shevardnadze] report to the Supreme Soviet on what he had done at the United Nations Security Council. Or Georgy Borovikov, who proposed a retroactive withdrawal of support from the Security Council resolution, at least with respect to the deadline. Shevardnadze was also accused of giving the green light to an armed conflict by signing the resolution. Everyone is looking for the reasons why Shevardnadze resigned. But they are evident at every step. It is difficult to refuse to take up arms when everyone around you is armed and ready to fire.

It seems that the fragile balance between our aggressiveness and our attempts to think in a new way has been shaken. A proposed draft of a Supreme Soviet resolution stated that the Ministry of Foreign Affairs is obliged to inform the parliament of the steps it has taken to resolve the crisis. It's as if we have no other ministries with interests in the Persian Gulf, such as the Ministry of Defense or the Ministry of Foreign Economic Relations, particularly its agencies linked to the defense industry. Even the scandal with the ship *Dmitry Furmanov*, which according to some reports was carrying spare parts for tanks to Jordan, did not cause the parliament to stop and think.[1]

We haven't healed ourselves. And morality has not yet become the basis of our actions. We are still a nation that bows down to dictatorship and relies on force, to the extent that we have enough of it. When Galina Starovoitova asked whether the parliament had the moral right to go on vacation when the world was on the brink of war and blood was flowing in the Baltic states, nobody understood her. She was surrounded by people speaking a different language.

Nobody knows how much I wanted to go to Iraq. Please forgive me for this desire. It's sinful, because it contains an element of selfishness. I wanted to understand something there so I could explain here why we have a warlike consciousness and why we still perceive ourselves as dictators, with respect to both ourselves and the rest of the world. I wanted the people of my country to be free of the desire to fight. But I don't know how to tell them about it.

[1]The U.S. Navy, carrying out the UN-sanctioned blockade of Iraq, turned this Soviet ship back from the Jordanian port of Akaba.

"Army and Society: Who Is Serving Whom?" *Sovetskaya Kultura*, March 31, 1990.

A roundtable discussion of the role of the armed forces in the age of *perestroika*, of the advantages of a professional army, and of criticism of the Soviet armed forces.

Ilyin, Yuri. "Do We Have the Need for a Strong Army?" *Molodaya Gvardiya*, no. 3, 1990.

This penetrating criticism of the Soviet armed forces over the past seventy years printed in a conservative publication proves that dissatisfaction with the military in the USSR is universal.

Karaganov, Sergei. "Problems of the USSR's European Policies." *Mezhdunarodnaya Zhizn*, no. 6, 1990.

A philosophical and political interpretation of the new realities in Europe.

Kasatonov, Yuri. "The Architects of Cardboard Walls." *Molodaya Gvardiya*, no. 7, 1990.

A severe conservative criticism of Soviet foreign and military policy. Georgy Arbatov is singled out for strong condemnation as an agent of Western, particularly American, influence. Alexander Yakovlev is also criticized, and Eduard Shevardnadze is not even mentioned.

Kolesnikov, Sergei; Nekrasov, Vadim; and Shashkov, Yevgeny. "Eastern Europe: The Road to Redemption." *Kommunist*, no. 2, 1990.

A strikingly reasonable and positive analysis of the historic changes in Eastern Europe.

Kondrashov, A. "An Alarming Vacation in Tbilisi." *Kommunist Vooruzhennykh Sil*, no. 24, 1989.

A Russian officer's opinion concerning the situation in Georgia.

Kornilov, Yuri. "Is the Decision-Making Process the Only Reason?" *Ogonyok*, nos. 4 and 5, 1989.

Who was responsible for the faulty and disastrous decision to invade Afghanistan?

Lavrentiev, S. "Secrets of the N—skii Court." *Kommunist Vooruzhennykh Sil*, no. 19, 1989.

An exposé of widespread corruption among officers in charge of the draft.

Maksimychev, I., and Menshikov, P. "A United German Fatherland." *Mezhdunarodnaya Zhizn*, no. 6, 1990.

The authors criticize the former leaders of the German Democratic Republic for having committed flagrant errors in their social policies by building a "Prussian variety" of the command socialist system.

Medvedev, Roy. "In the Second Echelon: L. I. Brezhnev during the War Years." *Nedelya*, no. 11, 1990.

A description of the insignificant role Leonid Brezhnev played in World War II and how it was exaggerated while he was in power.

Mirsky, Georgy. "A Common Sense Approach." *Pravda*, January 25, 1989.

The author tries to reconcile old Soviet perceptions with the concept of deideologization of international relations.

Pushkov, Alexei. "Is a Harmony of Ideologies Possible?" *Mezhdunarodnaya Zhizn*, no. 6, 1990.

An evolutionary convergence of socialist and capitalist ideologies on the basis of general human values, unnoticed by most of us, philosophically exonerates current Soviet foreign policy.

Shashkov, Yevgeny. "A Guarantee of Threat or Security?" *Pravda*, April 8, 1990.

Discusses the anxiety on the part of Soviet society, especially among older people, about the new military strategic balance in Europe. The author advances a theory that Soviet troops in Eastern Europe would have been vulnerable in conditions of modern warfare.

Teplyakov, Yuri. "Prisoners of War." *Moscow News*, no. 19, 1990.

A critique of the Soviet Union's attitude toward its six million World War II prisoners of war and of Stalin's rejection of the Geneva Convention.

Yazov, Dmitry. "The Army of Friendship and Brotherhood of Peoples." *Kommunist Vooruzhennykh Sil*, no. 20, 1989.

A highly authoritative assessment by Defense Minister Yazov of the magnitude of the ethnic problem in the Soviet armed forces.

I think that the future is not predictable and is not determined. It is created by all of us—step by step in our endlessly complex interaction. But it is man who retains the freedom of choice. That is why the role of the personality that destiny placed in some of the key moments of history is so important.[1]

Andrei Sakharov

Chapter Five

Personalities

As a result of *perestroika* and *glasnost*, the role of personality in Soviet politics is beginning to be appreciated. For the first time since World War II, individual Soviet politicians can be observed openly expressing their views in public and in the mass media. Five of today's most important political figures, each of whom holds independent views and has greatly influenced recent events in contemporary Soviet politics, are discussed in this chapter. Four of them are or were Communist party members; the fifth, the late Andrei Sakharov, was the country's most prominent dissident.

Mikhail Gorbachev

In most countries, reforms are initiated by an opposition force, which often has had time (when not in power) to think through its policies. In the USSR the situation is different. Seemingly out of nowhere one of the leaders of the Communist party, Mikhail Gorbachev, proclaimed his intention to reform the Soviet Union, thereby attracting worldwide attention. At first, Gorbachev was not taken seriously, then he was overestimated, and now many are disappointed in him. After more than six years, his activities and their results make a dramatic multifaceted story, one that is still being written. Events and personalities have been interwoven into this evolutionary process.

---

[1] *Molodyozh Estonii*, October 11, 1988.

The first question about Gorbachev concerns his true political credo. Is he a radical reformer or a closet conservative (a party *apparatchik* turned militant reformer by the pressure of events)? He has stated many times that he does not intend to abandon socialism in favor of capitalism. Gorbachev's initial objectives for reforms were modest, neither revolution nor modernization but rather a cosmetic reform. The aim was to improve the existing system, with the Communist party retaining control. Even with such limited goals, he went much further than did Nikita Khrushchev. Gorbachev coined and promoted several slogans and expressions including *perestroika*, *glasnost*, and "new thinking." Some of them reflect his wishes but do not make sense in practice, such as "strong center and strong republics" and the idea of a "regulated socialist market."

Initially, it was helpful for him to maintain a middle ground in policy debates. Both reformers and conservatives have wanted to believe that Gorbachev is with them in his heart, no matter what his official position. After all, it was a tradition to believe blindly in the leader in the Soviet Union, just as it was in Russia before. This Gorbachev strategy might have been rooted in his life as a party *apparatchik*, during which the party line often changed. An impartial observer might interpret Gorbachev's rationale as "let left and right devour each other, and I will stay an arbiter forever." This tactic, however, created the danger of losing the respect of both political blocs. Without their support the only instrument of power left at Gorbachev's disposal would be the army and the KGB. The Soviet leader often accuses his opponents of not having a clearly spelled-out program of action. His own program borrows its ideas from the left and its method of execution from the right.

Gorbachev is very sensitive to criticism in the press, and he has an uncanny ability to turn each defeat and disaster into a sort of political victory. He is a master of small gestures, which are sometimes interpreted as important developments. His political style seems to ensure that the political circus will never disappear from Soviet life. To influence events, Gorbachev has masterfully manipulated three basic elements: domestic policy, foreign policy, and *glasnost*.

To distract attention from economic failures, Gorbachev's chief political tactics have been 1) to announce that a new party *plenum* or congress will be called in the future to deal with an urgent issue, raising hopes that a solution is near, and 2) to throw some conservatives out of the Politburo. The results of these actions are usually far below expectations. The referendum on March 17, 1991, regarding the future of the Soviet Union was a classic example of Gorbachev in action. Everything about this undertaking was dubious, including its results.

The power of the man in the Kremlin is often greatly exaggerated. In many ways he has much less power than do legitimately elected Western leaders. The best evidence of that is the ephemeral consolidation-of-power process that Gorbachev has had to go through. It has taken years for him to do what democratic leaders accomplish shortly after being popularly elected, since they almost automatically have a consensus or mandate to rule.

Gorbachev's consolidation of power has gone through three successive stages. First, he gained control of the Politburo; at the end of this stage control was achieved by diluting the Politburo to twenty-four members and thus greatly diminishing the importance of each individual Politburo member; hardly anyone knows their names anymore. Second, he introduced an electoral system and a new parliament while preserving the party's preponderance and maintaining the same socialist ideology. Gorbachev has clearly enjoyed playing the roles of legislator and parliamentarian, although, in fact, little has been achieved. The third stage has been to introduce a presidential system. How long this stage will last is unclear, since it seems obvious that more democracy may mean loss of control by the Communist party and by Gorbachev himself.

On March 15, 1990, Mikhail Gorbachev became the first appointed president of the USSR, exactly five years after he came to power. He has continuously expressed his desire for more power, asking the Supreme Soviet for it several times. In September 1990 the Supreme Soviet again gave President Gorbachev special powers to handle the political situation and to conduct a transition to a market economy. He has by now obtained virtually dictatorial powers. He has also started to demand more respect for his office, by introducing a law against insulting the integrity of the presidency. This intolerance is not a good sign. One thing he has not done is test his popularity with the public in an election.

Some people say that Gorbachev is liberal in the spring and conservative in the winter. This was true in the winter of 1990–91. His policies, called in Russian *otkat*, were really directed against democratic forces and relied on the party, the armed forces, and the KGB. The hiatus occurred on March 28, 1991, when Gorbachev called on fifty thousand troops in Moscow to prevent the demonstration in support of Boris Yeltsin that almost caused an outbreak of civil war. However, since the April meeting in Novo-Ogarevo, he turned around 180 degrees. One might ask the question: for how long?

Few leaders have managed so skillfully to avoid criticism for their mistakes as has Mikhail Gorbachev during his six years in power. A major criticism of Gorbachev is that he has devoted too much time to foreign policy while neglecting domestic affairs and the economy. Two of his most crucial mistakes have made reform especially difficult: 1) his continuing reliance on old institutions and mechanisms, and 2) his use of an extremely narrow pool of talent and leadership restricted basically to the party—the wrong place to look for entrepreneurship and talent. The people whom Gorbachev prefers are usually dull, such as Nikolai Ryzhkov, who presided over the final destruction of the economy, or his right hand, Anatoly Lukyanov, who studied with him at Moscow Law School.

The Kremlin is not 10 Downing Street. Soviet leaders have always been surrounded by mystery, and the world seems always to hope for the best from any new Soviet leader.[2] But rarely has there been so much excitement in the West as there was when Gorbachev came to power. Energetic and relatively young, coming after three Soviet leaders died in a three-year period, he represented a generational change. The Western press analyzed Gorbachev's actions through rose-colored glasses, viewing him as an ardent reformer with few supporters, fighting against enemies on the right and the left. The two latest inventions of the Western press are that Gorbachev has abandoned the reformers and joined the conservatives, and that to rule such a huge country as Russia one needs truly effective tools: the party, the army, and the KGB.

Gorbachev's biggest achievement has been to acknowledge problems and to face up to them; he is the first Soviet leader to do this in several decades. His significant contributions in the areas of foreign policy and *glasnost* should be greatly appreciated. However, naming Mikhail Gorbachev the Nobel Peace Prize winner for 1990 was obviously a mistake, given the level of violence inside the Soviet Union and the political and economic havoc in the USSR. His speech on June 5, 1991, upon receiving this award, was devoted to the obligation of the West to help the USSR for its peaceful policies. But his stubborn attempt to preserve the Soviet socialist system and an unreformed Communist party has doomed his and the country's efforts to get out of this historic impasse. It is like trying to jump out of a swamp: the more energy a person applies, the deeper in he sinks.

Boris Yeltsin

Boris Yeltsin is unquestionably the most popular politician in the Soviet Union today. Yeltsin has fully recovered from his dismissal from the Politburo in 1987. He has surrounded himself with highly respected intellectuals and economists, and he has shown himself to be a mature, thoughtful politician. Yeltsin is the first individual to be chosen president of Russia by a direct popular election in one thousand years of Russian history.

One of Yeltsin's favorite targets is the special treatment accorded to members of the Communist party apparatus. In his book, *Against the Grain*, he goes into great detail about the benefits and luxuries he enjoyed as a member of the Politburo. Although it is clear that Yeltsin himself never refused any of these privileges, he points out that life in such luxury distorts perceptions about the realities of Soviet daily life.

---

[2]For example, when Yuri Andropov, who had been chief of the KGB for fifteen years, came to power, many Western newspapers dutifully reported the KGB leaks about how appreciative Andropov was of Western culture, how he read in English, maybe even spoke it.

His almost-two-year rule as Moscow party chief in 1986 and 1987 demonstrated his brand of populism. In a way he was imitating Mikhail Gorbachev by meeting with ordinary people, entering vegetable stores, and riding public transportation. And he fired almost half of all party bureaucrats under his control. Put simply, he took his job seriously. Then came the October 1987 *plenum* of the CPSU and Yeltsin's rebellion, which drastically and forever changed his life. This rebellion had no connection with his previous experiences. Yeltsin did not represent the radicals of the party. It is still difficult to understand why he took so much risk. His major opponent, Yegor Ligachev, was surprised and noted that Yeltsin had sat quietly for almost a year. It is possible that Yeltsin had an arrangement with Gorbachev to take a resolute stand. If so, at the very last moment, probably, Gorbachev withdrew his support from Yeltsin, fearing a conservative backlash. In a major test of *glasnost*, it took eighteen months to publish the speech he made at this *plenum*. The events of the *plenum* and Yeltsin's subsequent dismissal from the Politburo were widely interpreted as the end of Yeltsin as a politician in the Soviet Union.

Then, in March 1989, came the first almost-free elections in Soviet history, for the new Congress of People's Deputies. Displaying great courage, Yeltsin mounted a strong campaign against the party and its privileges. In contrast to tradition, he did not shy away from the Western press, nor did he hesitate to speak his mind with Western journalists. Communist party *apparatchiks* turned against him, in one instance trying to frighten voters with a poster warning: "If you miss Stalin, vote for Yeltsin." In the end, Yeltsin resoundingly defeated the Moscow bureaucrats. Muscovites voted for him in such overwhelming numbers that the entire political landscape of the country has changed.

Yeltsin has an ability to attract talent, he is willing to work with other people, and he knows how to delegate responsibility. From the beginning it was very unclear, however, whether the conservatives would permit him to function effectively as a leader. Nevertheless, he made an effort to work with them in the Russian parliament.

His dramatic walkout at the 28th Congress of the CPSU in July 1990 was more belated than premature—it is probably hopeless to expect that the party can play any constructive role in the reform process. Yeltsin walking out of the congress, and resigning from the Communist party, symbolically sentenced the party to self-destruction. It was a dramatic gesture from one who had advanced his career and built his entire life through the party.

The results of Yeltsin's work in the Russian parliament have been more symbolic than practical, since the laws and regulations approved there have been mostly ignored by the Kremlin. True power still belongs to the Kremlin, not to the republics.

Day by day, Yeltsin's popularity is growing, while Mikhail Gorbachev's is diminishing. Yeltsin has become more serious and is now less likely to shoot from the hip; he has become more a leader than a gadfly. There is a strong possibility that, out of the impending havoc in the USSR, Yeltsin might become the national leader. However, many Soviets have hoped that these two strong leaders—Gorbachev and Yeltsin—will join forces to save their country from the abyss. Several recent events have nurtured that hope—a joint appearance at Lenin's mausoleum on November 7, 1990, followed by a private meeting on November 11 that lasted for five hours.

However, this pair went into their worst quarrel when, in February 1991 in his television appearance, Yeltsin demanded Gorbachev's resignation. When faced with the increased pressure from the party conservatives, Gorbachev made another salto mortale to obtain Yeltsin's support. He transferred to the Russian Republic the management of the striking mines at the meeting at Novo-Ogarevo on April 23, 1991. This does not preclude new surprises in this turbulent relationship.

It is difficult to predict how, if he did take over the country, Yeltsin would conduct national affairs. He is inexperienced in foreign policy, vague on many internal issues, and has made many promises that might be hard to keep. His demagogic streak and tendency to exaggerate have been noted by many observers.

Despite his critics' assertions that he is not a serious thinker, it should be emphasized that Boris Yeltsin has at each historical juncture raised the most pivotal political issues. In 1987 he rightly asserted that reforms were stalled, in 1989 he urged that the party should transfer power to the Soviets, and in 1990 he asserted that the 500-day plan should be accepted. Whether he can overcome his thirty years of being a party man is a matter of concern. It is likely that Yeltsin will continue to surprise us in the future. If he becomes the country's new leader, he will encounter great resistance from the party apparatus and from the Soviet military.

Alexander Yakovlev

An éminence grise of *perestroika*, Alexander Yakovlev was an exchange student at Columbia University in 1958 and then served as Soviet ambassador to Canada for ten years.[3] He rose quickly under Gorbachev, becoming a full member of the Politburo in June 1987. In a party that executed all of its leftist members in the thirties, he is a rare bird—a person with a liberal outlook. However, this theoretician of democratic socialism has never made a dent in the conservative party environment and has preferred to work outside of it. He, rather than

---

[3]Princeton University's Professor Stephen Cohen claims that the ambassadorship in Canada was a kind of political exile, a punishment meted out by the conservative Brezhnev regime. It seems more likely that it was a promotion for Alexander Yakovlev, who at that time was not even a member of the Central Committee; at any rate it definitely influenced his political outlook toward liberalism.

Gorbachev, can rightfully be called the spiritual father of *glasnost*, since it is he who has succeeded in creating a liberal press. Alexander Yakovlev, as a head of the Propaganda Department of the Central Committee, had a great influence over all aspects of the mass media, including appointments and material resources. He is the only senior member of the leadership and the Politburo (until July 1990) who is incessantly and openly attacked by the conservative press. His reply in *Pravda* on April 5, 1988, to Nina Andreyeva's famous letter was a stern rebuke to the conservatives; it may have saved the reform process.[4] Undoubtedly he has great influence over Gorbachev, and possibly he has helped him to formulate his ideas on more than one occasion.

Yakovlev chaired the commission researching the treaty negotiated by Viacheslav Molotov and German diplomat Joachim von Ribbentrop in 1939. In a very courageous step, Yakovlev announced that the Soviet Union and Nazi Germany had indeed signed a secret protocol that allowed Stalin to occupy the three Baltic republics of Lithuania, Latvia, and Estonia. Although the rest of the world had not doubted this for the last fifty years, Soviet conservatives had a hard time swallowing Yakovlev's "revelation." Yakovlev is often viciously attacked by conservatives. He is accused of being part of a Jewish-Mason conspiracy. (If an opponent is not Jewish, then he is considered to be a Mason.) It is interesting that Gorbachev, who has on many occasions publicly defended Nikolai Ryzhkov, has not once raised his voice in defense of Yakovlev. Nor is Boris Yeltsin a supporter of Yakovlev.

Many of Yakovlev's views concerning the leading role of the party in *perestroika*, the regulated socialist market, and socialism in general contain more rhetoric than substance. He has not usually been as outspoken as either Yeltsin or Sakharov. Yakovlev is often unjustly accused of anti-American feelings by American conservatives. He sometimes criticizes U.S. foreign policy, but so too do the Democrats in Congress. He fully supports the Soviet policy of improving Soviet-American relations, and he defended the Soviet reform press, which had a significant impact on changing for the better the Soviet perceptions of the United States.

He is an odd choice to be the leading theoretician of the CPSU, which has few followers of his liberal ideas—not even his boss Mikhail Gorbachev. In his article "On the Threshold of Momentous Changes" (Doc. 30) Yakovlev points out that, no matter how much has been accomplished, the Soviet Union is only just beginning to do what is needed to build a new society based on principles of common sense.

---

[4]Nina Andreyeva, "Polemics: I Cannot Waive Principles," reprinted in Isaac J. Tarasulo, ed., *Gorbachev and Glasnost: Viewpoints from the Soviet Press* (Wilmington, DE: Scholarly Resources, 1989), pp. 277–90. See also Document 13 above.

Yegor Ligachev

Although an engineer by education, Yegor Ligachev looks more like an average worker. Physically strong and an outspoken Great Russian, he has worked most of his life in Siberia. He is a true conservative, a stubborn defender of socialism who still believes that if everything were done right, there would be no need for such momentous changes as the introduction of private property. He stands behind his words, "The party can express the profound essence of *perestroika* with clear wording—more socialism."[5] One of the staunchest defenders of the antialcoholism campaign, he insisted to the bitter end that it was the right thing to do. That is in spite of the fact that it was one of the major political and economic mistakes of the Gorbachev years.

In a 1989 interview in *Argumenty i Fakty* he declared that socialism cannot be modernized by capitalist methods, although many useful elements of capitalism can be adopted.[6] According to Ligachev, Soviet agriculture could have been best improved by utilizing the positive elements of the collectivized agriculture of Czechoslovakia and East Germany. No matter what the circumstances have been, Yegor Kuzmich Ligachev has continued to make dogmatic ideological speeches unconditionally defending socialism.

His relationship with Mikhail Gorbachev is a subject for psychological study. How could these two men, so different in so many respects, work so closely together for five years? Ligachev was considered to be the most influential conservative figure in the Politburo—indeed, in the whole country. He also was the second most powerful politician, right after Gorbachev. Ligachev always claimed that he never had any substantial disagreements with Gorbachev. His downfall began in June 1988 when, at the 19th Party Conference, he became responsible for Soviet agriculture. He became bold enough in the spring of 1990 to criticize Gorbachev. However, in a tactical error, he lost the opportunity at the beginning of the July 1990 28th Party Congress to state clearly his intentions. Meanwhile, Gorbachev marshaled his forces and took over the work of the congress. Ligachev openly challenged Gorbachev, competing for the position of Gorbachev's deputy with the unknown Ukrainian *apparatchik* Vladimir Ivashko, and lost. Gorbachev thus dispensed with Ligachev mercilessly, humiliating him at the end—finally, Ligachev's fellow *apparatchiks* betrayed him without any oscillation. Obviously, Gorbachev and Ligachev shared many views, including a belief in socialism and a dislike of private property and democrats. Ligachev also served as a convenient scapegoat for Gorbachev, who attributed

---

[5]Speech delivered on November 6, 1986, in *Ye. K. Ligachev: Selected Speeches and Articles* (Moscow, 1989), p. 148.

[6]Natalia Zhelnorova, *Argumenty i Fakty*, no. 42, 1989.

to him responsibility for a variety of unpopular and unpleasant events, such as the killing of demonstrators in Tbilisi.

Andrei Sakharov

Andrei Sakharov's life was quite unusual. One of the most respected and decorated of Soviet scientists, a father of the hydrogen bomb, and a recipient of the Gold Star Hero of Labor and the Lenin and Stalin prizes, he transformed himself into the country's leading dissident. Throughout his career, he managed to avoid the main hypocrisies of Soviet life, although he never regretted his contribution to the nuclear arms race. He was never a Young Pioneer, a participant in Communist youth groups, or a party member. His relationships with people demonstrated great personal compassion, and he defended his political credo and philosophy with remarkable strength and firmness. Sakharov projected such integrity that he was respected by friends and enemies alike. The majority of Soviet intellectuals and scientists, who slavishly cooperated with the authorities, were nevertheless ready to fight for the protection of Andrei Sakharov. He enjoyed a special kind of immunity in Soviet society.

His "second life," as a dissenter, started in 1958. In the end his contribution to Soviet political life was even greater than his contribution to science. In 1968, Sakharov wrote *Reflections on Progress, Peaceful Coexistence, and Intellectual Freedom*, a treatise on the convergence of socialism and capitalism adapted to Soviet reality. He was becoming an active dissenter.

It can be argued that Andrei Sakharov did more for the cause of dissent in the USSR than did all the other dissidents taken together. He and author Alexander Solzhenitsyn were very important for the survival of the human pride of the Soviet people. However, he was not as lucky as Solzhenitsyn, who was expelled in 1973.

There was no insignificant cause for Sakharov if it involved human suffering; he was ready to respond to every single case of human injustice in his totalitarian society. He wholeheartedly supported the cause of minorities and of individuals as well. He consistently spoke up in defense of the Crimean Tatars. He stood outside the court with Anatoly Sharansky's mother during Sharansky's July 1978 espionage trial. His personal modesty, his house open for any visitor, and his desire to help any person who was persecuted made him a legend among the Soviet people. For his public activities, Andrei Sakharov was awarded the Nobel Peace Prize in 1975.

For his condemnation of the December 1979 Soviet invasion of Afghanistan, Sakharov was exiled to Gorky, a city of more than one million inhabitants that was closed to foreigners. The aim of this internal exile was to isolate him from the Western press. These were difficult years for Sakharov; his health was undermined by several prolonged hunger strikes and by KGB mistreatment. During these years he never stopped his fundamental theoretical research in physics. It took a telephone call from Gorbachev himself, in December 1986, to return the academician to political life.

Sakharov actively participated in the first session of the Congress of People's Deputies. A living legend, he became a magnet for the liberal deputies. He correctly addressed the main shortcomings of the new electoral system and insisted on the abolition of Article 6 of the constitution, which asserted the leading role of the Communist party in the Soviet Union. Some of his former comrades accused him of betraying his firm principles and supporting Gorbachev. He protested against the concentration of power in Gorbachev's hands, trying to explain to Gorbachev that without being elected he would not have the authority to govern. He wanted to continue his fight when he died on December 14, 1989. His last words were: "Tomorrow there will be a big fight."

Gorbachev's attendance at Sakharov's funeral was a certain recognition, a triumph for a person so often maligned by the official repressive machine. Sakharov applied his immense scientific talent to obtain knowledge about science and society; for the first he was richly rewarded, for the second—cruelly punished. Sakharov was, in fact, a national treasure, possibly the last hope of nascent Soviet democracy, and the only person in the last seventy years who can be placed side by side with Leo Tolstoy and Mahatma Gandhi. His last work was a prototype for a constitution of the Union of Soviet Republics of Europe and Asia, an idealistic project for a troubled union.

28

Gorbachev Talks to Workers at the Izhora Plant

Mikhail Gorbachev

Sovetskaya Rossiya
August 20, 1989

These notes were not published until almost six weeks after this July 11, 1989, meeting. As a result, this event escaped the attention of the Western press. Judging by the workers' tough questions, the claim by the newspaper *Moskovskie Novosti* that Gorbachev went to the plant to avert a general strike sounds like a realistic appraisal.[1] If so, he succeeded in his goal. Gorbachev tried hard to convince the workers of the benefits of his policies of *glasnost* and *perestroika*; he repeated these magic words many times. The talk was completely devoted to domestic policies. In general, he tried to placate the conservative workers of this plant in Leningrad on issues such as cooperatives, introduction of the market, and private property. For example, he did not defend cooperatives, which were introduced in an attempt to alleviate the scarcity of services and consumer goods, but which have not been successful. In this talk, Gorbachev opposed the institution of the presidency, which shows that his views changed considerably in the year following this talk. His positions on the party and on elections were more conservative than were those of the workers. Gorbachev was very evasive concerning "perks" for party and state bureaucrats, and he refused to repudiate them. He expressed his faith in socialist public ownership and the socialist centralized economy and spoke out emphatically against private property. It is quite possible that among his listeners was Alexander Shmonov, a worker in shop no. 30, who tried to assassinate him on November 7, 1990.

Gorbachev: Right now I am comparing my impressions of this and past trips to Leningrad. It seems that today I am meeting with different people, people who are apparently still the same Leningraders but are already different. In this brief period all of us, not just the Izhora workers and Leningraders, but the entire country, have gone through a great deal of change. We have stuck with our *perestroika*, and now we are probably all troubled by and concerned with the

[1]*Moskovskie Novosti*, no. 46, November 18, 1990.

same thing: how to continue our reform so as to make it more decisive and capable of producing noticeable results. This has been the subject of my brief but, I would say, very frank and meaningful conversations with Leningraders.

I can provide a very simple answer to the question of why we need *perestroika*. We want to accomplish very simple goals. We want people to live better in the country, we want them to feel confident and free, and we want them to feel that they can take part in all the processes under way in the country and feel like owners of the country. This seems like a simple formula, but its realization has proven to be quite difficult. Hence it became necessary to carry out economic and political reforms.

The main point of economic reform is to shatter the old bureaucratic and administrative system for managing the economy, a system which has exhausted itself. It is impossible to decide everything and issue all commands from the center in such a complex, vast, and diverse economy as ours. Hence we must reform our economy and reform it radically, because in this case, comrades, any kind of partial solutions is completely incapable of helping us.

We began reforms in the past, but we started them at the top, and ultimately they bogged down and were devalued and emasculated, and everything remained the same. This was the case in the 1950s and 1960s, when Nikita Khrushchev took the initiative in planning programs for reorganizing both the economy and the party. At first these programs produced good results, but then everything went back to square one. The same thing happened in 1965, when the March and September plenary sessions of the Central Committee were held. The decisions of these sessions gave us hope for major change, but once again we were incapable of carrying out to the end the reforms we had started.

Hence when we acknowledged the need to reform the economy, the political system, and the way we manage all of public life, we returned to past experience and pondered it a great deal. We would not be able to devise correct policies if we did not analyze our past activity. That is why you and I are so attentively and self-critically analyzing our history today, even with a certain amount of excess emotionalism and self-flagellation, because the situation we had come to in the early 1980s was rooted very deeply in the past.

An analysis of past experience indicated that we must begin with the workplace and get workers actively involved in real life by reforming our entire economic system, and thus unlock the potential of the socialist system of management. That is why the Law on State-Owned Enterprises [which took effect on January 1, 1988] was passed. Despite all its shortcomings, it constituted a very important step. Now we are hearing a great deal of criticism implying that this law has not gone into effect and is not working. This may be true, but it was important to make a beginning.

And now it seems that we have rejected the old system but have failed to think through and resolve many aspects of the new system. As a result the situation at many plants is very uneasy. People believe that their expectations have not been justified and that the provisions of the law have been emasculated by different kinds of directives and the preservation of the old bureaucratic and administrative methods. All of this is true. This is the reality of our current transitional phase and all of its complexity.

In short, now we are going through perhaps the most complex and difficult stage in the country's life. It is important for us to keep our cool in this situation, even more so now that life is presenting us with many new problems in the form of different kinds of shortages, strains, and breakdowns in retail distribution. This is our current reality, and people are justifiably raising these issues.

We will cope with these problems, but first of all we must put our finances and the marketplace in order. Here we have several ways to proceed. The most important is to expand the supply of consumer goods. We must take immediate steps to bring the money supply and the supply of goods into balance. Hence, now we must introduce a very strict austerity program. As the situation stands right now, dear comrades (and you should be aware of this), labor productivity is rising at a rate of 3 to 5 percent a year, while wages are increasing at a rate of 6 to 10 percent a year. And this is making the situation in the retail market even worse. Consumer demand has grown even more, while the possibilities of meeting this demand are increasing at a slower pace.

You might ask why it has to be this way. Why are there fewer goods available? I must tell you that with the exception of several kinds of food commodities and manufactured goods, total output has risen during this period; it has risen considerably and is continuing to rise. But this growth is lagging far behind consumer demand, which is where the problem lies.

Could we consider going back to the old command system? Could we clamp down and halt the processes associated with reform? No, I think we must have adjustments to reform but continue to carry it out energetically.

Currently the economy is the most important and central issue facing us. The solution of our economic problems will make it possible for us to proceed with greater confidence in other areas. And first of all we must resolve social problems more successfully.

In the next two years we must lay the groundwork for attaining a level in the next five-year plan period which would make it possible for us to guarantee a normal supply of food. Such possibilities do exist. This, I would say, is a priority task. Now we are opening up extensive opportunities for collective farms and state farms to manage their own affairs and enter into leasing agreements and contracts, and we are providing incentives for individually operated subsidiary farms and for the integration of industrial plants with collective and state farms. This is the first point.

Second, we must do everything possible to improve rural living conditions, because without this no capital investment or resources sent to the countryside would help one bit. We need to provide suitable living conditions for people in the country and get them interested in the results of their work and thus proceed to solve the food problem. This will require a tremendous effort on the part of all of society.

And, finally, we must modernize the agricultural infrastructure, primarily the food-processing industry. After all, at present up to 30 percent and sometimes more of our agricultural losses are due to defects in the storage and processing of agricultural products. This is absurd. That is why we have developed a seven-year plan for the development of the food-processing industry, have involved defense plants in its implementation, and are now monitoring its progress and becoming more demanding with respect to its execution. In our opinion the food situation will change for the better in the near future.

The Congress of People's Deputies, among other forums, has raised the issue of relieving the tension in the marketplace by purchasing imported goods. Well, first of all, we are already buying some food with hard currency. Second, we are spending some hard currency on consumer goods. But some economists have suggested obtaining major credits for purchasing consumer goods. This would be acceptable as a temporary measure for relieving the tension in the marketplace, but it would be unacceptable as a policy for the future. Our policy for the future should provide for the development of our own infrastructure for increasing the production of food and manufactured goods. That is why today, no matter what kind of job a group of workers may have, they must make their own contribution toward solving the consumer goods problem. In essence this is our common, national responsibility, and this is what I am asking of you, the workers of the Izhora plant.

In summation, I would like to conclude this portion of my talk with an appeal to you. Comrades, we must firmly proceed on the path of economic reform that we have taken. We cannot count on some advantageous, divine bounty falling our way. We have no stockpiles to draw on. We've expended them all. Hence we must hold to our main course, that is, soberly and firmly taking the path of *perestroika* step by step, developing new economic forms, new administrative forms, and new and more rational and efficient forms of management. There is no other way.

People ask why we immediately took on both economic and political reform at the same time.

I have already mentioned the weaknesses of previous economic reforms. Their weaknesses lay in the fact that they were bureaucratic in nature and were carried out at the level of administrators and managers. The public never saw these reforms and never took part in them, which is why they died. And most importantly, as long as the public is not involved in these changes, the public will not be interested in defending reforms. But how can people become involved in *perestroika*? Only in terms of their interests and through *glasnost*. People must be aware of everything that is going on in the country. People must be aware of what is going on in their areas and their towns. They not only must keep current with what decisions are being made, they must also take part in making these decisions through their representatives and thus guarantee that changes will take place and that the policies in force are realistic. And this has necessitated a new look at all the ways in which our society operates. How are the councils working? What is the role of the party? What is the role of workers? What is the role of trade unions, the Komsomol, and other public organizations, and most importantly, what is the role of each group of workers and each individual?

That is why we need political reform. Without it we will not be able to stick to the policies of *perestroika*. The primary actor of reform is the individual, our individual. *Perestroika* will be successful if we use democracy and political reform to get people genuinely involved in all affairs of society and the state. This is the only way. And only then will *perestroika* become irreversible and impossible to stop. And this would be guaranteed within the framework of democracy and *glasnost*.

What are the criteria of *glasnost* and democracy? They include our socialist values, namely, our social system, our public property in different forms, the absence of the exploitation of man by man, and social security. And democracy and *glasnost* must serve the interests of affirming all our values.

You'll say that sometimes openness and democracy are exploited for purposes which are completely contrary to the interests of socialism and the people. And it's true! So what conclusion should we draw from this? Should we eliminate democratic processes? Absolutely not. We should use the framework of openness and democracy to put the people who are trying to impose alien values, banners, and slogans on us in their place. Our rejection of *glasnost* and democracy would constitute evidence of a lack of confidence and a lack of trust in people. That's the only way I would evaluate the situation if we were to surrender to the appeals to eliminate democracy.

We must pay attention to the opinions which workers have expressed with respect to the nomination of candidates for the legislature. We must draw lessons from the past electoral campaign when, in some cases, workers were seemingly aloof from democratic processes.

I believe that you have already figured it out, have rid yourselves of this needless reticence, and have gained experience in the past campaign. But what's most important is for the opinion of groups of workers to become a reality. My meetings with many representatives of the working class at the Supreme Soviet have persuaded me that they are splendid people who are intelligent and capable of evaluating the most important political issues of the day while remaining faithful to the cause of socialism and the working class.

We are all troubled by the fact that interethnic problems have become worse in recent years. They will be discussed at the forthcoming plenary session of the Central Committee. I believe that the solution to our interethnic problems lies not in the disintegration or emasculation of our federation but in fully unlocking its potential. This is a key idea. We must make the sovereignty of the union republics and the autonomy of national entities a reality. We must do what we can to make sure that people of all nationalities and ethnic groups, no matter where they live, feel calm and confident both now and in the future.

This is a realistic and humane course which will harmonize the interests of society and the peoples who populate our vast country. Those who are pushing people in the other direction are playing with fire. Dividing and separating our people and carving up the federation are simply irresponsible acts. And the Central Committee plenary session will speak in greater detail on this issue. I think that it will also discuss problems of the development of the Russian Federation. They also exist.

Voice: I have a question.

Gorbachev: So you don't want me to leave, huh? (Laughter.) Well, I won't leave until I give you an answer. (Applause.)

In short, you can see, comrades, that we are now in the most difficult and transitional stage of *perestroika* when all our policies are becoming a reality. Now there is so much that is new that it is causing people to become agitated, worried, and troubled. I consider this worry quite normal, as a sign that people care about the country. But we must all be very responsible and we must all understand one another. And no matter how our discussions proceed, in our discussions we must always unite in the interest of the success of reform, in the interest of social revitalization, and in our common interests. This is what I wanted to summarize for you. (Applause.)

(Then Mikhail Gorbachev answered written and oral questions from the audience.)

Question: Don't you believe that we must take timely action to eliminate speculative cooperatives?

Gorbachev: We need cooperatives. We are in favor of cooperatives that produce goods and that help repair equipment and renovate housing and apartments, that help in matters which the government system cannot always handle. There are cooperatives that are generally indispensable.

Voice: But cooperative operators are involved in buying up scarce goods and speculation.

Gorbachev: Cooperatives that buy up food and certain manufactured goods are another matter. They might buy up some T-shirts, paint some flowers on them, and then raise the price.

Voice: Ninety percent of the cooperatives are like that.

Gorbachev: And these are the cooperatives we have to deal with. So who should deal with them? And how should the cooperative movement in general be managed? We in the Central Committee and government have discussed these issues and have arrived at a conclusion on which a decision of the Council of Ministers was based: issues of regulating the cooperatives, namely, what kind of cooperatives should be allowed, what kind should not be allowed, and what kind of taxes should be imposed on them, are matters that should be left up to the local authorities.

(Clamor in the auditorium.)

Gorbachev: I understand that you doubt the possibility of resolving the issue in this way.

Voices: You're right!

Gorbachev: The Leningrad press has already published proposals on cooperatives and an entire newspaper column has been devoted to them. It's true that I haven't read it, but I've seen it. From what I hear, it contains information on cooperatives which are necessary and should be allowed to operate and on cooperatives which must be closed. So what? This means that Leningraders themselves are intent on deciding what cooperatives should be allowed to exist and what cooperatives should be closed. And this, comrades, is the way it should be.

Question: Why, when [Alexander] Obolensky announced his candidacy for the chairmanship of the Supreme Soviet at the Congress of People's Deputies, did you not get up and say that democracy must be defended in this case? After all, his candidacy posed no threat to you.[2]

Gorbachev: Three candidates were nominated: Gorbachev, Obolensky, and [Boris] Yeltsin. Yeltsin withdrew his

---

[2]Obolensky, an engineer from Leningrad province, unexpectedly challenged Gorbachev for this position when the Supreme Soviet convened for the first time on May 25, 1989.

candidacy, and the congress did not include Obolensky on the ballot. And I just sat and listened. Why? Comrades, I believe that we must have confidence in the process that is under way. And to me there is no question as to whether the democratic process applies to me or not. It does apply, and you could not help but notice this in the four years of reform. Everything which society has at its disposal today and all information are available under *glasnost* and democracy. And I have probably made some contribution to this. (Applause.) I don't want you to feel sympathy for me. Please understand that I am devoted to the cause of democracy. If I was faced with the choice of returning to the past system under which the country was ruled and managed, I would resign immediately.

After all, if we look at current social processes, all of them involve democratization: the democratization of economic life, the democratization of political life, the democratization of culture, and the democratization of all social forces. And I am devoted to this choice and will defend it to the end. I will do everything I can to democratize society. I see the goal of my activity as creating conditions under which it would be impossible to return to the command-administrative system or, moreover, to any kind of personality cult. This goes against my convictions. I don't want the sweeping powers that have been conferred on me in the name of the people to be used for any other purposes than in the interests of the people and in the interests of *perestroika* and democratic development in the country. (Applause.)

At the Congress of People's Deputies we heard a wide variety of opinions and judgments, and you and I saw a genuine crosssection of our society. I believe that, in this, the congress provided an important service. On the other hand, the congress marked the beginning of a genuine transfer of power to the councils. This process will be further developed in elections to the local councils, and this will be of vast importance for the destiny of our country.

We need democracy in order to change our life for the better. And therefore simply playing parliamentary games and parliamentary tricks is unworthy of a People's Deputy. I am also profoundly convinced of this. You'll notice that a great deal of time is spent on discussing nominees for ministerial positions. The deputies are trying to clarify each question and want to hear the right answer in order to make a conscious choice instead of simply approving candidates for ministerial positions by a mechanical majority. This takes a lot of time, but I believe that it is simply necessary for all of us, including the ministers, the deputies, and all of society.

Question: Do you believe, and if so, how soon, that truly equal rights will be granted to different forms of property, be it government, cooperative, or private?

Gorbachev: We will do everything we can to unlock the potential of socialist property, be it by means of self-financing, leasing, or cooperatives. I myself can't imagine, and I think it would be difficult for any of us to imagine, that we will begin to pass laws making factories private property.

Voice: But what about cooperative property?

Gorbachev: As far as cooperative property, of course!

Voice: But what about land?

Gorbachev: Land, too. Let it belong to all the people, but it might be used in different ways, including leasing to peasants, cooperatives, and other associations. In this case we must be frank, bold, and decisive. When we adopt a lease law, we must add a rule stating that the councils are granted the rights of property holders, that is, the right to lease land regardless of whether certain officials like it or not.

But I am opposed to private property. To us private property is unacceptable. In general, I am against private property. (Applause.)

Voice: But, Mikhail Sergeyevich . . .

Gorbachev: So you, comrade, are already prepared to go to work for the capitalists?

Voice: If the pay was right, I would!

Gorbachev: That's your opinion. I am convinced that the working class will not reject socialism, because it is through public property that the working class can accomplish its far-reaching social objectives. But we are using and will continue to use socialist property within the framework of the managerial autonomy of enterprises, the reform of the relations of production, and in different organizational forms for economic life. In this case the possibilities are unlimited. I believe that very few people here want to return to capitalism.

Voice: So what was the purpose of your visit to the Izhora plant?

Gorbachev: I have wanted to visit this place for a long time. Your association is one concern where a very important experiment is under way. We are placing the hopes for the future of our economy on it.

Question: Do you have any information on the performance of concerns such as ours?

Gorbachev: Yes, I do. Perhaps the best results have come out of Kvantemp in Moscow. Its prospects for the future look quite good. It is breaking down the barriers between industries and between science and industry. As a result it is gaining a great deal of flexibility.

Question: How many years, according to the economists, will it take to solve our urgent social and economic problems?

Gorbachev: I have basically answered the question of how we are viewing these problems. I think that we don't have a whole lot of time. We must solve the problems of food and other consumer goods immediately, without delay. People "at the bottom" and "at the top" realize this, and we must do everything we can to solve the problem by combining our efforts. Commissions and committees of the Supreme Soviet and the Council of Ministers are working on the problem; some committees are working on the budget, while others are working on emergency measures, and so forth. We are tackling the problem right now.

We have a great deal of potential, including human, intellectual, natural, and technical potential. We must give it room and set it in motion. If we do this, we will be able to turn our country into a thriving place. I have no doubts in this regard. So why is it still important for us to buy less and not place so much of our hopes on imports? We must do this in order not to condemn ourselves to dependence. We must solve our own problems and learn how to live and work differently. We live the way we work. If we work better, we'll live better. If we're smarter, we'll change! It's all up to us! We ourselves must change, and then all of society will change.

Question: Will a free-trade zone be allowed in Leningrad province?

Gorbachev: This issue must be discussed.

Voice: Why is Comrade [Nikolai] Ryzhkov nominating for ministerial positions the people who have led the country to economic collapse?[3]

Gorbachev: I can't agree with you. First of all, our government led by Comrade Ryzhkov was organized in the last four years; hence, it would be incorrect to say that this government is responsible for the collapse in the country.

---

[3]Gorbachev's dogged defense of Prime Minister Ryzhkov has considerably decreased his own popularity.

Moreover, some of the ministers who worked in the old government were not proposed by Comrade Ryzhkov and some of the candidates were rejected by the Supreme Soviet.

Question: Mikhail Sergeyevich, why were the live television broadcasts of the Supreme Soviet sessions stopped? I consider this a step backward.

Gorbachev: Here, there are different points of view. The 1st Congress of People's Deputies and the first session of the Supreme Soviet had to receive full coverage. And we are still in favor of this. The congress was broadcast live, while the Supreme Soviet sessions were taped, but practically everything was broadcast. But there are certain limits. People keep talking, and so the broadcast ends at two in the morning. It was suggested that the Supreme Soviet sessions be broadcast in the evening, when most people are home. Let the people themselves decide whether to watch or not. I must say that when the congress was in session, many people didn't go to work. (Laughter.) And you'll probably back me up on this. But we are in favor of providing full coverage. And in the future, when the Supreme Soviet is in session, we will stick to the principle of providing complete information—not continuous coverage, but complete coverage. I will say once again that basically television is showing practically everything.

Question: What is your attitude with respect to elections solely on the basis of national and national territorial districts, without public organizations?

Gorbachev: You should know, although there were quite a few arguments, that the nomination of candidates from public organizations was accompanied by a diversity of opinions, judgments, and interests. In general we have received quite strong reinforcements from the public organizations. Just take the economists and representatives of other branches of our intelligentsia: after all, most of them came through the public organizations. There has been criticism of the process of nominating candidates from the party. But with respect to the comrades who were nominated, there was practically no criticism. It was a very formidable contingent!

Well, why did the general secretary supposedly "leave the people" during the elections? I would like to take you into the mind of the general secretary. Initially I wanted to run for election from a territorial district, but then they would have said that the general secretary was abandoning the party. There would have been more misinterpretations. So I said, let us discuss and analyze everything and we'll find the right solution.

Question: What is your attitude toward religion?

Gorbachev: In this matter I take the position expressed in the constitution and believe that we must consistently make constitutional principles a reality.

Question: Do you personally believe in God?

Gorbachev: Of course not! I only know that I was baptized and that my name was changed.

Question: What is your attitude toward direct elections to the councils and in the party?

Gorbachev: What are you talking about? Elections to the highest positions?

Voice: That's right.

Gorbachev: I believe that everything is in our hands. But I am not impressed by the practice of presidential elections, and the word "president" itself does not agree with many of my convictions. I am more in favor of concepts such as the council, the collegium, and the presidium, which include representatives of all the republics. I think that this is more appropriate for our democracy and the needs of our federation. But ultimately we could discuss this and resolve it by a referendum: Do we need this kind of power or another kind?

With respect to elections in the party, we have traditions that come from Lenin, and we must not ignore them. It's important that our election campaigns be democratic. And this is becoming increasingly evident now. And I think that the forthcoming electoral campaign in the party will be much different from previous campaigns. The process of democracy within the party is gaining momentum.

Question: What is your opinion on state quality control?

Gorbachev: When self-financing triumphs and every plant becomes interested in producing high-quality goods, then this agency will be unnecessary. If you've already grown up, then we could get rid of it here, right now.

Question: Comrade General Secretary, what is your attitude toward the statements made by the economist [Wassily] Leontieff, the Russian-American, who has advocated using foreign specialists as consultants at our plants?

Gorbachev: I have a favorable attitude toward it, in the same way that I do toward drawing on foreign experience in technology, in finance, in credit, and in banking, where foreigners have gained a great deal of useful experience. And this experience will be useful to us as we make the transition to economic methods of managing the economy. By the way, we have already made these contacts, and this kind of cooperation is already under way.

Question: What is your opinion with respect to reviewing privileges and benefits?

Gorbachev: We, comrades, have already agreed on some points. There has been a great deal of discussion of privileges and benefits. I consider myself an even-handed person who is nonetheless in favor of radical solutions of major issues. And before I thought that this could all be resolved by a stroke of the pen. And then I requested the appropriate information and was astounded by the system that had emerged in this area during the reign of Soviet power.

We asked for information from the trade unions on the privileges at their disposal and at the disposal of the enterprises. We discovered that the introduction of self-financing at the republic, provincial, and plant levels had expanded the opportunities for the plants and that privileges and benefits would continue to grow. And many enterprises that have their own "plums" have already emerged in both the republics and the provinces. They have medical departments that are superior to any of ours, and there are enterprises that have their own health resorts on the Black Sea and guest houses on the Gulf of Riga and the Gulf of Finland. But after all, they earned it, so let them keep it.

On the other hand, science has its own system of incentives, which includes titles, certain bonuses, and privileges for academicians. There are privileges for active-duty military personnel, for some veterans, for Heroes of Socialist Labor, and so forth.

In short, there is a very diversified system of legitimate privileges and benefits. This issue is so complex that it cannot be boiled down to closing certain dining halls or stores. Or, for example, the Supreme Soviet raised the issue of the Fourth Department of the USSR Ministry of Public Health. But after all, these polyclinics provide services not only to party members but also to a very wide range of people, including ministry employees, the creative intelligentsia, veterans, and so forth.

The latest currents of opinion call for eliminating all of this. But I think, and we have already started studying this, that we must first of all take an inventory. We must carefully analyze everything that has taken root under the reign of Soviet power and what system of benefits and privileges has emerged. And everything that is considered legal should be left in place, while everything that is considered illegal should be eliminated.

Voice: Mikhail Sergeyevich, this was probably not the point of the question.

Gorbachev: Well, what was the point?

Voice: If we are now living through such difficult times, then everyone should live through them to an equal extent, including us and the academicians. If, as the saying goes, we're scraping by on black bread, then both we and they should do it! That was the point.

Gorbachev: But we must provide for different pay scales in order to keep our best scientists from running off to America, as is the case in the Third World. These are great talents! Therefore, comrades, we must stick to socialist principles. We must pay for the quantity and quality of labor. But we must provide a certain level of social security that must apply to all workers, and above this level we should provide incentives for talents, abilities, work and so forth. And I believe that all of this should be encouraged in the form of higher pay. This should become the basic privilege, namely, let everyone have the opportunity to acquire goods with his wages.

Voice: That's exactly what we've been saying! (Applause.)

Question: In the city of Leningrad all manufactured goods that are in very short supply are distributed on the basis of preliminary applications only to veterans of the war in Afghanistan. I am not against their privileges, but what are people like me, who don't have any relatives or acquaintances who are war veterans, supposed to do? I can't buy a washing machine, a television, or a refrigerator if I don't find a dishonest veteran who would be willing to render this service for a certain amount of money. Let some of the goods go to satisfying their needs and let some go on sale to the general public.

Gorbachev: But I'm sure that there are some. Some of them are sold to the general public.

Voices: No.

Gorbachev: That's a serious matter. In addition I have also received the following note: "What steps are being taken to crack down on Soviet millionaires?" Do you believe that they exist?

Voices: Yes, we do.

Gorbachev: We must firmly take these steps. What's most important is that as we abandon the system of wage leveling, we must pay out only money that has been earned.[4] And we must crack down on unearned income.

Questions may arise with respect to the cooperatives. In Moscow there was a case when a party member came to pay party dues from an income of three million rubles. I would say that this is abnormal. And we must be firm in combating this.

By the way, we have instituted a system of taxation for cooperatives. This system of taxation should be adjusted so as to avoid excessive polarization in income levels. But there will be and should be a certain amount of polarization. Otherwise, the entire principle of compensating labor on the basis of quantity and quality would come to nothing.

Question: What is your attitude with respect to political strikes? For example, if the legislature should adopt an undemocratic law on elections to the local councils?

Gorbachev: I think that there won't be an undemocratic law on elections to local councils.

Question: You say that we must put an end to the command-administrative system. So how, then, could we understand your policy of support for the ministries?

Gorbachev: I hope that you do not suspect or assume that the general secretary is opposed to the success of *perestroika*? No, I am very much interested in making it faster and more effective. But faster doesn't mean that it can happen overnight, in a week, in a year, or even two years. There are immediate problems that must be resolved immediately, while others will be resolved in five, seven, or ten years. The issue of a transition from a command-administrative system to economic methods is very complex and cannot be resolved by a single stroke of the pen.

Question: So how was the question of taxing the cooperatives resolved? Why, despite all our openness, wasn't there a national discussion?

Gorbachev: The issue of taxing the cooperatives was discussed very energetically and, I would even say, passionately. It even reached the point of fighting.

---

[4]"Wage leveling" means that skilled and industrious workers are paid the same wages as the unskilled and lazy.

Cooperative operators and finance agencies took part in the discussions. I believe that the fact that it wasn't submitted to the general public for discussion was a mistake, but it's the kind of mistake that can easily be corrected. Now the Supreme Soviet is watching over the public interest, and if any sort of revisions are needed, it will not approve the taxation system in its current form.

Question: What are the current prospects for the development of nuclear power?

Gorbachev: In the world there is the opinion, and I share it, that we cannot do without nuclear power. But what its importance in our overall energy system should be is another question. And, of course, safety must be guaranteed. But we will not survive without nuclear power.

Question: What is your attitude toward the construction of recreation centers in Leningrad?

Gorbachev: I have confidence in your decision. (Applause.)

Question: What will happen to our twenty-million-member party? What kind of future and destiny do you see for it? You are involved in affairs of state, so my question is: Shouldn't you entrust intraparty affairs to a Politburo member?

Gorbachev: If we were to allow the party to become weaker and allow its progressive activity to decline, we would inflict irreparable damage on socialism. The party, its policies, and its organizational activity express the interests of the entire nation and constitute a very reliable tool which integrates and consolidates our society. On the other hand, the party today should operate on the basis of the actual situation that characterizes the phase in which our society finds itself.

The party must take the process of democratization into account and stimulate it. The party must relieve itself of unnatural functions and of matters related to economic activity or the activity of the councils. These issues should be the concern of the councils and the appropriate administrative agencies. Because of the fact that the party had taken on many inappropriate functions, we overlooked and omitted a great deal. We should have analyzed the development of our society a long time ago. We should have provided the right answers, drawn conclusions, and devised appropriate policies a long time ago. We didn't do this, because party committees were too busy mowing, plowing, planting, harvesting, making steel, and so forth.

You might ask if the party is divorcing itself from all of this now. No, it's not. But the party must first of all resolve political issues, open up prospects for society, note the problems which are emerging, and suggest ways of solving them. If we had done this, our problems wouldn't have accumulated to the extent that they have now. With respect to political leadership, no one will take the party's place. All societies have political organizations. Moreover, a socialist society built by the workers can and should realize its potential under the condition of reliable political leadership, but this must be political leadership. And the party should act as a political vanguard by developing economic, social, and personnel policies, providing ideological support for these policies, and carrying on organizational activity among the masses. In this respect no one will replace the party. And I believe that once the party reforms itself, it will acquire new strength and augment and consolidate its authority.

Now I would like to answer the question of delegating the responsibility for managing political affairs to a Politburo member. The Politburo makes collective decisions on all political issues. We try not to take the place of the Council of Ministers and, of course, the Supreme Soviet, but we do discuss all urgent political matters and devise strategies which party members working in the Supreme Soviet and the government do take into consideration.

Question: Isn't it time to follow the precedent of the October Revolution in cracking down on saboteurs of the reform process?

Gorbachev: Comrades, I believe that the best way is to follow the path we have taken of involving the people in all social processes. And if we do this, the saboteurs and reactionaries will find it increasingly difficult to operate now, and in the future they will find it impossible. The process of democratization at both the factory level and the level of any council is the best way. But we know what special squads for imposing order—"threes," "fours," and "sevens"—led to in their day.[5] We should continue to strive for the rule of law, instead of having telephone calls from officials determining the fates of individuals, groups, cadres, and so forth. And this process involves democracy and is proceeding at a fast pace here.

---

[5]Gorbachev refers here to special tribunals which, in a parody of justice, sentenced people during the Stalin-era repressions.

Voice: And I have one final question . . .

Gorbachev: What do you mean by final? (Laughter.)

Question: Prices are going up practically every day, the cooperatives are responsible for driving them up even further, but nevertheless you and the government have spoken of the need to raise procurement and retail prices.

Gorbachev: No, comrades. With respect to retail prices, the situation in the marketplace over the next two to three years will not make it possible for us to approve a rise in retail prices. This is my first point. Second, you and I will resolve this issue together, and, moreover, the Supreme Soviet is keeping an eye on all of these processes. Retail prices will not be reformed without a broad public discussion. We must also think of how to keep this from adversely affecting the people's standard of living. This means that we must consider different kinds of compensation. But this is a matter for the future.[6]

Question: How do you evaluate the urgency of the environmental problem?

Gorbachev: I'll say right out that the environment has us by the throat. We cannot fool around. Hence we must have a carefully planned national program which provides for major investment in the environment. And not one industry can ignore the solution of environmental problems. Any new plant under construction must meet environmental standards, and plants which are already in operation should be modernized so as to bring the environmental situation at them up to standards. We will introduce agencies, some of which are already functioning, which will not permit a single plant to make its balance sheet look good by ignoring environmental problems. This is unacceptable. And I believe that society will insist on this.

We are working on a national program that will include the entire range of issues in order to effect positive changes in the environment. This does not eliminate the need to act now, including efforts by public initiative groups, which should raise these issues in places where the environmental situation has taken an alarming course without waiting for any final decisions.

---

[6]After six years of procrastination, Gorbachev finally raised prices on April 2, 1991, for most consumer goods, including food. Many items' prices were raised by several hundred percent.

Here I have a note thanking me for visiting the plant. This is the first point. And second, the author is convinced that we must have *perestroika*. (Applause.)

I was very glad to meet with you. I feel that you are in the mood for work. I wish you much success! (Applause.)

Voices: Thank you very much, Mikhail Sergeyevich.

Gorbachev: Good-bye.

29

There Won't Be a Civil War

Boris Yeltsin

Ogonyok
no. 12, March 16–23, 1991

The towering figure of the president of the Russian Republic is the very embodiment of confidence. He fiercely defends the interests of Russia in disagreement with the Kremlin's boss, Mikhail Gorbachev. However, their disagreements are but a continuation of the personal contest between them. The efforts of the party hacks to prevent Yeltsin's return to politics greatly contributed to his spectacular electoral successes. His newly acquired tactful manner of presiding over the Russian parliament makes him the most popular politician in the Soviet Union. A secret wish of the demoralized country is that Gorbachev and Yeltsin will join their efforts to find a way out of the current impasse. This article is the most comprehensive exposé of Yeltsin's views by himself. His direct and forceful manner is not yet supported by any philosophical foundation.

I realize that a degree of caution should be exercised with respect to public opinion polls that rate the popularity of and confidence in a political figure and his leadership. At least there is no need to become excessively euphoric when you become, as I have, the hero of the "Man of the Month" department. First of all, public opinion is fickle, and in addition it's impossible and just plain indecent to try to please everyone.

But what's the point of trying to hide the fact that it's obviously pleasant when your deeds and actions don't go unnoticed? For me February was a difficult, stressful, and exhausting month, and when I heard that Professor Grushin's sociological service called me the "man of February," he made it possible for me to arrive at the comforting conclusion that I hadn't survived the month in vain. In addition, I am happy to get the opportunity to address the readers of *Ogonyok*. During the information blockade that the Russian parliament is now under, it's particularly important for me to engage in a direct dialogue with the readers without any intermediaries, interpreters, Communist commentators, or other narrators.

Quite recently I spoke to very different audiences in Yaroslavl, Kaliningrad, and Novgorod provinces. And although I met with workers, intellectuals, peasants, military men, party employees, and managerial employees, people with diverse political views, sympathies, and passions, it will be a long time before I will be able to recall such unanimity on the most important point, that is, the understanding that the country has reached the very final stage of collapse and that there is no longer anywhere to fall back to.

The people who led one of the wealthiest and most talented countries on the planet to a state of destitution and degradation must always have a face of the "enemy" to fall back on, someone they can blame for everything that is going on. We have always had an "enemy" in the seventy-three years of Soviet power: at first we had the bourgeoisie, the gentry, and the capitalists; then we had the counterrevolutionaries, the Trotskyites, and the left- and right-wing deviationists, and also the kulaks; then came the CIA, imperialism, and the Zionist conspiracy. And now we need a new "enemy," because no one believes in the CIA, the Trotskyites, or the capitalists anymore. The new "enemy" is the so-called democrats, who are destabilizing, tormenting, subverting, disorienting, and committing all other kinds of vile acts in their lust for power. On the basis of this logic, all we would have to do to make everything good in the country would be to remove the democrats and get rid of them somehow, and then there would ensue a glorious time known as the "Communist future," "the socialist choice," or the "radiant future."

After I was elected chairman of the Supreme Soviet of Russia, I committed one very important tactical blunder. I trusted Gorbachev. It seemed to me that an alliance with Gorbachev might become very important in stabilizing the situation both in the republics and in the country as a whole. And many people urged me on. Our joint work on the 500-day program brought the interests of a renewed union of republics and the center even closer together. Gorbachev had admitted publicly that the Shatalin-Yavlinsky program looked very interesting and promising to him. It seemed to me that all we had to do was take one more step, and we could walk together onto the road which would lead us out of the crisis. But that didn't happen. He suddenly changed his position drastically, and the 500-day program collapsed, burying any hopes with it for a way out of the impasse.

Instead of breaking with Gorbachev and firmly divorcing myself from the president's policies of half steps, half measures, and half reforms, I fell prey to the illusion that we could still reach an agreement. But, as it turned out, it was impossible to make an agreement with a president who is simultaneously the general secretary of the Central Committee of the Communist party and to whom the interests of the party caste and the party elite will always take precedence over any other interests.

And so we lost four months. We didn't get anywhere by supporting Moscow indirectly by our silence.

On February 19, in a live broadcast on Central Television, I had enough courage to tell the viewers that I was dissociating myself from Gorbachev's policies. It would have been impossible and immoral for me to continue to watch without a murmur while the current leadership dragged the country toward chaos and catastrophe by trying to preserve the rotten system.

Yes, for me February became a month of choice, a month when I had to make a hard but unambiguous and necessary choice. Before then I believed that the time was not yet right for the left-wing forces to form their own political organization and that, after I left the Communist party, I had rid myself forever of the need to join any kind of party. Now I realize that this was just another one of my illusions. Without a powerful, well-organized party of the left based on the democratic platform and other democratic movements, we will never be able to stand up to the Communist party. The Communists have rushed to the attack, and already we are beginning to hear "front-line" terminology from the highest tribunals in the land. The president is trying to scare us with a civil war. An appeal has been made to party members to "come out of the trenches." Already it seems that the old stereotypes of class hatred and class struggle, which had supposedly been buried in the archives forever because they were no longer needed, have suddenly been pulled out into the light.

Everywhere we see them whipping up hysteria and manipulating the public. At this point creating an atmosphere of fear, uncertainty, and hysteria is the only way the bankrupt authorities have to stay at the top a little longer. And this means that now is the time for us to say clearly and succinctly that this is the year of decision. Either democracy will be strangled, or we will win and pull the country out of the terrible state that it's in. If the democrats are defeated, the country won't wake up in 1985, which was a relatively placid and calm year by comparison with now, but in much worse times.

But I personally believe in a different future. I believe, because the people are behind us, because hundreds of thousands of people are coming to rallies in support of democratic ideas in response to a call from the heart, not because they were told to march there in formation on orders from the commanders of military units.

At this time the miners are engaged in a desperate battle for democratic ideas. The fact that they had to resort to such a hard and difficult step for everyone as a strike says only one thing: that the people's supply of patience has dried up. Now they will get pressure from all sides, a torrent of slanders and disinformation will rain down on the strikers, and the authorities will try to intimidate the leaders of the strike committees with trials and fines. It's very important that the strikers should feel the support of all kinds of people standing behind them. And we must support them.

I have already said that "the democrats are to blame for it all" is a very convenient formula. In particular we "are to blame for the collapse of the Union." I realize that the people who conjure up these kinds of incantations are themselves very well aware of who is really to blame for what. Who alienated seven republics to the point that they left the union, who considers the phrase "renewed union" to be nothing more than a smoke screen for cosmetic repairs of the same old command-bureaucratic system, and who is using the same old imperial thinking as the basis for relations between the republics and Moscow? The republics are just small children who can be slapped hard on the hands, like Lithuania, or given candy for good behavior (such as getting a hefty line of credit in hard currency). What's important is that there is an uncle who knows all, decides everything for everyone, and whom everyone has to obey.

That's what they call a renewed union. That's what they call sovereign states and republics.

One more mistake I made and one more illusion I fell prey to was deciding, along with my allies, that when I won a majority of the delegates in the elections to the Russian Congress of People's Deputies and when I became chairman of the Supreme Soviet of the Republic, we had won. Now, we decided, we can pass good laws and appoint energetic and talented executives and begin to build a normal human life for ourselves. But nothing of the kind happened. All of the power in the country and in the republic continued to remain in the hands of people who had successfully sold off and plundered the country and were not prepared to share power, namely the party bureaucratic center.

Thus, I, the leader of the parliament of a very important republic with millions and millions of people, vast territory, and tremendous potential, had no idea of what a president who had very little public confidence and a government which had absolutely none would do with Russia and everything else. I would lie down to sleep [at night] and have no idea where, in what circumstances, and how I would wake up the next morning. Would they confiscate my money and the money of my fellow citizens under the guise of changing denominations, would they put a freeze on bank deposits for the purpose of fighting inflation, would they seize the Russian television and radio company at night or simply take it off the air, would they put tanks and paratroopers on the streets, or what? All of this is decided at the Kremlin, at Old Square, at the KGB, at the Ministry of Defense, wherever you like, but not with any input from the Russian parliament. We could only watch in terror as the center made its next agonizing move. And all of this is known as "the sovereignty of a republic."

I will refuse to sign the recently published version of the union treaty which the center prepared and which was supposedly approved by nine tenths of all the republics that took part in discussing it. Ruslan Khasbulatov, the leader of the working group, never signed the draft. And I hope that the Congress of People's Deputies of Russia and the peoples of Russia will support me in this. We have dozens of major complaints concerning the text of the treaty, starting with the title of the document and ending with its basic principles; in particular, who the subjects of the federation are, how they propose to delineate republican and federal property, the division of administrative functions among the country and the republics, and so forth. All of these are very important problems that must be resolved before we can even think about any kind of treaty. And that also means any kind of union.

Although I already know what kind of scenario they are preparing in order to avoid the necessity of my signature on the union treaty. The "Communists of Russia" bloc has proposed the creation of a group of plenipotentiaries at an extraordinary congress for the purpose of signing the new union treaty in the name of Russia. By the way, they have lots of other preparations to make at this congress. They will try to engage us in a decisive battle and will try to change the leadership of the parliament's republic. And right now, at Old Square, there are entire groups of people engaged in conjuring up and preparing compromising materials on unwanted leaders, developing different tactics for the congress, and screening candidates for leadership positions in the parliament and government of the republic. In general, they're very, very busy.

In this situation our main argument in the struggle against the party bureaucratic structures is a direct appeal for popular support. People are not drawn to us because we democrats are a head taller, better built, or generally look nicer than the party *apparatchiks*. Perhaps it's just the opposite. They're drawn to us because of our ideas, which unite all of us and are attractive and simple: A man should have the right to work freely and dispose freely of the results of his work. And that's it. You don't need anything else.

The first secretaries of the party provincial committees, who are at the same time the chairmen of the provincial councils, are sabotaging most of the decisions made by the Russian parliament and the government. Each of them will have to decide between one post or the other by March 15. Russian law prohibits combining a council leadership position with a leadership position in any other public organization. This is very important for the whole republic. In places where the provincial councils are still, in essence, branch offices of the party provincial committees, no land is being allocated for private farming and any attempts to develop new forms of management are being blocked. But in places where bold and energetic people have taken power into their own hands, privatization has proceeded apace, hundreds and thousands of farmers with their own land have emerged, and life is becoming normal, full, and creative.

I am placing my hopes on the results of the Russian referendum. I have always believed and still believe that the president of the republic should be elected by a direct popular vote. I am confident that most of the voters in the referendum will support this civilized and democratic procedure for electing the leader of the republic. And then it will be necessary to take the next step: The leaders of all the councils should be elected by direct popular vote. Only then will we have strong executive and legislative powers. And in general the entire power structure would be reinforced and sustained by the direct expression of the popular will.

I am convinced that despite the tragedy of the situation now afflicting the country, we still have a chance of getting out of this rotting quagmire if they would just stop interfering with our work. In the near future our economists will submit a Russian version of the 500-day program for discussion. And one more very important matter: This month we will do everything we can to make sure that everyone who wants to can get land this spring and start to work on it. I have confidence in Russians, we all deserve a better fate, and it seems to me that the time has come for us to build our own lives with our own hands.

But I don't believe in a civil war. No matter how agitated the atmosphere gets and no matter how hard the president and his advisers try to aggravate the situation, I am absolutely confident of the people's common sense.

And what else is there left to believe in?

30

On the Threshold of Momentous Changes

Alexander Yakovlev

Izvestiya
May 31, 1990

This is the work of the preeminent theoretician in the current party leadership. According to Yakovlev, a qualitatively new stage of reform is only now beginning with the switch to a market economy, which should put an end to the lack of economic freedom for the individual. Yakovlev analyzes the results of the political reforms of 1989 and 1990, the main achievement of which was a step from *glasnost* to action, toward the rule of law and toward freedom of thought that cannot be reversed. He pays lip service to the "socialist idea" and would like to see it as an integral part of world civilization. He often takes reasonable positions that are not supported by his boss, Gorbachev, and which have not been implemented.

The Soviet Union now finds itself in a period of a qualitatively new alternative. Our country is huge, diverse, and rich. The situation is not simple in many respects, and it is influenced by the strong inertia of the past. A fundamental shift was made in April of 1985. However, a qualitatively new chronology for *perestroika* starts only now. And this frontier is a transition to a market economy.

I speak about this in order to emphasize once more that, in a certain sense, *perestroika* is still just beginning. All that has happened until now, in spite of its revolutionary significance, is no more than an overture to what will have to be done now. In recent years, it was necessary to take stock of the problems, and honestly and impartially to analyze them. As a result, the politically and socially active members of society had to complete this work independently in order to arrive at their own solutions and to gain the necessary determination. Now comes the moment of truth, the moment to arrive at a position of common sense—neither to the left nor to the right—and to overcome the uproar of emotions, mean egoism, and ambitious fervor.

Any practical task, particularly concerning economic relations, requires realism. My remarks are motivated by the need for realism, not by a wish to continue old disputes or to start new ideological disputes. Reality is more complex than are mechanical schemes. For our society to attain a higher level of quality, we must operate on the basis of attachment to the socialist idea. This idea is founded on the values of justice, which have been cherished throughout the millennia and which have contributed to creating the essence of modern civilization.

Where, then, lies the difference between the practice of *perestroika* and the ideas we inherited from our own past?

First, our society has resolutely and categorically thrown away everything that is, by its essence or its form, incompatible with natural morality. Certainly, we cannot rearrange the past, but it is necessary to understand it. It is necessary to free our conscience and our actions from vestiges of the past—whether they occurred because of the country's low general level of development, or because of excessive ideological zeal, exaggerations of external threat, or real difficulties. There were enough of those for several generations, many of them caused by one individual's mean spirit. Precisely for this reason, we condemn Stalinism as a phenomenon and as a specific state of social institutions, affairs, and morality.

Second, it is not abstract formulas, attractive as they may be, that should be used as reference points or criteria for our future actions. Instead, we should use the concrete welfare of the individual in society now and in the near future as our criterion, as measured by the following indexes: the elevation of personality, freedom, democratization, *glasnost*, solid moral foundations, provision of life's necessities, and creation of the unrestricted possibility for rational choices and self-fulfillment.

Third, the realization of the socialist idea should not be isolated from the rest of human experience. It is unacceptable to view the socialist idea as either separate from or opposed to human development. Socialism is a component of world civilization. Its future is embedded in economics, culture, science and technology, way of life, forms of social organization—in everything connected with world processes. We must include here its significance for foreign policy, legal issues, economic management, and in general for all the technological aspects of society.

The political reform introduced in 1989 and 1990 had several objectives. It took a step from *glasnost* to realistic, institutionalized democracy. From a command-administrative system dominated by the leaders of the party-state apparatus and industrial monopolies, we have moved toward a legalistic system of power with a clear distribution of functions and with the supreme power for each belonging to the appropriate soviet. Political reform is gradually dismantling the overly bureaucratized structures. Possessed of inherent value, it must nevertheless stimulate the execution of economic reform. And, most essential, it must lay a foundation for a democratic state of law. What and how much has been accomplished?

A great deal has been accomplished, and little has been accomplished. A great deal, if we reflect on how far society has moved away from the very recent past. Everything is changing, most especially people's consciousness, albeit slowly. Monopolies on thought, truth, the right to evaluate, and the right to propose have been broken down. I think this is irreversible. Indeed, we now look differently at ourselves, at our actions, at our problems, at the external world and our place in it.

However, there is great apprehension about how much we still need to accomplish. The question of joint ventures offers one immediate example. A law of property is needed for their healthy functioning. We approved it only recently. We do not yet have a law on entrepreneurship. Nor do we yet have laws addressing land ownership, currency controls, market relations (we don't even have a market), and laws about many other things. We do not yet have all of this. It would have been impossible to have created them in such a brief period, and equally impossible to write laws speculatively, a priori, and in isolation from life processes that we are only just beginning to experience.

Even in the domain of political reform (which has far outstripped economic reform), we are still learning about political culture. The newly elected soviets are beginning to show signs of getting it right. Individuals, groups, and parties are beginning to adjust to one another and are learning to work under new conditions. We must still reorganize the federation, conclude a new union treaty, and approve a new constitution.

Society is moving ahead with all due speed. The presidency, an absolutely new institution for us, has been introduced. The primary goal of this step is to ensure the consolidation of society and all of its forces on the basis of democratic development. Democracy is the key to everything.

It creates an opportunity for a historical turn in the fate of the country and its peoples. Too many obstacles prevented us from making this turn earlier. But now it has become an imperative for further development.

What are the barriers standing in the way of the democratic process? Of course, there is some organized resistance. But that is not the most threatening factor. It is the resistance by the forces of inertia and habit that poses the most serious obstacles, but these too can be conquered. I would also like to mention obstacles of a systemic nature.

The growth of democracy in our way of life is strongly inhibited by a persistent lack of economic freedom. The essential functions of both individuals and collectives still depend on the state. Their self-reliance, independence, and sovereignty are, in practice, considerably restricted. In my view, freedom has been retarded by a high degree of freeloading that has undermined the motivation to work and allowed one to exist without worrying too much about the material sources of life. The level and quality of life in the majority of such cases are dissociated from the results of the work of the particular person or collective. This split will be overcome with the help of a transition to a socially just market.

We must now develop, strengthen, and nurture democracy in every way, but we must also be firm in our insistence that it stand on the solid ground of realism and law. Democracy, *perestroika*, and the market demand exactly such rational thinking and action. To be sure, it would be unwise to go to the opposite extreme, to fall prey to pure rationalism and nearsighted pragmatism; such a tendency also exists.

Today the growth of democratic potential is endangered by interethnic tensions. This came as a surprise, although an unpleasant one. The problems have accumulated for decades, and once *perestroika* removed the previous fear and silence they manifested themselves. It is even possible that these tensions are being deliberately fanned.

I believe that this explosion of interethnic passions reflects not only previous mistakes and well-intended stupidities but also the objective difficulties of the general situation in the country. The establishment of true democracy and a modern market economy has required a struggle with nationalism everywhere. Classical European feudalism as well as our bureaucratic feudalism objectively divides nations, and even cities and provinces, by erecting customs barriers between them. With time, the market will break down these barriers, but for that to occur it must reach a certain level of development.

Naturally, all of the above is influencing economic relations with the outside world. We have overcome in ourselves—although perhaps not completely—the past psychology of autarky. Subjectively, we are striving to achieve the most active connections with the external world, and we need them. We understand how useful such connections will be in all respects.

Based on my understanding of society and its economic structures, it would appear that we are not yet prepared for these connections. I will not discuss the purely professional matters addressed by your conference.[1] However, it is absolutely clear that, during a period when the old economic system is breaking down and a new one is not yet formed, it is a difficult time for economic ties. When many vitally important political, legal, administrative, and arbitration structures are still in the process of formation, it is also a difficult time for honest business relations.

It is necessary to raise another issue. Decades of confrontation, cold war, antagonism, and mutual suspicion cannot be eradicated without a trace. The psychology of the people has been shaped by such an existence, and the result is that we are severely handicapped by this way of life. We encounter diverse expressions of its consequences, and we will continue to encounter them for some time. This is also an integral part of modern complex realities.

It is necessary to pay our respects to those Western businessmen who are striving to expand relations with us in spite of difficult conditions. I think I understand in general the risks they are taking and their difficulties as well as the potential benefits. I am sure that the progress of *perestroika*, economic reform, and the transition to the market will result in a situation in which business relations will be influenced only by the usual problems, without extraneous issues. I believe in that.

And I am also sure that not only our country but also the whole world is at a turning point. It seems that man and mankind, speaking in a broad philosophical sense, have come

---

[1]This document is derived from a speech made by Yakovlev at an international conference on financing investments and trade with the Soviet Union, held in Moscow in May 1990.

to understand that disunity carries the potential to cause general destruction. Men, very likely, have also come to understand their primal kinship.

A mutual, intensive gravitation toward one another is especially strong now. I think many factors are intertwined here: a natural human and political interest, after decades of hostility and alienation; weariness of confrontation and awareness not only of its dangers but also that we had come to an impasse and were unable to deal constructively with any question; the drama of *perestroika* and the possibilities it opened; a desire to find something new and useful for yourself in someone else; and a satisfaction deriving from mutual discovery and recognition, from the realization that we can do things together—a seemingly hopeless fantasy only a few years ago. Thus we have the essence of *perestroika*:

—to place the country decisively on the trajectory of accelerating economic progress;

—to work out in practice a model of effective development corresponding to modern internal and external realities;

—to begin a broad international cooperation that is in our own interests as well as for the sake of the whole civilized world;

—above all, to contribute to creating conditions for a qualitatively new world that can be built together and not by a single country, not in conflict but in unity.

This is the beautiful dream of all social romantics, but it shows every sign of becoming a reality worthy of man in our time.

31

"I Believe in the People's Soul and Reason"

Yegor Ligachev

Pravda
June 18, 1990

This interview with *Pravda* correspondent O. Stepanenko is devoted to agricultural problems. It is essentially a conversation between two conservatives. Ligachev approves of the creation of a new organization, the Peasants Union. (He speaks the old language; for him everyone is either a worker or peasant.) Ligachev sees himself as a defender of peasants' interests; he is worried that their representation in the Supreme Soviet has declined, but he neglects to say in comparison to what. His peasants are the chairmen of the collective and state farms, the rural bureaucracy. Nevertheless, he believes that the majority of peasants support the party, and that this should help during the introduction of a multiparty system. Similarly, Czar Nicholas II and his government mistakenly assumed that the naive peasants would certainly support their czar. Ligachev stands for diversity of forms of ownership, but only socialist forms. He still insists that collective and state farms have great potential, and he does not support the privatization of land. Not even his visit to Sweden in June 1990—his only visit to a capitalist country—changed his mind; he noticed only that the Swedish government assists and regulates agriculture, nothing that spoke of capitalist superiority.

Pravda: It would clearly be useful to begin with our domestic event—the formation of the Peasants Union.

Ligachev: Indisputably. I expressed my attitude toward it at the union's congress. I think you will agree: A fundamentally new sociopolitical organization has been set up in the country, uniting an entire class—the peasant class—together with that part of the working class and the intelligentsia that works in the agro-industrial complex. This organization is destined to strengthen and develop. If we had had such an agrarian union before, I am confident that we would have made fewer mistakes with regard to peasants, the countryside, and agriculture as a whole.

Pravda: Different opinions exist on why the union was set up and what its purpose is.

Ligachev: I think it was set up because the peasantry's role in society has increased. It has undergone politicization, and the need to defend its interests is more keenly felt than ever before. And, of course, the formation of the union is primarily associated with the rapid and, let me be frank, contradictory processes of democratization of our society. The peasantry, like the working class, is very concerned that it is poorly represented in the highest organs of power.

I will not deny that I was most gratified by the fact that, despite the difficult processes unleashed by the very first steps toward the market system—the increasing costs of industrial output and industrial services—the Peasants Union did not enter into confrontation with the working class. It was firmly declared at the union's congress that the countryside and the city are a single whole and that the conflicts between them, created in past years and greatly strengthened in the context of the transition to market relations, must be eliminated. It is gratifying that the Peasants Union sees the only solution in the unity of workers, peasants, and intelligentsia.

Pravda: Yegor Kuzmich, what, in your view, should be the attitude of the CPSU and the Communists toward the agrarian union?

Ligachev: I would like to divide the question into two parts. First: What is the attitude of the peasantry itself toward the Communist party? I think that the vast majority of our peasantry supports the party and is on its side. Second: I am convinced that rural Communists will join the agrarian union, set about working, win over the masses, and strengthen the party's prestige. I repeat—win over the masses, which is very important in the period of an incipient multiparty system. I hope that the Peasants Union will help the party to strengthen its influence among the rural population; after all, this union is a powerful force consolidating the peasantry. I personally would advise party committees actively to help it to find its feet, so to speak, to form the corresponding organizations, and to give them every possible assistance.

Pravda: And what is the [Communist party] Central Committee's attitude toward the agrarian union?

Ligachev: That a Peasants Union is being set up was discussed at the Politburo and at a session of our agrarian commission. Everyone took a positive view of it. I would also like to mention one of the main questions that was debated at the agrarian congress: the diversity of forms of ownership.

Pravda: I think that this question is being debated in society as a whole, not just at the agrarian congress.

Ligachev: True. Because of the attempts to represent my speech in a certain light, I would like to refresh memories. At the congress I was not talking about forms of ownership in general, but about forms of socialist ownership. That is very important. I said that I am decisively in favor of a diversity of forms of socialist ownership. At the same time, I am profoundly convinced that at present and in the future the basis of our agriculture will be social ownership (in the form of state and cooperative enterprises) integrated with individual labor ownership (personal plots, family farms). I added that I cannot conceive of the policy of *perestroika* without continuity. From my viewpoint, this is of fundamental significance.

Many of our troubles stem from the fact that our policy doesn't ensure the necessary combination of transformations and continuity. The system of collective and state farms has enormous potential for the successful development of production, for the economy, and for the social sphere in agriculture. And we are only just beginning to remove administrative edicts, chains and fetters, so as to release this enormous—I repeat, enormous—economic and moral potential. Many delegates to the agrarian congress spoke of this.

Pravda: I believe that you were elected to the Peasants Union Central Council.

Ligachev: And I regard it as a great honor. I am grateful for this expression of trust, and I regard it as an assessment of my position on agrarian questions.

Pravda: Incidentally, readers express anxiety: No parliament in the world would ever adopt a law under which anyone can just leave an enterprise and take some of its resources with him. Yet our Soviet parliament has done just that. Under the Law on Land everyone, on leaving a *sovkhoz* [state farm], for instance—and a *sovkhoz* is an enterprise—can take part of the land. Many people note that this is downright anarchy. In a society of free enterprise and "freedom" of the individual, no legislator and no boss would ever tolerate such a thing.

Ligachev: Well, that is a fair comment. The principle of freedom to the detriment of others is highly dangerous, and it has already brought mankind to the brink of catastrophe, which was avoided, if you look at it objectively, by socialism, however deformed it may have been. At the macro level, when large entities, republics, withdraw from a whole community to the detriment of other republics and peoples, we have already realized how ruinous this kind of "freedom" is. And we are working out a mechanism for secession taking everyone's interests into account. Yet at the micro level, which is the basic foundation of economic and social processes and which determines their orientation either toward destruction or toward creation, we are reluctant to grasp it. It was no accident that the Peasants Union delegates also spoke of the need for economic substantiation when innovations are introduced.

Pravda: Yegor Kuzmich, did your trip to Sweden change your views and your approach to rural problems?

Ligachev: On the contrary, if anything it reinforced them.

Pravda: Yet Sweden bases its life on private ownership of the means of production, and its agriculture has achieved great successes on the basis of private farming.

Ligachev: Who is denying it? But there are many reasons for these successes. The Swedes joke, for instance, and not without reason, that Russia (or specifically Peter the Great) helped them a good deal.

Pravda: What do they mean?

Ligachev: He taught them to fight, and nearly three centuries of peace helped the entire economy to grow strong. But there are, you realize, other reasons, too. In Sweden once again we were firmly convinced that along with the type of ownership and the form of economic management, exceptional significance is attached to material, technical, and social factors for development.

I would like to say that the Swedish National Farmers Union has very broad rights. In particular, in the middle of the year its representatives assemble without fail for a round table, along with representatives of consumers, trade unions, and the state. And every year they examine questions relating to purchase prices for agricultural products and the price correlation between agricultural and industrial output, to ensure that economic equality and price parity are strictly observed.

Pravda: The parity which for decades our peasants have been telling us, loud and clear, has been violated?

Ligachev: That is bitter for us, but true. This evaluation alone undermines the countryside at its roots. In Sweden the state strictly regulates purchase prices for such important types of agricultural produce as grain, milk, meat, eggs, and a number of other food products as well as agricultural raw materials in light of the interests of rural workers.

The level of social security is also important. There, the farmer has the same pension as a city dweller, and his living conditions are better than the city dweller's.

Pravda: The impression is created that the free market that certain economists propose for us does not exist in Sweden.

Ligachev: That is not an impression. It is a fact. Those of our esteemed economists who propose so-called free-market relations, which will undoubtedly lead to mass unemployment—let them be the first unemployed, let them find out what it means. I am sure that it is possible to create a system of material assistance for the unemployed, but to compensate a capable person for losing participation in socially useful activity—that is impossible. And there is no greater disaster for anyone than to be discarded from the sphere of social production.

Pravda: And the second question: Do you not think that in the Swedish experience (at least what you have spoken about it) the most important thing is the organization of the struggle against the consequences of the same old capitalist economy, the same old market relations, albeit regulated by the state? But scientific socialism offers different approaches, structures, and principles.

Ligachev: You are right. In general, it provides for the combination of interests and the formation of equal, fair relations, beginning with the most basic levels, the cells of production and of life. And this, let me tell you, accords with the spirit of our people, who have a very keen sense of injustice and inequality. Take the question of ownership of the land. I would like to quote a remark by [Alexander] Chayanov. "For the people, what matters is not ownership of the land, but that they should have access to the land and that they should not be prevented from working steadily and productively on the land. It also matters to them that the land should not accumulate in the hands of the nouveaux riches. Yet when there is private ownership, land slips very easily from the hands of the poorest farmers and accumulates in the hands of the rich."

Private ownership of the means of production, in any form, leads to divisions between people and differentiation of their interests. There is nothing innovative in the fact that private ownership is being proposed; all of this has happened before. Those who call for a free market invariably push us back toward private-ownership appropriation of the results of other people's labor, toward its exploitation.

Let us in the end ask the people's opinion on what path we should follow in restructuring society—the socialist or the capitalist path. Let us hold a nationwide referendum.

As for my opinion, I am in favor of a planned market economy based on social ownership of the means of production in all the diversity of its forms. I am in favor of a market guaranteeing firm prices for the main consumer goods and with real guarantees against unemployment. I am in favor of the consistent, gradual, and steady implementation of the socialist reform of society. Gradual—that does not mean slow. It means stage by stage, from one milestone to the next, devoting the maximum time and effort to preparing for the transformations—legal, organizational, and educational preparation.

Once again: I believe in the people's soul and reason. That is what I am taking to the Russian Party Conference and the Party Congress.

32

Ligachev Addresses the Constituent Congress of Russian Communists

Yegor Ligachev

"Moscow TV Service"
[television program]
June 20, 1990

Alarmed by the electoral successes of reformers in 1989 and 1990, conservatives decided to call a June 1990 meeting of the Russian delegates to the 28th CPSU Congress (which met in July 1990) to discuss the possibility of forming a conservative-dominated separate party—the Communist Party of Russia. Ligachev, clearly one of the instigators of this move, strongly indicated his support for it in this televised speech to the meeting. The delegates so overwhelmingly favored founding a separate party that they declared their meeting to be the founding congress of the new party.

In his speech, Ligachev states that the country and the party are in disarray, and he confesses that he did not realize that reforms would weaken the party and lead to the disintegration of the Soviet federation and a loss of faith in socialism. He indirectly accuses Gorbachev of abandoning the collective principle of leadership and of not consulting the Politburo and the Central Committee on such important issues as the shift to a regulated market economy, the events in Eastern Europe, and the German question. He claims that his objections and those raised by party organizations in many cities were ignored. Ligachev asserts that it is impossible to combine a party post with other obligations, referring to the fact that Gorbachev simultaneously occupies the posts of Communist party first secretary and president of the Soviet Union. It is quite likely that Gorbachev has not forgiven him for these public comments.

Esteemed comrades, like many of you I back the formation of a Russian Communist party within the CPSU, and also the election at our congress of its ruling bodies and the setting up of printed publications. Why do I back this? It is because I believe in the strong internationalist traditions of the Communists of Russia and of all its peoples. I believe that the Communist party of Russia, like the whole of Soviet Russia, will strengthen the unity of the CPSU and the integrity of the Soviet federation and will genuinely become a catalyst for the processes of renewal. That is the first thing I wanted to say.

Second, whatever problems we happen to discuss—and there really is a multitude of them today—one literally cannot get the two main ones out of one's head: What is to happen to the country and to the Soviet federation, and what is to happen to the party. No, there is no alternative to *perestroika*. We cannot go on living as we did up to 1985. We all embarked on *perestroika* with enthusiasm. In the early years, things were on the up and up. Both gains and failures are evident. The social reorientation of the economy, democratization of the soviets, changes in the party, and the elimination of the threat of nuclear war—I think you will agree that each of these taken individually has been an enormous advance.

But at the same time the political situation in society remains extremely difficult, and the most alarming thing is that it is tending to get even worse. The country is in disarray. The economy is moving backward, and living costs are increasing. National separatism is spreading. The Soviet federation is being dismembered. People are dying. The question on literally everyone's lips is: What sort of a state is it that is incapable of defending its citizens?

In reply, one can frequently hear appeals to the effect that one should not panic. Of course panic does not help, but I think we must resolutely get rid of the sentiment that everything will come out all right in the end, and that things could be worse. The question that arises is: Why did all this happen? Are these inevitable concomitants of the policy of *perestroika*, or are they the consequences of the mistakes and errors of the present leadership? Today, as was mentioned here, it really is not a question of repentance, but one of honest and open analysis and of a self-critical assessment of the activity of the political leadership, of which I am a member, and I bear—I would like to say this in all honesty, too—my full measure of responsibility. And I consider the demand of delegates that members of the Politburo should give an account of themselves at the Party Congress to be quite proper, and I shall make such a report myself at the 28th Congress.

I'd now like to say this: The party's strategy and its principal positions geared to the renewal of society are correct. And I think that the boldness and farsightedness of the leadership were manifested in this. And I want to say honestly here—despite it being a generally known fact—that the political initiative here belongs to Mikhail Sergeyevich Gorbachev.

But serious omissions and grave mistakes indeed have been made in the tactics, methods, and approaches to reform. I believe that, as a Politburo member, I did not realize fully and with due attentiveness the main danger for the policy of *perestroika*, namely the systematic and ever-increasing work of antisocialist forces aimed at weakening and, eventually, destroying from within—I would like to stress "from within"—the Communist party and, consequently, the socialist union of the republics. It is customary now to divide the opposition forces into left-wingers and right-wingers, radicals and conservatives. Frankly speaking, I have a different approach. I think one should put it as follows: The majority of Communists in the party adhere to Marxist-Leninist positions and to platforms of scientific socialism. At the same time, social-democratic, revisionist, centrist, and national-separatist movements are in evidence in the party.

There are quite a few of those who are nostalgic for Stalin's times. Many advocate private ownership, a market-based environment, and factions in the party, and reject the principle of democratic centralism. What is all of this, comrades? Is it radicalism? No, it is pure revisionism, there is not a grain of anything new, we have seen it all before.

But, comrades, I would like to talk about something else. We often, and not without deep satisfaction, have said that collectivism, democratism, and taking others' opinions into account are inherent characteristics of the present political leadership of the country. Of late, in the work of the Politburo these features have begun to be lost. One example: The government measures for changing over to a regulated market economy—and this you must agree is some policy—were not discussed, and I would like to say this, either in the Politburo or at a *plenum* of the party Central Committee. Thus, the political leadership was left out.

Here is another serious example: Up to now, no analysis has been made at the Central Committee level of the events in Eastern Europe. The German question has not been examined. And this is also major politics, for the socialist community has disintegrated, and the positions of imperialism have grown incredibly stronger. The question inevitably arises: Did I raise these problems in the Politburo? Yes, I did, and more than once. I wrote memos to the Politburo giving grounds for the discussion of the questions of the current moment, the market economy and the integrity of the state, at a *plenum* of the Central Committee.

My proposals are not what is at issue. Many such proposals were made, by the Moscow, Leningrad, Sverdlovsk, Novosibirsk, and other party organizations of Russia. But no *plenum* was held on these important questions. I would like to ask: Is this democratic? The collective nature of the leadership is a very important principle of party building which proceeds from Vladimir Ilyich Lenin. In the past the party has paid a heavy price when it retreated from it. We cannot allow a repetition. One cannot lead the party, this leading force, without giving it all one's time—or perhaps it is possible to do without it.

33

Dimensions of Freedom

Andrei Sakharov

Ogonyok
no. 31, 1989

This interview was conducted by *Ogonyok* correspondent Grigory Tsitrinyak in June 1989. Events since then have shown how far ahead of changes in the Soviet Union Sakharov's thought was and continues to be. Academician Andrei Sakharov, patron saint of reformers, was not much appreciated by his country during the last thirty years of his life. His presence in the Congress of People's Deputies from May 1989 until his death on December 14, 1989, made him a natural leader of the democratic forces. His modesty, his readiness to give everything to others and to his country, and his lucid analysis and personal courage made his death a loss of great proportions for the future of democracy in Russia.

Ogonyok: Before my conversation with Academician Andrei Sakharov, People's Deputy of the USSR, I wanted to take his photograph. With no offense meant to our renowned generals, such a picture is called a "general's photograph." The picture would have shown all of his orders and medals, most especially the three gold stars of the Hero of Socialist Labor, of which he was so shamefully deprived during that disgraceful seven-year exile in Gorky. It seemed to me that readers would have been pleased to learn that the injustice had ended and that truth was triumphant.

Sakharov: They did not return them to me.

Ogonyok: How could they not return them? How is this possible?

Sakharov: It is so. They called me from the Presidium of the Supreme Soviet and said that this question is being considered. I answered that restoring these honors to me is a question of rehabilitation, and I personally don't think that I have the right to get these awards back while others are not yet rehabilitated, and that includes everyone who suffered repression for their beliefs during the stagnation period.

Ogonyok: Andrei Dmitriyevich, you donated money for the construction of an oncological center.

Sakharov: In 1969, I donated money for construction of an oncological center and an equal amount to the Red Cross.

Ogonyok: An equal amount—what sum?

Sakharov: One hundred thirty-nine thousand rubles, and I received thanks from the Red Cross. I wanted to divide my contribution into three parts, with one third allocated to children's charities, but I did not succeed because it was not allowed. The authorities said that some kind of legal problem arose. Therefore I was not successful.

Ogonyok: And what other charitable actions are connected with your name? Tell us about them; after all, it is not known.

Sakharov: Well, I didn't have any more to give.

Yelena Bonner: Why not? (Yelena Georgievna, the wife of Andrei Dmitriyevich, had returned from shopping.) Didn't you receive the international prize of Chino Del Duka in 1974?

Sakharov: True, I forgot.

Bonner: He entrusted me to create a fund to help children of political prisoners. That is what I did.

Ogonyok: What was the sum of the prize?

Bonner: Twenty-five thousand dollars. Despite the fact that the money was heavily taxed, we continued to send money to Czechoslovakia and Poland, both before and during the exile to Gorky.

Sakharov: She did not hold any of it in her own hands. She only filled out the bank forms. All the financial transfers were made without our involvement; we only supplied the addresses.

(Time was passing. It was now time to begin the formal interview.)

We, the Representatives

Ogonyok: Andrei Dmitriyevich, did you not present a general appraisal of the Congress of People's Deputies in your address at the last congress meeting?

Sakharov: Not completely, I did not manage to say everything. On the whole, I think that the congress became a very important affair. It very much politicized our society. The political excitement began even before the elections. People awoke to a more active political life; they stopped being cogs deprived of their rights and showed that they wanted to do something for their country. The process of politicization greatly intensified as a result of twelve days of live televised sessions, when the position of the majority became evident, when it became clear that there were in the hall those who were able to propose real alternatives and who, as a result, inspired the minds of the people. In addition, the congress demonstrated the tragedy of our situation in all regions with greater clarity than our press was able to do during the entire period of *glasnost*. We somehow achieved a new level of understanding about ourselves. This proved to be the most important accomplishment of the congress.

I stated that the congress, in my opinion, did not fulfill the fundamental task that history had placed before it, as expressed in the slogan "All power to the Soviets!" The congress might have been unable to do this by virtue of its composition, but it is good that, in any case, the problem was highlighted. Power is the key element; without power it is impossible to address economic, social, or any other problems facing our country. Without power in the soviets, it will be impossible to overcome the arbitrary rule of the ministries; there will be no way. It will not be possible to create truly free, self-governing enterprises, or to implement land reforms, and in general to carry out agricultural policies that depart from pointless infusions of capital into the unprofitable collective farms, which are falling apart.

And, of course, the solution of economic problems will also be impossible: They must be solved by the soviets at all levels. For that, they must be independent.

The congress also did not settle the extraordinarily acute problems of the nationalities. As our inheritance from Stalinism, we received an imperial system with an imperial ideology and an imperial policy, summed up in the words "divide and conquer." We also inherited a system of oppression of the small republics and of the small national political entities that are part of the union republics. The union republics were turned into empires on a smaller scale.

This system oppressed large national groups as well, in particular the Russians, who became one of its main victims. On its shoulders rested the major weight of all our historical development, of all our imperial ambitions, of dogmatism, of adventures in foreign as well as domestic politics. The people have had to pay for all that has happened.

Ogonyok: Do you have any concrete suggestions in this area?

Sakharov: I suggest a confederation. Equal rights with the preservation of present territorial borders should be granted to all the republics—both union and autonomous, autonomous provinces, and national districts. All of them should receive the maximum degree of independence. Their sovereignty should be minimally restricted by issues of common defense, foreign policy, transportation, communications, and perhaps a few other things. The fundamental requirement is that they possess full independence in all other respects and on this basis enter into the relations of a union treaty.

Ogonyok: The popular front movements of the Baltics advance a similar reconstruction project.

Sakharov: It seems to me perfectly correct. I would only supplement their proposal by including not only union republics but also all existing national entities. Thus, for example, the autonomous republics of Yakutia, Chuvashia, Bashkiria, Tataria, and Komi would have the same rights as the Ukraine or Estonia.

Ogonyok: At the congress, you said that you intend to propose an alternative constitution.

Sakharov: I said that when the question of my participation on the commission for development of the constitution was discussed. I said that I am sure that on all fundamental questions I will remain in the minority or alone, and that therefore I can take part only in work on alternatives to the constitution or on separate articles—in any case, to present alternative opinions. But I didn't intend to participate in the main project. This was my view.

Ogonyok: Have you, as yet, formulated the first article of the constitution?

Sakharov: I can only say, "We, the representatives of the following republics, hereby state our intention to enter into a union treaty." Of course, I do not yet have the final wording.

Ogonyok: Is this similar to the preamble of the constitution of the United States, "We the people of the United States . . ."?

Sakharov: Yes, it presents the idea of a unification of independent states. I think that this will be the first article, and on this foundation the remainder should be developed. What must be determined is which rights the republics will retain and which they will delegate. In addition, we should adopt the Universal Declaration of the Rights of Man, which was accepted by the United Nations in the year 1948, as one of the elements of our constitution.

Ogonyok: Thank you for that clarification. My questions arose because it is the first time that I have had a chance to speak to a person proposing an alternative constitution for the USSR. Let's return to the congress.

Sakharov: Yes, I called for the adoption of an appeal to China. It seems to me that events of huge importance for all the world occurred in China.[1] The question of democratization of the largest country on earth is, in effect, a question of the fate of mankind. We here in another powerful country, located next door, should be guided by the principles of internationalism and defense of democracy. We must not equate those who, by means of peaceful student and civilian demonstrations, demanded democracy, a free press, and a fight against corruption, with those who implemented bloody, harsh reprisals against them.

Therefore, I supported the appeal of the interregional group of deputies concerning the events in China. It was quite different from the resolution passed by the congress by a simple vote and without discussion. In that resolution, there wasn't even an appeal to the Chinese government to stop the bloodshed and executions. It appeared that the Soviet government in the name of the Soviet people allegedly supported those who carried out the bloody actions in Beijing. The same type of harsh reprisals occurred in Tbilisi on April 9, 1989, and in Novocherkassk in 1962.[2] And in different cities all over our country, but in Tbilisi it was a most tragic moment.

What Happened to the Armed Forces?

Ogonyok: At the congress, you also spoke about the army.

Sakharov: I spoke about a reduction in the length of service and a reduction of our army by five hundred thousand men, as was announced in December of last year by Mikhail

---

[1]Sakharov is referring to the massacre by government troops of prodemocracy demonstrators in Tiananmen Square, Beijing.

[2]In Tbilisi, on April 9, 1989, army units attacked a demonstration calling for the independence of Georgia, killing twenty people, mostly women and children. A massacre took place in Novocherkassk when troops fired on a workers' demonstration in front of the provincial party committee headquarters.

Gorbachev during his speech in New York. This very important step is being carried out, but it is not radical enough to affect the international and domestic situation in a fundamental way. Our present armed forces are far too big, bigger than any other three countries taken together.

Ogonyok: At the congress, you named only two countries, the United States and China.

Sakharov: You may add any other—for example, Germany.

Ogonyok: What kind of army should it be? It is strange that no one has asked the defense minister, "What should the size of our army be at a time when we have adopted a new doctrine of reasonable sufficiency?" "As much as the stomach will hold," as people used to say. But to support the army "as much as the stomach will hold" is too expensive. Yes, and pity the boys—they use up their best years. Shouldn't there be scientific studies on this subject?

Sakharov: Even without such studies it is clear that the army is much too big. At the present time, there is no real danger of a military attack on the USSR, and the unilateral reduction of the army, if we implement it, will fundamentally change the whole situation. The USSR's initiative will create a completely new international situation grounded in the spirit of new political thinking.

Ogonyok: Andrei Dmitriyevich, in many countries the ministers of war go around in civilian dress; they are, in fact, civilians. Do you think that this is advisable?

Sakharov: We had, I think, Dmitry Ustinov, who was a civilian.

Ogonyok: He was immediately made a marshal of the Soviet Union.

Sakharov: Yes, he became a marshal, although his military rank was a secondary factor.

Ogonyok: But in principle?

Sakharov: I think that the army shouldn't be the political force in any country. It always creates a serious danger if the army independently enters the political arena. When the minister of war is a civilian, that kind of danger is, to some extent, diminished. But it is essential to decrease the probability of a military coup.

Ogonyok: We will return to the subject of coups, but now I would like to ask you a question that you might not want to answer. How is it that you, a laureate of the Nobel Peace Prize, could have once been a developer of atomic and hydrogen bombs? At that time, was your thinking different? You don't have to answer.

Sakharov: No, I will answer. You asked me the question that will always burden me. I was not a creator of atomic arms. I entered the system in 1948, when atomic arms in our country were already on the way out; work on it continued, of course, but I did not directly participate.

As far as hydrogen arms are concerned, I did play an active role in this collective effort, which involved a huge number of people. I invested a great effort because I thought it was necessary for world stability. You see, I, along with others, thought that this was the only way to prevent a third world war.

Certainly, since that time my opinions have evolved. But I think that my position during that period, in that historical situation, was justified. It was the possession of hydrogen arms by many countries—the USSR, United States, and the other nuclear powers—that protected the world from slipping into a new world war. This danger arose more than once, and we don't know with certainty how events would have developed if the threat of mutual annihilation had not existed. Of course, such a balance is unstable, as if on the point of a knife. And to maintain peace on such a basis for an unlimited period of time is impossible. Therefore our work was historically justified, despite the fact that we gave arms to Stalin and [Lavrenty] Beria. However, nuclear arms did not acquire a global role until later, until the fall of 1953.

Ogonyok: Andrei Dmitriyevich, do you really think that it is possible to obtain a universal ban on nuclear weapons and effectively to remove them from the hands of mankind?

Sakharov: Yes, I think so; moreover, a full ban is clearly a very important goal. This was declared by Mikhail Gorbachev. I also think that conditions must favor such a sociopolitical evolution throughout the world. A step such as a ban and a disavowal of nuclear arms must be approached very carefully. Not only the West but all countries must exercise caution in this matter.

Ogonyok: Shouldn't a ban on nuclear arms also include an immediate halt to any research in this field? Otherwise miniaturization, simplification of the manufacturing technology, and so forth will negate such a ban. Tomorrow will be too late.

Sakharov: A ban on research and development will never be possible or effective. We can only request that such work be made public if it exceeds some kind of dangerous limits. That is, society must move further and further away from secrecy in military research. There should be fewer and fewer secrets, and that will be possible only if there is a radical improvement in the international atmosphere. One of the preconditions for this improvement is convergence—that is, elimination of the state of confrontation between the two economic systems.

I am convinced that there can never be a solid solution to the problems of global danger without convergence, without a pluralistic rapprochement of the socialist and capitalist systems. I am told that this is impossible. However, this process is already taking place. For example, we can say that a country like Sweden is, as a matter of fact, an exemplary socialist country. This is what is happening in capitalist countries.

This process is taking place in our country as well, and it is called *perestroika*. Objectively, *perestroika* is the movement of our society toward "pluralism," no matter what our leaders say. They are often afraid of the word "pluralism," but in fact this is what we need. We need a pluralization of the economy so that all forms of property will finally become legally and economically equal. In any case, I think that *perestroika* means pluralism in all spheres of life. And that is convergence.

Coup d'état, Dictatorship—Are They Possible?

Ogonyok: Let's return to another issue. Do you think that there is a danger of a rightist coup d'état, staged by the military or the party and similar to that of October 1964, when Nikita Khrushchev was removed?

Sakharov: The country now stands on the eve of an economic catastrophe, so the economists say. People are worse off now than they were during the time of stagnation. A dramatic and tragic intensification of national tensions has occurred. All of this leads to extraordinarily powerful hidden processes. One of these is the crisis of trust on the part of the people toward the leaders of the country, a matter of which I spoke at the congress.

This is a very dangerous, unstable situation in which could happen terrible and tragic things, both predictable and unpredictable. The system could explode, because tensions have reached their limit at the same time that some of the props of the system are beginning to crumble. I believe that a coup d'état by the military or by a right-wing party is a possibility in the current situation.

An analogous situation could arise that would not be linked to a change in the country's leadership. The leadership could become hostage to forces using such levers as personal information, connections, threats, or God knows what else. Then, even without a change in leadership, a move toward the right would be possible. Moreover, the power in our country is in the hands of one person, who could fall prey to incredible pressure. I have the greatest respect for Mikhail Sergeyevich Gorbachev, but this is a political issue, not a personal one. Nobody lives forever, and I am speaking about a head of state and about a situation that could arise.

Ogonyok: Is there a danger that Gorbachev will become a dictator? There was some talk at the congress.

Sakharov: It was circulating, and we see that the constitution is structured so that Gorbachev received all the power (and, by the way, without direct elections). He also became a People's Deputy without alternative candidates; there were one hundred candidates for one hundred places.[3] He was not elected to the Supreme Soviet: We have here the paradoxical situation in which the chairman of the Supreme Soviet of the USSR is not among its elected members; that is, he was elected chairman without being elected as a member. This procedure was established in the December amendments to the constitution of the USSR. Thus, Mikhail Gorbachev was given the opportunity to occupy his present post without the danger that elections, and especially contested elections, always present.

In contrast, [Boris] Yeltsin was voted down in his contest for the Supreme Soviet, even though millions of Muscovites had voted for him in the general elections. Based on the number of electoral votes he won, he had the greatest support in the country.

We are now facing a complex situation fraught with great dangers. There are many possibilities for backstage pressure on Gorbachev. It is also possible that he himself will move to the right, having accumulated so much personal power. We

---

[3]For the elections to the 1st Congress of People's Deputies, 750 seats were set aside for public organizations. These 750 included 100 seats for the CPSU, which nominated exactly 100 candidates. The remaining 1,500 seats were filled by general election.

have seen that happen many times in history. I repeat: A concentration of so much personal power in the hands of one man is dangerous, no matter who he is, even if he is the initiator of *perestroika*. In addition, there is the danger that he could be replaced, and virtually unlimited power would fall into someone else's hands, we do not know whose.

Ogonyok: Do I understand you correctly, that we do not have legal guarantees preventing the possibility of establishing a personal dictatorship at this time?

Sakharov: You are absolutely correct, there are no legal guarantees. But there is the most important fact that Gorbachev himself was the initiator of *perestroika* four years ago. We all should remember what he has already done for the country. It is a historical, political, and psychological fact. We cannot ignore him. Besides, what I have described is only a potential danger. Nevertheless, we all should act to make it easier for Gorbachev to advance on the road of *perestroika* and to make a retreat to the right impossible. This is unrelated to our evaluation of Gorbachev's personality; right now, it is a historical necessity.

Bibliography

"Andrei Sakharov: The Man and the Scientist." *Priroda*, no. 8, August 1990, special issue.

Reminiscences of the Soviet scientists who worked with Sakharov and who admired and defended him from the Soviet bureaucracy.

Ligachev, Yegor. "From Recollections." *Argumenty i Fakty*, nos. 3–6, 1991.

Autobiographical account of an *apparatchik*'s life.

Tretyakov, Vitaly. "A Good Man from the Politburo." *Moskovskie Novosti*, no. 26, July 1, 1990.

Alexander Yakovlev is described as a typical Russian liberal whose loyalty does not allow him to criticize Gorbachev.

Yakovlev, Alexander. "The Politics Are Fascinating at the Turning Point." *Komsomolskaya Pravda*, June 5, 1990.

Conversation about Yakovlev's life and his political views concerning *perestroika*.

Zhelnorova, Natalya. "Life Is More Complicated than Decisions." *Argumenty i Fakty*, no. 33, 1989.

An interview with Premier Nikolai Ryzhkov.

———. "Socialism Possesses Colossal Resources; It Does Not Need to Be Improved by Capitalism." *Argumenty i Fakty*, no. 42, 1989.

Interview with Yegor Ligachev on September 26, 1989.

Glossary

apparat	the machinery of government
apparatchik	a functionary, a member of the *apparat*
Black Hundreds	squads of Russian rightists who attacked Jews and intellectuals after the revolution of 1905
Congress of People's Deputies	the Soviet parliament, first elections for which were held in March 1989
CPSU	the Communist Party of the Soviet Union
Democratic Russia	a voting bloc of many democratic and reformist organizations
glasnost	openness, publicity
Great Russian	ethnic Russian, as distinguished from Ukrainian and Byelorussian; can carry a connotation of imperialist ambition
Komsomol	the Soviet organization for Communist youth ages fourteen to twenty-eight
New Economic Policy (NEP)	a relatively liberal Soviet economic program followed from 1921 to 1928
nomenklatura	a select group of party members occupying key positions
oblast	a unit of government roughly at the level of a U.S. county

Pamyat	"Memory," the name of an extreme and openly anti-Semitic Russian nationalist organization
Party Congress	a regularly scheduled meeting of party delegates from all over the USSR at which party leadership is discussed
Party Conference	an irregularly scheduled meeting at which party delegates from all over the USSR discuss an agenda of issues listed by the party leadership
perestroika	"restructuring," a slogan signifying Gorbachev's agenda for changing the structure of the Soviet economic, social, and political system
plenum	a plenary meeting of the Central Committee of the CPSU
State Planning Agency (Gosplan)	the powerful agency in charge of determining the yearly quotas for various industries and enterprises

Index